William Haven Daniels

The temperance reform and its great reformers

William Haven Daniels

The temperance reform and its great reformers

ISBN/EAN: 9783742834072

Manufactured in Europe, USA, Canada, Australia, Japa

Cover: Foto ©Thomas Meinert / pixelio.de

Manufactured and distributed by brebook publishing software
(www.brebook.com)

William Haven Daniels

The temperance reform and its great reformers

HON. NEAL DOW.

HON. HENRY WILSON.

THE
TEMPERANCE REFORM
AND ITS GREAT REFORMERS.

AN ILLUSTRATED HISTORY,

INCLUDING THE TEMPERANCE "BLUE LAWS" OF THE NEW ENGLAND COL-
ONIES; THE LIQUOR LAWS OF THE STATES; A SKETCH OF THE
VARIOUS TEMPERANCE ORGANIZATIONS; BIOGRAPHIES OF
LYMAN BEECHER, JOHN B. GOUGH, DR. JEWETT,
ETC., A CHAPTER ON THE MEDICAL AND
CHEMICAL PHASES OF THE MOVE-
MENT; "THE CRUSADES;" THE
WOMAN'S CHRISTIAN
TEMPERANCE
UNIONS; "RED RIBBON"
REFORM UNDER DR. REYNOLDS;
THE EVANGELISTIC TEMPERANCE WORK
UNDER MESSRS. MOODY, SAWYER, ETC.; HISTORY OF
THE MURPHY TEMPERANCE MOVEMENT; WITH THRILLING
EXPERIENCES OF REFORMED AND CONVERTED DRUNKARDS;
WITH OVER TWENTY PORTRAITS OF THE CHIEF REFORMERS, AND
CHARACTERISTIC SELECTIONS FROM THEIR BEST WRITINGS AND ADDRESSES.

EDITED BY
REV. W. H. DANIELS, A.M.

WITH AN INTRODUCTION BY REV. THEODORE L. CUYLER, D.D.

PUBLISHED BY SUBSCRIPTION.

NELSON & PHILLIPS,
NEW YORK, BOSTON, BUFFALO, PITTSBURGH, AND SAN FRANCISCO.
HITCHCOCK & WALDEN.
CINCINNATI, CHICAGO, AND ST. LOUIS.
1878.

Table of Contents.

SECTION V.

THE CRUSADES, AND THE WOMAN'S CHRISTIAN TEMPERANCE UNION.

SECTION VI.

DR. REYNOLDS, AND THE RED RIBBON REFORM CLUBS.

SECTION VII.

THE MURPHY MOVEMENT.

SECTION VIII.

EVANGELISTIC, OR "GOSPEL TEMPERANCE."

SECTION IX.

TEMPERANCE LITERATURE.

List of Illustrations.

INTRODUCTION.

BY REV. THEODORE L. CUYLER, D.D.

AMERICA is the birthplace of the modern Temperance Reform. Just as the idea of foreign missions —although contained in God's word — seemed to lie latent in the Evangelical Churches until the eighteenth century brought the idea out into organic action, so the seed-corn of Bible-temperance remained latent until the plowshare of effort turned it up to the sunlight. In Great Britain there were a few sporadic movements early in this century; but on our American soil the first temperance society of modern times was organized.

A single locality in the "Empire State" has been most remarkably identified with the rise and progress of this beneficent reform. It is the locality which is linked with the healthful efficacy of *water* the world over—Saratoga. In the county of that name, not far from the spot where the most decisive battle of the Revolution was fought, the first organization for arresting the drinking custom by a pledge was established just seventy years ago. In the borough of Saratoga Springs a national convention (held in 1835) placed the movement on the impregnable basis of total abstinence. Several similar conventions have been held in that beautiful town; at one of them (in 1866) the initiatory steps were taken for organizing the present "National Temperance Society

and Publication House." Saratoga County was the residence of those early pioneers of our reform—Billy J.
Clark, Chancellor Walworth, and Edward C. Delavan.

The temperance reform has had several phases in the
course of its seventy years of development. The first
pledge, adopted at Moreau, in Saratoga County, only
forbade the use of ardent spirits under the penalty of a
fine. It was the drinker, and not the vender, who was
compelled to " pay damages." Thirty years elapsed before the discovery was made that the only logical basis
of the temperance movement is entire abstinence from
all intoxicants. Five years later the " Washingtonian "
movement originated in Baltimore. It was very soon
followed by the organization of the " Sons of Temperance," (in 1842.) Attempts had been made to suppress
tippling houses by law in several States; but the first
thorough statute of prohibition went into operation in
the year 1851 in that gallant north-eastern State whose
motto is the proud word "*Dirigo*." That original
" Maine Law " has been altered and improved, but *never
repealed*.

Since 1873 the most remarkable developments in the
temperance reform have been the " Woman's Crusade " or
the " Ohio movement," and those extraordinary campaigns carried forward under the name of " Gospel Temperance " by such noble workers as Dr. Reynolds, Mr.
Gough, Miss Willard, Mr. Murphy, Mrs. Wittenmyer,
Mr. Moody, and Mr. Sawyer. The most complete record of these latest phases of the great reform yet given
to the public will be found in the following pages of this
volume.

In penning a few words of introduction to this elaborate work of Mr. Daniels, it may not be indelicate for me to note down two or three personal reminiscences which are intimately connected with the progress of the temperance enterprise. It has been the privilege and joy of my life to bear a humble part in advancing a movement so intimately linked with the welfare of humanity and the kingdom of Christ. From my early childhood I have been a teetotaler. My first public addresses were at temperance meetings. While a youth of twenty years of age I was permitted to bear a part with FATHER MATHEW in his first day's work in the city of Glasgow. My recollections of that brave and benevolent philanthropist— whose merit was only equaled by his modesty—are most vivid and delightful. He was then in the prime of his power and his manly beauty. The fame of his wonderful successes in Ireland had preceded him, and secured for him a tumultuous welcome by a multitude of 50,000 souls on Glasgow Green. During that exciting day I witnessed his peculiar method of administering the pledge to the hundreds who thronged around him to receive his medals and his priestly blessing. However widely I differ from Theobald Mathew in theology, I am happy to pay this cordial tribute to him as one of the purest philanthropists of modern times. "The Father Mathew T. A. B. Societies" are a prodigious power for good in America.

During the year 1852 and 1853 the prohibition movement came to the front. Several States followed the wise example of Maine, and passed laws for the suppression of tippling-houses. The father of the Maine Law,

1*

General Neal Dow, made a tour through the land, addressing ecclesiastical bodies and Legislatures in favor of the principles of prohibition. It was my good fortune to labor with my friend Dow in that campaign, and we were allowed to address the Legislatures of New York and New Jersey in company. The principles we then advocated, although sorely assailed and gainsaid in this generation, are destined to an ultimate triumph.

One of the most important movements of the last dozen years was the organization of the National Temperance Society and Publication House, in 1866. This has furnished a central point of radiation of temperance truth, as the "Book Concern" has been for the diffusion of American Methodism. In organizing that Society I gladly bore a part; its constitution was drafted and its name selected under my own roof. Those of us who have rejoiced to bestow our gratuitous labor in behalf of this truly Christian crusade against the decanter, the dram-shop, and the distillery, have already reaped a large reward. The good cause is yet under the mid-vollies of hot encounter, but as surely as God holds the helm of the universe our cause shall win a final and substantial victory.

> "For right is right, as God is God,
>   And right the day shall win;
> To doubt would be disloyalty,
>   To falter would be sin."

In my humble judgment the three *Thermopylæs* of our conflict are the legal veto of the rum-traffic, the medical argument against alcohol, and the individual effort to save the tempted by God's grace and the abstinence pledge. At these three decisive points the battle rages. Defeat at any one of these points would be disastrous; defeat at all of them would be death.

One object of this volume is to furnish the bulletins of the score of temperance campaigns already fought. It also aims to present a personal narrative of the foremost actors. The author has labored diligently to make his history full, accurate, and inspiring; he tells well a noble story of brave Christian effort; and we wish a hearty *God-speed* to his volume over all this broad Continent.

LAFAYETTE AVENUE CHURCH,
BROOKLYN, *Jan.*, 1878.

SECTION I.

TEMPERANCE ACCORDING TO LAW.
LIQUOR LAWS OF AMERICA.

THE TEMPERANCE REFORM

AND ITS

GREAT REFORMERS.

————•————

CHAPTER I.

EARLY COLONIAL LAWS, ALIAS "BLUE LAWS."

FROM the earliest period of American history until now Alcohol has been treated as a criminal, against whose crimes and ravages society has sought to protect itself by law. He has, indeed, been upheld and defended by those who enjoy his society, and by those who make gain out of him, just as a great many other rich and powerful public enemies have been upheld and defended; but the attitude toward him of the best men, and of almost all women, has always been that of armed resistance.

This is a fact worth the attention of those who hold strong drink to be "one of the good creatures of God, to be received with thanksgiving." There are no laws to be found against raising or selling too much bread, or meat, or fruit, or wool, or cotton, or silk, or lumber; all the "good creatures of God," for the body at least, are, by universal consent, allowed the fullest liberty; but alcoholic drinks no sooner make their appearance in a community than somebody cries out against them.

Shepherds put a dog with the flock not to hinder the sheep and lambs from killing each other, but to keep the wolf from killing the sheep and lambs. So in the history of all American legislation, in colonial as well as in Federal days, Alcohol has been treated as a wolf, on which, from time to time, as his ravages become more awful and cruel, the colony or State has been forced to set the sharp teeth and the strong muscles of the law.

Such an act, especially for the protection of the lambs, that is, children and Indians—the adult colonists being presumed to be able to fight the wolf without the help of the dog—is the law passed in the settlement of East Hampton, on Long Island, as early as the year 1651.

This provided "that no man may sell any liquor but such as are deputed thereto by the town. Such men shall not let youths, or such as are under other men's management, remain drinking at unseasonable hours, and such persons shall not have above one half pint at a time among four men."

In 1655 it was forbidden in the same town to sell liquor to Indians above two drams at one time; and to sell to no Indian unless he was sent by the Sachem, or brought a written ticket with him of the kind which were furnished by the town; and even then he could not have above a quart of liquor at one time.

Somewhere about the year 1655 the infant colony of New Haven, finding that drunkenness was making sad havoc in their feeble settlement, enacted the following as a part of its Impost Laws: "And that no person at any time shall re-tale any sort of strong liquor within this jurisdiction without express license from the authority of the plantation within the limits where he so sells; and that the selling of a lessened quantity than three gallands at a time is to be accounted re-tale; and that due moderation be attended in prisas [prices] when it is so retailed, but that none of any sort be at any time sold above 3 sh. and 6 pence a quart "—which at this distance of time appears to be, instead of a temperance statute, a provision for securing to the people of New Haven a part, at least, of what the anti-temperance men at a recent election in Chicago demanded, and which was proposed as the watchword, or rallying cry, of the campaign; namely, " Cheap liquor, good liquor, and plenty of it."

INN-KEEPERS, TIPPLING, AND DRUNKENNESS.

It is ordered: " That no person or persons shall at any time hereafter, under any practice or call whatsoever, undertake or become a Common Victualer, keeper of a Cooke-shop, or house for common entertainment, tavern, or publick seller of wine, ale, or strong beere, or strong liquor, by retaile within this jurisdiction; nor shall any, either directly or indirectly, sell any sorte of wine privately in his house, cellar, etc., or out of doores, by a lesse quantity, or under three gallands at a time, without approbation and license of the plantation court to which he belongeth; or, where there is no such court, without the license of the constable and major part of the freemen, under the penalty of five pounds, to be paid to the plantation for the first miscarriage complained of, and proved; and ten pounds for the second miscarriage so proved; and when payment cannot or will not be made, imprisonment during the court's pleasure, for the first

offence, and for the second offence such further punishment as the court shall order. And that no person so
licensed shall sell any beere, or ale, above three pence
an ale quart, under the penalty of three shillings and
four pence for such miscarriage, proved the first time,
and six shillings and eight pence the second time. But
it is allowed and ordered, that any man that will may
sell beere or ale out of doores at a penny a quart, or
cheaper.

"It is further ordered, That whosoever licensed as before, selleth any sort of wine by retaile, that is, by any
less quantity than three gallons at a time, he shall pay to
the jurisdiction treasurer over and above the custome
before mentioned, after the rate of forty shillings for
every butt or pipe so re-tailed; and every one, that so
selleth by re-tale, shall give a true account and notice to
the said treasurer, or to some other officer appointed for
that purpose in each plantation, of the true or ful quantity, which he either buyeth or receiveth into his custody,
and that within one week after he is possessed of it,
upon paine of forfeiting the same, or the value thereof;
and shal further every six months, truly account with
the jurisdiction's treasurer, or other officer as aforesaid,
for what he hath sold by re-tale as aforesaid, and discharge the same, having due allowance for what he hath
sold by greater parcels than by this order is accounted
re-tale, and in case of delay, or neglect of payment after
demand, the treasurer or officer shal recover it by action
as other debts, provided that if any person shall give in
a false account to defraud the jurisdiction, upon due

proof, he shal pay double the value of what he would so have kept back.

"And it is further ordered, That every person so licensed to draw and sel strong beer, ale, and wine, or strong liquour, do see, and take care that good order, and all rules of sobriety be duly attended in his course, and house, and about the same; and that neither see, nor suffer any to be drunken, or to drink excessively, or to continue tippling above the space of half an hour, or at unseasonable times; or after nine of the clock at night without weighty cause, nor that any children or servants without the consent of parents, or governors, be permitted to sit, or stay there drinking or unnecessarily to spend their time there, especially at late or unseasonable hours.

" But every person found drunken, namely, so that he be thereby for the present bereaved, or disabled in the use of his understanding, appearing in his speech, jesture, or carriage, in any of the said houses or elsewhere, shall forfeit for the first time, ten shillings ; and for excess of drinking, or continuing in any such place unnecessarily, at unseasonable times, or after nine of the clock at night, five shillings; and for continuing tippling there, above the space of an hour, two shillings six pence for the first offence, and for the second offence in each kind, and for all further disorder, quarelling, or disturbance, whether a first or second time, such further fine or punishment as the court shall determine.

"And for that God may be much dishonoured, and many inconveniences may grow by the Indians' disorderly drinking of wine, strong water, and strong beere, unto which they are much addicted; it is ordered, That no person whatsoever shall either directly or indirectly within this jurisdiction, sel any wine, strong water, or strong beere, to any Indian or Indians, or procure any for them, either to drink within this jurisdiction, or upon any pretence to carry away without special license under the hand of some magistrate of this jurisdiction, or in any plantation where there is no magistrate, under the hand of one of the deputies, or constables where he lives; and that no license so given shall serve, or be of force anny longer than for that one particular time, and for the limited quantity then granted, under the penalty of five shillings for the first offence, and ten shillings for the second; but if any shal offend the third time therein, it is left to the plantation court where the offence is committed to consider the case, and to inflict such punishment or increase of fine as shal be meet; and in any plantation, where at present there is no court kept, the deputies last chosen for the general court, or constable, shall require the forfeitures, and for defect of payment, make seizure of so much out of the delinquent's estate; but, if any person shall offend the third time, every such person shal by the said deputies, or constable, be bound over to answer it before the next court of magistrates."

One of the orders of the General Court in the Colonies of Connecticut is as follows: 1659.—"It is ordered by this court, that if any person be found drunk, and convicted so to be, in any private house, he shall pay twenty shillings for every transgression of this nature, unto the public treasury, and the owner of the house where the person is found and proved to be made drunk shall pay ten shillings."

In 1654 the court granted special privilege to one Cullick "to draw and sell one hogshead of claret and a quarter cask of red wine to his friends and neighbors free from the country's excise."

What great public service Mr. Cullick had rendered whereby this court privilege was accorded him the record does not show.

STRONG WATER.

"*Whereas*, Many complaints are brought in court by reason of divers abuses that fall out by several persons that sell wine and strong water, as well in vessels on the river as also in several houses; for the prevention thereof, it is now ordered by the authority of this court: That no person or persons, after the publication of this order, shall neither sell wine or strong water by re-tale, in any place within these liberties, without license from a particular court, or any two magistrates; and where there is but one magistrate, by a magistrate and one of those appointed to order the affairs of the town."

INNKEEPERS.

"It is ordered by this court that no person or persons licensed for giving entertainment shall suffer any to be drunken, or to drink excessively; namely, above one half pint of wine for one person at a time, or to continue tippling above the space of one half hour, or at unseasonable times, and after nine of the clock at night, in or about any of their houses, on penalty of five shillings for every such offence ; and every person found drunken, namely, so that he thereby is bereaved or disabled of the use of his understanding, appearing in his speech or gesture in any said house or elsewhere to be so bereaved and disabled, shall forfeit ten shillings, and for excessive drinking, three shilling, four pence, and for continuing above one half hour tippling, two shillings and six pence, and for tippling at unseasonable times, after nine of the clock, five shillings. And for want of payment such shall be imprisoned until they pay, or be set in the stocks one hour or more in some open place as the weather will permit, not exceeding three hours at a time."

It would appear that sea-faring men and travelers occasionally need above " one half pint of wine at a time," and ought to be permitted "to tipple for above one half hour at a time," for it is " provided, notwithstanding such license, that persons may entertain sea-faring men, or land travelers in the night season, when they come first on shore, or from their journey, if their necessary refreshment demand, or when they prepare for their voyage or journey next day, if there be no disorder amongst them ; and also strangers and other persons, in an orderly way, may continue in such houses of quiet enter tainment what time their occasions shall require."

For the second offense of any of the above the fine was doubled, the third time it was trebled, and "if the parties be not able to pay their fines, then he that is found drunk shall be punished by whipping, to the num-

ber of ten stripes, or put in the stocks for three hours;"
for the fourth offense, "imprisonment until they give
sufficient sureties for future good behaviour."

The Connecticut code provided that in each town one
Ordinary, or Inn, or Lodging-house, should be maintained, the keepers of which should be chosen by the
magistrates.

"It is ordered by the authority aforesaid that all constables may, and shall, from time to time, duly make
search throughout the limits of their town, upon Lord's
days and lecture days, in times of exercise, [that is,
times of meeting,] and also at other times, so oft as they
shall see cause, for all offences and offenders against
this law, in any of the particulars thereof; and it is
ordered further by this court and authority that no
inn-keeper, victualer, wine-drawer, or other, shall deliver
any wine, nor suffer any to be delivered out of his house
to any which come for it, unless they bring a note under
the hand of some one master of some family."

The following curious reason for restricting gaming
will be of interest:—

GAMING.

"Upon complaint of great disorder by the use of the
game called shuffle-board, in houses of common entertainment, whereby much precious time is spent unfruit-
fully, and *much waste of wine and beer occasioned;*

"It is ordered and enacted, by the authority of this
court, that no person shall henceforth use the said game
of shuffle-board in any such house, nor in any other
house used as common for such purpose, upon pain of
every keeper of such house to forfeit for every such

offence twenty shillings; and for every person playing at the said game in any such house to forfeit for every such offence five shillings. The like penalty shall be for playing in any place at any unlawful game."

These statutes are from the first code of laws established by the General Court of Connecticut in May, 1650.

COURT RECORDS.

"Judgments of the New Haven Courts from 1639 to 1660:—

"Joseph B. and Joseph C. were accused for drinking to excess. Joseph B. confessed that he had sack out of his father's cellar, out of the bung with a tobacco pipe, and after that, that he went to an ordinary and there drank a quart of beer.

"Sister Linge testified that she saw them as they came from the ordinary, and that Joseph B. did lead Joseph C. by the arm, and she, speaking to them, asked whether Joseph C. were drunk; whereupon Joseph B. let him go, and then she saw him stagger and reel, and she said again he was drunk, because he could not go nor stand.

"The court being fully satisfied in the evidence given by Sister Linge, and the governor testifying that upon [the] examination they, and especially Joseph B., had told abundance of lies, the court conceived that they deserved to be severely whipped, but referred it to Mr. Evance [probably guardian of Joseph C.] and Mr. B. to give them correction in their families."

Thus, as would appear, domestic and colonial government was presumed to walk hand in hand.

At a court of magistrates held January 26, 1654, Law-

rence Cornelinsson, a Dutchman, at Milford, and another
Dutchman who had been scandalously, and for himself
dangerously, drunk, were sent for by the magistrate, but
refused to come. From the record it appears that Cornelinsson used severe words against the marshal, who
was sent for him, and his rebellion and wickedness are
set forth at large in the account; but some one naving
struck him and broken his head, they succeeded in bringing him before the magistrate, who "repeated his miscarriages to him." He told the magistrate he lied.

Then he demanded to see the law against drunkenness
and swearing, which being read, he said, "'This is the law
of man, but not of God.' When he was gone from the
magistrate he asked those who were about him whether
they knew the story of Samson's revenge upon the
Philistines, how he tied the fire-brands betwixt the tails
of foxes, and burned their corn? as if he thought the
English were Philistines and he purposed a revenge;
adding he would rather be cast into the sea than to be
buried in Milford; his bones should not be in Milford, re-
peating the story of Joseph, who would have his bones
carried out of Egypt, as if Milford were as Egypt to him.
To defend the aforesaid Dutchman, he, the said Lawrence, professed himself to be a drunkard, and asked the
English about him, if they were not so, 'Have not you,
and you been drunk?' adding that at *Mannadoes* [New
York] they were not punished for drunkenness."

It appears from the record that the Dutchman when
he became sober was ashamed of himself, "after which
the court, considering how he had contemned and trampled upon authority, and disturbed the peace of the

2

jurisdiction, (besides his slighting or censuring the English,) Lawrence Cornelinsson was sentenced to pay a fine of forty pounds, and that he make a due and public acknowledgment of his miscarriages at Milford, where they were committed, owning his sin and shame for it, which if not performed to satisfaction there, he is to be sent back to New Haven, and the court will further consider it."

TOBACCO.

At this early day a war against tobacco seems to have been waged, for in 1655 "It was ordered, that no tobacco shall be taken in the streets, yards, or houses, or in any plantation or farm in this jurisdiction, or without doors near or about the town, or in the meeting-house, or about any of the train-soldiers, or in any other place where they may do a mischief thereby, under penalty of sixpence a pipe or time ; but if he be a poor servant and hath not to pay, and his master will not pay for him, he shall then be punished by sitting in the stocks one hour."

The following is a record of a complaint made against one of the "train-soldiers:"—

October, 1657.—"William East was told there was a sad fame spread abroad of his excessive drinking and drunkenness, so that people as they go in the street do say that Sergeant East was drunk yesterday before ten o'clock, and now he is drunk again to-day already. He says he dares not say he is clear, but is sorry he hath given cause for such reports. He was told he hath now a black eye, and whither it came not by some such course he best knows; of which he said nothing to clear himself, yet said he had some distemper which fell into his eye.

Some of Milford being present, as Richard Baldwin, William Fowler, and Steven Treman, were called to speak what they know or have heard in the case; but first, Mr. Fenn, the magistrate, said that he thinks he hath been twice dealt with at Milford for drunkenness."

In the printed Colony Records of Massachusetts, 1630, " It is ordered that all Rich Cloughe's stronge water shall presently be seazed upon, for his selling greate quantitie thereof, to severall men's servants, which was the occasion of much disorder, drunckenes, and misdemeanor."

" It is ordered that the remainder of Mr. Allen's stronge water, being estimated about 2 gallands, shall be delivered into the hands of the deacons of Dorchester for the benefit of the poore there, for his selling of it dyvers tymes to such as were drunke with it, hee knowing thereof."

1633.—" Robert Coles is fined 10 lbs. and enjoyned to stand with a white sheete of paper on his back, wherein A DRUNKARD shall be written in greate letters, and to stand therewith soe longe as the Court thinks meete, for abusing himselfe shamefully with drinke . . . and other misdemeanor."

1634.—" Tymothy Hawkins and John Vauhan fined 20s. a peece for misspending their tyme in company, keeping and drinking stronge water, and selling other contrary to order of the Court."

" It is ordered that Robert Coles, for drunckenes by him committed att Rocksbury, shall be disfranchised, weare aboute his necke, and soe [as] to hang upon his outward garment, a D made of redd cloath, and sett upon white; to contynue this for a yeare, and nott to leave it off att any tyme when hee comes amongst company, under the penalty of 40s. for the first offence, and £5 the second, and after to be punished by the Court as they thinke meete. Also hee is to weare the D outwards; and is enjoyned to appear att the next Generall Court, and contynue there until the Court be ended."

This singular penalty, which will not fail to recall to those who have read it that sorrowful yet beautiful story of Hawthorne's entitled " The Scarlet Letter," was soon remitted upon the evidence of the offender's good behavior.

The price of entertainment in an Ordinary is thus regulated in the early laws of Maryland :—

1699.—" Every Ordinary keeper that shall demand or take above 10 lbs. of tobacco for a gallon of small beer, 20 lbs. of tobacco for a gallon of strong beer, 4 lbs. of tobacco for a night's lodging in a bed, 12 lbs. of tobacco for a peck of Indian corn or oats, 6 lbs. of tobacco for a night's grass for a horse, 10 lbs. for a night's hay or straw, shall forfeit for every such offence 500 lbs. of tobacco.'

November, 1637.—" Whereas it hath appeared unto this Court, upon many sad complaints, that much drunckenes, and waste of the good creatures of God, mispence of precious time, and other disorders, have frequently fallen out in the inns and common victualing houses within this jurisdiction, whereby God is much dishonored, the profession of religion reproached, and the welfare of this commonwealth greatly impaired, and the true use of such houses (being the necessary releefe of travellers) subverted ; for redress hearof, it is now ordered that after the last day of this present month it shall not bee lawful for any person that shall keep any such inne, or common victualing house, to sell or have in their houses any wine or stronge waters, nor any beare, nor other drinke, other than such as may and shall be sould for one penny the quart at the most." It is presumed that cheap liquors would necessarily be weak liquors, and therefore comparatively harmless.

" And it is further ordered that no common brewer shall sell or utter to any inne or common victualing house within this jurisdiction any beere or other drink of any stronger size than such as may and shall be afforded at the rate of 8sh. the barrel, upon paine of £20 for every offence against this order."

Thus it appears that even in this new country, among a people exposed to hardships and given to sturdy toil in the woods and fields—conditions under which it is claimed that strong drink is most requisite and beneficial —and in that early day, before the vile arts of adulteration were known, even the pure liquors which our forefathers drank were not "good creatures, to be received with thanksgiving," but open enemies of peace and good order of society; savage beasts, preying upon the bodies and souls of men.

Note.—These extracts from the Blue Laws of Connecticut are from the volume of Mr. J. Hammond Trumbull, by permission of The American Publishing Company.

CHAPTER II.

TEMPERANCE LAWS IN THE STATES.

MAINE was the first State of the Union to adopt a prohibitory liquor law. As early as the year 1837 the name of Neil Dow appears as a leader in the temperance reform, in connection with the Maine Temperance Union, organized that year, and which, as the result of his efforts, was established on a total abstinence basis. As a prosperous merchant, he was highly respected; as mayor of Portland, he was honored with the praise of good men and the wrath of evil men; as general in the armies of the Union, his record is fair and stainless; but as author of "The Maine Law," his name has been for years a household word throughout the English-speaking temperance world. This famous statute, enacted in 1846, concerning the success of which there has been no little dispute even in the ranks of the reformers themselves, aimed at the absolute crushing out of the traffic in intoxicating drinks, and placed the sale thereof for purposes of indulgence among the other infamous crimes punishable both by fine and imprisonment. The law provided for the establishment of an agency, the officer in charge to be appointed by the governor, for the sale of pure liquors for medicinal, mechanical, and manufacturing purposes. This agency furnished the town officers or corporation with liquors for such uses; but the sale of intoxicating liquors was prohibited to all others.

This law was amended in 1851 so as to confiscate all liquors stored for sale by private parties. In February 27, 1873, it was further revised. It now provides that " No person shall be allowed at any time to sell by his clerk, servant, or agent, directly or indirectly, any intoxicating liquors, except as hereinafter provided. Ale, porter, strong beer, lager beer, or other malt liquors; wine and cider, shall be considered intoxicating liquors, and coming within the meaning of this charge as well as also distilled spirits; but this enumeration shall not prevent any other beer, or mixed liquors of any kind, from being considered as intoxicating."

Also, the provision of this chapter shall not extend to the manufacture and sale of unadulterated cider by the manufacturer, nor to the sale, by agents appointed under the provisions of this chapter, of pure wine for sacramental and medicinal uses.

The selectmen of any town, and mayor and aldermen of any city, shall, on the first Monday of May, annually, or as soon thereafter as may be convenient, purchase such quantity of intoxicating liquors as may be necessary, to be sold under the provisions of this chapter, and shall appoint some suitable person as the agent of said town or city to sell the same at some convenient place within said town or city, to be used for medicinal, mechanical, and manufacturing purposes, and no other; and such agent shall receive such compensation for his services, and in the sale of such liquors shall conform to such regulations, not inconsistent with the provisions of law as the board appointing him shall prescribe.

Also, that no person shall keep a drinking-house and

tippling-shop within this State. If any person shall sell
any intoxicating liquors in any building, vessel, or boat
in this State contrary to the provisions of law, and the
same are there drunk, he shall be deemed and held to be
guilty of keeping a drinking-house and tippling-shop.
Any person convicted of keeping a drinking-house and
tippling-shop within this State shall be punished by a
fine of one hundred dollars and costs of prosecution, and,
in default of payment thereof, by imprisonment in the
county jail three months ; or, instead of such fine, shall
be imprisoned in the county jail three months on the first
conviction, and on every subsequent conviction he shall
be imprisoned six months in addition to the fine and costs.

Also, every wife, child, parent, husband, or other
person who shall be injured in person, property, means
of support, or otherwise by any intoxicated person, or
by reason of the intoxication of any person, shall have a
right of action in his or her own name against any person
or persons who shall, by selling or giving any intoxicating
liquors, or otherwise, have caused or contributed to the
intoxication of such person or persons ; and in any such
action the plaintiff shall have a right to recover actual
and exemplary damages. And the owner or lessee, or
person or persons renting or leasing any building or
premises, having knowledge that intoxicating liquors are
sold therein in violation of law, shall be liable, severally
or jointly, with the persons so selling or giving intoxicating liquors as aforesaid.

Also, all liquors declared forfeited by any Court by
virtue of the provisions of this chapter shall, by order of
the Court rendering final judgment thereon, be destroyed

by any officer competent to serve the process on which they were forfeited, and he shall make return accordingly to such Court or magistrate. And such liquors shall be destroyed by pouring the same upon the ground.

Also, no person authorized as aforesaid to sell intoxicating liquors shall sell such liquors to any minor without the direction in writing of his parent, master, or guardian, to any Indian, to any soldier in the army, to any drunkard, to any intoxicated person, nor to any intemperate person of whose intemperate habits he has been notified by the relatives of such person, or by the aldermen, selectmen, or assessors, respectively, of any city, town, or plantation."

The above are the most prominent provisions of this famous instrument, which is drawn up at great length and with much exactness, and is regarded by the advocates of prohibition as the most perfect form of statute prohibition now in existence.

The following testimony will show the working of that law. Governor Nelson Dingley, Jun., in reference to the working of the law prohibiting dram-shops and tippling-houses in this State, says:—

"These laws have accomplished great good, and have proved far more effective in suppressing dram-shops, and in restraining the evils of intemperance, than any other system of legislative restraint ever tried in this State. For more than two hundred years, first in the parent province and commonwealth, and subsequently in the State of Maine, a thorough trial was made of what is popularly known as the license system in every form that could be devised.

2*

" So powerful was the system in restraining the evils of
the dram-shops and tippling-houses, that in 1851 the
State of Maine adopted the policy of prohibiting dram-
shops altogether. We have twenty-three years' experience of the policy of prohibition, and the results have
been, on the whole, far greater than those of any other
system of liquor restraint, and so far greater that
the prohibition policy is accepted as a settled fact in
this State, and no considerable body of men favor its
repeal.

" In more than three fourths of the State, particularly
in the rural sections, open dram-shops are almost un-
known, and secret sales comparatively rare.

" In some of the cities and larger villages, where public
sentiment on the temperance question is not so well
sustained as in the rural districts, the law is not so effi-
ciently enforced as to prevent open sales to some extent,
although even in such places prohibition is not without
some influence for good.

" Statistics show that under the influence of our prohibitory system, and the moral efforts which have been
put forth to increase its efficiency, the sale and use of
liquor in this State has been so largely decreased that
drinking habits have ceased to be fashionable, and that
total abstinence has come to be a common thing instead
of, as formerly, a rare exception."

The Hon. Hannibal Hamlin, United States Senator
from Maine, says :—

· " In my judgment, less than one half of the liquor has
been consumed in the State that would have been consumed had there been no prohibitory law."

Hon. William P. Fry, member of Congress from Maine, says:—

" Since the enactment of the prohibitory liquor law, the sales of liquor have fallen off more than two thirds. More than one half of the State is absolutely free from it, and the ' corner groceries ' are gone forever.

" The jails in the three counties adjoining—Franklin, Oxford, and Somerset—have been tenantless for more than a year, and, I presume, the same is true of several other counties. In my own city, (Lewiston,) of 18,000 population now, and in Auburn, just across the river, of 10,000 more, not a hotel keeper, druggist, or grocer sells a drop of liquor. Of course with our large population liquor is sold in shanties, but it is a precarious business, for our warfare against the seller is constant and vigorous."

Hon. Lot M. Morrill, United States Senator from Maine, says of the prohibitory liquor law:—

" I think it has been most efficient and salutary, as attested in the statistics of pauperism and crime. The number of persons supported at the public charge in 1870 was 4,607, as against 8,966 in 1860; and the statistics of crime, it is believed, would show about the same reduction."

NEW HAMPSHIRE. Hon. Justin Edwards, of the Supreme Court, says :—

" New Hampshire has a prohibitory law which needs to be better enforced."

VERMONT has, in addition to the prohibitory law, a Civil Damage act, adopted in 1869, which provides " that whenever any person in a state of intoxication shall wil-

fully commit any injury upon the person or property of
another individual ; any person who by himself, his clerk
or servant, shall have unlawfully sold or furnished any
part of the liquor causing such intoxication, shall be liable
to pay for all damage occasioned by the injury so done."

The Legislature of 1876 enacted the following :—

"AN ACT TO ABATE AND SUPPRESS NUISANCES.

" *It is hereby enacted, etc. :—*

"SECTION 1. Every saloon, restaurant, grocery, cellar,
shop, billiard-room, bar-room, and every drinking place
or room used as a place of public resort, where spirituous
or malt liquor or any kind of intoxicating drink is unlawfully sold, furnished, or given away, or kept for selling,
or giving away unlawfully, shall be held and regarded as
a common nuisance, kept in violation of law.

"SEC. 2. When, upon due trial, it shall be proved that
any such liquor or intoxicating drink is kept for unlawful sale, furnishing, or giving away, or is unlawfully sold,
furnished, or given away, in any such place of public resort as is named in the preceding section, the Court having jurisdiction in the case shall adjudge such place to
be a common nuisance, and the same shall be shut up
and abated by the order of such Court, in the manner
and form hereinafter provided, and shall not be reopened
by the person convicted as the keeper thereof until he
shall file with such Court a bond, with sufficient surety
or sureties, payable to the treasurer of the State, in the
sum of not less than three hundred dollars nor more than
five hundred dollars, conditioned that he will not thereafter keep for unlawful sale, furnishing, or giving away,

nor unlawfully sell, furnish, or give away, therein any such liquor or intoxicating drink as herein named. And if such person so convicted shall reopen or reoccupy such place before giving such bond, he shall be liable to a fine of ten dollars, payable to the State treasury, for each day in which he shall keep open such place before giving such bond, with the costs of prosecution.

"SEC. 3. Whenever any person is duly convicted of keeping and maintaining any such place or room used as a place of public resort, in which any such spirituous or malt liquor, or any kind of intoxicating drink, is unlawfully sold, furnished, or given away, or kept for unlawful sale, furnishing, or giving away, he shall be adjudged by the Court before which he is so convicted to be guilty of keeping and maintaining a common nuisance, and upon any conviction of such offense he shall forfeit and pay into the State treasury a fine of not less than twenty dollars nor more than two hundred dollars, or he shall be liable to a fine of not exceeding twenty dollars and imprisonment in the county jail not less than one month nor more than three months, in the discretion of the Court."

The bill then gives the forms necessary for the carrying out of the provision.

An amendment authorizes the arrest of intoxicated persons and detention till sober, and that the persons so detained shall upon oath disclose where the liquor was obtained, and on refusal may be committed to jail.

MASSACHUSETTS has been and still is one of the hotly, contested points along the temperance line of battle.

The City of Boston, so rich in Revolutionary traditions, so happy in its possession of the cradle of liberty, so full of "notions" and so prolific in reforms, has long been a chief seat of this beast of drunkenness, by which the power of both law and Gospel has been defied.

One of the first notable attempts to control this evil by means of legislation was the famous Fifteen Gallon law, so called from its prohibition of the sale of ardent spirits in less quantities than fifteen gallons, producing no small stir among the opponents of the temperance reform.

This appears to have been a scheme for serving the Lord with one hand and the devil with the other.

New England rum was one of the principal products of Massachusetts, as well as one of its most profitable articles of commerce, and this law seems to have been framed to prevent the sale of liquor in small quantities for tippling and drunkard-making, while at the same time the wholesale traffic in this commodity might go on undisturbed. It was, also, thought that a man who could afford to buy fifteen gallons of liquor at one time, and take it home for use in his own family, would make a more judicious use thereof than the poor tippler, who could only afford to buy three cents' worth of liquor at a time.

This law was passed on the petition of a very large and honorable body of delegates to the convention which was held in Boston, February 20, 1808 ; but, after all their fine and pious rhetoric, it seems both pitiful and ridiculous that so lame and impotent a conclusion should have been reached, as to insist only that when intoxicating liquors were sold, they should be sold in very large quantities.

Immediately on the passage of this law the liquor dealers met in Boston to contrive means to nullify its operation, and to prevent its being executed at all. They failed to procure its repeal for a considerable length of time ; but, as may be imagined, the law which allowed wholesale and prohibited retail traffic in liquors could never accomplish very much in the way of moral reform.

The next year Mississippi enacted what was called the One Gallon law, which was evidently a stroke at the bar-rooms, but encouraged the consumption of liquor " in the bosom of the family." These laws, and all others like them, aiming at the *regulation* of the evils attendant on the use of ardent spirits, though they raised no small stir in their day, have passed into temperance history as miserable failures. Like all other compromises between might and right, they have only served to show how impossible it is to mingle fire and gunpowder, or to establish a fraternity between Christ and Belial.

In 1852 " The Maine Law," in its most stringent form, was enacted by the Massachusetts Legislature, and under its provisions large quantities of liquors were seized and poured out into the streets by temperance prosecutors, who, from their work as detectives, were nicknamed " Smelling Committees." But the defiance of the powerful liquor interest in Boston, where the law was never enforced, and the Yankee ingenuity which devised a variety of methods of evading it, made the law unpopular, and after a short trial it was suffered to become a dead letter.

After various efforts by an organized political temperance party to secure and enforce anti-liquor laws, Massachusetts now has a kind of half-and-half prohibitory and license law.

One section classifies the licenses to be given as follows:—

"*First class.* To sell liquors of any kind, to be drunk on the premises.

"*Second class.* To sell malt liquors, cider, and light wines containing not more than fifteen *per centum* of alcohol, to be drunk on the premises.

"*Third class.* To sell malt liquors and cider, to be drunk on the premises.

"*Fourth class.* To sell liquors of any kind, not to be drunk on the premises.

"*Fifth class.* To sell malt liquors, cider, and light wines, containing not more than fifteen *per centum* of alcohol, not to be drunk on the premises.

"SEC. 8. The fees for a license shall be as follows:—

"For a license of the first class, not less than one hundred dollars nor more than one thousand dollars.

"For a license of the second or third class, not less than fifty dollars nor more than two hundred and fifty.

"For a license of the fourth class, not less than fifty dollars nor more than five hundred dollars. *Provided*, *however*, That a distiller shall pay not less than three hundred dollars nor more than five hundred dollars. *Provided*, *secondly*, That distillers distilling not over fifty barrels annually shall pay a license fee of fifty dollars.

"For a license of the fifth class, not less than fifty dollars nor more than one hundred and fifty dollars. *Pro-*

vided, however, That a brewer shall pay not less than two hundred dollars nor more than four hundred dollars."

Section 11 of the Massachusetts law provides that " The mayor and aldermen of a city, or the selectmen of a town, or any police officer or constable especially authorized by them, may at any time enter upon the premises of any person licensed to sell under this act, to ascertain the manner in which such person conducts his business, and to preserve order. And such police officers or constables may at any time take samples for analysis from any liquors kept on such premises, and the vessel or vessels containing such samples shall be sealed on the premises by the seal of the vender, and shall remain so sealed until presented to the assayer for analysis. The city or town shall pay for the samples so taken. *Provided*, Such liquors are found to be of good quality, and free from adulteration."

The law is carefully drawn, apparently with a view to protect the liquor seller quite as much as to maintain the peace and good order of the State.

Of course, such a law is not enforced in Boston, or the other large cities, if, indeed, it is thoroughly enforced in any single county in the State.

RHODE ISLAND has a license law of forty-six sections, passed June 25, 1875.

Town councils of the several towns, and the boards of aldermen in the several cities, are empowered to grant or to refuse to grant annual licenses to sell liquor, to such extent as they may think proper. The sale of intoxicating liquors is prohibited " on Sundays, or to any minor,

or person of notoriously intemperate habits." A bond
of $1,000 is required, and other provision is made to
prevent violations of the law.   Licenses are to be posted
in a conspicuous position in the room or place where the
liquor is sold.   There is a civil damage proviso, and pay-
ments for liquors unlawfully sold cannot be enforced.

CONNECTICUT licenses the sale of liquor.   Licenses
may be granted by the County Commissioners on the
recommendation of a majority of the selectmen of a town.

NEW YORK licenses the sale of liquor, but has a Civil
Damage law, and a Landlord and Tenant bill; the latter
of which makes void the lease of any tenant who sells
liquor contrary to the law of the State, and holds the
landlord, or owner of the house or property, responsible,
if it can be proved that he rented the place for such unlawful traffic.

One peculiarity of the New York law is in Section 6,
which provides that—

"License shall not be granted to any person to sell
strong and spirituous liquors and wines to be drunk on
the premises of the persons licensed, unless such person
proposes to keep an inn, tavern, or hotel, nor unless the
commissioners are satisfied that the applicant is of good
moral character, that he has sufficient ability to keep an
inn, tavern, or hotel, and the necessary accommodations
to entertain travelers, and that an inn, tavern, or hotel
is required for the actual accommodation of travelers at
the place where such applicant resides or proposes to
keep the same, all which shall be expressly stated in
such license; and no such license shall be granted except

on the petition of not less than twenty respectable free-holders of this State residing in the election district where such inn, tavern, or hotel is proposed to be kept, by them duly signed and verified by the oath of a subscribing witness, and not then unless, in the opinion of the commissioners, such inn, tavern, or hotel is necessary or proper, and not more than one license shall be granted on the memorial of the same petitioners or any of them.

An "Inn" is thus defined in Section 8 :—

"Every keeper of an inn, tavern, or hotel, in any of the towns or villages of this State, shall keep in his house at least three spare beds for his guests, with good and sufficient bedding, and shall provide and keep good and sufficient stabling, and provender of hay in the winter, and hay or pasturage in the summer, and grain for four horses or other cattle more than his own stock, for the accommodation of travelers."

In cities the "Inn" is required to have the "three spare beds and bedding" only.

The following is the text of the Landlord and Tenant Bill, passed May, 1873 :—

"AN ACT TO DEFINE SOME OF THE RIGHTS AND RESPONSIBILITIES OF LANDLORDS AND TENANTS.

"*The People of the State of New York, represented in Senate and Assembly, do enact as follows : —*

"SECTION 1. Whenever the lessee or occupant other than the owner of any building or premises shall use or occupy the same, or any part thereof, for any illegal trade, manufacture, or other business, the lease or agreement for the letting or occupancy of such building or premises shall thereupon become void, and the landlord of such lessee or occupant may enter upon the premises so let or occupied, and shall have the same remedies to secure possession thereof as are given by law in the case of a tenant holding over after the expiration of his lease.

" SEC. 2. The owner or owners of any building or premises knowingly leasing or giving possession of the same, to be used or occupied, in whole or in part, for any illegal trade, manufacture, or business, or knowingly permitting the same to be used for any illegal trade, manufacture, or business, shall be jointly and severally liable with the tenant or tenants, occupant or occupants, for any damage that may result by reason of such illegal use, occupancy, trade, manufacture, or business.

" SEC. 3. This act shall take effect immediately."

The following is the first section of the new Civil Damage bill passed by the New York Legislature, May, 1873:—

" AN ACT TO SUPPRESS INTEMPERANCE, PAUPERISM, AND CRIME.

"*The People of the State of New York, represented in Senate and Assembly, do enact as follows :—*

" SECTION 1. Every husband, wife, child, parent, guardian, employer, or other person, who shall be injured in person, or property, or means of support, by any intoxicated person, or in consequence of the intoxication, habitual or otherwise, of any person, shall have a right of action in his or her name against any person or persons who shall, by selling or giving away intoxicating liquors, have caused the intoxication, in whole or in part, of such person or persons ; and any person or persons owning and renting or permitting the occupation of any building or premises, and having knowledge that intoxicating liquors are to be sold therein, shall be liable, severally or jointly with the person or persons selling or giving intoxicating liquors aforesaid, for all damages sustained and for exemplary damages ; and all damages recovered by a minor shall be paid either to such minor or his or her parent, guardian, or next friend, as the Court shall direct ; and the unlawful sale or giving away of intoxicating liquors shall work a forfeiture of all rights of the lessee or tenant under any lease or contract of rent upon the premises."

NEW JERSEY has a license law similar to that of New York, except the town of Vineland, and a few other townships which are centers of the prohibition movement.

Special acts of the Legislature have been passed to allow certain cities and towns to license or prohibit the sale of liquors according to local option.

"A "local option" law was passed for the town of Chatham, which voted " no license ;" and on an appeal to the Supreme Court, the law was declared constitutional.

PENNSYLVANIA. In 1760 among the Friends in Pennsylvania the effort was made to abolish the practice of furnishing liquor at funerals.

On the assembling of the first American Congress in Philadelphia the evils arising from the use of distilled liquors were seen to be so great that the following resolution was unanimously passed .—

"*Resolved*, That it be recommended to the several

legislatures of the U. S. immediately to pass laws most effective for putting an immediate stop to the pernicious practice of distilling grain, by which the most extensive evils are likely to be derived, if not quickly prevented."

Thus it appears that a majority, at least, of the fathers of our country were temperance men in theory if not in practice; and after passing such a resolution they could hardly have allowed a liquor saloon to be set up in Independence Hall during the sessions of Congress, as some of their degenerate descendants have done under the dome of the Capitol.

In 1855 Pennsylvania passed an ordinance which was called, in derision, the " Jug law," which was in substance a prohibition of the sale of liquors to be drunk on the premises, but giving permission to sell it by the quart, to be carried home and drank at leisure. This was so obnoxious to the temperance sentiment of the State that it was presently repealed.

This State formerly had a Local Option law which permitted the inhabitants of any town or county to vote on the question of license every three years. Desperate efforts were made by the liquor interest to secure its repeal, which in April, 1875, were successful.

OHIO in 1870 passed the Adair law, which makes the liquor seller and owner of the premises on which the liquor is sold jointly responsible for injury caused by intoxicating drinks. It also gives the right of action to the husband, wife, child, parent, or guardian, to sue for injury done by intoxicating drinks ; but, like other good laws, this is a partial failure for want of being enforced.

INDIANA has a very strict license law, known from its author as the Baxter law. This act, passed in February, 1873, forbids the sale of liquor except by virtue of a license from the County Commissioners, to obtain which the applicant must file a petition for the same, signed by a majority of the legal voters of the ward or township in which he proposes to sell, and also give bonds in the sum of three thousand dollars, with good freehold security thereon, for the payment of all fines, penalties, and forfeitures which may be adjudged against him.

No such license is granted for more than one year.

The sale of liquor to minors or habitual drunkards is forbidden, and all places where liquor is sold in violation of this act are to be closed as public nuisances.

Intoxication is a penal offense, and if proved, the person may be compelled to give the name of the person of whom he bought the liquor.

The keeper of a saloon is liable for the cost of caring for an intoxicated person.

The same right of action for damages caused by intoxication is given as in the Adair law.

In case an intoxicated person has no relatives, it is the duty of the Overseer of the Poor in any township to bring action against the saloon keeper for injury arising out of intoxication caused by liquor sold by him, the fines to go to the benefit of the poor of his ward or township.

This law has succeeded admirably in country districts, but has failed to be enforced in the cities of the State.

ILLINOIS is a license State. Its laws are framed with a view to *regulate* rather than to prohibit the sale of intoxicating drinks, the result of which is a regular and enormous sale and use of all kinds of liquors. The immense penitentiary overflowing with criminals, and the new penitentiary about to be erected in the southern part of the State, are a sufficient comment on the workings of this system.

This State has a Civil Damage law, and a law against the sale of liquors to any minor without the written order of his parent, guardian, or physician ; or to any person intoxicated, or who is in the habit of getting intoxicated, under which provisions a recent movement has been started to save the young men of Chicago.

MICHIGAN has a Liquor Tax law, with Civil Damage law attached ; but mightier than all law has been the great moral and religious reform, under the leadership of Dr. Henry A. Reynolds, whose work in this one State has resulted in securing the signatures of 80,000 drinking men and women to the total abstinence pledge. [See Section IX.]

IOWA has a prohibitory law of thirty-six sections. The manfacture and sale of intoxicating liquors is prohibited, except for " mechanical, medicinal, culinary, or sacramental purposes ; " except also foreign importations of such liquors under the authority of the laws of the United States ; except also the manufacture and sale of beer, cider from apples, wine from grapes, currants, or other fruits grown in the State. Violations of the law either in manufacturing or selling intoxicating liquors are punished by fines varying from twenty to two hundred dollars, and by imprisonment from ten days to six months. Common carriers are liable for bringing liquors into the State except upon a proper certificate, penalties are prescribed for evasions of the law, and there is a civil damage proviso for injuries resulting from the illegal sale of intoxicating liquors. Hotel-keepers, keepers of saloons and eating-houses, grocery keepers, and confectioners, are not allowed to sell intoxicating liquors under any circumstances. Only such persons can sell for " mechanical, medicinal, culinary, and sacramental purposes " as first obtain permission from the board of supervisors of the county in which the business is to be conducted, and upon the certificates of a majority of the legal electors of the town, township, or ward. A bond of three thousand dollars, with two or more sureties who shall justify in double the amount of said bond, is required of every applicant to whom a permit is thus granted.

WISCONSIN, which has hitherto been a lager beer State, and some of whose cities are still absolutely under the control of the beer interest, is also enjoying a temperance revival under the auspices of the Temple of Honor. It has a license law like that of Illinois.

MINNESOTA places the question of the issuance of license in the hands of the aldermen or selectmen.

CALIFORNIA, a wine growing State, where the advocates of the common use of wine, as a means of preventing drunkenness, have had an excellent opportunity of testing their theories, has become so cursed by intemperance as to produce a very general alarm. It has a License and Local Option law.

3

In OREGON there is a law prohibiting the sale of liquor unless the majority of citizens of a town sign a petition for the sale to be licensed therein ; the converse of the local option idea. A bond of two thousand dollars is required, and the sale of all liquor prohibited on election day.

VIRGINIA.   As early as 1676 the Colony of Virginia in its new constitution prohibited the sale of wines and ardent spirits.   It appears, however, that the *State* of Virginia fell from its colonial grace, for until recently it has not been known as a leading temperance community. Of late there has been a great revival of interest in this reform under the lead of the Woman's Christian Temperance Union.

The new temperance law of Virginia, in providing for the estimates of liquor sales on which a heavy tax is levied, requires all liquor sellers to use a sort of bell-punch, or register, on which the dealer is required to turn a crank once round for the purpose of registering every drink he sells.

Thus the success of this scheme depends upon the liquor dealers themselves.

Some of the dealers have attempted to block the law by showing that the registering machine was an infringement upon another man's patent ; but the injunction was dissolved, and, for the present, Virginia liquor dealers must go on grinding out the evidence of their own shame.

NORTH CAROLINA has the Local Option law, as follows :—

" SEC. I. *The General Assembly of North Carolina do*

enact : That it shall be the duty of the county commissioners of any county, upon petition of one fourth of the qualified voters of any township in their respective counties, to order an election, to be held on the first Monday in May in every year, to ascertain whether or not spirituous liquors shall or may be sold in said township or townships.

" SEC. 2. That it shall be the duty of the sheriffs of each county to hold such township elections when so ordered, under the same rules and regulations as are prescribed by law for holding elections for members of the General Assembly, so far as the same may be applicable, except as herein modified.

" SEC. 3. That any person allowed by law to vote for members of the General Assembly shall have the right to vote at such elections in the township where he is allowed by law to vote, and every such voter who favors the prohibition of the sale of spirituous liquors in his township shall vote a ticket on which shall be written or printed the word "prohibition," and every such voter who shall favor such sale shall vote a ticket on which shall be written or printed the word " license."

" SEC. 4. That on the day next after any such election shall be held, the inspectors of such election and a justice of the peace of the township shall compare the votes polled in the township, and certify the number of votes cast in favor of " prohibition" and the number in favor of " license," and the result of such election, to the Register of Deeds of the county, who shall first carefully copy such certificates in a book to be prepared and kept for that purpose, and then file the same among the pa-

pers of his office; and a certified copy from the book in
which such certificate is so registered, under the hand of
the Register of Deeds, and the seal of the county, shall
be sufficient evidence in all cases and courts in this State
of the result of such election in the township to which
the same may refer.

"SEC. 5. That if a majority of the votes cast at any
such election in any township shall have written or
printed on the same the word "prohibition," then and in
that case it shall not be lawful for the county commissioners to license the sale of spirituous liquors, or for any
person to sell any spirituous liquors within such township for one year next after any such election; and if any
person so prohibited shall sell any spirituous liquors
within such township, such person offending shall be
deemed guilty of a misdemeanor, and, on conviction of
such offense, shall be fined not exceeding fifty dollars, or
imprisoned not exceeding one month; but if a majority of the votes so cast shall have written or printed on
the same the word "license," then spirituous liquors may
be sold in such townships as now provided by law, and
not otherwise; provided that nothing herein contained
shall affect localities in which the sales of spirituous liquors are prohibited by law.

"SEC. 6. The sheriff shall designate the justice of the
peace in each township to aid in comparing and certify-
ing the vote cast at any such election, and the Register
of Deeds shall designate inspectors of elections in each
township. In case he shall fail, the sheriff or his deputies
shall make such appointments; and if any officer or
other person shall fail to discharge any duty imposed

by this act, such person offending shall be guilty of a misdemeanor, and, on conviction in the Superior Court, fined in the discretion of the Court.

"SEC. 7. This act shall take effect and be in force from and after the first day of April, 1874."

SOUTH CAROLINA has a stringent license law.

TEXAS has a Local Option law, passed in 1876, similar to that of North Carolina given above.

In GEORGIA, in 1874, a Bill passed the Legislature prohibiting the sale of liquors unless two thirds of the property owners of a county agreed thereto.

ALABAMA has a Local Option bill, applying to certain counties.

FLORIDA passed a Civil Damage bill through the House, but it was lost by one vote in the Senate.

MISSISSIPPI. The Legislature of Mississippi has recently passed an act requiring rum sellers to obtain the written consent of the men and women of legal age, in a town where they propose to sell, before license can be granted. Very few licenses have been granted in this State under the operation of this law, which, with a proper local public sentiment, seems to be the best possible legislation on this difficult subject. It is the prevailing practice in law to give the prisoner the benefit of all doubts arising in his case, and to count him innocent until he has been proven guilty. On this basis, therefore, the dram seller has been treated as a citizen holding certain inalienable rights, which could not be taken away except by due process of law. The Mississippi law holds the dram seller to be an outlaw, having no rights that any one is bound to respect; or a wild beast, to be killed on sight, unless he is taken under the especial protection of a majority of the citizens of some community.

NEVADA has no law upon the statute book relating to the traffic in alcoholic liquors.

ARKANSAS has a Local Option license law.

KANSAS in 1866 passed a Prohibitory and Local Option law, in connection with which the following incident is worthy of record :—

"The Legislature were in session at Topeka, where, at the time their bill was to come up, the temperance men held a State Temperance Convention. The Local Option bill was opposed at every stage by the party of the liquor sellers, but they were feeble, and it seemed likely that it would become a law. In this emergency a dispatch was sent over the wires to the liquor-traders of Leavenworth, the great center of the liquor interest in Kansas, stating the condition of things in the capital, and urging them to come on with all possible speed and appliances to check, if possible, the impending disaster.

"The liquor fraternity were thoroughly alarmed, and a full car load of them reached Topeka the next morning, confident that by such influences as they might bring to bear on the members of the House or Senate they could prevent the passage of the bill.

"But here they learned the truth of the divine word, 'The expectation of the wicked shall perish.' Topeka was on the west bank of the Kansas River, and the

State-house on the east, and the bridge had been carried away, so that there was no crossing except by boats.
During the night it happened that the ice in the trib-
utary of the Kansas had broken up, and was being
whirled along toward the Missouri at a rate which rendered it impossible to cross the river in a boat. Not all
the money in those liquor sellers' pockets—and they were
well lined, undoubtedly—could tempt a boatman to risk
his boat and life in an attempt to cross.

"They fumed, and raved, and swore, but all in vain.
They were compelled to remain in plain sight of the
State-house while the bill passed through the several
stages and was enacted by an overwhelming majority in
both branches, and received the signature of the governor."

The peculiarity of the Kansas Bill is, that no license
is to be granted to any individual to sell intoxicating liquors in the State until the party applying for license shall
present to the proper authorities a petition for the same,
signed by a majority of the adult citizens, *both male and
female*, of any city or ward in which he proposes to engage in the business.

Thus, to the young State of Kansas belongs the
honor of having first accorded to woman, the greatest
sufferer from the liquor system, a potential voice in
reference to its continuance or suppression.

It is not the purpose of this work to treat of the different political questions growing out of the temperance
reform. In some of the States of the Union, notably in
Maine, Massachusetts, Kansas etc., there are well-organ
ized political parties endeavoring to secure the election

of State officers pledged to carry out the temperance laws, which almost every-where, for want of magisterial sympathy, vigilance, and vigor are far less effective than they ought to be.

In the last presidential election, the temperance party had its candidate in the field, though but very little temperance was heard in the great struggle between the supporters of Mr. Hayes and Mr. Tilden.

On the 17th of May, 1876, the National Prohibition Convention, at Cleveland, Ohio, nominated Gen. Green Clay Smith as the temperance candidate for President of the United States. The general, who is also a reverend by virtue of his ministry in the Baptist denomination, is an ex-congressman, a prominent Son of Temperance, and Grand Worthy Chief Templar of the Good Templars of Kentucky.

This chapter on legal temperance may not be appropriately closed without mention of the Congressional Temperance Society, which owes its existence chiefly to the efforts of that veteran temperance statesman, the late Hon. Henry Wilson, for many years United States Senator from Massachusetts. Senator Wilson was the first president of this society, and was most ably seconded by the Hon. William E. Dodge, President of the National Temperance Society, and at one time member of Congress from New York.

REV. LYMAN BEECHER, D.D.

SECTION II.

FIRST TEMPERANCE SOCIETIES IN AMERICA.

CHAPTER III.

THE FIRST TEMPERANCE SOCIETIES IN AMERICA.

THE first assault upon the enemy by the temperance people of America was, as we have seen, along the lines of the law.

The second was by means of local associations, called Temperance or Temperate Societies, whose members were so deeply impressed with the evils resulting from the use of intoxicating drinks that they resolved *not to drink more than was good for them*, and not to make themselves responsible for drunkenness in others by furnishing liquor *on ordinary occasions*, either at their tables or in their fields.

The first of these temperate societies of which any record appears was organized in the County of Litchfield, Connecticut, in 1789, nineteen years earlier than that in Saratoga County, New York, which is set down in some of the authorities as the beginning of organized social temperance reform. Upward of two hundred of the most respectable Litchfield farmers formed themselves into " an association to discourage the use of spirituous liquors." They determined not to furnish any kind of *distilled* liquors to their farm hands, though it may be fairly inferred that cider, both hard and soft, and any kind of home-brewed liquors, were not considered objectionable.

Such a reform, which in our times seems rather a

weak affair, was in those days a notable domestic revolution, and the reformers were in no small danger of becoming martyrs to the cause. Among the laborers, who had no farms of their own to till, the withholding of the usual " 'leven o'clock bitters," and the absence of rum from the plowing matches, raisings, and husking bees, was regarded as an infringement of their inalienable rights, which, if it might not be resisted with fire and sword, could be, and usually was, resisted with derision, denunciation, and various petty annoyances. Temperance farmers of that day, not only in Connecticut, but throughout the country, were marked men. Nobody would work for them who could find employment with more " liberal " masters. They were jeered at in public places ; accused of being stingy hypocrites, who merely wanted to cheat their help out of the cost of the liquor ; their fences were broken down, their horses' tails were sheared, their houses were disfigured with filth, and every indignity which the lovers of bad spirits could invent, short of actual violence, was plentifully heaped upon them. Notwithstanding the very moderate views of the early temperance men, they were scouted as " fanatics," a word of common use in our day for describing teetotalers and advocates of prohibition by persons who claimed to hold substantially the same moderate views for which the early temperance fathers were so berated. Thus temperance "fanaticism " appears to be a variable term, changing its meanings with the changing front of the friends of the temperance reform.

In 1797 a Conference of the Methodist Episcopal Church, in Virginia, passed the following resolution :—

" *Resolved*, That we, the members of this Conference, do pledge our honor, as well as our word as Christians, not only to abandon the use of ardent spirits ourselves, except as a medicine, but also to use our influence to induce others to do the same."

Similar resolutions were passed by the Presbyterian Synod of Pennsylvania also enjoining ministers to preach against the sin of intemperance.

The next notable event in the history of temperance was the formation of the Union Temperance Society of Moreau and Northumberland, organized in Saratoga County, N. Y., April 13th, 1808. Dr. B. J. Clark and Rev. Lebbeus Armstrong were the leaders in this movement. They drafted the constitution for the society, and secured the signatures of forty-three gentlemen thereto.

The following extract from the constitution of the society shows the feebleness of this beginning:—

"Article IV, Section 1. No member shall drink rum, gin, whisky, wine, or any distilled spirits, or composition of the same, or any of them, except by advice of a physician, or in case of actual disease, (also excepting at public dinners,) under the penalty of twenty-five cents, provided that this article shall not infringe on any religious rite.

"Section 2. No member shall be intoxicated under penalty of fifty cents."

[This may be presumed to have reference to *ordinary* drunks, and not to the hilarities of public dinners and religious rites above mentioned.]

"Section 3. No member shall offer any of the above

liquors to any person to drink thereof under penalty of twenty-five cents for each offense."

Among the " religious rites " excepted in the constitution of this temperance society, at which a member might be drunk without loss of membership, provided he paid twenty-five cents for that privilege, were funerals, weddings, dedications of churches, and the like ; it being then the universal custom to furnish very strong refreshments for such great occasions, where not unfrequently the clergyman, as well as the lay members of the company, was badly under the influence of these evil spirits.

It was presumed that the ministers could pray and preach better for using a little strong drink ; while anniversaries, civic festivals, military displays, municipal elections, and all public and social assemblies, were nothing without plenty of liquor.

The ordination and installation of pastors of Churches, on which occasions the people of the parish kept open house for all comers, were occasions on which particularly large quantities of liquor were consumed ; the reputation of the town for good fellowship and hospitality being in exact proportion to the quantity and quality of the rum, brandy, gin, and wine set forth. With such exceptions to the binding force of their pledge, it would seem as if it were not necessary to persecute as fanatics the members of these early " Temperate Societies." They were certainly very temperate with their temperance.

In 1813 the first temperance society in Massachusetts was formed.

Its purpose, as stated in its constitution, was " to suppress the too free use of ardent spirit and its kindred

vices, and to encourage temperance and general morality;" but the Rev. Dr. Marsh declares, that "the society did little beyond observing its anniversary, by the
preaching of a sermon, after which preacher and hearers
would repair to tables richly laden with wine. It was,
therefore, without efficacy in rooting out the evil."

In describing the indifference of the country at that
time to the evil of intemperance, Henry Ware, of Boston, says: "The moral pestilence which scatters suffering worse than death spreads itself every-where around
us, but we are unaffected by its terrific magnitude and
fearful devastation.

"It would be comparatively a little thing if the plague
should sweep these thousands from our cities. It would
be a comfort to know that they perished by the hand
of God; but now they fall by their own hand — rush
downward of their own will into the corrupting grave,
and we stand by unmoved.

"Two things only appear certain: first, that the principal object must be to draw the public attention frequently and earnestly to the subject. In the second
place, it seems at the same time equally clear that there
is no man, or body of men, that can strike at the root of
the evil but the Legislature of the nation."

Among the advocates of temperance in these early
days we find such eminent names as Rev. Justin Edwards, the Rev. Joshua Leavitt, Rev. Leonard Woods,
Rev. Nathaniel Hewett, and Rev. Dr. Eliphalet Nott.

The year 1826 was a memorable one in the temperance reform. On the tenth of January, through the
agency of Dr. Edwards, a few friends met in the city of

Boston to consider the question, "What shall be done to banish the enemy from the United States?" The result of this meeting was the formation of a society whose pledge was *total abstinence from ardent spirits.* Of this society the Hon. Marcus Morton, for a long term of years governor of Massachusetts, was President; Hon. Samuel Hubbard, Vice-President; William Ropes, Esq., Treasurer; and John Tappan, Esq., Auditor.

Here was a new departure: it was also the basis of the first substantial success. There was evidently no salvation in the doctrine of "Temperance, not total abstinence;" which, in spite of its long trial in New England and New York, from 1789 till 1826, and its absolute and often ridiculous failure, is still the doctrine of the moderation men, from whom most of the drunkards are made.

If the members of the temperate societies were "fanatics," what word could describe the total abstinence men? If the first were hooted and annoyed, these last were sometimes actually in danger of their lives. The whole power of the rum fiend was aroused to meet this great uprising of conscience against him. Safe enough in possession of his spoils under the moderation theory, total abstinence was a blow at his vitals.

There was a great contrast between this Boston society and its immediate predecessor. That was a respectable show of morality, following the lead of public opinion; this was an organized army fighting the King's great enemy in the King's almighty name. It knew nothing of compromise. In its eyes drunkenness at "public dinners" was as much a shame as drunkenness anywhere else; perhaps more. It began to lay the ax at the root of the tree, and no wonder there was a mighty shaking among the branches.

One of the first acts of the American Temperance Society, as it was called, was to put into the field a temperance advocate to travel, lecture, organize branch societies, etc. For this purpose the sum of eight thousand dollars was raised in Boston and vicinity, and the Rev. Dr. Hewitt was engaged for this service. This first professional temperance advocate made a tour through some of the New England and Middle States, every-where enlisting the sympathies of the people and organizing numerous branches, so that the society at its first anniversary, held that year, was able to report a total of two hundred and twenty-two societies, besides thirty thousand signers of the total abstinence pledge. Many distilleries had to close for want of business, and a number of ship-brokers sent their vessels to sea under the temperance flag.

So energetically was the work pushed forward during the years 1828 and 1829, that at the end of the latter year four hundred merchants had given up the traffic in liquor, fifty distilleries had closed, the number of societies had increased to one thousand, and the number of pledged members to *one hundred thousand*, of whom about twelve thousand had been drunkards.

On the seventeenth of January, 1828, principally through the influence of the Hon. Edward C. Delavan, a wealthy and retired business man, the New York State Temperance Society was organized; and on the twentieth of May a similar society was formed in Hartford,

Connecticut, with the Rev. Jeremiah Day, President of
Yale College, as its President, and Rev. John Marsh as
Secretary and General Agent.

"The National Philanthropist," the first distinctively
temperance newspaper in the world, was established in
Boston, by the Rev. William Collier in 1828; but it was
shortly after removed to New York, where it gave place
to " The Journal of Humanity," established by the New
York State Temperance Society in 1829, and edited by
Rev. W. W. Hooker.

This notable year of temperance revival was also sig-
nalized by the entrance into the temperance ranks of the
Hon. Lewis Cass, of Michigan, who was twice a member
of the Cabinet of the United States.   In his addresses
on the temperance platform he declared that he had all
his life been a cold-water man, and that in the severe
trials his constitution had undergone in youth from the
exposure and the severe weather he had encountered
during the last war, he had remained strictly a total abstinence man.

Three years later General Cass, then Secretary of
War, issued an order "forbidding the introduction of
ardent spirits into any fort, camp, or garrison in the
United States, and prohibiting their sale by any sutler
to the troops.   As a substitute for the ardent spirits issued previously, and for the commutation in money prescribed thereby, eight pounds of sugar and four pounds
of coffee will be allowed to every one hundred rations."
The Secretary of the Navy likewise discouraged the
use of spirits by the seamen, and directed that coffee,
tea, sugar, and money be offered in their place.

It was claimed that from one half to two thirds of all the distilleries in the State of New York had closed; and the committee of the State society estimated that that commonwealth had saved during twelve months, in the lessened use of ardent spirits, the sum of $6,250,000.

During that period there was also a marked improvement in public morals, and increased prosperity in trade and every branch of industry; while, better than all, the Spirit of the Lord had wrought wonderful things in revivals of religion throughout the State.

At the beginning of 1833 it was estimated that there were more than five thousand temperance societies in the United States, with a membership of a million and a quarter, of whom ten thousand had been drunkards. Four thousand distilleries had been stopped, six thousand merchants had given up the sale of ardent spirits, and their use had been abandoned on over four thousand vessels.

There was still a weak point in the platform of the Temperance Society. It pledged its members to total abstinence from all distilled liquors, but little or nothing was said against the use of the lighter stimulants. In some high and influential quarters this was thought to be the full extent to which the pledge could be carried without impertinent interference.

The distinguished Dr. Hitchcock, President of Amherst College, in his Hygienic Lectures before the students, published in 1829, declared that he had considered it extremely injudicious and " Quixotic " for any temperance society to require total abstinence from the milder stimulants; but the good doctor was afterward converted from the error of his ways, and became an advocate of total abstinence from *all* intoxicating drinks.

The relapse of multitudes of reformed men into drunkenness through the use of milder drinks, such as wine, ale, and cider, led to the conviction that this, also, must be abandoned. The rich must give up their wine, if the common people were to give up their rum and whisky. As a thrust at the reformers aimed at this joint in their armor, a satirical preamble and resolution, adopted at a meeting of old topers, produced not only a great deal of laughter at their expense, but provoked them to more vigorous and sweeping measures of reform. The document was widely circulated, and read as follows:—

"*Whereas*, The object of all drinking is to produce intoxication in the cheapest and most expeditious manner possible; and,

"*Whereas*, The substitution of the more costly drinks, such as wine and beer, has a tendency to increase the expense of the operation without lessening the disposition to drink; therefore,

"*Resolved*, That we recommend to all true friends of temperance to quit the use of every other intoxicating beverage except whisky, rum, gin, or brandy."

The excitement produced by this insignificant squib is said to have been one of the chief causes which led to the holding of the first National Temperance Convention in America. It took place in the city of Philadelphia, commencing on the 24th of May, 1833, and continuing in session three days.

There were four hundred and forty delegates present, representing nineteen States and one Territory.

The two leading conclusions reached by the discussions were: First, "That the traffic in ardent spirits to be used as a beverage is morally wrong, and ought to be universally abandoned." Second, "That an advance in the cause is demanded, and that it is expedient to adopt the total abstinence pledge as soon as possible."

There was a weakness about this language which destroyed the influence of this first National Temperance Congress. There was, indeed, a National Society formed, but it was scarcely ever heard of afterward; and not till the organization of the American Temperance Union on a strict total abstinence basis was there ever a *national* temperance society in America worthy of the name.

If there is any one doctrine established by the history of the temperance reform in America, it is the doctrine that *temperance which does not mean total abstinence is powerless for permanent good.*

CHAPTER IV.

REV. LYMAN BEECHER, D.D.

ONE of the most prominent characters in the early history of the total abstinence reform is the Rev. Lyman Beecher, of whom it has been said that "he was the father of more brains than any other man in America."

Mr. Beecher was born October 12th, 1775, in the town of Guilford, Conn.; educated in the classics and in theology at Yale College; commenced his ministry in Easthampton, Conn., and in 1810 was called to the pastorate of the Congregational Church in Litchfield, Conn.

Soon after his arrival in this parish he became impressed with the evils arising from the use of liquor among the clergy, which was almost universal.

The following picture of a drinking scene at the ordination of a minister at Plymouth is from that delightful book, "The Autobiography of Lyman Beecher," which, with other extracts from the same volume, is here inserted by permission of Harper & Brothers, the publishers thereof :—

"At the ordination at Plymouth, the preparation for our creature comforts, besides food, was a broad sideboard covered with decanters, liquor and sugar, pitchers of water, etc.   There were found all the various kinds of liquor then in vogue, for when the Consociation arrived they always took something to drink around; also before public services, and always on their return.   As they could not all drink at once, they would be obliged to stand and wait, as people do when they go to mill. There was a decanter of spirits on the dinner table, also, 'to help digestion,' and the side-board, with the spillings of sugar, water, and liquor, looked like the bar of a very active grog-shop.

"None of the Consociation were drunk, but that there was not at times a considerable amount of exhilaration I cannot affirm.

"When they had all done drinking, and taken pipes and tobacco, in less than fifteen minutes there was such a smoke you could not see, and the noise I cannot describe—it was the *maximum* of hilarity.

"They were not the old-fashioned Puritans—they had run down; they had a great deal of spirituality on the Sabbath, and not much when they were where there was something good to drink.

"I think I recollect some animadversions were made at that time by the people on the amount of the liquor drunk, for the tide was swelling on the drinking habits of society."

The following extracts from the records of the South Society, in Hartford, in the year 1784, are given by the Rev. J. B. Dunn, D.D., in his history of the temperance movement; the record being a portion of the account for the entertainment of ministers at the ordination of the pastor of that Society:—

May 4th.	£	s.	d.
To keeping ministers, etc.:			
2 mugs tody,	0	2	4
5 segars,	0	5	10
1 pint wine,	0	3	0
3 lodgings,	0	9	0

The wants of the preachers on this the first day of their session, were very moderate; probably they met in the evening, as there is no mention of any meals, and there were but three persons, and this was their night-cap.

The next day, as the following records show, they did justice to the hospitalities of the occasion, and their numbers were increased after breakfast :—

		£	s.	d.
May 5th.				
To	3 bitters,	0	0	9
"	3 breakfasts,	0	3	6
"	15 boles punch,	1	10	0
"	24 dinners,	1	16	0
"	11 bottles of wine,	3	6	0
"	5 mugs flip,	0	5	10
"	3 boles punch,	0	6	0
"	3 boles tody,	0	3	6
		8	3	11

"The next ordination," continues Dr. Beecher, "was of Mr. Harvey, in Goshen, where there was some hard drinking, and some complaint on account of the amount of liquor consumed. Those two meetings were near together, and in both my alarm, and shame, and indignation were intense. It was that which woke me up for the work, and silently I took an oath before God that I would never attend another ordination of that kind.

"I was full. My heart kindles up at the thoughts of it now.

"There had been already so much alarm on the subject, that, at the General Association, at Fairfield, in

1811, a committee of three had been appointed in order to take into consideration some means of allaying the evil. A committee was also appointed by the Association of Massachusetts, for a similar purpose, that same month.

"I was a member of the General Association, which met the following year at Sharon. In 1812, when said committee reported, they said they had taken the subject into careful consideration; that intemperance had been for some time increasing in the most alarming manner, but that, after the most faithful and prayerful inquiry, they were obliged to confess that they did not perceive that any thing could be done.

"The blood started from my heart when I heard this, and I arose instantly and moved that another committee of three be appointed to report at this meeting on ways and means of arresting the tide of intemperance. This was immediately done. I was chairman, and on the following day brought in the report, the most important paper that ever I wrote."

This report, after referring to the alarming increase of intemperance, and its effect in nullifying the means of grace and in destroying souls, recommended, first, that all the ministers of the Association should preach on the subject; secondly, that they should abstain from the use of ardent spirits at ecclesiastical meetings; thirdly, that church-members should abstain from unlawful traffic in ardent spirits, and should cease to follow the fashion of furnishing them as a part of hospitable entertainment in social visits; fourthly, that parents should cease from the ordinary use of ardent spirits in the family, and should warn their children of the evils and dangers of intemper-

4

ance ; fifth, that employers should cease to give liquor to their employes, but give them other and better drinks and additional money ; also to circulate documents and form associations to aid the magistrates in the execution of the temperance laws.

The arguments of this report have the true temperance ring, and are among the strongest sentences ever written by that sturdy pen.

" I was not headstrong then," he goes on to say, " but I was heartstrong.

" We did not say a word then about wine, because we thought that it was best, in this sudden onset, to tackle that which was most prevalent and deadly, and that it was as much as would be safe to take hold of one such dragon by the horn without tackling another.

" However, we resolved upon abstaining from wine, and generally did so in our families.'

Dr. Beecher records with great satisfaction that as a result of these efforts ardent spirits were banished from the ecclesiastical meetings ; the use of spirits in families had diminished ; a temperance literature commenced ; and from that time the movement went on, " marching through New England, and marching through the world. Glory to God ! how it wakes up my old heart to think of it ! "

On election days, as well as at ordinations, liquor always flowed freely, and the ministers in those times being all of them politicians, were foremost in the caucus as well as the tippling.

The doctor says the ministers had always managed things to suit themselves. On election days they had a festival, and all the clergy used to go, walk in procession, smoke pipes, drink, talk over who should be governor, lieutenant-governor, and who in the upper house, and their councils would prevail as a matter of course.

In those days the justices of the peace were usually deacons of the Church; and so, what with ministers and deacons, the Standing Order of Religion, as it is called, almost amounted to a State Church; and this ecclesiastical power in politics the wise Dr. Beecher called to his aid to help on the temperance reform.

The following extract from one of his great sermons on the sins of the times, preached at New Haven, will give a good idea of the style of this temperance Boanerges:—

"Our vices are digging the grave of our liberties, and preparing to entomb our glory. We may despise admonition, but our destruction slumbereth not. The enormous consumption of ardent spirits in our land will produce neither bodies nor minds like those which are the offspring of temperance and virtue. Our institutions, civil and religious, have outlived that domestic discipline and official vigilance in magistrates which render obedience easy and habitual. Drunkards reel through the streets day after day, and year after year, with entire impunity. Profane swearing is heard, even by magistrates, as though they heard it not. . . .

"Truly we do stand on the confines of destruction · we are becoming another people. So many hands have so long been employed to pull away foundations, so few to repair the breaches, that the building totters. It is easy to recede, easy to retreat; but when the abomination of desolation has once passed over, who is to rear again the prostrate altars, and gather again the fragments, and build up demolished institutions? . . .

"Can we lawfully amass property by a course of trade which fills the land with beggars, and widows, and orphans, and crimes—which peoples the graveyard with premature mortality, and the world of woe with its victims of despair? Could all the forms of evil produced in the land by intemperance come upon us in one horrid array, it would appall the nation and put an end to the traffic in ardent spirits. If, in every dwelling built by blood, the stone from the wall should utter all the cries which the bloody traffic extorts, and the beam out of the timber should echo them back, who would build such a house? What if in every part of the dwelling, from the cellar upward, through all the halls and chambers, babblings, and contentions, and voices, and groans, and shrieks, and wailings were heard day and night! What if the cold blood oozed out, and stood in drops upon the walls, and, by preternatural art, all the ghastly skulls and bones of the victims destroyed by intemperance were dimly seen haunting the distilleries and stores where they received their bane, following the track of the ship engaged in the commerce, walking the waves, flitting athwart the deck, sitting upon the rigging, and sending up from the hold within, and from the waves without, groans and loud laments and wailings! Who would attend such stores? Who would labor in such distilleries? Who would navigate such ships? O! were the sky over our heads one great whispering gallery, bringing down about us all the lamentation and woe which intemperance creates, and the firm earth one sonorous medium of sound, bringing up around us from beneath the wailing of the damned whom the commerce in ardent spirits had sent thither, these tremendous realities, assailing our sense, would invigorate our conscience, and give decision to our purpose of reformation.

" But these evils are as real as if the stone did cry out of the wall, and the beam did answer it ; as real as if day and night wailings were heard in every part of the dwelling, and blood and skeletons were seen upon every wall ; as real as if the ghostly forms of departed victims flitted about the ship as she passed over the billows, and showed themselves nightly about stores and distilleries, and with unearthly voices screamed in our ears their loud laments. They are as real as if the sky over our heads collected and brought down about us all the notes of sorrow in the land, and the firm earth should open a passage for the wailings of despair to come up from beneath."

This radical doctrine was regarded by many as impracticable and ridiculous ; nevertheless it was the beginning of the great reform which now teaches total abstinence, as the first letter of its alphabet, and which declares the traffic in intoxicating drinks to be a nuisance, an outlaw, and under the curse of Almighty God.

THE FAMOUS SIX SERMONS.

Dr. Beecher's "Six Sermons on the Sin of Intemperance" have scarcely ever been equaled, and never excelled; and when we take into account the fact that these mighty discourses were delivered at a time when the free use of ardent spirits was almost universal, their author stands forth, not only as an advocate, but as a prophet in the early history of the temperance reform.

The following is his own account of the occasion of these sermons, as given in his autobiography:—

"There was a neighborhood about four miles out called Bradleysville, where I used to preach on Sabbath afternoon and have a lecture in the week. The first time I went was during a revival of religion, in which Mr. —— and his wife became pious. He was nearly the first male convert I had after I went to Litchfield, and he was always most affectionate and kind. His house was my home when I went out there to preach and spend the night. He gave me more presents than any two or three, and was one of my most useful and excellent young men. The meetings about this time had been discontinued for some cause, and on setting them up again I preached at his house as usual; but it did not go as it used to, and the second time the same. After lecture I went out-doors a few moments, and when I came in found he was abed, and his wife was weeping. I felt a shock of presentiment. I drew up my chair by her side, and said, 'What is the matter?'

"'O, matter enough,' said she.

"'Who is it? Is it your father?'

"I knew he had some liabilities that way. She told me it was her husband too.

"'Is it possible? is it possible?'

"'Yes, it is possible!'

"I thought to myself as I rode home, It is now or never. I must go about it immediately, or there is no chance of their salvation. These sermons I had projected early. I rather think it was at Easthampton that I struck out a considerable skeleton. They were laid by to be finished when I could get time. I knew where they were. I had laid them up. So I began the next Sabbath, and continued as fast as I could write them—one every Sabbath, I think. I wrote under such a power of feeling as never before or since—never could have written it under other circumstances. They took hold of the whole congregation. Sabbath after Sabbath the interest grew, and became the most absorbing thing ever heard of before—a wonder, of weekly conversation and interest, and when I got through, of eulogy. All the old farmers that brought in their wood to sell, and used to set up their cart-whips at the groggery, talked about it, and said, many of them, they would never drink again.

" The father was rescued, but the son was carried away; but when he died he was in possession of his mind, and seemed to have Christian feelings. And there is this hope about it : his mother was an habitual drinker, and he was nursed on milk-punch, and the thirst was in his constitution. He was a retailer, and so became bound hand and foot. He reformed for a season but went back. Still, I indulge the hope that God ·saw it was a constitutional infirmity, like any other disease."

CHAPTER V.

LYMAN BEECHER'S TEMPERANCE SERMONS.

THE following selections from Dr. Beecher's famous "Six Sermons on Intemperance"—perhaps the most powerful and successful temperance document ever produced—are here inserted by the kind permission of The American Tract Society. These discourses were preached at Litchfield in 1826, but their echoes have, for half a century, been heard half round the world:—

THE SIGNS OF INTEMPERANCE.

"Who hath woe? who hath sorrow? who hath contentions? who hath babbling? who hath wounds without cause? who hath redness of eyes?

"They that tarry long at the wine; they that go to seek mixed wine.

"Look not thou upon the wine when it is red, when it giveth his color in the cup, when it moveth itself aright. At the last it biteth like a serpent, and stingeth like an adder. Thine eyes shall behold strange women, and thine heart shall utter perverse things. Yea, thou shalt be as he that lieth down in the midst of the sea, or as he that lieth upon the top of a mast. They have stricken me, shalt thou say, and I was not sick; they have beaten me, and I felt it not; when shall I awake? I will seek it yet again."—PROVERBS xxiii, 29-35.

      *   *   *   *   *   *

We now approach some of those symptoms of intemperance which abused nature, first or last, never fails to give.

Who hath redness of eyes? All are not, of course, intemperate whose visual organs become inflamed and weak. But there are few intemperate persons who escape this malady; and yet, when it comes, they have no suspicion of the cause—speak of it without embarrassment, and wonder what the matter can be—apply to the physician for eye-water, and drink on. But every man who is accustomed to drink ardent spirits freely, whose eye begins to redden and to weep, ought to know what the matter is and to take warning; it is one of the signals which distressed nature holds out and waves in token of distress.

Another indication of intemperance is found in the fullness and redness of the countenance. It is not the fullness and freshness of health, but rather the plethora of a relaxed fiber and peccant humors, which come to occupy the vacancy of healthful nutrition, and to mar the countenance with pimples and inflammation. All are not intemperate, of course, who are affected with diseases of the skin. But no hard drinker carries such a face without a guilty and specific cause, and it is another signal of distress which abused nature holds out, while she cries for help.

Another indication of intemperance may be found in impaired muscular strength and tremor of the hand. Now the destroyer in his mining process approaches the citadel of life, and is advancing fast to make the keepers of the house tremble, and the strong men bow themselves. This relaxation of the joints and trembling of the nerves will be experienced especially in the morning, when the system, unsustained by sleep, has run down. The fire which sparkled in the eye the evening before is quenched, the courage which dilated the heart is passed

4*

away, and the tones of eloquence which dwelt on the inspired tongue are turned into pusillanimous complainings, until opium, or bitters, or both, are thrown into the
stomach to wind up again the run-down machine.

And now the liver, steeped in fire, begins to contract,
and refuses to perform its functions, and loss of appetite
ensues; and indigestion and fermentation and acidity
begin to rob the system of nutrition, and to vex and
irritate the vital organs, filling the stomach with air
and the head with fumes and the soul with darkness
and terror.

This reiterated irritation extends by sympathy to the
lungs, which become inflamed and lacerated, until hem-
orrhage ensues. And now the terrified victim hastens
to the physician to stay the progress of a consumption
which intemperance has begun, and which medical treatment, while the cause continues, cannot arrest.

About this time the fumes of the scalding furnace below begin to lacerate the throat, and blister the tongue
and the lip. Here, again, the physician is called in to
ease these torments; but until the fires beneath are ex-
tinct, what can the physician do? He can no more alle-
viate these woes than he can carry alleviation to the tormented in the flames for which these are the sad preparations.

Another indication of intemperance is irritability, pet-
ulance, and violent anger. The great organ of nervous
sensibility has been brought into a state of tremulous excitement. The slightest touch causes painful vibrations
and irritations, which defy self-government. The temper becomes like the flash of powder, or ungovernable

and violent as the helm driven hither and thither by raging winds and mountain waves.

Another indication of intemperance is to be found in the extinction of all the finer feelings and amiable dispositions of the soul; and if there have ever seemed to be religious affections, of these also. The fiery *stimulus* has raised the organ of sensibility above the power of excitement by motives addressed to the finer feelings of the soul and of the moral nature, and left the man a prey to animal sensation. You might as well fling out music upon the whirlwind to stay its course, as to govern the storm within by the gentler feelings of humanity. The only stimulant which now has power to move is ardent spirits, and he who has arrived at this condition is lost. The sea has made a clear breach over him, and swept away forever whatsoever things are pure and lovely and of good report.

And as to religion, if he ever seemed to have any, all such affections declined as the emotions of artificial stimulants arose, until conscience has lost its power, or survives only with vulture scream to flap the wing and terrify the soul. His religious affections are dead when he is sober, and rise only to emotion and loquacity and tears when he is drunk. Dead, twice dead is he, whatever may have been the hopes he once indulged, or the evidence he once gave, or the hopes he once inspired. For drunkards, no more than murderers, shall inherit the kingdom of God.

As the disease makes progress rheumatic pains diffuse themselves throughout the system. The man wonders what can be the reason that he should be visited by such a complication of diseases, and again betakes himself to the physician, and tries every remedy but the simple one of temperance. For these pains are only the murmurings and complainings of nature, through all the system giving signs of woe that all is lost. For to rheumatic pains ensues a debility of the system, which becoming unable to sustain the circulation, the fluids fall first upon the feet, and as the deluge rises the chest is invaded, and the breath is shortened, until by a sudden inundation it is stopped. Or, if in this form death is avoided, it is only to be met in another, more dilatory but no less terrific; for now comes on the last catastrophe—the sudden prostration of strength and appetite—an increased difficulty of raising the ebbing tide of life by stimulants —a few panic-struck reformations, just on the sides of the pit, until the last sinking comes from which there is no resurrection but by the trump of God and at the judgment-day.

And now the woes and the sorrows and the contentions and the wounds and babblings are over—the red eye sleeps—the tortured body rests—the deformed visage is hid from human observation—and the soul, while the dust crumbles back to dust, returns to God who gave it, to receive according to the deeds done in the body.

　　*　　　　*　　　　*　　　　*　　　　*　　　　*

But it will be said, What can be done? and ten thousand voices will reply, "Nothing, O, nothing; men always have drunk to excess, and they always will; there is so much capital embarked in the business of importation and distillation, and so much supposed gain in vending ardent spirits, and such an insatiable demand for them, and such ability to pay for them by high-minded, willful, independent freemen, that nothing can be done." Then farewell, a long farewell, to all our greatness!

The seasons are not more sure to roll, the sun to shine, or the rivers to flow, than the present enormous consumption of ardent spirits is sure to produce the most deadly consequences to the nation. They will be consumed in a compound ratio, and there is a physical certainty of the dreadful consequences. Have you taken the dimensions of the evil, its manifold and magnifying miseries, its sure-paced and tremendous ruin? And shall it come unresisted by prayer, and without a finger lifted to stay the desolation?

What if all men had cried out, as some did, at the commencement of the revolutionary struggle, "Alas! we must submit; we must be taxed; nothing can be done. O, the fleets and armies of England, we cannot stand before them!" Had such counsels prevailed we should have abandoned a righteous cause, and forfeited that aid of Heaven for which men are always authorized to trust in God, who are disposed to do his will.

Nothing can be done! Why can nothing be done? Because the intemperate will not stop drinking, shall the temperate keep on and become drunkards? Because the intemperate cannot be reasoned with, shall the temperate become madmen? And because force will not avail with men of independence and property, does it follow that reason and conscience and the fear of the Lord will have no influence? And because the public mind is now unenlightened and unawakened and unconcentrated, does it follow that it cannot be enlightened

and aroused, and concentrated in one simultaneous **and**
successful effort?   Reformations as much resisted **by**
popular feeling, and impeded by ignorance, interest, and
depraved obstinacy, have been accomplished through
the medium of a rectified public opinion ; and no nation
ever possessed the opportunities and the means that we
possess of correctly forming the public opinion, nor was
a nation ever called upon to attempt it by motives of
such imperious necessity.   Our all is at stake ; we shall
perish if we do not effect it.   There is nothing **that**
ought to be done which a free people cannot do.

THE REMEDY OF INTEMPERANCE.

" Woe to him that coveteth an evil covetousness to his house, that
he may set his nest on high, that he may be delivered from the power
of evil! Thou hast consulted shame to thy house by cutting off
many people, and hast sinned against thy soul. For the stone shall
cry out of the wall, and the beam out of the timber shall answer it.

" Woe unto him that giveth his neighbor drink, that puttest thy
bottle to him, and makest him drunken also, that thou mayest look
on their nakedness! Thou art filled with shame for glory: drink
thou also, and let thy foreskin be uncovered: the cup of the Lord's
right hand shall be turned unto thee, and shameful spewing shall be
on thy glory."—HABAKKUK 2 : 9–11, 15, 16.

LET us now take an inventory of the things which can
be done to resist the progress of intemperance. I shall
set down nothing which is chimerical, nothing which will
not commend itself to every man's judgment as entirely
practicable.

1. It is entirely practicable to extend universal information on the subject of intemperance. Every pulpit and
every newspaper in the land may be put in requisition
to give line upon line on this subject. The national
Tract Society may, with great propriety, volunteer in
this glorious work, and send out its warning voice by
winged messengers all over the land. And would all this
accomplish nothing? It would prevent the formation of
intemperate habits in millions of instances, and it would
reclaim thousands in the early stages of this sin.

2. It is practicable to form an association for the special purpose of superintending this great subject, whose
untiring energies shall be exerted in sending out agents

to pass through the land, collect information, confer with influential individuals and bodies of men, deliver addresses at popular meetings, and form societies auxiliary to the parent institution. This not only may be done, but I am persuaded will be done before another year shall have passed away.

3. Something has been done, and more may be done, by agricultural, commercial, and manufacturing establishments, in the exclusion of ardent spirits as an auxiliary to labor. Every experiment which has been made by capitalists to exclude ardent spirits and intemperance has succeeded, and greatly to the profit and satisfaction both of the laborer and his employer. And what is more natural and easy than the extension of such examples by capitalists, and by voluntary associations — in cities, towns, and parishes—of mechanics and farmers, whose resolutions and success may from time to time be published, to raise the flagging tone of hope, and assure the land of her own self-preserving powers? Most assuredly it is not too late to achieve a reformation. Our hands are not bound, our feet are not put in fetters; and the nation is not so fully set upon destruction as that warning and exertion will be in vain. It is not too much to be hoped, that the entire business of the nation, by land and by sea, shall yet move on without the aid of ardent spirits, and by the impulse alone of temperate freemen. This would cut off one of the most fruitful occasions of intemperance, and give to our morals and to our liberties an earthly immortality.

The young men of our land may set glorious examples of voluntary abstinence from ardent spirits, and, by associations for that purpose, may array a phalanx of opposition against the encroachments of the destroyer; while men of high official standing and influence may cheer us by sending down the good example of their firmness and independence in the abolition of long-established, but corrupting habits.

All the professions, too, may volunteer in this holy cause, and each lift up its warning voice, and each concentrate the power of its own blessed example. Already from all clerical meetings the use of ardent spirits is excluded; and the medical profession have also commenced a reform in this respect which, we doubt not, will prevail. Nor is it to be expected that the bar, or the agricultural interest as represented in agricultural societies, will be deficient in magnanimity and patriotic zeal, in purifying the morals and perpetuating the liberties of the nation. A host may be enlisted against intemperance which no man can number, and a moral power be arrayed against it which nothing can resist.

All denominations of Christians in the nation may with great ease be united in the effort to exclude the use and the commerce in ardent spirits. They alike feel and deplore the evil, and, united, have it in their power to put a stop to it. This union may be accomplished through the medium of a national society. There is no object for which a national society is more imperiously demanded, or for which it can be reared under happier auspices. God grant that three years may not pass away before the entire land shall be marshaled, and the evils of intemperance be seen like a dark cloud passing off, and leaving behind a cloudless day!

The Churches of our Lord Jesus Christ of every name can do much to aid in this reformation. They are organized to shine as lights in the world, and to avoid the
• very appearance of evil. A vigilant discipline is doubtless demanded in the cases of members who are of a lax and doubtful morality in respect to intemperance. It is not enough to cut off those who are past reformation, and to keep those who, by close watching, can be preserved in the use of their feet and tongue. Men who are mighty to consume strong drink are unfit members of that kingdom which consisteth not in "meat and drink," but in "righteousness and peace." The time, we trust, is not distant, when the use of ardent spirits will be proscribed by a vote of all the Churches in our land, and when the commerce in that article shall, equally with the slave-trade, be regarded as inconsistent with a creditable profession of Christianity.

The Friends, in excluding ardent spirits from the list of lawful articles of commerce, have done themselves immortal honor; and in the temperance of their families, and their thrift in business, have set an example which is worthy the admiration and imitation of all the Churches in our land.

When the preceding measures have been carried, something may be done by legislation to discourage the distillation and importation of ardent spirits, and to discountenance improper modes of vending them. Then the suffrage of the community may be expected to put in requisition men of talents and integrity, who, sustained by their constituents, will not hesitate to frame the requisite laws, and to give to them their salutary power.

Even now there may be an amount of suffrage sufficient, could it be concentrated and expressed, to sustain laws which might go to limit the evil; but it is scattered, it is a dispersed, unorganized influence, and any effort to suppress intemperance by legislation now, before the public is prepared for an efficient co-operation, could terminate only in defeat. Republics must be prepared by moral sentiment for efficient legislation.

Much may be accomplished to discountenance the commerce in ardent spirits by a silent, judicious distribution of patronage in trade.

Let that portion of the community who would exile from society the traffic in ardent spirits bestow their custom upon those who will agree to abandon it, and a regard to interest will soon produce a competition in well-doing. The temperate population of a city or town are the best customers, and have it in their power to render the commerce in ardent spirits disadvantageous to those who engage in it. This would throw an irresistible argument upon the side of reformation. There are many now who would gladly be released from the necessity of dealing in spirituous liquors, but they think that their customers would not bear it. Let their sober customers, then, take off their fears on this hand and array them on the other, and a glorious reformation is achieved. When the temperate part of the community shall not only declaim against mercantile establishments which thrive by the dissemination of moral contagion, but shall begin to act with a silent but determined discrimination, the work is done; and can any conscientious man fail to make the experiment? " To him that

knoweth to do good and doeth it not, to him it is sin."
If we countenance establishments in extending and perpetuating a national calamity, are we not partakers in
other men's sins? How many thousands may be saved
from entering into temptation, and how many thousands
rescued who have entered, if temperate families will give
their custom to those who have abandoned the traffic in
ardent spirits. And to how much crime and suffering
and blood shall we be accessory if we fail to do our duty
in this respect. Let every man, then, bestow his custom
in the fear of the Lord, and as he expects to give an account with joy or grief, of the improvement or neglect
of that powerful means of effecting moral good.

When all these preliminary steps have been taken, petitions may be addressed to the Legislatures of the States
and to Congress, by all denominations, each under their
own proper name, praying for legislative interference to
protect the health and morals of the nation. This will
call to the subject the attention of the ablest men in the
nation, and enable them to touch some of the springs of
general action with compendious energy. They can
reach the causes of disastrous action when the public
sentiment will bear them out in it, and can introduce
principles which, like the great laws of nature, will with
silent simplicity reform and purify the land.

And now, could my voice be extended through the
land to all orders and descriptions of men, I would " cry
aloud and spare not." To the watchmen upon Zion's
walls, appointed to announce the approach of danger,
and to say unto the wicked man, " Thou shalt surely
die," I would say, Can we hold our peace, or withhold

the influence of our example in such an emergency as this, and be guiltless of blood? Are we not called upon to set examples of entire abstinence? How otherwise shall we be able to preach against intemperance, and reprove, rebuke, and exhort? Talk not of "habit," and of "prudent use," and a little for the "stomach's sake." This is the way in which men become drunkards. Our security and our influence demand immediate and entire abstinence. If nature would receive a shock by such a reformation, it proves that it has already been too long delayed, and can safely be deferred no longer.

To the Churches of our Lord Jesus Christ—whom he hath purchased with his blood, that he might redeem them from all iniquity, and purify them to himself a peculiar people—I would say, Beloved in the Lord, the world hath need of your purified example; for who will make a stand against the encroachments of intemperance if professors of religion will not? Will you not, then, abstain from the use of it entirely, and exile it from your families? Will you not watch over one another with keener vigilance, and lift an earlier note of admonition, and draw tighter the bands of brotherly discipline, and with a more determined fidelity cut off those whom admonition cannot reclaim? Separate, brethren, between the precious and the vile, the living and the dead, and burn incense between them, that the plague may be stayed.

To the physicians of the land I would cry for help in this attempt to stay the march of ruin. Beloved men, possessing our confidence by your skill and our hearts by your assiduities in seasons of alarm and distress, com-

bine, I beseech you, and exert, systematically and vigorously, the mighty power you possess on this subject
over the national understanding and will. Beware of
planting the seeds of intemperance in the course of your
professional labors, but become our guardian angels to
conduct us in the paths of health and of virtue. Fear
not the consequences of fidelity in admonishing your patients, when diseased by intemperance, of the cause and
the remedy of this malady : and whenever one of you
shall be rejected for your faithfulness, and another be
called in to prophesy smooth things, let all the intemperate and all the land know, that in the whole nation
there are no false prophets among physicians, who for
filthy lucre will cry peace to their intemperate patients,
when there is no peace to them but in reformation. Will
you not speak out on this subject in all your medical societies, and provide tracts, sanctioned by your high professional authority, to be spread over the land?

Ye magistrates, to whom the law has confided the dis-
cretionary power of giving license for the vending of
ardent spirits, and the sword for the punishment of the
violations of law, though you alone could not resist the
burning tide, yet, when the nation is moved with fear,
and is putting in requisition her energies to strengthen
your hands, will you not stand up to your duty and do
it fearlessly and firmly? No class of men in the community possess as much direct power as you possess ; and,
when sustained by public sentiment, your official influence and authority may be made irresistible. Remember,
then, your designation by Heaven to office for this self-
same thing ; and, as you would maintain a conscience

void of offense, and give up to God a joyful account, be faithful. Through you let the violated law speak out, and righteousness and peace become the stability of our times.

The friends of the Lord and his Christ, with laudable enterprise, are rearing temples to Jehovah, and extending his word and ordinances through the land; while the irreligious influence of this single crime balances, or nearly balances, the entire account.

And now, ye venerable and honorable men, raised to seats of legislation in a nation which is the freest, and is destined to become the greatest, and may become the happiest upon earth, can you, will you behold unmoved the march of the mighty evil? Shall it mine in darkness, and lift fearlessly its giant form in daylight, and deliberately dig the grave of our liberties, and entomb the last hope of enslaved nations, and nothing be done by the national government to stop the destroyer? With the concurrent aid of an enlightened public sentiment, you possess the power of a most efficacious legislation; and, by your example and influence, you of all men possess the best opportunities of forming a correct and irresistible public sentiment on the side of temperance. Much power to you is given to check and extirpate this evil, and to roll down to distant ages, broader and deeper and purer, the streams of national prosperity. Save us by your wisdom and firmness, save us by your own example, and, " as in duty bound, we will ever pray."

This sermon, in which the future steps of this great reform were pointed out with almost prophetic wisdom, concludes as follows :—

" To the affectionate husband I would say, Behold the
wife of thy bosom, young and beautiful as the morning;
and yet her day may be overcast with clouds, and all thy
early hopes be blasted. Upon her the fell destroyer may
lay his hand, and plant in that healthful frame the seeds
of disease, and transmit to successive generations the inheritance of crime and woe. Will you not watch over
her with ever-wakeful affection, and keep far from your
abode the occasions of temptation and ruin ? Call around
you the circle of your healthful and beautiful children.
Will you bring contagion into such a circle as this?
Shall those sparkling eyes become inflamed, those rosy
cheeks purpled and bloated, that sweet breath be tainted,
those ruby lips blistered, and that vital tone of unceasing
cheerfulness be turned into tremor and melancholy?
Shall those joints so compact be unstrung, that dawning
intellect be clouded, those affectionate sensibilities be-
numbed, and those capacities for holiness and heaven be
filled with sin and "fitted for destruction?" O, thou
father, was it for this that the Son of God shed his blood
for thy precious offspring ; that, abandoned, and even
tempted, by thee, they should destroy themselves and
pierce thy heart with many sorrows? Wouldst thou let
the wolf into thy sheep-fold among the tender lambs?
wouldst thou send thy flock to graze about a den of lions ?
Close, then, thy doors against a more ferocious destroyer,
and withhold the footsteps of thy immortal progeny
from places of resort more dangerous than the lions' den.
Should a serpent of vast dimensions surprise in the field
one of your little group, and wreath about his body its
cold, elastic folds—tightening with every yielding breath

its deadly grip—how would his cries pierce your soul, and his strained eyeballs and convulsive agonies and imploring hands add wings to your feet, and supernatural strength to your arms! But in this case you could approach with hope to his rescue. The keen edge of steel might sunder the elastic fold and rescue the victim, who, the moment he is released, breathes freely and is well again. But the serpent Intemperance twines about the body of your child a deadlier grip, and extorts a keener cry of distress, and mocks your effort to relieve him by a fiber which no steel can sunder. Like Laocoon, you can only look on while bone after bone of your child is crushed, till his agonies are over and his cries are hushed in death.

And now, I would say, Resolve upon reformation by entire abstinence while the argument is clear, and the impression of it is fresh, and your judgment is convinced, and your conscience is awake, be persuaded, not almost, but altogether. The present moment may be the one which decides your destiny forever. As you decide now upon abstinence or continued indulgence, so may your character be through time and through eternity. Resolve, also, instantly to exclude ardent spirits from your family, and put out of sight the memorials of past folly and danger. And if for medical purposes you retain ardent spirits in your house, let it be among other drugs, and labeled, "Touch not, taste not, handle not."

As you would regulate your conduct by the Gospel, and give up your last account with joy, weigh well the arguments for abandoning the traffic in ardent spirits as

5

unlawful in the sight of God. And "if thy right hand offend thee, cut it off. If thy right eye offend thee, pluck it out." Talk not of loss and gain; for who can answer for the blood of souls? and " what shall it profit a man, if he gain the whole world and lose his own soul?" "Woe to him that coveteth an evil covetousness to his house, that he may set his nest on high, that he may be delivered from the power of evil! Thou hast consulted shame to thy house by cutting off many people, and hast sinned against thy soul. For the stone shall cry out of the wall, and the beam out of the timber shall answer it. Woe to him that buildeth a town with blood, and establisheth a city by iniquity! Behold, is it not of the Lord of hosts that the people shall labor in the very fire, and the people shall weary themselves for very vanity?"

JOHN B. GOUGH

SECTION III.

THE WASHINGTONIANS.

CHAPTER VI.

THE WASHINGTONIANS.—JOHN HAWKINS.

THE Washingtonian movement had its origin in a tippling house, in the city of Baltimore, in the year 1840, with a company of half a dozen hard drinkers who had formed themselves into a club, and who used to meet for drinking bouts at Chase's tavern.

One night the Rev. Matthew Hale Smith, a noted lecturer on temperance, was announced to speak in one of the churches, and they appointed two of their number a committee to go and hear him. The committee brought back a favorable report of the man and his doctrines, upon which a warm discussion arose. This being overheard by the landlord, he at once broke out into a tirade against all temperance lecturers, and denounced them as hypocrites and fools.

To this storm of abuse one of the old topers replied, "Of course it is for your interest to cry them down;" whereupon the discussion waxed hotter and hotter, and resulted in the six men forming themselves into a temperance club, which they styled the "Washingtonian Total Abstinence Society," and adopted a pledge requiring total abstinence from the use of all intoxicating liquors.

The names of these six individuals were William Mitchell, David Hoss, Charles Anderson, George Steer, Bill M'Curdy, and Tom Campbell. John Hawkins early became a member, but was not one of the original six.

They then voted to meet the next night in a carpenter shop, and each agreed to bring a new member. These meetings were held almost nightly, at which each man related his own experience at the court of death. As might be expected, the meetings soon began to attract public attention.

These reformed men were soon invited to visit other cities and towns; and who of our older citizens has not listened to the thrilling and simple experience of John Hawkins as he portrayed the misery of the drunkard, and told the touching story of his little daughter, Hannah, persuading him to reform? This new movement spread from city to city, and from town to town, until there was scarcely a place in the United States that did not have its Washingtonian Total Abstinence Society. Men who had been drunkards for years burst the bands that had so long bound them, and became temperance reformers. The name being quite long, it soon became shortened by daily use, and these organizations became known throughout the country as " Washingtonians."

This was a rebellion of the subjects of King Alcohol against his tyranny, and as such it immediately became famous. It was a reform, commencing with the people who most needed reformation, and carried with it so much of sound sense, and so little of mere rhetoric, that every-where the reformed men who went about telling their own experience and salvation from the power of liquor found large and attentive audiences, and the Washingtonian movement became the chief topic both in religious and social circles.

It was quite a wonderful thing to hear a man in plain clothes, and without any of the graces of speech, declare what had been done for him, and exhorting with all simplicity and boldness that others should give up liquor as he had done.

The common people heard these men gladly, and drunkards by thousands and tens of thousands signed the total abstinence pledge.

In this movement there was no exception made in favor of the man who could buy fifteen gallons over the man who could buy a single glass.

Ale, wine, beer, cider, every thing else that had alcohol in it, was rejected, and for motives of domestic peace and plenty, self-respect and personal honor, men were persuaded to sign this pledge.

It was assumed that every man who wished to do so was able to break off his habits of drink. The religious feature of the movement, which is its latest and crowning glory, had not then appeared. Personal experiences, droll stories, and sharp jokes at the expense of drunkards and drunkard makers; imitations of the antics and fooleries of men under the influence of liquor; sharp thrusts at the avariciousness and meanness of the liquor sellers, and at the tricks of liquor makers, formed the staple of the lecturing under the Washingtonian movement.

When this movement began, Dr. Jewitt, who was himself one of the chief agents of the reformation in Massachusetts, says, " Nineteen twentieths of the clergy were total abstainers;" and what was true of Massachusetts was substantially true throughout New England.

The progress of the temperance reform for the nine

years from 1831 to 1840 may be indicated by the following figures: In the first-mentioned year twelve millions
of people drank seventy millions of gallons of liquor—an
average of six gallons a year to every man, woman, and
child—besides wine, beer, and cider.   In 1840 seventeen
millions of people drank forty-three millions of gallons—
a reduction of more than one half *per capita*.

Still more manifest were the signs of progress after
the Washingtonian movement fairly got under way, and
the reformed men had commenced their tour of the principal cities, relating their experience to assembled multitudes, and gathering in the people by thousands to the
new society.   It is estimated that under the impetus of
this movement one hundred and fifty thousand drunkards signed the pledge, besides uncounted thousands of
other classes of society.

Some of the leaders in this movement, so far from feeling the need of religion, declared that religious exercises
of every kind were out of place in temperance meetings.
They were not even opened with prayer.

It seemed to be a part of the policy to avoid every
possible question that might arise concerning religion, in
order that men might be the more deeply impressed with
the duty of temperance.   But this effort to divorce temperance from religion was the chief weakness of the
Washingtonian movement.   Nevertheless, in spite of
this coldness toward Christ and his Church, the actual
reform wrought by this means was oftentimes the forerunner of revivals of religion in local churches, and many
a man was saved from his other sins through his effort
to save himself from drunkenness.

.

JOHN H. W. HAWKINS.

Few names were more familiar to the people of the United States during the early years of the great Washingtonian movement than that of John Hawkins, of Baltimore.   He was not one of the original club by which the reform was inaugurated, but joined them soon after, and presently developed such talent for temperance oratory that his services were in demand from Maine to Louisiana.   During the eighteen years of his life after his reformation he spoke and organized Washingtonian societies in all the principal cities and towns of New England; and in New York, Philadelphia, Washington, Harrisburgh, Cincinnati, Louisville, Ky., Charleston, S. C., New Orleans, La., etc.

In his journal, which was published after his death, the record of the number of signers of the total abstinence pledge at a large number of his meetings are given, usually reaching into the hundreds, a considerable proportion of them being men whose bloated countenances and trembling nerves showed how much they were in need of this salvation.

At Springfield, Mass., Newport, R. I., Sáratoga, N. Y., and Portland, Maine, his efforts were notably blessed; but perhaps his most remarkable triumph was in Boston, then a city of a hundred thousand inhabitants, in which it was declared at one of the Washingtonian Conventions that "*four fifths of all the Boston drunkards had signed the temperance pledge.*"

5*

The enthusiasm of these Washingtonian meetings was something wonderful. The experiences of men actually reformed from the lowest depths of drunkenness were arguments that nothing could resist, and the presence of such a man before an audience was as if one had risen from the dead. Poor wretches would rise to their feet in the midst of great assemblies, and, with a look of desperation on their bloated faces, would ask,

" Do you think I could reform? Do you think there is any hope for me?"

" Yes, brother. Sign the pledge, and it will make a sober man of you," would be the reply. Then, amid the sobs, and "God bless yous!" of his family and friends, the poor drunkard would crowd up to the platform, take the pen in his trembling hand, and sign, the vast congregation holding their breath as they watched him through their tears. Then, with a heavy sigh, the man, with a new hope in him, would, perhaps, try to speak a few words, confessing his own sins, and the sorrows he had brought upon his wife and children—always the same sad story, but always new and touching—and then the older Washingtonians would gather round him, talk encouragingly to him, find out his most pressing necessities and relieve them, and the poor, lost wretch would feel as if he had suddenly been lifted to a mountain top where on the one hand he could look down into the abyss from which he had just been taken, and on the other he could catch a glimpse of the distant glories of the city of God, whose snowy, shining towers he dimly remembered in childhood's visions, but which he had wholly lost sight of in his long years of degradation, and which he had never again expected to see

The following, from one of Mr. Hawkins's addresses at Faneuil Hall, Boston, shows the tone and spirit of that brotherly work :—

"When I compare the past with the present, my days of intemperance with my present peace and sobriety, my past degradation with my present position in this hall— the Cradle of Liberty—I am overwhelmed. It seems to me holy ground.

" I never expected to see this hall. I heard of it in my boyhood. 'Twas here that Otis and the elder Adams argued the principles of independence, and we now meet here to make a second declaration of independence, not quite so lengthy as the old one, but it promises life, liberty, and the pursuit of happiness. Our forefathers pledged their lives, their fortunes, and their sacred honor ; we, too, will pledge our honor and our lives, but our fortunes—they have gone for rum !

"Drunkard! come up here, you can reform. I met a gentleman this morning who reformed four weeks ago, rejoicing in his reformation ; he brought a man with him who took the pledge, and this man brought two others. This is the way we do the business up in Baltimore ; we reformed drunkards are a Committee of the Whole on the State of the Union. We are all missionaries. We don't slight the drunkard ; we love him, we nurse him, as a mother does her infant learning to walk.

"I tell you, be kind to those men ; they have peculiar feelings when the boys run after them and hoot at them. Don't lay a stumbling-block in the way of such a man ; he has better feelings than many a moderate drinker.

Go up to him, stretch out your hand to him, and say,
'How do you do, sir?'

"Just let me tell you about one of our reformed men.
We all of us changed a great deal in our appearance :
some grew thin, some grew pale, but a certain dark com-
plexioned man grew yellow; and the old grog-seller
noticing the change in the others and seeing this old
customer not becoming *white*, declared he did not believe
but what he was a hypocrite, still drinking behind the
door.   One day the two men met, and the taverner
said to the teetotaler,

"'It appears to me you don't alter quite so much as
the rest.'

"'Don't I?   Well, why don't I?'

"'Why you don't grow pale, you only grow yaller.'

"'Yes,' said the reformed drunkard, putting his hand
in his pocket and pulling out a handful of gold pieces,
'these look *yaller*, too, but you don't get any more of
'em from me.'

"Go to Baltimore now and see our happy wives and
children.   Just think of our procession on the 5th of
April, when we celebrated our anniversary.   Six thousand men, nearly half of them reformed within a year,
followed by two thousand boys of all ages, to give assurance to the world that the next generation shall be sober.

"But where were our wives on that occasion?   At
home, shut up with hungry children in rags, the way
they were a year ago?   No, no; but in carriages, riding
round the streets to see and rejoice over their sober
husbands!"

Mr. Hawkins, like the other temperance orators of

those days, relied chiefly on the force and value of his
own experience before the great crowds that flocked to
hear him; but all the time he had new miracles of de-
liverances to relate, new stories of reformation to tell
out of the rich successes that crowned his temperance
ministry.

The following, gathered mostly from his published
memoirs, is the story of his life:—

"I was born in Baltimore, on the 28th of September,
1797. After some years at the school of the Rev. Mr.
Coxe, at the age of fourteen I was apprenticed for eight
years to learn the trade of a hatter with a master whose
place of business was a regular den of drunkenness. A
few days ago I found the old books of my master; there
were the names of sixty men upon them, and we could
not recollect but one who did not go to a drunkard's
grave."

When the British made a landing at Baltimore during
the war of 1812, young Hawkins borrowed a musket
and joined the ranks of the volunteers, exposing himself
with all the rashness and *abandon* of southern youth in
the very front of the battle, from which, however, he
escaped unhurt. In 1815 he was brought under the influence of divine grace in a revival of religion, united on
probation with the Methodist Episcopal Church, and for
some years was a zealous and useful Sunday-school
teacher and Christian worker. But hard times came,
employment failed, and in 1818 he went to seek his fortune at the West.

Of these days he says: "As soon as I was away from
paternal care I fell away. All went by the board, and my

sufferings commenced. For six months I had no shoes, and only one shirt and one pair of pantaloons. Then I was a vagabond indeed. But I returned, ragged and bloated, to my mother's home. It was customary in those days to let the young people drink with their parents, but neither they nor I thought of my becoming a miserable drunkard.

"When I got to the edge of my native town I was so ashamed that I waited till the dusk of the evening, and then I crept along to the house of my mother. She dressed me up decently, did not upbraid me, but only said, ' John, I am afraid you are bloated!' "

Mr. Hawkins having temporarily reformed, was married on Christmas day, 1822, to Miss Rachel Thompson, of Baltimore, of which marriage two children were born, Elizabeth and Hannah. The latter name will recall to many of the readers of this history a little temperance book of Washingtonian days entitled " Hannah Hawkins; or, the Reformed Drunkard's Daughter," a book over which many tears have been shed and many good resolutions made.

"For fifteen years," continues Mr. H., " I rose and fell, was up and down. I would earn fifteen dollars a week and be well and happy, and with my money in hand would start for home, but in some unaccountable way would fall into a tavern, thinking one glass would do me good. But a single glass would conquer all my resolutions. I appeal to all my fellow-drunkards if it is not exactly so.

"During the first two weeks of June (1840) I drank dreadfully, bought liquor by the gallon and drank and drank. I cannot tell how I suffered: in body every thing, but in mind more!

"By the fourteenth of the month—drunk all the time —I was a wonder to myself, astonished that I had any mind left; and yet it seemed, in the goodness of God, uncommonly clear. My conscience drove me to madness. I hated the darkness of the night, and when morning came I hated the light, I hated myself, hated existence; was about taking my own life. I asked myself, 'Can I restrain? Is it possible?' But there was no one to take me by the hand and say *you can*. I had a pint of whisky in my room, where I lay in bed, and thought I would drink it, but this seemed to be a turning point with me. I knew it was life or death as I decided to drink it or not.

"My wife came up knowing how I was suffering, and asked me to come down to breakfast. I said I would come presently. Then my daughter, Hannah, came up— my only friend, I always loved her the most—and she said,

"'Father, don't send me after whisky to-day!'

"I was tormented before; this was agony. I could not stand it, so I told her to leave, and she went down stairs crying, and saying, 'Father is angry with me.' My wife came up again and asked me to take some coffee. I told her I did not want any thing of her and covered myself up in the bed. Pretty soon I heard some one in the room, and, peeping out, I saw it was my daughter.

"'Hannah,' said I, 'I am not angry with you—and—*I shall not drink any more.*' Then we wept together.

"I got up, went to the cupboard, and looked on my

enemy, the whisky bottle, and thought, 'Is it possible I can be restored?' Several times while dressing I looked at the bottle, but I thought, 'I shall be lost if I yield.'

"Poor drunkard! there is hope for you. You cannot be worse off than I was, not more degraded or more of a slave to appetite. You can return if you will. Try it! *Try it!*

"Well, I went to the society of reformed drunkards, where I found all my old bottle companions. I did not tell any one, not even my wife, that I was going. I had got out of difficulty, but did not know how long I could keep out.

"The six founders of the society were there. We had worked together, got drunk together, we stuck together like brothers; and so we do now that we are sober.

"One of them said, 'Here's Hawkins, the regulator, the old bruiser,' and they clapped and laughed. But there was no laugh in me, I was too solemn and sober for that. Then they read the pledge:—

"'We, whose names are annexed, desirous of forming a society for our mutual benefit and to guard against a pernicious practice which is injurious to our health, standing, and families, do pledge ourselves, as gentlemen, that we will not drink any spirituous or malt liquors, wine, or cider.'

"They all looked over my shoulder to see me write my name. It was a great battle. I never had such feelings before.

"At eleven o'clock I went home. Before when I stayed out late I always went home drunk. My yard is covered with brick, and my wife could easily tell as I walked over it whether I were drunk or sober. She could even tell whether the gate opened drunk or sober.

"Well, this time it opened sober, and when I entered she was astonished. I smiled, and she smiled; and then I told her quick—I could not keep it back:—

"*'I have put my name to the temperance pledge, never to drink as long as I live.'*

"It was a happy time. I cried and she cried—we couldn't help it; the crying woke up my daughter, and she cried too for joy. I slept none that night; my thoughts were better than sleep. Next morning I went to see my mother. She had been praying twenty years for her drunken son. When she heard the good news she said, ' It is enough. Now I am ready to die.'

"Now what was I to do? My mind was blunted, my character gone; I was bloated, and getting old; but men who had slighted me came to my help again, took me by the hand, encouraged me, held me up, and comforted me.

"I'll never slight a drunkard as long as I live; he needs sympathy and is worthy of it. Poor and miserable as he is, he did not design to become a drunkard, and people have too long told him he cannot reform. But now we assure him he can reform, and we show ourselves, the Baltimore Washingtonians, two hundred in one year, as evidence of that fact.

"Drunkard, come up here! You can reform. Take the pledge and be forever free!"

The Washingtonian meetings might have been called temperance class-meetings, with a missionary outlook. One of the first records of the work is a letter to the original Baltimore Washingtonians, asking them to send a delegation of reformed men to New York, "to tell their experience." Five men were sent, men wholly without oratorical powers, but who had been slaves to drink, and had felt how good it was to be free; and the testimony of these five men was all that was required to kindle the enthusiasm in that great city.

A number of new temperance newspapers sprang into existence. Nineteen such publications are named in Mr. Hawkins' memoirs, while the regular newspaper press was largely occupied with the strange work of reform among the drunkards and the individual histories that the meetings developed. Some of the ablest speakers and writers of the day, in prose and poetry, devoted their genius to this great moral reform; among them Rev. Mr. Pierpont, of Boston, Wm. B. Tappen, Rev. Edward N. Kirk, D.D., and a large number of other leading clergymen. Dr. Lyman Beecher, in his mature age, saw and rejoiced over this temperance tidal wave, which was a fulfillment of his own prophecy, and a result for which he had well prepared the way.

Mr. Hawkins, toward the close of his brilliant career as a temperance worker, was licensed as a preacher of the Gospel by the Methodist Protestant Church, though he seems to have made little use of his commission.

His death occurred suddenly at Piqua, Pa., August 26, 1858, in the sixty-first year of his age, in the full possession of his mental power, and in the glorious hope of everlasting life.

CHAPTER VII.

JOHN B. GOUGH, THE TEMPERANCE APOSTLE.*

AMONG the men who were reached by the Washingtonian movement was that great temperance apostle whose name is a household word throughout the English-speaking world, and whose influence in favor of temperance, as well as of righteousness, has been one of the greatest blessings which God has vouchsafed to the people of this country in this age.

John B. Gough was born at Sandgate, on the Straits of Dover, in the county of Kent, England, on the twenty-seventh day of August, 1817. His father was a soldier, who, after his discharge from the army, with a pension of twenty pounds a year, used to delight in fighting his battles over again in common with his son, with whom he shared his faded military trappings and his love of military glory. His mother was a Christian woman, who long occupied the humble position of school-mistress in the village, and under whose instruction John made good progress, until he was able to enter the Seminary of Mr. Davis, of Folkestone. In his tenth year the finances of the family did not admit of this expense, and the boy left the school, which was the last he ever saw of the regular appliances of education.

---

* The thanks of the Editor of this volume are hereby expressed to Mr. Gough for his kind permission to make use of his Autobiography in preparing this sketch.

Before he was eleven years old, desiring to make a fortune for himself and relieve his father and mother, the boy joined a family about emigrating to America, who, for the sum of ten pounds, undertook to transport him across the Atlantic, give him a place on their prospective farm in Oneida County, New York, and help him in his beginnings to make a man of himself. This separation, which occurred on the tenth of June, 1829, nearly broke his mother's heart; however, she sent him away with her blessing, with many tears, and with sundry pieces of paper pinned to the articles of his scanty wardrobe in his small portmanteau on which were written texts of Scripture, which she thus brought home to his attention.

Why his guardians never sent him either to day-school or Sabbath-school is not explained, but, in consequence of this neglect, the lad determined to strike out alone, and in his eleventh year he left Oneida County for New York city, where he found a situation in the old Methodist Book Concern in Crosby-street, in which he was engaged as errand boy, and apprenticed to the book-binding business.

During his two years on the farm he had attended some meetings of the Methodists in Oneida County, and believing himself to be a subject of divine grace, he united on probation with the Methodist Episcopal Church—the Allen-street Church—where his brightness and talents induced some gentlemen in the congregation to make a proposal for his education; but circumstances led to his removal from the Book Concern to another place of employment, and the plans for his education were never carried out.

It appears that he had already become careless and thoughtless about religious things, and from that time for many long years he experienced the truth of that sad saying, " The way of the transgressor is hard."

In the year 1833 he sent for his mother and sister to come over to New York; but the mother soon after died in the miserable garret where they had lived together in the midst of the deepest privations, and John and his sister were the only mourners over her grave in the Potter's Field.

Five years after his arrival in the city of New York he had sunk so far as to connect himself with a low theater in Chatham-street as a comic singer, in which line he possessed unusual talents. Of this business, and of every thing connected with theaters, he formerly, through the influence of his mother, had entertained especial horror.

For several years he led this precarious life, obtaining situations in New York, Boston, Newburyport, Lowell, Providence, and several smaller New England cities, almost always cheated out of his pay, living by his wits rather than by his earnings, and all the while sinking lower and lower in the abyss of drunkenness.

A part of his performance in the actor's line was in a play called " The Departed Spirits; or, The Temperance Hoax," a composition in which those eminent temperance lecturers, Dr. Lyman Beecher, and Deacon Moses Grant, of Boston, were held up to ridicule.

Young Gough was a good workman at his trade, and but for the habit of drink, which had completely enslaved him, he might have risen to the first place in his business.

After his marriage he opened a bindery on his own account in Newburyport; but he spent the larger part of his earnings for brandy, which had now come to be the first necessity, and it was not long before his wife and infant child were taken away from him by the merciful Father above, where they could no longer suffer from poverty and neglect.

In a fit of *delirium tremens*, which came upon him as a result of a three days' debauch, he was near burning himself to death by dropping a lighted candle on his miserable bed, upon which he almost instantly fell in a drunken stupor, and from which he was aroused by his neighbors, who were attracted by the smell of fire.

The death of his wife and child he celebrated as drunkards are wont to celebrate their sorrows—spending part of his time between the death and the funeral in maudlin melancholy, and part in drunken stupor.

From Newburyport he removed to Worcester, still keeping the lowest company, and continuing the lowest habits. It was his custom to visit the saloons at night, where he entertained a wretched crowd with droll stories, comic songs, tricks, and ventriloquism, to the great delight and wonder of the loafers, who paid him for their pleasure with drink.

When under the influence of liquor Gough was sometimes almost insane with merriment, at which times he would do and say the most ridiculous things, whereby he gained a kind of reputation for talent and genius in the low society in which he moved.

As a specimen of this, he records in his Autobiography his visit to a Millerite meeting, which was held in one of the Methodist churches of Worcester, where he gave himself up to the most noisy religious exercises, and finished his performance by passing around a wooden spittoon filled with saw-dust, with a view to taking up a collection. For this trick he was brought before the justice next morning and fined five dollars for disturbing public worship, which fine, as it appears, was paid by some of his pals, who could not think of losing the company of their most talented *confrere* while he should be sent to jail for his offense.

In 1842 the Washingtonian movement was under full headway in New England, and Gough became its chiefest trophy. He declares that at that time he had become so utterly lost to all hope, both for this life and the next, that, even with a fearful sense of the truth of God's Word, " No drunkard shall enter the kingdom of God," he was on the point of committing suicide, because whatever there might be hereafter, the whip of scorpions which he had made for himself, and which now perpetually lashed him, seemed to be more than he could possibly bear.

One Sunday evening, in the month of October, 1842, as he was wandering about the streets, half drunk and half clad, some one tapped him on the shoulder and said, " Mr. Gough, I believe."

A kindly voice, to which he was not accustomed, arrested his attention and awakened his conscience. To the invitation of the stranger to sign the pledge as a means of escape from his troubles, he at length gave the reluctant promise that he would sign it on the following evening at a temperance meeting which was to be held in the Worcester town hall.

The demands of his appetite were such that he spent the intervening time under the influence of liquor, but at the time for the appointed meeting he appeared, closely buttoned up to the chin in an old brown surtout, in order to hide his ragged habilaments beneath.

His friend, Mr. Joel Stratton, was there to receive him, and, under an inspiration which seems to have been divine, the poor drunkard arose when the opportunity for speaking was offered and requested that he might be heard. He was invited to the stand, where he related the sad story of his experience in a manner so touching and powerful that the great audience was overwhelmed with emotion. He exhibited himself as a specimen of the work of ruin that rum was all the while engaged in; showed them his trembling hands, his nerves all unstrung by alcohol, and told them he was a houseless, miserable, blighted outcast from society, with scarce a hope remaining to him of ever becoming any thing better.

"But," said he, "I have promised to sign the pledge, and I am determined not to break my word."

At the close of his remarks, while hundreds in the audience were weeping, the pledge was passed to him, and, in sight of the whole congregation, he took the pen in his unsteady hand, and, in characters almost as crooked as those of old Stephen Hopkins on the Declaration of Independence, he wrote himself down a free man—free from the power of the inexorable tyrant, Rum.

Of this act Mr. Gough says:—

" I had exerted a moral power which had long remained lying by perfectly useless, and the very idea of
what I had done strengthened and encouraged me.

" Many who witnessed my signing and heard my simple statement came forward and kindly grasped my
hand, and expressed their satisfaction at the step I had
taken.   And now a better day seemed already to have
dawned upon me.   As I left the hall, agitated and ener-
vated, I remembered chuckling to myself with great
gratification, 'I have done it! I have done it!' When I
got up in the morning my brain seemed as though it
would burst.   My throat was on fire, and in my stomach
I experienced a dreadful burning sensation, as if the fires
of the pit had been kindled there.   My hands trembled
so that I could not raise a drink of water to my feverish
lips.   I literally gasped for my accustomed *stimulus*, and
felt that I should die if I did not have it.   Still I experienced a feeling somewhat akin to satisfaction at the position I had taken.   I had made at least one step toward
reform.   I was exceedingly weak, and fancied, as I almost reeled about my shop, that every eye was fixed
upon me.   I was suffering, and those who have never
suffered thus cannot comprehend what it means.   The
shivering of the spine; then the flashes of heat, causing
every pore of the body to sting as if punctured with some
sharp instrument; the horrible whispering in the ear,
combined with the longing cry of the whole system for
stimulants—one glass of brandy would steady my shaking nerves, but I would not touch it.   I said to myself:
' Here I am a young man, but twenty-five years of age,
but I have no control of my nerves; I cannot stand still,

6

I cannot hold my hands still. One glass of brandy would relieve this gnawing, aching, throbbing system; but I have signed the pledge, and I *must* fight it out.

"How I got through the day I cannot tell.

"I went to my employer, and said, 'I signed the pledge last night.'

"'I know you did.'

"'I mean to keep it.'

"'So they all say. I hope you will.'

"'You don't believe I will? You have no confidence in me?'

"'None whatever.'

"I turned to my work broken-hearted, crushed in spirit, paralyzed in energy, feeling how low I had sunk in the esteem of prudent and sober-minded men. Suddenly the small bar I held in my hand began to move; I felt it move; I griped it; still it moved and twisted; I griped it still harder; yet the thing would move till I could feel it—yes, *feel* it—tearing the palm out of my hand; then I dropped it, and there it lay a curling, slimy snake! I could hear the paper shavings rustle as the horrible thing writhed before me! If it *had been* a snake I should not have minded it; I was never afraid of a snake; I should have called some one to look at it; I could have killed it. I should not have been terrified at a *thing;* but I knew it was a cold, dead bar of iron, and there it was, with its green eyes, its forked, darting tongue, curling in all its slimy loathsomeness! and the horror filled me so that my hair seemed to stand up and shiver, and my skin lift from the scalp to the ancles, and I groaned out, 'I cannot fight this through! O, my

God! I shall die! I cannot fight it! —when a gentleman came into the shop with a cheerful,

"'Good-morning, Mr. Gough.'

"'Good-morning, sir.'

"'I saw you sign the pledge last night.'

"'Yes, sir; I did it.'

"'I was very glad to see you do it, and many young
men followed your example. It is just such men as you
that we want, and I hope you will be the means of doing
a great deal of good. My office is in the Exchange;
come and see me. I shall be happy to make your acquaintance. I have only a minute or two to spare, but
I thought I would just call and tell you to keep up a
brave heart. Good-bye! God bless you! come and see
me.'

"This was Jesse Goodrich, then a practicing attorney
and counselor at law in Worcester, now dead, but to
the last of his life my true and faithful friend. It would
be impossible to describe how this little act of kindness
cheered me. With the exception of Joel Stratton, who
was a waiter at a temperance hotel, and who had asked
me to sign the pledge, no one had accosted me for
months in a manner which would lead me to think any
one cared what might be my fate. *Now* I was not altogether alone in the world! I felt that the fountain of
human kindness was not utterly sealed up; and again a
green spot, an oasis, small, indeed, but cheering, appeared in the desert of life. I had something now to live
for; a new desire for life seemed suddenly to spring up.

"All these sensations were generated by a few kind
words at the right time. Yes, now I can fight, and I

did fight, six days and nights, encouraged and helped by these few words of sympathy. He said, 'Come and see me.' I will. He said he would be pleased to make my acquaintance. He shall. He said, 'Keep up a brave heart.' By God's help I will. And so encouraged I fought on, not one particle of food passing my lips for six days and nights. What a lesson of love should not this teach us! How know we but some trifling sacrifice, some little act of kindness, some, it may be, unconsidered word, may heal a bruised heart, or cheer a drooping spirit.

" Never shall I forget my exquisite pleasure when first asked to call and see Mr. Goodrich ; and how I did love him, from my very heart, for the pleasure he afforded me in the knowledge that *some one* on the broad face of the earth cared for me, for me, who had given myself up as a castaway ; who two days before had been friendless in the widest signification of the word, and willing, nay, wishing to die.

"Any man who has suddenly broken a habit such as mine was, may imagine what my sufferings were during the week which followed my abandoning the use of alcohol.

"On the evening of the day following that on which I signed the pledge, I went straight home from my workshop with a dreadful feeling of some impending calamity haunting me. In spite of the encouragement I had received, the presentiment of coming evil was so strong that it bowed me almost to the dust with apprehension. The slakeless thirst still clung to me, and water, instead of allaying it, seemed only to increase its intensity.

" I was fated to encounter one struggle more with my enemy before I became free. God in his mercy forbid that any young man should endure but a tenth part of the torture which racked my frame and agonized my heart! As in the former attack, horrible faces glared upon me from the walls—faces ever changing, and displaying new and still more horrible features ; black, bloated insects crawled over my face, and myriads of burning concentric rings were revolving incessantly. At one moment the chamber appeared as red as blood, and in a twinkling it was dark as the charnel-house. I seemed to have a knife with hundreds of blades in my hand, every blade driven through the flesh, and all so inextricably bent and tangled together that I could not withdraw them for some time ; and when I did, from my lacerated fingers the bloody fibers would stretch out all quivering with pain.

" After a frightful paroxysm of this kind I would start like a maniac from my bed, and beg for life, life! What I of late thought so worthless seemed now to be of unappreciable value. I dreaded to die, and clung to existence with a feeling that my soul's salvation depended upon a little more of life. A great portion of this time I spent alone ; no mother's hand was near to wipe the big drops of perspiration from my brow, no kind voice cheered me in my solitude. Alone I encountered all the host of demoniac forms which crowded my chamber. No one witnessed my agonies, or counted my woes, and yet I recovered ; *how*, still remains a mystery to myself, and still more mysterious was the fact of my concealing my suffering from every mortal eye.

" In about a week I gained, in a great degree, the mastery over my accursed appetite ; but the strife had made me dreadfully weak. Gradually my health improved; I recovered my spirits, and ceased to despair. Once more was I enabled to crawl into the sunshine; but, O, how changed ! Wan cheeks and hollow eyes, feeble limbs and almost powerless hands, plainly enough indicated that between me and death there had been indeed but a step ; and those who saw me might say as was said of Dante when he passed through the streets of Florence : ' There's the man that has been in hell ! ' "

The name of Mr. Gough now was one of the most familiar to the friends of the Washingtonian movement throughout Worcester County. His talents as an actor and singer, which he had abused so shamefully, were now devoted to the temperance reform, and first throughout his own county and then throughout the eastern part of New England he went, telling his strange experiences, singing temperance songs, exhorting drunkards to reform, and taking the names of thousands to the temperance pledge.

In the midst of this career, under the influence of a medicine which he had taken by the prescription of a doctor, and also under severe nervous prostration, the young advocate stumbled and fell, but only for a few days. His old friends rallied round him, and from that time he stood firm, tortured, indeed, by the sense of shame at his new disgrace, which, however, was ever after an added warning and an added reason of faithfulness.

Taking advantage of this sad fact, the opponents of

the temperance reform now and then published false statements, to the effect that he had fallen here and drank there; but all these calumnies were successfully hunted down.

On this subject Mr. Gough says:—

"On some temperaments one glass of liquor will mount to the brain instantly, weaken the power of the will, affecting self-control, stimulating perception, while it destroys its accuracy, and the man is not the same. That one glass has caused partial insanity. His judgment being perverted he is not so able to resist temptation, and the appetite being roused takes hold of him and drags him down in its fearful embrace. The only safety for such a man is total abstinence. A man who has been a victim, bound by the cords of this fierce desire, will find it a life struggle when, at times, the old appetite comes over him like a wave."

Thus it appears that in the Washingtonian movement the modern miracle of saving the drunkard from the appetite for drink, by the power of the grace of God, had not entered his mind as a resource in this time of trial.

Mr. Gough, writing of this early period, says:—

"Let a man do any thing but drink. Let him run; it is not cowardly to run. I know a man who was strongly tempted. He grew nervous; every fiber of his system seemed to cry out; but when he thought of his wife and children, of the former ruin and disgrace, and of his present prosperity and reputation, he rushed out from his place of business, ran through the streets until he reached his home, and cried out, 'Wife, shut me up for mercy's

sake! shut me up, and don't let me out!   Ask no questions, but shut me up!'"

His wife was a wise wife, and she locked him in a
room, and there he remained for thirty hours before he
dared to venture out to his work again.   He also mentions a lawyer who had been intemperate who declared
that he could hardly read the newspaper, because if he
only read of drinking it seemed as if he must drink.

Thus in that early day the chief counsel and comfort
there was for a struggling reformed inebriate was contained in the single word Resistance; now, under the better light of the Gospel Temperance Reform, the comfort
and counsel for such seasons comes in the words of the
apostle: "If any is afflicted let him pray."

The record of Mr. Gough's first year of temperance
work shows three hundred and eighty-three addresses,
fifteen thousand two hundred and eighteen signatures
to the pledge, six thousand eight hundred and forty
miles of travel, for all which he received scarcely money
enough to pay his traveling and living expenses.

In 1843 Mr. Gough married again, the lady of his
choice being Miss Mary Whitcomb, of Boylston, Mass.

In speaking of this marriage he says:—

"When I had paid the minister [Rev. Mr. Smalley, of
Worcester] five dollars, and our fare to Boston, I had
just three dollars and a half left; but Mary was perfectly
willing to risk it with me, though, in addition, I was
somewhat in debt.

"I had a book called 'Daily Food,' with passages of
Scripture for every day in the year, and the passage for
the day after my wedding was, 'He shall cover thee with

his feathers, and under his wings shalt thou trust : his truth shall be thy shield and buckler.' Psa. xci, 4. Truly he has covered us until now, and caused our cup to run over with good. He has set our table for us in the sight of all our enemies, and given us a goodly heritage."

His wife seems to have been his good angel. She traveled with him constantly, and aided him by her loving presence to resist his old enemy and to improve his methods of work.

Mr. Gough's oratory, so familiar to the great audiences both of England and America, is indescribable. On this subject he says :—

"I know I am ungraceful and awkward. I never studied grace of action or gesture. A German in Philadelphia once said to his employer, ' *I goes to hear dot Meester Gough vot dalks mit his goat dails !* '

"I have often been amused by the committee erecting a platform for me to speak on perhaps twenty by fifteen feet, asking me if I should have room enough, or whether the president would be in the way if he remained in the chair."

A lecturer who was rather jealous of Gough, and who was unable to draw equal audiences, complained that they did not give him room enough. "Only let me have a platform as big as you gave Mr. Gough, and I will make as good a speech, and draw as many people. It is nothing in Gough, it is the platform that does it."

The intensity of excitement which attends Mr. Gough's speaking is the genuine outflow of his intense feeling. Of this he says :—

"It is burned into my memory from years of suffer-

6*

ing and degradation, and I do feel, and must ever feel, on this great question."

After entertaining an immense audience for an hour and a half or two hours with a perfect torrent of wit, pathos, argument, and persuasion, Mr. Gough frequently goes home to the place of his stay, and with a select party of friends about him keeps up their entertainment for two or three hours more; thus cooling off gradually, and in the process giving out light, heat, and power enough to set up half a dozen lecturers in business.

Throughout the Eastern and Western States of the Union, and over into the British Provinces, this great apostle of temperance traveled, lectured, and sung, increasing crowds every-where attending him, until he was confessedly the first orator in America.

TEMPERANCE TOUR IN GREAT BRITAIN.

In 1853 Mr. Gough received an invitation from the London Temperance League to visit England and speak for temperance. He consented to spend a month in this work, but so kindly was his reception, and so great was his success, that he did not return for over two years.

Both in England and in Scotland, under the *Scottish Temperance League, The British Association*, and the London *Temperance League*, he labored with wonderful success ; his hundred nights on temperance in the city of London being the greatest effort in that direction recorded of any of the great temperance reformers.

The temperance brethren in England being anxious that the experiment of bringing the American advocate should be successful, prepared and published in great numbers an edition of Mr. Gough's autobiography, which were sent to the provincial newspapers. An extensive system of advertising was also resorted to. Exeter Hall was engaged, and the committee confidently waited the result.

Mr. and Mrs. Gough arrived in Liverpool July 31st, 1853, and on the next day, by a committee of the League, were received in London in the house of George Cruikshank, Esq., where the *élite* of the temperance body had assembled to welcome the long-anticipated guests.

The first lecture was announced in Exeter Hall for eight o'clock, but as early as four o'clock in the afternoon persons were waiting to obtain admission to the hall, and at six, when the doors were opened, every part of the auditorium commanding a view of the speaker was immediately filled. Over the platform the national flags of England and America waved harmoniously together, and united choirs of the temperance societies occupied the vast platform in front of the great organ.

When Mr. Gough came forward attended by the leaders of the temperance cause the enthusiasm was unbounded, many actually weeping for joy.

Dr. Campbell says of this occasion: "It was a night of trial, yet he was equal to the task. Great as had been the expectations created, Mr. Gough surpassed them all. He swayed the vast multitude as with an enchanter's wand. As he willed, it was moved to laughter or melted to tears."

Of Mr. Gough himself, the press spoke as follows:—

"Some twenty-four years back a poor lad, without money or learning, almost without friends, was shipped for America to try his fortunes in the new world.   Arriving there, the lad became a man living by the sweat of his brow.   He learned to drink; he fell, as must fall all others who learn to love the flowing bowl, and look upon the wine when it is red.

"Friends left him; he became an outcast, a wanderer; he sank lower and lower.   He walked in rags; he loathed life.   His frame became emaciated with disease, and there was none to pity or to save.   It seemed for that man there was nothing left but to lie down and die.

"That man in his degradation and despair, so wretched and miserable, so near the final wreck, signed the temperance pledge!   He became an advocate of the temperance cause.   His words were words of power.   They touched men's hearts.   They fired men's souls.   He lived the life of an apostle.   Wherever he went drunkards were reclaimed, zeal was excited, the spell of the cup was broken, humanity was saved; and now, as he returns for a while to his native land to advocate the cause which has been salvation to his own soul, and life to many men and women, thousands open to him the tenderest hearts, and haste to give him welcome.

"The first sentence, as it falls easily and gently from his lips, tells us that Gough has that true oratorical power which neither money, nor industry, nor persevering study can ever win."   Like the poet, the orator must be born, and Gough is an orator born.

There are some men who have prodigious advantages on account of appearance alone.   Some one has said "It was impossible for any one to be as wise as Lord

Thurlow looked ;" but Mr. Gough has nothing of this; he is just as plain a personage as George Dawson of Birmingham would be if he would only cut his hair and shave his mustache. Gough is a real original. We have no one in England we can compare him to. He seems to speak by inspiration. In what he said there was nothing new, there could be nothing new. The tale he told was as old as the hills, yet as he spoke an immense audience grew hushed and still. Their hearts were melted, tears glistened, and that human mass became knit together by a common spell.

D'Israeli says, " Sir Robert Peel played upon the House of Commons like an old fiddle." Gough did the same upon his audience at Exeter Hall.

The Scotchmen compared Mr. Gough to Father Gavazzi, the great Italian orator, whom Mr. Gough resembles in his style and power more than any other speaker now living.

On the 28th of September the League appointed an address for Mr. Gough at Folkestone, near his old home, only a mile and a half from Sandgate, his birth-place, where he was received with ecstatic joy not only by his old school-fellows, but by the older citizens, who remembered him as a little boy, and who were both astonished and delighted to see him come back again such a great man.

The success of Mr. Gough's lectures, as may naturally be supposed, raised no small uproar of opposition.

Total abstinence was not yet popular even with the clergy, and the religious as well as secular press contained many attacks upon the man and his doctrines. The Saviour's command to his disciples at the Passover,

"Drink ye all of it," was one of the Bible texts on which the anti-teetotalers founded their opposition.

Occasionally, after he had delivered a lecture, a sermon would be preached to expose the errors of total abstinence on the ground that it tended to infidelity.

In many places astonishment was expressed that Mr. and Mrs. Gough drank no wine.

They were once the guests of a gentleman who afterward became their warm friend. On the arrival of their train, dinner being over, a lunch was set for them, and the travelers asked for a glass of water.

"O, I will give you something better than water," said their host; "a glass of wine would be better for you than cold water."

"But I never drink wine," said Mr. Gough.

'What!" answered his host, in great surprise, "you don't drink wine? I suppose you are, of course, opposed to brandy, gin, and other strong liquors, but you cannot, I am sure, be afraid of a glass of wine or ale?"

"I think," commented Mr. Gough afterward, "that the gentleman looked upon us as curiosities."

On another occasion he says:—

"One gentleman who entertained us at his house invited a large party to dinner, and when the cloth was being removed he said:—

"'I hardly know how to explain; that is, I—I—hem! Well, you will get no wine, gentlemen, to-day. I ordered the butler to decant no wine, as a compliment to our guest, Mr. Gough.'

"All looked at me, some rather discontentedly. So I said:—

"'I am very sorry that you have deprived these gentlemen of their accustomed beverage on my account. Please allow me to say that if it is *right* to place wine on your table, do it without regard to any man's prejudice or whims. If it is *wrong*, never place it there. And if you have the slightest doubt whether it is right or wrong, put the wine away until you have settled that question, and give the doubt the benefit.'

"Another person brought me a passage in Deuteronomy, where the children of Israel are told to obtain what their souls lusted for—sheep, oxen, wine, and strong drink; by which he understood that God commended the people to use not only wine but whisky. I turned at once and read the words :—

"'If a man have a rebellious son, he shall bring him to the elders of the people, who shall take him without the gates of the city, and they shall stone him with stones until he die.'

"'Ah!' said the objector, 'but that was under the old dispensation.'

"'So were your sheep, oxen, wine, and strong drink,' I answered, upon which the objector was angry and the argument closed."

Mr. Gough always disliked the term orator and oration as applied to himself and his addresses, and the English formalities of introduction, etc., were particularly distasteful to him. He had, he said, some curious introductions. Once a chairman said : " I rise to introduce Mr. Gough, famous in both hemispheres for his sublime, as well as his ridiculous ! "

Another gentleman, who aspirated his h's, wishing to

compliment Mr. Gough, and to show off his own scripture knowledge, said:—

" Ladies and gentlemen, hi rise to hintroduce the horator of the hevening. 'E comes from the hother side of
the Hatlantic. 'E is to speak hon the subject of temperance—a very dry subject ; but when we 'ear the horator
discuss hon the subject of temperance we may himagine
the miracle again performed by which the prophet was
refreshed with water from the jaw-bone of the hass."

On one occasion, at a lecture in a country town, an Independent minister opened the exercises with prayer,
after which he began his introduction of the speaker thus :
" Ladies and gentlemen, as I have informed you in my
prayer, the temperance cause is in a healthy state,"
etc., etc.

At another time he found a platform erected on the
top of a high pulpit, lifting him out of reach of his audience on the floor, and bringing him unpleasantly close to
those in the gallery. Mr. Gough declared that he could
not speak there, that he would be dizzy in looking down.
" Ah ! " said the gentleman, " but the people in the gallery pay the highest price, and they would like to look
at your feet."

Upon this Mr. Gough grew desperate, remembering
what a reputation he had for walking the platform ; but
what was his surprise to hear the minister of the church,
when called upon for the introductory prayer, apologize
to the Lord for the platform, which he regretted was not
satisfactory to the speaker, with these words : " We pray
thee, O Lord, that the height of the platform may not so
interfere with the comfort of the lecturer but that he

will be able to give us as good a lecture here as it is reported in the newspapers he has done in other towns in the country."

Among the singular experiences of Mr. Gough was his lecture in Oxford, where a certain class of students had been in the habit of disturbing public assemblies for fun. They had recently smoked out a gentleman who came to lecture on tobacco, and it was thought that a temperance lecture would be too good an opportunity to be lost. However, Mr. Gough ventured an appointment, and on entering the hall found a good many caps and gowns awaiting him. Presently the students began to cheer, and to behave in such a manner as to produce universal laughter. There was no abuse of the speaker, but simply rollicking fun, so that the chairman, who tried to be grave, was obliged to yield to merriment, and even Mr. Gough himself had the greatest difficulty in keeping serious.

After a while they began to ask questions, some of them serious, some ridiculous, and some of them profane, and whenever he began to answer they would begin to cheer. At length their questions became more serious. One asked who it was that turned the water into wine? to which he gave the reply: "We have no objection to wine that is made of water."

At last, in the midst of the confusion, he called for fair play, which he said was an Englishman's motto, and then offered a proposition that the audience should choose a champion who should take the platform and debate with him, turn about, for ten minutes each, to decide who was victor in the contest. This sounded fair enough, but as no one could be agreed upon as champion, Mr. Gough had the evening pretty much to himself.

The next evening one of the proctors came to the platform to shake hands with Mr. Gough before the whole audience, and to thank him for the manner in which he had managed the students.

During his work in Great Britain he was sometimes called upon to address crowds of roughs and outcasts, whose rags, filth, and degradation he mentions as being beyond description.

"On one such occasion, as I came in, the minister of the town said to me:—

" ' Mr. Gough, you have " Fire " in the house to-night.'

" I asked, 'What do you mean?'

" ' Do you see that tall woman near the platform?'

" 'Yes.'

" ' Her nickname is " Hell-fire." She is known by no other name in the vicinity of her residence. When she appears in the street the boys cry, " Fire! fire!" She is the most incorrigible woman in the neighborhood; she is ripe for mischief now; and if she makes a disturbance, you will see such a row as you never saw before. The power of the woman's tongue in blasphemy is something horrible.' "

Mr. Gough said: " I expected a row, and confess to a nervous feeling of apprehension; but I spoke to them as men and women, not as outcasts. I told them that poverty was hard to bear, but that there might be peace with poverty. I told them that I had been poor, very poor. I spoke to them of my mother and her struggles; then of her faith, and love, and hope. I said that there was no disgrace in poverty; that ·the only thing that was de-grading was *sin.*

"Presently I saw a naked arm and hand lifted in the crowd, and heard a voice cry out : ' That's all true.

"The woman that was called 'Hell-fire,' rose to her feet, and facing me, said : "That's a' true, mon : ye're tellin' the truth,' and stretching her arms to the audience, said : ' The mon kens what he's talkin' aboot.'

"When I concluded she came on the platform, and I almost thought she was going to tackle me ; but, after looking at me a moment, she said : ' Tak' a gude look at me, mon. I'm a bit of a beauty, aint I ?' Then, coming up close to me, she said : ' Would ye gi'e the pledge to a puir body like me ?'

"I answered at once, ' Yes, ma'am. Can you keep it ?"

"' Can I ? If I say I wull I wull.'

"' Give me your hand on that,' said I, and I shook hands with her. She signed the pledge, and I said to her, ' I know you will keep it, and before I go to Amer-ica I will come and see you.'

"' Come when you will,' she replied, ' an' you'll find I ha'e keepit it.'

"Two years from that time I was again in the town. A gentleman approached me and said, ' I wish to intro-duce to you Mrs. Archer.' It was the same ' Hell-fire who had signed the pledge on the occasion of my last visit, but how changed ! I went down to her house, and this is a part of what she said to me :—

"' Ah ! Mr. Gough, I'm a puir body. I dinna ken much, and what little I ha'e kenned has a' ben knokit out o' me by the staffs o' the policemen ; for they beat me about the head a good deal, and knockit prutty much a' the sense out o' me; but sometimes I ha'e a dream. I dream I'm drunk, and fichting, and the police ha'e got me agen, and then I get out o' my bed, and I go down on my knees, and I don't go back to my bed 'till the daylight comes, an' I keep a ' sayin : ' God keep me, for I canna get drunk any mair.' "

Mr. Gough mentions receiving a letter from this woman, Mrs. Archer, years afterward. She was keeping a small shop, had become a Christian, and employed all her spare time in trying to reform others.

Mr. Gough's first temperance tour in Great Britain lasted two years and fourteen days, but before leaving Great Britain he had made arrangements to return again in two years, for three years more of temperance lectures in England, Scotland, and Ireland.

Gough's sharp eyes, his great knowledge of and sympathy with human nature in suffering, as well as his great appreciation of striking elements of character, fitted him to observe the manners and customs of the people among whom he traveled, not only for his own pleasure and profit, but for the instruction of others, to whom, in his admirable Lyceum Lectures, he related the results of his observations.

Of the beggars and tramps he says: "I found the lowest class, in London; but in Ireland one finds the poetry of begging ; even the poorest of the Irish beggars being in a rollicking humor, and quick to retort if I chaffed them.

" A beggar thus accosted a gentleman : 'Ah ! yer honor, have compassion on the lame, the blind, and the lazy ! ' "

" ' How is that?'

" ' Please, yer honor, I am lame, me wife is blind, and me daughter is lazy.'

" Another time, ' Ah! ye're good-looking, yer honor; have pity on a poor crathur, bliss yer handsome face!'

" ' No,' says the person approached, ' I wont give you any thing at all, you are a flatterer;' upon which another beggar responded, ' Judy, go way with ye, that's all ye git for yer blarneyin' paple; shure an' doesn't his honor know he's as ugly a piece ov furniture as I've seen for many a day?' then coming up to his honor, and thrusting out her hand, said: ' Now, give me a penny for my honesty.' "

The results of Mr. Gough's lectures during his second tour were somewhat interfered with by an unpleasant newspaper controversy over a letter written by him in which he criticised the operation of the Maine Law; but this was overborne in the enthusiasm infused into the temperance movement, and the six hundred lectures in three years to all classes of people in all parts of the United Kingdom could not fail of great and beneficial results.

For some years past Mr. Gough has been known to us as the prince of the lecture platform, giving to delighted audiences an account of his experiences in London, and portraitures of the many different characters he met there and elsewhere; but through them all we never forget that Mr. Gough is, over and above every thing else, a temperance lecturer. "All roads lead to Rome," it is said, and so of Mr. Gough's lecturing. Whatever be the subject, sooner or later the audience find themselves listening to a lecture on temperance.

"Street Life in London," "London by Night," "The great Metropolis," "Here and There in Britain," "Curiosity," "Habit," are the titles of some of the Lyceum Lectures which Mr. Gough has delivered hundreds of times over, and in consequence of which he has the reputation of having become rich; but the generous nature of the man is incompatible with the hoarding of money for himself; and those who know him best are best prepared to believe his statement that it is only by his hard work, even with the large prices paid him, that he is able to maintain his quiet but beautiful home in the town of Boylston, near Worcester, and keep up the various works of charity to which he has given his heart and his purse.

Of himself he says, in view of the great change that has taken place in him and his fortunes since those sad days when he roamed the streets of Worcester, played the clown in low drinking dens, and hid himself away in shame at the thought of his degradation, and his present position as the foremost temperance orator, aye, and the foremost orator of America: "If there is a man on the face of the earth who has cause for deep and humble gratitude, and who can say with the Psalmist, 'Praise the Lord, O my soul! while I live will I praise the Lord; I will sing praises to God while I have any being;' I am that man."

CHAPTER VIII.

JOHN B. GOUGH'S TEMPERANCE ADDRESSES.

DURING the progress of Mr. Moody's meetings in the Boston Tabernacle, Mr. Gough gave frequent and valuable assistance. He did not quite agree with Mr. Moody, that signing the pledge was of no value, having seen and experienced such great and good results therefrom; but he bore testimony to the power of divine grace to save those men who had become utterly powerless to save themselves.

The following extracts from Mr. Gough's lecture in aid of the North End Mission on the evening of the first of May, 1877, will show that this great orator of the Washingtonian movement has not lost either his love or his power.

Mr. Gough said: " Ladies and gentlemen, the committee have announced no particular theme for the evening, but simply requested me to deliver a lecture on behalf of the North End Mission. Some have suggested that I should speak altogether on temperance, and certainly I could not refer to the work of this mission without speaking of temperance. I suppose that every individual here is aware of the object of the North End Mission. It is to rescue the perishing, to lift up the degraded and the debased, to try to train their children, born under such adverse circumstances, to walk in the paths of truth, purity, and righteousness. I rejoice in the fact that the North End Mission recognizes the truth that while Christians are anxious for the souls of their fellow-men, they do not forget that they have bodies, and that its workers labor by personal intercourse with men as human beings, and so influence and lead them to a higher life. A man who was sent to the war on the work of the Christian Commission found, on his first visit to the hospital, a man very sick, suffering with intense thirst, and tossing upon a miserable bed.

"'Shall I pray with you, my friend?' he asked.

"'I don't care whether you pray or not,' was the reply; 'but I wish somebody would give me a clean shirt.'

"That made his work plain to him. He went and got clean linen for the poor man, and smoothed his pillow, and then offered prayer with the man whose attention he had enlisted by his sympathy. Now, just this principle should operate in our dealings with those whom we are accustomed to term 'the lower classes.'

" It is not just to judge a man merely by circumstances. Take a boy that is well dressed, with a neat frill about his neck, his hair combed, and place him beside another boy quite as good-looking, but in ragged clothes, his hair sticking out of his cap, wearing no shoes, dirty, and unkempt ; when you talk to the boys you don't use the same tone. To the rough-looking boy you will speak roughly : 'What are you doing about here, boy? What do you want?' To the other you will speak gently, pat him on the head, and say, 'Well, my fine boy, you are getting on to be a man, aren't you?'

" Change the rags and the dirt from the rough boy to the other, and you will change your tone and manner the moment the boy is clean and well dressed. But the one needs and yearns for sympathy as much as the other; and in no way like individual effort can men be held with so mighty a hold to truth.

"I would say to all who are engaged in religious work, Go on in your labors in the spirit of self-denial. It is a good work to distribute tracts among the poor; but when you come to a home where there has been a life-battle with hard, griping poverty, give to the man a loaf of bread in one hand and a tract in the other, and the man will not tear up your tract.

"As you take your boy to the Sunday-school, you will pass knots of boys at the street corners—boys who will swear, lie, and steal; and as you draw away from them you may thank God in your heart that your boy is not like them. But what makes the difference? Education and training. Take your own boy when a babe, and give him in charge of some horrible hag, and he will learn to swear, to lie, and blaspheme. Judge not according to circumstances; remember for how much degradation and crime bad training is responsible. The first thing to do is to try to remedy this evil. Go to these people with the Gospel and the gospel of temperance. Temperance is a part of Christianity with me; and to me—not necessarily to you—it means total abstinence.

"Some may say, 'You are putting temperance before the Gospel.' No, sir. Total abstinence does not pretend to make a man into a saint, but it does keep him from being a drunkard. It doesn't endow a man with all the cardinal virtues; some awfully mean men don't drink, and that is their only good point. As a
7

direct agency total abstinence only insures that a man shall not be a drunkard; but as an indirect agent I hold that temperance claims the sympathy and co-operation of all Christian men and women.

"The Gospel is a great power, but how can it be effective unless men hear? Drunkenness keeps more men from hearing the Gospel than any other one thing. Temperance cannot make men godly, but it is one of the agencies which God blesses.

"When Jesus stood before the tomb of Lazarus he might have commanded the stone to roll away from the sepulcher, but he commanded that men should roll it away. Total abstinence is the agency which is to roll away the stone from the sepulcher to-day; and on the incipient putrefaction Jesus will lay his hand, and the dead corpse of the drunkard shall be called to a higher and nobler life; not by temperance, but by God's grace.

"Drunkenness is the great curse of this nation, and we must battle with it on the platform that forbids the use of intoxicating liquors as a beverage. A man may say: 'Do you ask me to give up what to me is a lawful gratification because another man is a drunkard?' Every man knows the insidious effect of intoxicating liquor and its terrible results.

"'Would you banish it altogether from society?'

"Yes.

"'Wouldn't you allow it to be used as medicine?'

"Well, I wont take it as a medicine myself, and the doctors know it; and so they prescribe something else that does just as well. Some physicians prescribe liquor because they are fond of taking a little of the medicine with their patients, some because they believe it is good, others because they don't know any better.

"I have heard of a stingy old fellow who mixed a little of the ipecac and the assafœtida and the oils which he prescribed in a big black bottle.

"'What do you do with that stuff?' he was asked.

"'O, I use it. When I get a patient with a complication of diseases which I don't understand, I just take this black bottle and give him a dose of that.'

" A great many doctors are very fond of prescribing out of the black bottle. But in the use of intoxicants as medicine there is a terrible risk. It gives an unnatural *stimulus* to the system, which men are much better without, and, in many cases, it leads men and women of nervous temperaments to drunkenness and ruin.

" Men who have been led into drinking habits, men who are sorely tempted, cry unto God! Ask him who is able to save to the uttermost, and he will help you just as sure as he did Peter when he called upon him. In this tabernacle, every timber of which has been saturated by the holy eloquence which comes from the heart, and where many drunkards have been set free, we must all come back to the one theme. Let us go forward in the work, Christian men and women. Since ninety-nine out of every hundred ruined men are ruined by drink, let us 'rescue the perishing,' and carry to the drunkard the Gospel of hope and deliverance. Embody the self-denying principle which is the essence of Christianity in your life. If you do not need the total abstinence pledge for yourself, sign it for the sake of those who are weak and need help. Be positive, not negative, in the cause.

" An English clergyman once said to me, ' I believe in temperance, but I cannot accept total abstinence. My Master made wine by a special miracle on a festal occasion, and I cannot discredit what he then did.' I said, ' You wont stop with this, of course. You will wish to follow your Master in every thing?'

" ' Certainly.'

" ' Well, do you eat barley bread?'

" ' Why, no; I don't like it, and we only feed barley to the hogs.'

" ' But Christ made barley loaves by a special miracle for the feeding of five thousand people, and yet you don't eat barley bread because you don't like it, and are unwilling to give up wine because you do like it.' The only question for the Christian in this matter is, ' May I abstain?' and the whole Bible is full of words of encouragement. We are ' to bear the infirmities of our weaker brethren.' Let us go forward, then, in the work. We are God's agents, and the results rest in his hands. The day when drunkenness shall cease, and God's will be done on earth as it is in heaven, seems far off, but it is nearer than we think. The promise implies a fulfillment. Let us go forward, then, and let the motto be " Excelsior," and God shall have the glory.

WHY AM I A TEETOTALER?

An LL.D. (and I am very sorry to say he is a Massachusetts LL.D.) was dining at the table of a lady who never furnishes wine, no matter who is her guest, at whose house General Grant spent nearly two days, during which time not one drop of wine, ale, or spirits would she present to him or to his staff. This gentleman was at her dinner-table, and he said : " Now, madam, I cannot understand your position in reference to this matter ; I enjoy a glass of wine at my dinner ; it is my habit to use it. But you say to me, ' Doctor, I shall give you no wine because So-and-so makes a bad use of it.' Here is one person cannot drink with impunity, and here is another who makes a fool of himself. By and by you will take from us all our luxuries. I enjoy cheese. I like it with a cup of coffee and a cracker ; it promotes digestion. Would you say, ' Doctor, here is a man cannot eat cheese with impunity, and I shall give you no cheese ?' "

Is that the fair way of putting it ? Did you ever hear a man standing upon the gallows-tree saying to those who came to witness his execution, " Now, my friends, take warning by me ; never eat any cheese ?" Did you ever hear of a man murdering his wife, and giving a reason, or as an excuse, that he had been eating cheese ? Did you ever hear of a row in the streets where one man is murdered or several ribs broken of which the papers said : " Those men have been eating freely of cheese ?" You just show me that cheese produces eight tenths of the crime, seven eighths of the pauperism, and half the lunacy; show me that cheese produces the result that drink does, and, by the grace of God, I will battle the cheese as long as I live.

Now, we fight the drink wherever we find it, whether it is at the sideboard of the wealthy, in the social circle, or in the grog-shop. We fight it on principle. Our central principle is: " Total abstinence from all that can intoxicate." A certain minister in this city favors moderation. I know of a minister affirming that the Scriptures were in favor of wine. All I have to say is, that I would not give that [snapping his finger] for a command of the Bible, "Thou shalt abstain from intoxicating liquor." I don't want it. All I want from the Bible is the lawfulness of my principle. I do not go to the Bible to find " Thou shalt abstain from prize-fighting ; " " Thou shalt abstain from gambling ;" " Thou shalt abstain from horse-racing ; " " Thou shalt abstain from dog and cock-fighting." I abstain from these things because they are detrimental to the best interests of the community. I do not want to find these prohibitions in the Bible. All I want is to be sure of the lawfulness of my principle. I am no theologian, nor a learned man. I never was in school since I was eleven years old; but I stand upon that ground against the most learned minister in the city of New York. It is more lawful for me to abstain than for you to drink, by the Bible. If it is lawful for me to drink a glass of wine, what then ! By my allegiance to God, by my faith in Christ, I am bound to give up a lawful gratification if, by my giving up that which is lawful to me, I can stand beside the weaker brother and fulfill the law of Christ by bearing the infirmity of the weaker man. That is Bible, in my opinion; and that is the position I take with regard to the use of intoxicating drinks.

I believe a minister who used them in moderation published a sermon in which he recommended the young men to follow his example. I am not foolish enough to say here that every man who drinks must become a drunkard. There are moderate drinkers, and there are men who can be moderate drinkers. My father was a moderate drinker, and he lived to be ninety-four years of age. He drank his glass of ale every day for dinner, and his glass of ale every night for supper. When I was a boy, once in a great while, I remember, very seldom, he would take a glass of hot spirits and water before he went to bed; but he never was intoxicated in his life. My father was a moderate drinking Christian, and if there is a heaven for Christians he is in it. There are some men who can drink moderately and some men who cannot. My father drank moderately, and he could drink moderately. His son could no more drink moderately than you could blow up a powder magazine moderately, or fire a gun off a little at a time.

Then you will say, " You are a weak-minded man."

Well, let it go to that if you like. If I am so weak-minded that I cannot drink moderately, I am strong enough to let it alone altogether. The great fault of these ministers (and I am sure I am not the one to criticise the ministry) is in insisting that they are setting a good example. I deny it. They are not setting a good example to me. Suppose I should sit at the table

of one of these ministers, and he should say to me, " Is
it a sin to drink a glass of wine?"

" I do not know that it is."

" Is it a sin to take a glass of brandy?"

"I do not know that I can argue with you on that
point."

" Very well ; I take a glass of brandy ; it is no sin to
me. Will you take one?"

" No."

" Why?"

" I dare not."

" Then you are a foolish man."

Will these men undertake to argue this question and
maintain this position: "What is safe for one man is
safe for another?" When I went to see that beautiful
church they built in Owego I admired the beauty of the
immense spire. I saw a plank suspended on two ropes,
making a little platform, and then perceived a man get
out of the window of the spire, step on the platform,
and stand up. There was a man below who hallooed to
him. He put his hand to his knees and hallooed back.
Could you do that? How many of you could do it? If
I set my foot out of that window, the very moment I
touched my foot on the platform I would go off. No
logic, no argument, no will, no intellect, could help it.
You say, " You are a weak-minded man." I will keep
off the plank; that is all.

I say to the moderate drinker: You do not set a good
example ; you set an example that some men cannot
follow, and that is not a good example. You say that
these young men can follow your example. How do

you know? Suppose there is a bridge over a gulf which would hold a weight of one hundred and eighty pounds, but you are one hundred and fifty pounds. Here is a man who weighs two hundred pounds, and you say: " Follow my example, young man."

" I don't like the looks of that bridge."

" I have walked it forty years; it is perfectly safe."

" Yes, but they say—"

" Don't mind what they say; now, follow my example, prudently and in moderation; don't get excited; don't go with a rush; now, steady, with self-control, self-government, and discrimination; there you are; beautiful; you are doing it finely." But by-and-by his foot touches the center, and with a crash and a shriek he goes to destruction.

Did you set him a good example? No · you did not take into consideration the difference in the temperament, constitution, and nervous susceptibility of that man. It will take you a lifetime to study him before you can safely say, " I set you a good example."

There are some men who can be moderate drinkers, and some who cannot. I knew a man who joined the Church on profession of faith. I asked if he would sign the pledge, and he refused. He said: "The grace of God is able to keep me; I have come out from my young companions; I want them to understand the grace of God is able to keep me." Very good idea, very pretty, very beautiful. The grace of God has no power to prevent drink from affecting a man's brain and nervous system if he drinks, any more than it has to prevent laudanum if he takes it. You can poison a Christian to

7*

death just as quickly as you can a Hottentot. Give a man brimming over with the grace of God and a man who does not believe in the grace of God prussic acid, and they will go down together.

Have there been no men fallen to drunkenness who had grace in the heart? Have you never had Church-members disciplined for drunkenness? They have re-pented and confessed, and were disciplined again and again. Are they all self-deceived, or hypocrites, or what?

There was a poor wretch staggering through the streets of Albany, uttering Greek and Latin quotations. They put him in the station-house. Dr. Sprague, of Albany, went to see him, and recognized him as a minister of the Gospel who occupied one of the highest positions in the city of Glasgow, in Scotland, as the successor of Rev. Dr. Chalmers in the parish church of St. John's. I sup-pose he had no grace in his heart.

I spoke in this city in the year 1848, near Madison Square, in the pulpit of an eloquent man, of whom Dr. Eddy said that in some respects he was one of the most eloquent men he ever heard, who was so drunk that he could hardly get through the prayer. Dr. Skinner, of the Presbyterian Church, asked me if I would testify in the case as they were dealing with this man, saying, "You saw the state he was in." I did, but I did not appear as a witness. That poor man before he died visited the lowest grog-shops in the city. He had no grace in his heart.

I sat at the table of a doctor of divinity in New En-gland, knelt at his family altar and heard him pray, in 1851 and 1852, but to-day he is a drunken hostler in a stable at Boston. Let these men take care how they tell their brethren about example. There that man is to-day with his gray hairs and no grace in his heart. I know the wife of a clergyman, who, when she visited her friends, would take matches and scratch them on the wall to search for liquor, and then drink camphene. I can give you plenty of testimony, and can prove it. She died at the American House, in Boston, drunk, with a bottle of brandy half filled under her pillow. They heard her in the night crying, " O Christ, have mercy on me! O God, for Jesus' sake save me!" but she was dead, and a half-emptied bottle was found under her pillow. Do you tell me it is an example every body can follow, and that the grace of God is going to keep all harm away?

Men say to me, " Why don't you talk to an audience of drunkards?"

Will you get me such an audience? I tell you this, gentlemen, when I get such an audience as that I have got the most hopeless assemblage under the canopy of heaven, as things are now. It is almost impossible to save a confirmed drunkard. You have got inebriate asylums sustained by the State—good places for men to board and be kept clear of drink for a while; but three per cent. of the inmates of these institutions are not cured there. People are beginning to call them "bummers' retreats," because they come back, the same men, in three or six or twelve months, "cured." Look at the record and see if it is not so. It is almost impossible to save the drunkard. I tell you the conclusion I have come to within the last few years: after thirty-two years' experience and observation, when any drunkard comes to me I tell him plainly, "You have but little power in and of yourself," and I try to lead him to One that is able to save to the uttermost, and then I have some hope of his deliverance, because God will help him.

I was riding in the cars in Ohio last winter. The car into which I went was very full. There was one seat vacant. I said to a gentleman, "May I sit by you, sir?" He said, "Yes," and added,

"Mr. Gough, I heard you lecture last night. I went home to my wife and said, 'I will never drink a drop as long as I live.' She knew I meant it when I said it. She looked at me very earnestly, and went down on her knees. I am over forty years old, and have not been on my knees since I was ten years of age. I cannot remember when I have been on my knees. I never went to church; I am not of that sort. This morning I woke up and wanted whisky, and wanted nothing else." His lip quivered, and his whole face was convulsed as he said to me, "I have been on my knees myself this morning over an hour."

I replied, "Keep there, my friend, and you will keep sober." Away with your prayer-gauges and all that confounded nonsense! No man ever drank a glass of liquor while he was praying to God to keep him from it.

You do not know what the power of the appetite is. A gentleman said to me last winter: "It seems hard that drink should come into my house, when I have been fighting it. I have a family of six children, four daughters being married. My youngest son is twenty-six years of age; he has had *delirium tremens* twice, and is dying." The physician who related to me many of the circumstances of the case sat by his side, and said to him, "Charley, you know me and know that I am your friend. Now, my dear fellow, you have a terrible time before you; you have to suffer intolerably for ten days or a fortnight. I think I can see my way clear to get you on your feet and save your life. If I get you on your feet and you touch liquor again, do not send for me."

The young man looked in his face and said, "Doctor, you say I have to suffer. What do you know about it? Doctor, it is coming on me; I can feel it coming. What do you know about it? You could describe it, I suppose; you could tell your class in a medical school all about it. You could tell them how you amputated a limb, but could you tell them how the man felt when the saw touched the marrow? Doctor, if you can prove to me there is no physical suffering in hell, I will cut my throat; for there is no mental anguish to compare with what I know I have got to go through. Doctor, I have had great spiders draw their soft webs all over my face and in my mouth; I have had green flies buzz in my ears and crawl up my nostrils, and creep across my eyelashes. Ah! keep them off, doctor!"

In less than three minutes two men were holding him down. When he got on his feet he was weak and worn and wasted; he walked with two sticks, just able to keep himself up. On the third day he was out, and went into a saloon, exclaiming, "Give me a little brandy; just a table-spoonful, not much. Don't tell any body any thing about it; it will do me good." The man gave

it to him.   "And now," said the father, " that boy of mine
is dying."

Can you imagine an appetite like that?   God help
the poor men who are fighting this appetite!   It is an
awful thing to be a drunkard; the slavery of this appetite is intolerable.

Now, then, if drunkenness is such a curse, what are
you going to do about it?   That is the question.   We
fight the drink, not only in the grog-shop, but in the
social circle.   Ladies, we want your help, and are getting
it.   I had a letter from Cleveland from thirty-seven hundred women, inviting me to go on.   I believe there are
sixteen hundred young ladies belonging to the best
circles of society who have pledged themselves to
use no wine, and to discountenance its use in the
community.   That is what we want.   Young ladies, will
you help us?   .

It is pitiable to have a class of young ladies, such as
we have in Massachusetts, (I don't know whether you
have them in New York or not,) having intellect, genius,
and with the wonderful beauty with which God has endowed them, and for which he holds them responsible,
going the dull round of operas, parties, and balls, drifting
to the Dead Sea of a useless life.

A fashionable lady said to a young man: "O, my
daughter is very beautiful; she is very lovely and popular; she is constantly receiving invitations out, but her
physician has told her that she cannot endure the strain
of more than one party in a week.   The dear child went
away to her chamber, and she came back with tears in
her eyes, saying, ' We are required to take up our cross,

and I am perfectly willing to give up some of my parties.' Isn't it beautiful?"

What is that life in a world where humanity is crying out for help? That is what some people call "enjoyment." You hear a young man compliment you on your personal beauty. That is right. We are all open to that form of compliment. Although I am old and gray, I do like people to say, "You are looking remarkably well." It gratifies us. Did you ever hear a young gentleman compliment you on your accomplishments, on your musical ability, or on your conversational power? It is very pleasant, is it not? Did you ever hear a young man say, "God bless you; you strengthened me in a good resolution?" Did you ever hear a young gentleman say to you, "I thank you for the encouragement you gave me in the right direction? You remember the wine-party when I was about to drink; you lifted your finger and said one word. God bless you! I have never tasted it since, and I never will again."

We want to war against the social drinking customs of the community; we want to drive it out of the saloons and out of the grog-shops. I believe in prohibition; I believe it is coming to that by and by. I believe in law for the lawless, and although some men may accuse me of being a little lenient with regard to the liquor traffic, I will tell you how I feel about it. In view of the evils of drunkenness, and in view of that which I know by observation as well as by experience during the dark, bitter days of my life, I could say this: "Father in heaven, if it be thy will that man shall suffer, whatever of temporal evil is good in thy sight, impose it upon me;

let the bread of affliction be given me to eat; take from me the friends of my confidence; let the cold hut of poverty be my dwelling-place, and the wasting hand of disease inflict its painful torments; let me sow in the whirlwind and let me reap in the storm; let those have me in derision who are younger than I; let the passing away of my welfare be like the fleeting of a cloud, and the contempt of my enemies be like the rushing water; when I anticipate good let evil annoy me; when I look for light let darkness be upon me; let the terrors of death be ever before me; do all that, but save me, merciful God, save me from the fate of the drunkard." And yet, sir, as I shall answer it in the judgment-day, I would rather be the veriest drunkard that ever reeled blaspheming through your streets than I would be the man that sold him liquor for money. I hate that business, and when I wage war against it, I do so in the interests of the trader, as well as to promote the interests of humanity. We will fight liquor wherever we find it.

One word more, and that is this: I have not time to say what I would say with regard to the evils of drunkenness. You know we are very much in the habit of looking at drunkenness as a small thing; we make ourselves merry about it. By the way, we have a class of young ladies East—I don't know as you have them in New York—who when they get into the cars seem bent on informing every body in a very loud tone of voice of all their domestic affairs, telling how many beaux they have had, who has been married, and who wants to be married. I heard some young ladies talk about some young men who became drunk at a social gathering. One of them said :—

"O, it was perfectly splendid! I never had such a time in all my life. I laughed until I thought I would die. We had a sleigh-ride, and then went to a hotel. These young men went to the bar, and I never 'seen' such cuttings up in my life; the more they drank, the more they cut up. Ha! ha! ha! And what do you think—after we had three dances those young men had to go to bed. I never 'seen' such a sight in all my life. I thought I should die laughing the next morning." [Mr. Gough mimicked the young lady in his own characteristic style.] That is how some people look at drunkenness.

O, let us look at the awful degradation of drunkenness! To think of a man endowed with such wonderful capacities; with a mind capable of understanding in some degree the greatness of the Almighty; with a heart capable of loving him and a reason capable of worshiping him; with the fire of God in him—a spark of immortality that will never go out; with a destiny before him as high as heaven and vaster than eternity—to think of such a man as that extinguishing reason, talking sillily, with a blurred eye, and swollen lip, forgetting what he did every night! God help us and have mercy on us if we talk about such degradation as that as something to laugh about! We laugh at drunkenness, and that which we laugh at is one phase of that awful act.

I once heard a gentleman tell a story in Scotland which made me laugh immoderately. I cannot tell you the story, but will give you some idea of it. He said a laird went to pay his rent to the squire, and started in the morning on horseback, with his man Sandy following him. They were going home pretty full; and when the laird came to the water his horse pulled him in.

"Sandy, Sandy," says the laird, "something has fell off."

" No, laird, there is nothing fell off."

" Sandy, I heard a splash."

Sandy got off to see, and then, " It is yoursel is in the water."

"It can't be me, Sandy, for I am here."

Sandy got the laird on the horse wrong side foremost.

" Now, Sandy, give me the bridle."

" I cannot find the bridle ; there is not any bridle ; there is not any place for a bridle."

" Sandy, I *must* have a bridle to steer."

" Why, laird," said Sandy, " the horse's head is off, and I cannot find the place where it was ; there is nothing left but a long piece of his mane."

" Give me the mane, then, Sandy."

" O!" exclaimed Sandy, "you are going the wrong way."

I heard of a drunkard who came home very drunk in the dark. He was very thirsty, and found the water-pitcher, into which one of the children had dropped a spool of silk. He placed the pitcher to his lips and took a tremendous swallow, and finding the substance going down his throat, he got frightened and dropped it, but the thread caught on one of his teeth, and as he began to pull, it began to unwind from the depths of his stomach.

"Murder!" he cried; "Betsey, hurry up! I am all un-raveling."

Now that which we laugh at is one phase of an awful fact.

I will give you another phase of it. A man came into his house in Hartford, drunk. His boy, a little child three and a half years old, came to meet him, with arms extended. Had he been sober, the boy would have been nestling in his breast. He took him by the shoulder, lifted him over his head, dashed him through the window, and sash and all went out on the pavement, and amid broken glass lay the brains of that little boy. That is what a man is capable of doing when he is drunk. Whether you hold your sides in merriment, or your blood is chilled with horror, drunkenness is debasing, imbruting, blasting, scathing, mildewing, and damning to every thing that is bright, noble, manly and God-like in a human being.

What shall we do about it but to fight the evil? And you have heard to-night of ways by which you can do this. A great many persons try to discourage us by saying: "Do you ever expect the time to come when there will be no more drunkenness? Do you expect the time will come when men wont get tight? You will never see that day."

I was the guest of W. A. Reed, in Norfolk, Va., in 1846 and 1847, and one day I saw a woman standing on a hogshead, and heard a man say, "Three hundred and fifty-five for this wench; three fifty; turn around; look at her arm." I said, That is the most damnable sight a man ever saw in a Christian country; and when I got home I spoke about the enormity of the thing; but I was met with the query, "What are you going to do about it? You talk about the abolition of slavery, but it is so interwoven into the domestic life of our people that it is impossible to abolish it. Suppose you would attempt to buy them; it would cost you four thousand millions of dollars. There may be some evil in it, but you have got to submit to it. It is all nonsense, a Utopian scheme, to think to do away with it."

So men went on talking, until God saw fit to take it into his hand, and by the sacrifice of more than three hundred thousand men, and at a cost of more than four thousand millions of dollars, he swept with his own right hand slavery from our soil forever. It can be done when he takes the matter in his own hands, and, as one good lady said to-night, God will avenge us of our adversary. If he *can*, then he *will*.

He might send famine to this land, but that would not break up the liquor business. When I was in Ireland I was entertained by a brother of the Earl of Brandon. He told me at the dinner-table of the terrible famine, and showed me its tracks. A lady stood at a gate sprinkling chloride of lime where three hundred and fifty starving people were assembled, so as to prevent infection. Children were found by the sea-side dead, their little stomachs collapsed, and sea-weed that they had been sucking in their mouths. One lady said to me, "We were afraid to go out after dark, lest we should stumble over dead bodies." There were hardly enough people left to bury the dead.

Yet within that year of the famine in Ireland nine

millions of bushels of grain were distilled into whisky. In some cases the store-houses were overflowing. They bought up the grain in view of a rise, so that while the people were starving some of the store-houses were breaking down with the weight of it.

It needs something more than famine to awaken the people to the iniquity of this terrible curse that we are fighting on all sides by law; but the day of victory will come by and by.

We say, you know, in the Lord's Prayer, "Thy will be done on earth as it is in heaven." The Master never taught his disciples to pray for any thing that is not to be. His will is to be done on earth as it is in heaven. Will any people get "tight" then?

I shall not live to see it. What has that to do with it? What am I or you? It is in His hands. It is our business to work, and His province to give results. Let us who are engaged in this movement have faith in our principles and have faith in one another.

Let us not spend our energies in battling one another. Because one man makes moral suasion his specialty, and another makes prohibition his specialty, are these specialties going to knock their heads together? I work for moral suasion because I feel I am more at home in this department than any other; but I talk for prohibition. Let us have faith in our principles and faith in God. I mean *faith;* I do not mean what some people call faith. I do not mean the trust in Providence that was manifested by the old lady who said to the captain, "Are we in danger?"

To which he replied, "There is nothing left for us now but to trust in Providence."

"Goodness gracious!" she replied, "has it come to that?"

Some of us think we can treat the Lord as we see fit, as the poor washerwoman did when her shanty was burned down. "Now," said she, "you see if I don't work Sundays to pay for that."

We get lessons of faith where we hardly expect it. Two boys were in a hospital together—one of them with both legs broken, and the other a waif picked up in the public streets. They lay side by side with each other, and one crept up toward the other as the sun was going down, and said,

"Well, Bob, did you never hear of Jesus?"

"No, I never heard of him."

"Why, Bob, I went to the mission-school, and they told me that Jesus would take a feller to heaven when he died, where there would never be hunger any more, if a feller would only ax him."

"O, I couldn't ax such a big gentleman as him to do any thing for me. He wouldn't speak to a poor boy like me."

"But, Bob, don't you want your leg to stop aching? Don't you want to stop being hungry?"

"*Don't I!*"

"Well, ax him."

"How can I ax him, when I don't know where he is? And if I did know where he was, I couldn't go; my legs are broke."

"Bob, they told me in the mission-school that Jesus passes by. That means, you know, he comes around. How do you know but that he will be coming around this 'ere hospital? Just keep your eyes open. You would know him if you seed him, and then you could ax him."

"I can't keep my eyes open. My leg aches awfully, and the doctor says I will die."

"Bob, you can hold out your hand, and if he should come around he would see it."

The hand was raised again, and dropped. The third time the little fellow got it up, and as it dropped he burst out crying in his weakness.

"Bob, you just let me prop your elbow up with my pillow."

And he took his own pillow and propped up the child's hand.

In the morning the boy lay dead, with his little hand rigid, stiff, and cold, held up for Jesus.

That is faith; that is trust; that is absolute confidence. That is just what we want in this movement. Let us never mind results, but have faith in our principles, faith in each other, and faith in God, with the motto "Excelsior," and the hope that there is a better day coming by and by, and the prayer always offered in humble, reverent faith, "God speed the right."

SYMPATHY FOR THE DRUNKARD.

When I think of what I owe to the temperance movement, my sympathies go out to the poor victims of
intemperance.   No man or woman in this assembly,
perhaps, knows what it is to be a drunkard.   Can you
realize what it is to feel every nerve and fiber crying out
for stimulus?   " Ah," said a man to me, " I must have
it till I die; and I am as essentially damned to-day as
if sentence had been pronounced against me!"   When
I look back upon the past, and remember my own history, it seems to me as if my whole heart's sympathies
went out to the victims of this vice.   What shall we do
for the poor, debased, degraded, and almost hopeless
drunkards?   We look upon them as reckless and willfully
wicked.   Society throws them out of her superabundant
lap as things unworthy of pity or sympathy; and yet
these are men and women with hearts as warm and with
sensibilities as keen as yours.

I have in my house a small handkerchief, not worth
three cents to you, but you could not buy it from me.
A woman brought it, and said to my wife : " I am very
poor; I would give your husband a thousand pounds if
I had it, but I have brought this.   I married with the
fairest and brightest prospects before me ; but my husband took to drinking, and every thing went.   The
pianoforte my mother gave me and every thing were
sold, until at last I found myself in a miserable room.
My husband lay drunk in the corner, and my child, that

was lying on my knee, was restless. I sang 'The Light of Other Days has Faded,' and wet my handkerchief through with tears. My husband met yours. He spoke a few words and gave a grasp of the hand, and now for six years my husband has been to me all that a husband can be to a wife, and we are gathering our household goods together again. I have brought your husband the very handkerchief I wet through that night with my tears, and I want him when he is speaking to remember that he has wiped away those tears from me, I trust in God, forever." These are the trophies that make men glad.

Some say that the intemperate man is recklessly bent on on destroying himself. I know better, and so do you. Did you ever see a man take a glass of intoxicating liquor in his hands and apostrophize it: "Here I stand in vigorous health and fine physical development; I have a mother who loves me, and sisters who cling to me; I am respected; my ambition is high, and I lookinto the future with hope. With this I will now blast my reputation, ruin my prospects and my health, break the heart of my mother, and bring disgrace upon my sisters. Men shall speak of me in after years with bated breath, 'for the memory of the wicked shall rot.' I will take the first step to such a consummation by taking the first glass." Is there any man such a consummate fool as to deliberately say that? And yet men are doing just that thing in this city; doing it from the first commencement down the fatal sliding-scale to ruin—a ruin more awful than the imagination of man can describe.

If I ask a young man to stop drinking, he will say, " I can if I please." So you can; but you wont. There is

8

a man who can give it up, but he wont; there is another
man who would give it up with all his soul, but he cannot. I believe there are some men who cannot; I believe there are some men who have stepped across the
line, and that line is utter ruin. Some of you knew poor
Uniac. George H. Stuart knew and helped him, as one
Christian brother would help another. I knelt with
Uniac, and heard him with his hands clasped say, "O
God, help me! O Christ, help me!" The last words I
heard him say were, "I believe the Bible and in a future
state of retribution, and I will not live a drunkard. If I
fall again, I am a dead man." He did fall, and he was a
dead man before morning.

A glass of ale is a "little thing," a "small affair;" but
I care not what it is holds a man, so long as he is held
by it. Some men play with this "little thing" until
they are in the position of the poor fellow outside the
lines when he called out, "I've got a prisoner."

"Bring him in."

"He wont come in."

"Well, then, you had better come in without him."

"He wont let me."

In case there may be one young man in this assembly
who drinks, I would ask, "Do you not drink more now
than you did five years ago?" Every man who is in the
habit of drinking will say that he takes it oftener and
has a stronger craving for it. Some will say, "O yes!
this temperance is all right enough, but a man must not
be weak-minded." What are your ideas of weak-mind-
edness? I spoke in the city of New York, in the pulpit
of one of the most eloquent ministers of the Gospel in

this city. He was deposed from the ministry for drunkenness, and was seen two years afterward, with a
wretched, ragged shirt over his clothes, preaching sermons to loafers in a dram-shop for rum.

A minister told me, in 1847, one of the most thrilling
incidents I ever heard in my life. A member of his congregation came home for the first time in his life intoxicated, and his boy met him upon the door-step, clapping
his hands and exclaiming, " Papa has come home!" He
seized that boy by the shoulder, swung him around,
staggered, and fell with him in the hall. The minister
said to me: "I spent that night in that house. I went
to the door and bared my brow that the night air might
fall upon it and cool it; I walked up and down the hall.
There was his child dead; there was his wife in strong con-
vulsions, and he asleep. A man but thirty-five years of
age asleep, with a dead child in the house, having a blue
mark upon the temple where the corner of the marble
steps had come in contact with the head as he swung
him round, and a wife upon the very brink of the grave!
The doctor told me I must remain until he awoke, and I
did. When he awoke, he passed his hand over his face,
and exclaimed: 'What is the matter?   Where am I?
Where is my boy?'

"'You cannot see him.'

"'Where is my boy?' he inquired.

"'You cannot see him.'

"'Stand out of my way. I will see my boy!'

"To prevent confusion, I took him to that child's bed-
side, and as I turned down the sheet and showed him
the corpse, he uttered a shriek: 'Ah! my child.'"

That minister said further to me, "One year after
that he was brought from a lunatic asylum to lie side by
side with his wife, in one grave, and I attended his funeral." The minister of the Gospel who told me that
fact is to-day a drunken hostler in a stable in Boston!

Now tell me what drink will do. It will debase, de-
grade, imbrute, and damn every thing that is noble,
bright, glorious, and Godlike in a human being. There
is nothing drink will not do that is vile, dastardly, cowardly, sneaking, or hellish. We are united, brethren, are
we not, to fight it till the day of our death? O, may
God give me an increasing capacity to hate it as long as
I live!

You know as well as I do that it depends a great
deal more on the temperament of a man than upon the
strength of his mind, whether he becomes intemperate if
he drinks. Some men can drink moderately—those who
possess a cold, phlegmatic temperament. You have
seen such men—persons who could not understand a
joke.

A gentleman in St. Louis, an eminent joker, told me
that a friend of his was never able to understand a joke,
and whenever he perpetrated one upon him he informed
him that he would wink, so as to let him know that he
had been joking. The friend was very low with rheumatism—laid out stiff and straight, and could not move. The
joker came in, and said: "Jim, you are in the stationary
line," and winked. The old fellow lay there pondering
over the matter, saying: "How, in the name of common
sense, could that thing apply to me?" A friend came in,
to whom he said: "Bill has been here, and he got a joke

on me. I know he has, because he winked. He said, when I was laid out with rheumatism and could not move a single step, that I was keeping a book-store."

A man with this temperament may be a good husband, a good father, a good son, a good neighbor, and a good Christian, for aught I know; but if you give him a glass of drink he only feels "comfortable;" give him another, and he feels "comfortable;" give him another, and he feels "comfortabler." He will drop his chin on his chest, and his lower lip will lie over his chin; he will go to sleep "comfortable," and he will get up in the morning feeling "comfortable."

Now, the influence of drink upon such a man may be very disastrous to his vital organs, and may produce disease. But when such a person drinks, he does not stand with one foot upon the chair and the other upon the table, with a glass in his hand, calling upon the boys to give three cheers. He never hurrahs; he drinks "comfortably." Take a man with a nervous, susceptible temperament, who is easily excited, fond of society, full of music, with a very active brain, and give him a glass of liquor. He feels it in every nerve of his system, in every fiber of his frame, for it touches his brain instantly. What is the effect of drink upon the brain? It weakens the power of will, warps the judgment, and stimulates the perception, while it destroys its accuracy. A man is not what he was before; he is sensibly changed. There are men so nervously susceptible to the influence of stimulants that only one glass is to them not moderate, but excess. Say to a young man, "Come with me into that house," and he will respond, "No. Go into that house!

Never!" Coax him, argue with him, drive him, and he will rejoin: "No; by the love I bear my mother, by my sister's pure kiss upon my cheek, go across the threshold of that house, never! Here I stand, firm as a rock." But give him one glass of whisky or brandy, wait ten minutes, and then say: "Will you come with me now?" "Yes, go with you anywhere." And he will step across the threshold of her whose steps take hold on hell, when you could not have argued, forced, or ridiculed him into it without the influence of drink touching his brain. There are men as sensitive as that, and this is the class who are becoming intemperate. And they are not what many would call weak-minded.

But a man will tell me: "When I find out that it is injuring me, then I will give it up." No, you wont. When will a man find out that it is injuring him? and what is it to be injured by drink? There are young men in this city of whom it would be libelous to say that they are drunkards, but are they not drinking enough to injure them? It is natural for a young man to love his mother, isn't it? When I hear a young man speak contemptuously of his mother, I make up my mind to one of two things, either he is a bad man, or his mother is a bad woman. The love for a good mother is the last principle that will die out of a man. How many young men are there in the city of New York that, if I should say a word that would touch the feelings of a mother, would beat me like a dog! And yet these men are deliberately, willfully, and steadily breaking their mothers' hearts, and they know it. There are young men in this city who will press their lips upon their mother's cheek

in the evening, and, as they go out, she will say : " Don't
be late, my boy ; " and as that boy leaves his mother, he
knows that if he comes home at midnight, with the smell
of liquor upon his breath as he kisses his mother good-
night again, she will go to bed and weep till morning, and
wet the pillow with her tears.   Do you tell me that he
does not know that every step he takes he is planting a
thorn in her pillow?   And yet, when I ask him to quit
drinking, he will tell me that he does not drink enough
to hurt him.

I know a great many of our fashionable business men
say: " The fact is, you teetotalers are an ascetic set." No,
we are not.   We are the jolliest set of people that ever
lived, but when we laugh we have something to laugh
at.   You take a lot of men half-fuddled with wine, and
anything will make them laugh.   Temperance men like
fun and frolic.   Man is the only animal that can laugh,
and we teetotalers have a right to enjoy our privilege.
We are seeking happiness just as much as the intemperate ; but I want to say one thing, that happiness is not
worth the name unless you can thank God for it.   I was
asked by a lady in Cincinnati to go and hear Werner
play in his rooms.   I accepted the invitation, and listened while the weird, melancholy, minor discords resolved themselves into perfect harmonies.   I sat there
thrilled for two hours, and, by and by, I turned to the
lady, and said : "I thank God for such a capacity for enjoyment."   But no man ever dared to go down on his knees
and thank God for the gratification produced by intoxication.   We have sources of enjoyment around us, above
us, beneath, every-where.

(Mr. Gough then depicted in his characteristic and "unreportable" style the thrilling sensations he experienced several years ago when he visited Mont Blanc. He thanked God that, although but a speck amid those majestic mountains, he was a man.) The great God who created the universe formed me, and made me what he made no material thing—a living soul. There is a destiny before me as high as heaven and vast as eternity, for I am a man; and the universe, grand and glorious as it is, is but the nursery of my infant soul. The child is worth more than the nursery, and therefore I, as a man, am worth more than all God's material universe. Years have passed since I witnessed that spectacle, but I can at any time lie upon the sofa, cover my face in my hands, and dream it all back again, and thank God for the capacity for such enjoyment.

A short time ago a man came to me, and said: " I knew you twenty-seven years ago in Massachusetts, when you gave a concert at Haverhill. After the concert we went to Brown's Hotel, and continued to drink till four o'clock in the morning. I thought you were the happiest fellow I ever set my eyes on, and I said to my friends, 'If you want to see a happy fellow, there is one; it bubbles all over him.'" Are the flush and excitement that drink produces, and which leave a stain, real happiness? I am now fifty-three years old, and as I look back upon the past, as I mingle with the wise, the good, the pure, and the true, as I shake hands with such men as have grasped my hand to-night, I feel intense disgust and abhorrence of the days which that man spoke of as being happy. I would give my right hand to-night if I could forget them; if I could tear out from my memory the remembrance of the dark, black, damning days of degradation.

But some say, "You have recovered." No, we can never recover from the effects of such a life. What a man sows, that shall he reap. Little things show whether such men recover or not. One little thing I may say personally, if you please. I have tried to bring up some children—not my own—and two of them are on the platform to-night. One of the hinderances to my speech is that they are there and hear what I say. Last summer I heard one of those girls say to my wife, "Aunt Mary, is it not strange that Uncle John should have got drunk?" I felt ashamed of myself; and is that not some penalty for a man to pay all the days of his life? I do feel ashamed; I feel as if I could hide myself in the earth; I felt to-night, when I took hold of hands that never had been stained with the intoxicating cup, as if I could lie down and let them set their feet upon me. There is not a man so well known to the public so utterly lonesome and isolated as I am. Did you ever hear of my being at a party? Never. I have not attended two for twenty-five years. Did you ever hear of my calling upon great men? No. And when I invite them, I do it with so much timidity that I do not much expect them to accept the invitation. I have asked some of the gentlemen here to-night to come and see me, but I do not believe they ever will. If a man invites me to a dinner party I find an excuse. I never go to see people, because I stained the pages of my life's book. Though I may turn over ten thousand stainless pages, the stains on the other

pages will remain.   Yet I have one comfort: "I, even I
am He that blotteth out thine iniquities."   There is to be
a blotting-out, thank God!   But there never will be a
blotting-out in this life of wrong-doing: "What a man
sows, that shall he reap."   While I look back over the
past and look into the future, I trust with some confidence, and thank God for all he has enabled me to do,
though I have done it in a stumbling, blundering way.

A gentleman said to me the other day: "The Temperance Cause is dead."   It is not dead, for it was born in
the Church of Christ, and that which is born there can
never die.   Right is to triumph in the end.   You and I
shall not live to see it, but it will come.   Nero sat on
the throne, clothed in purple, and at his nod men trembled.   In the Mamertine dungeon a man was writing a
letter to Timothy to send him his cloak, for he was shivering in one of the dungeons of the Roman capital.
Years rolled on, and right and wrong contended with
each other.   Nero died a miserable suicide, but his prisoner wrote on and finished his letter: "I have fought a
good fight, I have finished my course, I have kept the
faith"—words which have comforted millions for generations.   And the world could better afford to lose all
the words of eloquence that ever fell from the lips of
Roman orators, than to lose one word of what the
chained prisoner wrote in his dungeon.

My experience has led me to this conclusion: that we
trust too much even to our organizations and to our efforts.   We are in too much of a hurry; we want results
immediately.   We do a thing and want results to come
at once, forgetting that with the Lord one day is as a

thousand years, and a thousand years as one day. It is God's work, and not ours; we are workers. If a man stands as a conscious machine, and if he is connected by a band of living faith with God Almighty, he is doing his work, as he wills, where he wills, and when he will, and occupies the highest position a man can occupy in this world. God is the motive power, and our work is simply nothing in comparison with his. Then, as we put forth our efforts, let us make our appeal to him.

Let us reverently ask God to help us for his great name's sake, and we with those we have worked for shall stand saved, not by our own efforts alone, but by our own efforts blessed and acknowledged by Him in whose hands are the destinies of all men.

TEMPERANCE ADDRESS.

The following address, by Mr. Gough, was delivered at the Twelfth Anniversary of the National Temperance and Publication Society, in New York. Being introduced by the President, Hon. Wm. E. Dodge, Mr. Gough spoke as follows:—

On the 9th day of May, 1844, at an anniversary of the American Temperance Union, I first appeared before a New York audience in the old Broadway Tabernacle, within two days of thirty-three years ago; and the cause that we advocate to-night is the same old theme—the evil of drunkenness and the instrumentalities and agencies to roll back this tide of evil from the land.

There are many persons who talk about us as being fanatics. They tell us we are rabid on this subject of temperance. I ask any reformed drunkard in this audience to-night if it is not right to be rabid against an evil that has scorched and blasted and scathed and scarred us, and we shall carry the marks of it to the grave with us.

Young men sometimes have an idea that a man can sow his wild oats and get over it. You put your hand in the hand of a giant and he crushes it. He may tear at your hand and it may be healed, and by and by in some sort it may be a useful one, but it is a mutilated hand; its beauty and symmetry have gone forever. We who have passed through this fire know something of its awful scourge; we know something of the terrible struggle to get out of it. I think we ought to be what they call rabid. They tell us that we exaggerate the evil of drunkenness. Do we? Let me appeal to this intelligent audience and ask the question, " Do we exaggerate the evil of drunkenness?"

A Voice : " No, sir."

Mr. Gough, (resuming:) No, sir, we cannot. God never gave a man a mind capable of grasping the extent of the awful evil of drunkenness for time and for eternity. You have a boy, a bright-eyed, beautiful fellow, round in limb, with his pearly teeth, ruby lip, and rosy cheek symmetrical and beautiful. O, how you love him as he springs into your arms in the morning, and puts his face to your cheek! You press him to your heart. How you love him as you say to a visitor, " Have you seen my boy?" and to him, " Come, old fellow." How he will spring into your arms! O, how you love him!

What would you do to save that child from curvature of the spine?

" Do any thing."

What would you give?

" All my property."

What would you sacrifice?

" Every luxury under heaven."

What would you suffer?

"Try me. That boy, so straight of limb, so beautiful, so perfect and symmetrical—that boy a poor little crawling cripple, deformed, upon the floor of my house? No, no; do not ask me what I would do or give or suffer—any thing!"

I was at the house of a family where there was a crippled child. When four years of age it had fallen out of a swing backward; the child was twenty-three years of age then. The body had developed, but it was a very strange case. Physicians came to see it. The limbs had grown but very little; it had a baby's hands and feet. I tell you, to see that little creature working over the carpet like a turtle made me shudder more than I ever shuddered to see a reptile. That child once said to the mother:

"Mamma, I sha'n't trouble you much longer."

"Trouble, my darling? Why, you are the light of our home! we are learning lessons of faith and trust and patience from you every day. Why, darling, when God takes you from us it will be a dark day in our home."

"Yes, mamma, but I want to go, because when I see Jesus I shall stand up straight, sha'n't I, mamma?"

There may be some beauty and glory around a crippled child; there may be something lovely and sweet and something to be desired about a crippled child. Is there anything about a drunken one? No, not a ray of light but such as comes lurid from hell. There is no comfort, nothing joyous or delightful, nothing you love to contemplate.

What would you do to save that child from epilepsy? That is worse than the other. "Do, give, or suffer? Anything; do not ask me." I stayed at the house of a clergyman whom many of you know—J. B. Wakeley, a noble Methodist minister. He had a boy afflicted with epilepsy. While we were conversing we heard a strange noise in the corner. The boy was twisting around, and his eyes were white. The mother rushed to the child, and the father kneeled down and offered one of the most pathetic prayers I ever heard. He said: "This is hard to bear when I see that child now, and remember what he was four years ago—the brightest in the school and at the head of his class, and now see him stand before me with fingers stretched and shoulders shrugged. I remember how he came to me once, saying, 'Papa, I cannot think, I cannot think!' The boy was growing idiotic. And yet, sir, as I am a man, as I am a minister of the Gospel, his mother and I would rather see that boy just like that than to see him a drunkard."

And so would you. There is not a father or mother in New York that dare stand up before God and say they would not rather the Almighty, in his providence, should smite that boy than that he should smite himself, with all his responsibility upon him.

I met Mr. Wakeley on Broadway some time after that.

"How do you do, Mr. Gough?"

"Very well. Is Harry well? is Harry cured?"

The minister and father responded: "The Saviour loved that suffering child and took him home. I have an anticipation that by and by, in the land where there is no more sighing, no more crying, no more suffering, and no more dying, I shall meet Harry."

Did you ever hear a father talk of a boy who died a drunkard like that? Did you ever hear a man talk comfortably of a boy who died a drunkard? No, sirs. I have been invited to houses where they have said to me before I went: "Look here! don't say any thing about their eldest son. Hush! hush! don't mention the name."

I have known them to take the photograph out of the album and to take the picture from the wall, lest there should be any thing to remind them of the boy whose beauty was once a glory, but who has passed into the blackness and darkness of drunkenness in another world.

Do we exaggerate the evil of drunkenness? Bring it home ; let it crawl across your threshold and sting you to death. Drunkenness is the terrible evil of the age, before which, it seems to me, (and you may say I am fanatical, if you will,) all other evils pale and sink out of sight. They tell us that this is our exaggeration when we speak of this as a great sin. Now, I am no theologian. I cannot talk about sin *per se*, like my friend, Dr. Taylor. I do not know what they mean when they say that. I know it is a sort of way of getting over things, but I do not know what it means. I am not one of those who believe in big sins and little sins. I am one of those who believe that the soul of man is bound to his God by the chain of the moral law, and if one link of that chain is broken the soul is as effectually severed as if all were broken. But the great evil of intemperance is the promoter of almost every other sin in the universe. It helps to every thing that is bad ; it stultifies man's moral perceptions as scarcely any thing in this world does. I wont detain you by speaking of this terrible evil of drunkenness. What I want is that people's minds should be impressed with the fact that what we war against is a terrible evil, and that it requires special efforts and special self-sacrifice.

Our first work is prevention. Prevention is better than cure. To build a barrier between the unpolluted lips and the intoxicating cup is the great work we aim at; therefore we are compelled to battle every influence and agency that stands between us and our great work.

Now, when men tell the world that temperance is a more manly virtue than total abstinence, I want to ask, in the first place, exactly what they mean. Sometimes we get at it in another form. A man once said to me:—

" I abominate excess."

" I hope you are with us," I replied.

He said : " No. Teetotalism is cowardly, and the other is beastly. I stand on the manly principle of moderation. Follow my example. I say to young men : Exercise self-control and self-government. Self-denial develops. You develop nothing in a man when he has nothing to resist. Don't you see that by the power of resistance a man's muscle grows stronger, but by running away no strength is gained. My principle develops a man."

I said to him : " What is excess?"

" Drinking too much."

" What is drinking too much?"

" Excess."

" I do not want to make you angry, but I want to ask you a plain question. Would six tumblers of whisky-punch be excess for you?"

" Well, no, not if I could stand it."

Don't you see? there the whole thing fell. According to that man's theory, if a man can drink as much as he can hold, and stands up, he is developing himself. If he drinks two quarts of whisky a day, and stands it, there is an exercise of self-control and a moderate use of

liquor; but if he takes two glasses, and does not stand
it, there is a rightful illustration of the want of self-denial and self-government, and of the excessive use of
intoxicating drinks. What is excess, in the common ac-
ceptation of the term? *A man's inability to stand it.*
You cannot judge of a man's drunkenness by the quantity he drinks. There are moderate drinkers in the city
of New York that drink more, day by day, than some
of the vilest drunkards brought up in the police courts,
because there are some men who can stand it. The
other men we call drunkards because they *cannot stand it.*

You take a man brimming over with the grace of God
— take Mr. Moody, (I consider that man full of the
grace of God and the Spirit of the Lord,) give Mr.
Moody prussic acid, and then give to a man who does
not believe in the grace of God prussic acid, and Mr.
Moody's grace wont save him; and—I say it with reverence—without a miracle it is beyond God's control to
save him. A man cannot undo a deed that he has accomplished, for it is the result of law, and law is inflexi-
ble. If a man takes drink into his system, whether he
is a Christian or infidel, whether he is a Buddhist or
Hottentot, it will produce the same effect upon the same
temperament and constitution.

But if I have grace it prompts me to pray, "Lead me
not into temptation." If, for the trial of my faith or patience He sees that I should be tempted, I have his
word I shall not be tempted over what I am able to
bear; but if I think I have so much grace as to voluntarily walk into temptation, and trust that grace to keep
me from falling, it is a kind of grace I do not under-

stand. I do not want to lower any man's opinion or appreciation of the grace of God. I want to come to these reformed drunkards. You stand up, some of you, all over the country, and say, " I am reformed by the grace of God ; God has taken away my appetite." Be very careful, my friend, that you do not ask God to take away your appetite, and then ask him for nothing else. When you ask the Lord in the agony of your desire for drink, " Take this away from me," yield yourself unreservedly to him, saying : " If I am to suffer, give me the grace to overcome and to glorify thee in my suffering."

I believe that this point is not enough insisted upon by good men, and I believe that this great and grand movement all over the country will fail of the success that we ought to expect from it, by its being ephemeral and shallow and not going deep enough. Men must understand what it is to be in Christ.

A man said to me: " I am fighting a hard battle, but I am safe in Christ." I could not help thinking if that man understood what he said. I have known men who have stood up and declared that they were safe in Christ, who would use profane language ten minutes after they had uttered that sentence in the meeting. Now, in this grand movement they must be instructed and trained. What we want now is for all the Churches in the land to come right up and unite in this reform movement, and be the balance-wheel, and, I was going to say, the very compass, by which they can steer right into the haven.

To come back again : this man trusted to the grace of God. He said he went for a load of goods, and on a drizzly November afternoon he took a glass of brandy and water to keep out the cold. When he came to the square in the village, he got off his wagon and backed up. People asked, "What is the matter with you?" Some one said, "Why, you are drunk." They got around him and said, "He was converted during the revival;" "That is a young convert; he made a speech in prayer-meeting last Thursday night. What are you going to say for yourself?" They set him up, and they were jeering a Church member who was so drunk that he could only babble.·

The Church had a duty to do. They disciplined him, and in consequence of that he suffered trouble. Now, what did that Church discipline that man for? It did so because he could not stand two glasses of brandy and water. If he had stood it, it would not have touched him. That Church disciplined that man for what he could not help, for a man cannot help getting drunk if he drinks. He can help drinking, but he cannot help the effect when he has drunk. The Church disciplined that man because he could not stand two glasses of brandy and water. But there are men in that Church who can drink more than two glasses. I would like to see the Church touch *them*. O! wouldn't there be a row?

I may be considered *ultra* and rabid, but I hold that a Church has no right to discipline a member for drunkenness which does not discipline its members for drinking. I will not belong to a Church that will not do it. I will ascertain first whether they discipline their members for drinking intoxicating drinks as a beverage, and if they say they do not I will never join the Church till, by the grace of God, I join the Church triumphant.

You say I am rabid? I have reason to be rabid. I often come to New York on a Saturday night for the purpose of enjoying such Sabbaths as I very seldom enjoy anywhere else. I come to hear my friend Dr. Taylor preach. I feel as if I was a member of the Tabernacle Church, yet not, as you would say, in full communion with them. But when on last Sunday noon (if he will excuse me for mentioning it here), after a sermon that melted our hearts within us, we sat down at the communion table, the very smell of that wine reminded me of days of damning degradation, and I would not have touched my lips to that wine to save my hand from being cut off at the wrist.

You will say: "You are a poor, weak man." There are multitudes like me.

I was conversing with a man from New Hampshire who has done an immense work. He has got over thirty thousand men to sign the pledge, and he said to me: " I would not dare to put my lips to a drop of wine. Mark me, I am not saying that if I took a glass I should go on drinking; I am not saying what is or is not the strength of my appetite. I say that I cannot consistently swallow alcoholic wine, because it contains the agency and instrumentality that ruined so many."

Do you know what I thought when the cup was handed to me? I looked at it and said to myself, " There is enough there to ruin me for time and eternity," and I passed it. I cannot help feeling so upon this subject. I knew that a great many persons would criticise me and say I was all wrong. I tell you my convictions are such that I cannot help it. You stand by the dying-bed of a

drunkard, as I have; you hear the stories of sorrow, suffering, and woe that I have; you have them come to you
in distress and anguish, as they have come to me, and you
would probably feel as I do about the terrible nature of
this evil of drunkenness.

I believe when I was here last I related an incident
that affected me wonderfully. A Scotchman, a fine-looking fellow, a graduate of Edinburgh University, showed
me his diploma as a physician. He was perhaps forty
years of age—a splendid specimen of a physical man.
When he left me he said: " I am very much obliged to
you, Mr. Gough; you have been very good to me, but it's
nae use; there is nae hope for me. Will ye shake hands
wi' me? I am a lost laddie;" and he went away. As I
saw him walk from me I thought of the "lost lad-
dies" in this country who were directly or indirectly lost
through the influence of intoxicating drink. Now, we
wage war against the use of it for the sake of prevention
—to save our young men from entering into the outer
circle of the whirlpool and being drawn into the vortex.

We have our enterprises to save and rescue men, and
it is a grand work to be engaged in. When I first began,
you know, it was in the height of the Washingtonian
movement. It was a grand movement, and many were
rescued; still, it did not seem to be all that was desired.
At any rate, it was as if we were so horrified at the sight
of men going over the rapids and down the awful cata-
ract that we were lining the banks with men, and building bridges over the rapids, and as they came down we
picked them up and passed them over to friends who
bound up their wounds. Still the stream of victims came

along in multitudes. We would pick up some whom we picked up six months before, as bad and even worse than they had been. The work of saving these men went on gloriously. But by and by we began to investigate. We went above the rapids, and there found men whose sole business it was *to push them in*—to entice them to enter upon that smooth, deceitful stream. We came to the conclusion that, while we manned our forces to save men, we must man other forces to stop the murderous business of inducing men to drink. This is our work in regard to saving the drunkard. It is a great but not an easy work. I know, in this grand movement that is going on over the land, perhaps it is wrong to say that it is a hard business to save drunkards; but when we consider the power and the permanency of the appetite the work *is* difficult, and nothing can secure it with safety but the grace of God in the heart of the victim.

I mean that, when I say it, in the largest sense of that expression—the grace of God in a man's heart. It is not by praying a little while, and supposing, as Dr. Chalmers once said, " by the expulsive power of a new affection that is in him" that his appetite is stayed; but we must be with these men and help them when the tug of war comes, when temptation and opportunity and inclination press upon them. While some may say that the appetite is dead, I do not believe it; it may be in some men, but that is not so, as a general thing. It is said that sixty thousand drunkards have signed the pledge in Pennsylvania. Let each of those sixty thousand drunkards drink one glass of whisky, and fifty-nine thousand five hundred of them will have another in spite of their pledges, and the other five hundred will begin to want it.

Is there any possibility of making a moderate drinker out of a drunkard? I know that some men by the power of their will can overcome this appetite for the time being and for the remainder of their lives. I would not stand up and say that a man cannot possibly reform unless he becomes a Christian. Men have reformed and have died total abstainers without the grace of God, but it is a risk to attempt to do so.

I will give you an illustration of what I mean. I know a gentleman who got so dissipated that he would drink a bottle of brandy a day—seven bottles a week. How he stood it no one knew. He was a splendid business man, but he went down rapidly. He married into a very nice family, and one day, when seated in the house conversing affectionately with his wife, she responded:

"I would be the happiest woman in this province if my husband did not drink."

"Well," he replied, "I married you to make you happy, and it is my duty to make you happy; I ought to make you happy, and if that will make you happy I will never drink a drop as long as I live."

That was seven years ago, and he has never tasted a drop since. He cut it off short and square, as you would cut off a piece of cheese; he did it by the power of his will.

I was walking along the street once with a friend, who said to me: "I have gone three squares out of my way for years to pass that saloon; for when I saw it I felt queer, but since I have got the grace of God in my heart

I can go right by, and if I feel the slightest inclination for drink I ejaculate a prayer, ' God help me!'" There is safety. I do not mean to say, I repeat, that a man cannot reform without being a Christian, but he runs a risk every day of his life in not having the grace of God to help him. I rejoice in this Christian movement.

There has been a great deal said about the woman's crusade. There have been articles in the newspapers ridiculing the woman's crusade movement, and some travelers have written letters about it. I have one in which the writer finds great fault with the woman's movement. I must confess that at first when I heard of women singing and praying in the street before saloons, it appeared a little odd and out of place, and I rather shrank from it; but after I saw what they were doing there was no shrinking. I first came in contact with the movement in Xenia. I waited at their prayer-meeting until the ladies came in from their work, when four hundred sat down and sang,

> "One more day's work for Jesus."

I have always loved that hymn ever since. The president of the meeting—a grand woman—said to me: " You may think this is very strange, but it has been a subject of great consideration among us, what we could do, when we saw our fathers, our brothers, our husbands, and our sons ruined. All we could do was to weep over our dead and walk to the tomb with them, and leave them there ; for we had no redress."

This out-door work among the saloons lasted but for a little time, and while it was being done many laughed

9

and ridiculed it, but it did its work. Then it was time to lay aside this instrumentality which roused the people of the country, whereupon the ladies quit their fighting and went to praying. And if I believe any thing in this world, I believe that the whole of this religious movement that has started from Maine to Louisiana, from the Atlantic to the Pacific, is the result of women's prayers to God.

People wonder at such an agency. It is "not by might, nor by power, but by My Spirit ; " and, therefore, this ought to be encouragement to the ladies. You say you can do nothing. You can pray in your closet, and you can assemble in little gatherings for prayer. Verily there is a God that heareth, and verily, there is a God that judgeth.

One of the speakers, in speaking of a fire on the prairie, reminded me of a story : A party was passing over the prairies toward their destination, and one of them cried out, " See, what is that lurid light yonder ? The prairie is on fire ; the flames are going on the dry grass at the rate of twenty miles an hour. We are lost ! and nothing will remain but our charred bones to tell the story of the sacrifice. We must fight fire with fire. Quick, quick ! Now for the matches ! " They came together, and examined their store, and found there were only two matches. In their haste they took one and struck it, but it failed. Their last earthly hope was only one match. The fire was running toward them at the rate of twenty miles an hour and only one match ! Reverently they gathered together, and with bowed heads they prayed :

" God help us, for his great name's sake. This is

our only hope, our only earthly trust. In this extremity save us."

They struck the match; it caught fire; the grass was ignited, and the flames went round them in every direction.

Remember, we are fighting fire with fire, and our instrumentalities are as feeble as that single match; but as we put them forth, asking God to help us, we shall be unharmed and saved while the flames rage harmlessly around us.

The following will serve to show the true religious spirit that inspires the words of this matchless temperance orator :—

"Sometimes these seasons of long-continued labor bring on a sort of depression of spirits; dark clouds seem to hover over me, and I begin to fear that the good cause is not prospering as it might. But at such times I try to examine my motives in advocating it; I try to look at the subject in the light of eternity, and ask God to give me strength to advocate it; and not strength only, but also patience and prudence and meekness and discretion, that I may be able to advocate these holy principles, not in a spirit of bigotry, but in the spirit of love to all.

"We do not put the temperance enterprise in the place of religion. No, no. Never! Never! But we believe that temperance may be the handmaid of Christianity. Total abstinence may not save a man from being a thief or a blasphemer, though I think it would help even to do that; but it will save him from being a drunkard;

and I would rather have a sober infidel than a drunken one. Some of you say that we are fostering the spirit of infidelity in our temperance movement. I tell you, there is more infidelity fostered and sustained by the inconsistencies of professing Christians than by all the teetotalism in the world.

"Let us carry on this reform in the spirit of that good old reformer, Nehemiah. He prayed while he worked. When the enemy came out and tried to stop his rebuilding the wall of Jerusalem, what does he say? He set a watch and so kept them off? No; but he says, 'We made our prayer unto God, and set a watch.' Prayer to God and work for our brothers' salvation belong together; and what God has joined together, let no man put asunder."

These admirable addresses of Mr. Gough are here inserted by the kind permission of the National Temperance and Publishing Society.

FATHER MATHEW.

SECTION IV.

FRATERNAL TEMPERANCE.

A SKETCH OF THE BROTHERHOODS AND SISTER-
HOODS OF THE TEMPERANCE REFORM.

CHAPTER IX.

FRATERNAL TEMPERANCE.

SONS OF TEMPERANCE. The Washingtonian movement, so called, was thought by some to be lack-
ing in the element of permanency. Many persons who
signed the pledge became again ensnared in the power
of strong drink, and it was thought that an organization
which should give greater fraternal care and watchful-
ness over its members would be the means of preventing these falls from the grace of temperance.

Accordingly, the Order of the Sons of Temperance,
and afterward of the Daughters of Temperance, was established, which contained the temperance doctrines of
the Washingtonian societies, with something of the fraternal elements of the Masons and Odd Fellows.

On the twenty-ninth of September, 1842, a select
meeting was called at Teetotaler's Hall, No. 71 Di-
vision-street, New York, to organize a beneficial society based on total abstinence, bearing the title of
The Sons of Temperance. It was proposed to make
the initiation fee at first one dollar, with dues of six
and a quarter cents a week; from which, in case of
sickness, members might receive $4 per week, and
in case of death $30, to be appropriated for funeral
expenses.

Of this meeting Daniel H. Sands was Chairman, and
John W. Oliver was Secretary, and here was formed New

York Division, No. 1, of the Order of the Sons of Temperance. The officers of this division were: *Worthy Patriarch*, Daniel H. Sands; *Worthy Associate*, Ephraim L. Snow; *Recording Scribe*, John W. Oliver; *Financial Scribe*, James Bale; *Treasurer*, George M'Kibbin.

An initiation ceremony and a ritual were arranged, which are both beautiful and impressive, and a pledge adopted, which may not be changed without the unanimous vote of the National Division of the Order. The pledge was as follows:—

"I will neither make, buy, sell, nor use as a beverage, any spirituous or malt liquors, wine, or cider."

Of this movement, Samuel W. Hodges, Most Worthy Scribe, says in his paper in the Centennial Volume:—

"It is hardly probable the originators of the Order foresaw the wide spread of the organization, but the very simplicity of the movement soon brought it into notice, and it immediately took the foremost ground as an aggressive temperance movement. Its pledge has been administered to three millions of men and women, and thousands of households in this and other countries have reason to bless the sixteen men to whom the credit of the organization belongs."

The Constitution provides for a National Division, which meets annually, composed of Past and Acting Grand Worthy Patriarchs of State Divisions, in which is vested the supreme power of the Order; for State Divisions, which meet quarterly, and are composed of all the Past and Acting Worthy Patriarchs of subordinate Divisions, under their respective jurisdictions; and for subordinate Divisions, with weekly temperance meetings

Concerning the objects of the Order, the paper already quoted has the following:—

"Up to this time all labors had been in the line of what is called moral suasion. The abolition of the rumshop had not been thought of; but the organization of determined men, having in view the salvation of their associates from the curse of drink, soon brought with it the question: Would it not be better to try to remove the temptation from the men, than to spend all the time in keeping the men from temptation?"

Thus the Sons of Temperance became a center of operations for the various efforts to procure prohibitory laws. The Order took the ground that the use of intoxicating liquors as a beverage is always useless, always dangerous, and that no law to *regulate* the sale of it as a beverage could ever make it any thing but a sin.

The National Division of the Sons of Temperance was organized in the State of New York, June 11th, 1843, at which the State Divisions of New York, New Jersey, Maryland, Pennsylvania, Connecticut, and Massachusetts were represented. The next year the District of Columbia, Maine, and Ohio were added, and the Order continued to expand until altogether, in 1855, it comprised forty-one Grand Divisions, 3,543 subordinate Divisions, and 134,177 members, besides seven Grand Divisions which failed to report.

The Sons of Temperance in this country operate in harmony with the Order in Great Britain and Ireland, and also in the British Provinces of North America. There are also two Divisions of the Order in Australia.

The latest census of the Order gives a total of about
9*

2,000 Divisions in North America. In Great Britain and Ireland the Order has a strong hold, while in Australia, under the two National Divisions, there are about 600 local Divisions, with about 35,000 members.

The members of the Divisions of the Sons of Temperance are initiated with solemn religious rites, with which are joined most delightful and appropriate fraternal exercises.

The amount of good accomplished by it cannot be estimated. One part of its work has been to bind the country more closely together, and to establish something like unity of effort in the work for the temperance reform, especially in the line of securing proper legislation. The falling off in the census of the Order may be accounted for by the rise and progress of other fraternal temperance organizations, though in the aggregate, the organized temperance force of the country is certainly and rapidly increasing.

DAUGHTERS OF TEMPERANCE.—The new Order at first only admitted " male persons, eighteen years of age and over," to its meetings, but in 1854 the wives, daughters, and sisters of members were admitted as visitors. Afterward ladies of fourteen years of age were admitted to full membership on the same terms as gentlemen.

There are separate divisions of this Order for people of the African race.

THE INDEPENDENT ORDER OF GOOD TEMPLARS.— The principles of the Order of Good Templars may be called the strictest orthodox temperance doctrine. It was found that while many real wants were relieved by the beneficiary system, it was frequently a source of difficulty, and in many instances became a temptation to fraud. The Good Templars accordingly ignored the benefit plan, and placed no motive before a person for joining them, but to be reclaimed, if fallen, or to assist in saving those who were fallen.

The Order takes the broadest ground upon all questions connected with the temperance reform. The following is its platform, as adopted in 1859:—

1. Total abstinence from all intoxicating liquors as a beverage.

2. No license, in any form or under any circumstances, for the sale of such liquors to be used as a beverage.

3. Absolute prohibition of the manufacture, importation, and sale of intoxicating liquors for such purposes— prohibition by the will of the people, expressed in due form of law, with the penalties deserved for a crime of such enormity.

4. The creation of a healthy public opinion upon the subject by the dissemination of the truth.

5. The election of good and honest men to administer the laws.

6. Persistence in efforts toward ultimate and universal success.

The Order of Good Templars takes the ground that alcohol is an outlaw, and its use in every form or degree is dangerous, ruinous, and hence immoral; that the traffic therein has no *status* in morals, and should have none in law.

"Total abstinence" to the Good Templar means abstinence from the use of sweet cider and unfermented wine, or the juice of the apple, grape, berry, in any state, as a beverage. The reason given for this is that it is impossible to tell the point at which fermentation commences. Hence, with a view to absolute safety, all liquors capable of fermentation are excluded by its pledge.

Another feature of the Order is that a Good Templar is pledged to total abstinence *for life*. The pledges of the Sons of Temperance are held binding only during membership of the Order. This membership may be canceled or forfeited ; but " Once a Good Templar always a Good Templar" is the doctrine of this organization.

Great stress is also laid on the social influence of the Good Templars' Lodge, where the youth of both sexes are brought together, and trained on strict total abstinence principles.

" I defend the Order of Good Templars," said a prominent Illinois divine, "on this ground, among others, that it promotes matrimony—a consummation devoutly to be wished in these days of celibacy and divorces."

The revenue of the Order, which is used to print and circulate tracts and papers, and to sustain lecturers in the field, is raised by a system of moderate fees and dues.

Its offices are all posts of labor and responsibility as well as honor. It has a system of committees to attend to the various practical temperance work, such as visiting the sick of the Order, distributing temperance literature, holding public meetings, and so forth.

The author of the ritual for initiatory and higher degrees is the Rev. D. W. Bristol, to whom, with Rev. H. P. Barnes, and Dr. C. S. Miles, belongs the honor of this new temperance work.

The supreme head of the Order is called the Right Worthy Grand Lodge, and is composed of delegates from the Grand Lodges of States and Territories.

This Lodge has held annual sessions since 1855, at which sixty Grand Lodges have been represented.

The Order has maintained an efficient lecture system, and has also sent out missionaries to organize Lodges in Great Britain and her colonies.

Prizes have been offered for productions on topics connected with the work of the Order, and, the financial basis of the Order not supplying ample funds, a tax of one cent per member of each subordinate Lodge (called the Moses Fund, from the name of the gentleman to whom the printing bill was due) was raised for printing the Grand Lodge ritual, which was composed by Mrs. F. D. B. Chase, of Pennsylvania.

The juvenile work of the Order is established in a separate branch, of which Mrs. M. B. O'Donnell is the chief superintendent. This department has a constitution and ritual of its own, which pledges its members against tobacco and profanity as well as against liquor. This juvenile department now numbers about 100,000 children.

In 1876 it was estimated that 2,900,804 persons had been initiated into the Order. Of this number 290,000 had been hard drinkers, half of whom have kept their pledge and become valuable laborers in the reform. The largest number of the members of the Order at any one time was in 1875, 617,733.

TEMPLE OF HONOR.—The Order of "Templars of Honor and Temperance" was originated by prominent members of the Sons of Temperance, as a kind of advanced degree of that organization, with a view to securing greater activity, influence, and perpetuity.

It may be called the Knighthood of the Sons of Temperance, to which those only may aspire who will dedicate to the cause their lives, their fortunes, and their sacred honor.

In 1846 delegates from twelve Temples met in the city of New York, and organized a Grand Temple. A ritual was secured, a regalia, jewels, and a seal were adopted, and officers elected, with titles similar to those of the Sons of Temperance, but with the word "Templar" in place of "Patriarch."

In November of the same year the National Temple of Honor was organized. It is the supreme head of the Order in the United States, and is composed of the Past and Acting G. W. Templars and Vice-Templars of the various State Lodges.

The ritual of the Order includes the initiation degree into what is called the Subordinate Temple, with its three sectional degrees, Love, Purity, and Fidelity.

The next is the Council Department, with the three degrees of Tried, Approved, and Select Templars.

The third is the Social Temple, with the three degrees of Love, Equality, and Fidelity.

The manual of the Order was prepared by the P. M. W. Templar, Rev. Geo. B. Jocelyn, of Michigan.

In 1876 this fraternity comprised twenty-one Grand Temples, and three hundred and fifty-seven subordinate Temples, with a total membership of both sexes of 16,229.

P. M. W. Templar Jocelyn, in his report of the Order
for the Centennial Volume, says:—

"The candidate for admission must profess his allegiance to Almighty God, and his willingness to assume a
vow that binds him to total and perpetual abstinence
from intoxicating beverages, and pledges him to all honorable means for the suppression of the use and the traffic thereof.

"The Order is not a religious or political one, but it is
a Christian, civil association.   The Bible is the great
store-house whence all the principles of the Order are
derived, and no Temple can transact its ordinary business unless, as symbolizing that fact, the Bible lies open
upon the altar."

THE INDEPENDENT ORDER OF RECHABITES.   The
title of this Order is taken from the thirty-fifth chapter
of the prophecy of Jeremiah, from the story of Jonadab
the son of Rechab, whose sons were commanded to
drink no wine forever, and who, for their obedience to
this injunction, were highly approved by Jehovah.

"Therefore thus saith the Lord of hosts, the God of
Israel; Jonadab the son of Rechab shall not want a man
to stand before me forever," in fulfillment whereof it is
declared that this family continue a distinct people even
unto this day.

The Order was established in the county of Lancaster,
in England, in 1835.   It is a friendly or benefit society,
providing for all its members in time of sickness and at
death, after the fashion of the Sons of Temperance, but,
like some other benevolent societies, it limits its mem-

bership to persons of healthy constitution and good moral character, between the ages of fifteen and fifty.

The sick and funeral fund is divided into shares, and each member on entering can take from one to six shares in the sick fund, and from one to four in the funeral fund. For every penny per week paid into the sick fund two shillings six pence were allowed in time of sickness ; and for every five pence per quarter paid into the funeral fund five pounds were paid at death. The local assemblies are called Tents, and the associations thereof are called Districts. The executive power is vested in a power of nine Directors, the president of which has the curious title of " High Chief Ruler," and the next in order, " High Deputy Ruler."

The Order has a reputation in England for dignity, respectability, and financial soundness. It was introduced into America from England in 1842, and spread with great rapidity throughout the United States, numbering at one time over 100,000 members.

THE INDEPENDENT ORDER OF GOOD SAMARITANS AND DAUGHTERS OF SAMARIA. This Order originated in the city of New York, in 1847. It is a small division of the temperance army, of only about fourteen thousand persons ; but in proportion to its membership it contains a very large number of reformed persons, its chief work being among those who, passing from Jerusalem to Jericho, have fallen among thieves. Its initiatory services are very charming, being the dramatized rendering of the parable of the Good Samaritan.

The Order has also a juvenile branch. It recognizes

no distinction of color, and does not permit political
questions to disturb its sessions, though it considers freely all questions and measures which can help a fallen
brother.

The present executive officers of the National Grand
Lodge are Sire, Rev. Geo. H. Hick; Secretary, W. H.
C. Curtis; Treasurer, Henry Russell, all of the State of
New York.

THE FRIENDS OF TEMPERANCE is the title of a separate and distinct organization of temperance workers,
which was formed at Petersburgh, Virginia, in November, 1865.

The reason given for this new organization was that
all the temperance organizations in the South had suffered immeasurable evils during the war, and at its close
only here and there a division of the Sons of Temperance
could be found, with a few widely scattered Tents of the
Rechabites.

The usual effects of war—that is, general corruption
among the soldiers—had taken place. Drunkenness prevailed among them to an alarming degree, and as many
of the old orders of temperance had lost their prestige
in the South, this new order was thought necessary to be
established.

They have already reached the number of twenty
thousand members. Their pledge is to total abstinence
from all intoxicating drinks. It is confined to white persons only, and a separate order, called "SONS OF THE
SOIL," has been organized for the colored people, which
is said to have done immense good among them.

Of the Supreme Council, which met at Jackson, Miss., June, 1876, the two principal officers were Rev. George B. Wetmore, of North Carolina, President, and the Rev. W. B. Wellous, D.D., of Virginia, Secretary.

The organ of this Order is a weekly paper called the "Friend of Temperance," published by R. H. Whittaker, of Raleigh, N. C.

There is also an order called the UNITED FRIENDS OF TEMPERANCE, which was organized at Chattanooga, Tennessee, in 1871, which is very strong in Virginia and North Carolina, and is rapidly extending into other Southern States.

It has a benevolent degree. Its motto is "Temperance, Friendship, and Benevolence," which three words also indicate the three principles or degrees of the Order.

THE CADETS OF TEMPERANCE grew out of the Order of the Sons of Temperance, being first organized in Philadelphia, at the Morning Star Division, Number 66, under the leadership of Robert N. Foust, Esq., now the Most Worthy Patron of the Order. There are also the juvenile temperance fraternities of THE COLD WATER ARMY and THE BAND OF HOPE, which have been promotive of untold good in preventing the beginnings of evil.

"If we are to stop having crime we must stop raising criminals," says Dr. Holland; a remark which is equally full of sound sense and vital force in respect to the wished-for end of the era of drunkenness. With a generation of boys and girls brought up to hate strong drink with all the strength of early impressions, to be at length ripened into sound convictions, there cannot fail to come a better day for our country, cursed so long by the crops of drunkards it has raised.

THE CATHOLIC TOTAL ABSTINENCE UNION OF AMERICA. The first Roman Catholic Convention on this continent for the promotion of total abstinence was held in the city of Baltimore, in the year 1872.

In the Catholic Church temperance has always been recognized as among the duties of religion, and, though often defined with considerable latitude, it is a duty to which the clergy and laity in all countries are bound. Abstinence from alcoholic drinks on the part of persons addicted to their excessive use is made the condition of approaching the sacraments of the Church, and the priests in the confessional sometimes administer the very strictest of total abstinence pledges.

But the abstinence required as a condition of approaching the sacrament is only a temporary one; and the pledges which are administered at the confessional are only for especial cases.

It was left for Father Mathew, the great Irish Catholic temperance reformer, to agitate and popularize the total abstinence movement in the Roman communion.

"We must cry down the vice, and make it odious in the eyes of society," said Father Mathew.

During his career as a temperance lecturer millions of medals bearing his effigy and the pledge which he wrote were worn upon the bosoms of the faithful; but after his death his people fell away, broke their pledges, and within ten years thereafter nine tenths of his work had apparently disappeared.

There were a few societies in Ireland and in America organized by him in 1849, which kept up their existence, and which served to form a link between the old and new era in Roman Catholic total abstinence work; but in 1860 only about twelve of these societies were in existence. However, it is in that year that the beginning of the present movement on a religious basis is to be dated.

James W. O'Brien, the Corresponding Secretary of the Catholic Total Abstinence Union of America, says :—

"In 1860 a young priest, lately ordained, became an assistant to one of the pastors in Jersey City. He asked permission of his superior to attempt the establishment of a religious total abstinence society, which was given, and the Parochial Total Abstinence Society was founded. It succeeded; and the young priest, removing to other parishes, founded in each one of them a similar organization.

"This system spread from the Diocese of Newark to the Diocese of New York, and as others in the region began to see the benefit of religious total abstinence, the movement was soon taken under the tutelage of the Church. Its progress was steady, and the societies multiplied, producing great fruits.

"Many years later this same priest, the Rev. Patrick Byrne, of Trenton, now President of the Catholic Total Abstinence Union of America, thus speaks of his experience in those days : 'I felt from the first the frightful nature of this vice, and I determined to combat it to the last limit allowed me by the Church; but I soon found that an occasional sermon, however powerful and scathing, or the administration of the pledge now and then, either within or without the tribunal of penance, was of little avail against a vice which had interlaced itself with all the social customs of our people. I therefore began to establish society against society, but when I reached this point I found myself opposed by many of my brethren far above me in learning, zeal, and piety. They thought that the ordinary means were sufficient to meet this, as all other vices. They looked upon the new scheme as unsafe. But as for me, I never could see the propriety of this view; as the " mission " (special religious service) awakens a habitual sinner, who, dead to grace and devotion, never hears the voice of his pastor, so, also, the total abstinence society becomes the means of recalling many an unfortunate to the path of sobriety and rectitude.' "

During the next ten years the new system of societies, under the sanction of the priests, gained very general approval.

In the years 1867–69, the orders of Passionists, Jesuits, and Paulists began to found total abstinence societies in parishes where they held " missions," or, as the Protestants call them, " revivals." In 1870 these societies had become so numerous that they began to combine in aggregate bodies, called " Unions," in cities, dioceses, and States. These unions were formed in New York city; in the States of Connecticut, Massachusetts, Rhode Island, New Jersey, and in the District of Columbia. The Bishop of Newark, the Most Reverend J. R. Bayley, gave the sanction of his great name to the movement, and made a "temperance speech" after witnessing a torch-light procession in which were a thousand brawny honest fellows of his parish who were pledged to total abstinence. This speech, which was reported in the "New York Herald," was published in all the Catholic papers, and printed as a Catholic temperance tract, and a hundred thousand copies of it were scattered all over the country.

"This," says Secretary O'Brien, "was the first speech we were able to get from a bishop of the Church." The result was glorious! From end to end of the land priests and people took up the work, and within the six succeeding months more societies were founded than had been in all the years since Father Mathew's death.

A scheme was now devised for a National Union of the Catholic Total Abstinence Society, which was formed at a convention held in Baltimore, February 22, 1872.

The Rev. Father M'Devitt was elected as head of the National Union movement, and James W. O'Brien as Secretary.

The Dominican preacher, Rev. Father Tom Burke, whose lectures on Irish history as against Mr. Froude produced so considerable an agitation in the Protestant world, and whose sermons were indescribably powerful among his own people, gave hearty assistance to this temperance work, speaking for its meetings again and again. These addresses of Father Burke were published and sent abroad as tracts, and under the impetus thus given new societies were formed and thousands of pledges taken.

In another year the Roman Catholic bishops throughout the country began to give the movement their confidence, and in an annual national convention, held in Chicago, October 6, 1874, letters of warmest approval were read from thirty of the most distinguished Roman Catholic prelates in this country. And, in addition to this, a very cheering letter was received from Cardinal Cullen, of Dublin, Ireland, congratulating the President of the National Union, and encouraging the American Catholics in their fight against intoxicating drinks.

The last report, given at the national convention in Buffalo, shows five hundred and seventy-three local societies, with over one hundred and fifty thousand members. Of the other Catholic total abstinence societies there are, perhaps, three hundred more, and Secretary O'Brien estimates the entire number of Roman Catholics in this country pledged to total abstinence at two hundred thousand persons.

Since 1870 over a million of Catholic temperance tracts have been circulated. A temperance journal, called after the name of the society—"The Catholic Total Abstinence Union," has been established in New York, being the first paper of the kind ever seen among the Roman Catholics of America.

CHAPTER X.

FATHER MATHEW, THE IRISH PRIEST OF TEMPERANCE.*

ALTHOUGH this volume treats only of the history of temperance in America, it would be incomplete without an ample record of the life and labors of that Irish Roman Catholic priest, Theobald Mathew, whose name is sacred to thousands of his countrymen on this side the ocean ; whose pledges were held to be almost sacramental, and whose temperance medals were actually worn as charms and amulets, like the holy relics which good Catholics delight to have upon their persons to keep all bad spirits away.

Father Mathew was a native of the county of Tipperary, Ireland, where he was born on the tenth of October, 1790. In childhood he showed the qualities of leadership and benevolence. He was tender-hearted and gentle, hating all such sports as hunting, coursing, and gunning, because of the pain they inflicted upon the game. No improper words were ever heard from his lips, and his behavior in all other respects was as orderly as his speech. His mother was a pious Catholic, and, like most good mothers of her creed in Ireland, wished to have a priest in her own family. One day, while her large household surrounded the ample dinner-table, she exclaimed :—

---

* From the admirable "Life of Father Mathew," by John Francis Maguire, M.P., of Cork, this sketch is prepared by the kind permission of the publishers, Messrs. Sadlier & Co., New York.

" Is it not unfortunate? I have nine sons, and not one of them to be a priest?"

Theobald, or Toby, as he was called, at once replied: " Mother, don't be uneasy, I shall be a priest;" and from that moment all the household regarded the question as forever settled. He was educated at the schools of Kilkenny and Maynooth, joined the order of Capuchin Friars, and was ordained priest on Easter Sunday, 1814. His youthful beauty, his winning speech, and his devotion to his holy office, at once made him a general favorite with the people of Kilkenny, his first place of labor; and on his removal to the little Capuchin Convent and chapel at Cork, it was not long till Father Mathew was the most popular priest, especially as a hearer of confessions, in all the country round. It used to be said that if a carman from Kerry brought a firkin of butter to Cork for market he would not return without going to Father Mathew's confessional; and as a great many of the country people spoke the Irish language, this zealous young priest mastered that tongue for their sake. He was a gentleman by birth as well as education and office, but his chief companions were the poor, in whom he said he could always see something to remind him of the world's Redeemer; for was not Jesus a poor man, too?

His first notable work was the establishment of an industrial school for girls, which, in that city swarming with ignorant and idle children, soon reached the number of five hundred pupils, for whom the good father found teachers among the educated and charitable ladies of his flock. As the income of his parish increased through

10

his personal popularity, his gifts to the poor increased, till it was said of him, " If the streets of Cork were paved with gold, and Father Mathew had control of them, there wouldn't be a paving stone in all Cork by the end of the year."

One who knew him well said of him, " He was the most irreproachable man I ever knew, and the pink of a gentleman;" and from the year 1820 he was one of the most popular preachers of his day. He was not a great theologian, but, what was better, he was familiar with the Scriptures from end to end, and excelled in portrayal of scriptural scenes, especially those in the life of Christ. There was nothing of sectarian bitterness about him, and Protestants as well as Papists were among his admirers, co-laborers, and friends.

In 1832 the city of Cork was swept by that terrible scourge, the cholera, and Father Mathew was just the man for the terrible emergency. Deaths at the cholera hospital were frequent at all hours of day and night, and in order that no poor wretch might die without the services of religion it was arranged that relays of priests should be always in attendance, and Father Mathew chose for his time the hours between midnight and six in the morning. Under his watchful eye no neglect or undue haste was permitted. He once actually saved a poor fellow from being buried alive, who had been taken to the dead house, and was about to be thrust into one of the rude cholera coffins by two of the overworked attendants, who were hardly able to keep pace with death in their preparations for burial, and who had no thought that a living man could ever be placed in their hands.

For some years that earnest Quaker, William Martin, sometimes called "the grandfather of the temperance cause" in Ireland, had looked upon this devoted priest as the man of all others to forward the temperance reform in Cork. "O Theobald Mathew, if thou would but take the cause in hand!" said he again and again, till at last it began to take hold of his conscience and his heart; and when that was reached the man was captured. He held a solemn vigil, laid the case before God in prayer, and at length, becoming satisfied that duty called him to do it, he put himself at the head of the temperance movement, and from 1838 till the day of his death he was a kind of teetotal saint in the Irish Catholic's calendar.

"*Here goes, in the name of God,*" said Father Mathew, as he approached the table on the opening of the first temperance meeting at which he ever presided, and signed his name to the total abstinence pledge. This was in April; by the following December *a hundred and thirty-one thousand* of his countrymen had followed his example, and in a month more the number reached *two hundred thousand*, all within the reach of Father Mathew's name and fame, and mostly in the county of Cork.

Then they began to pour into Cork from the adjoining counties of Kerry, Waterford, Limerick, Clare, Tipperary, and even from as far as Galway, eager to see Father Mathew, to receive his blessing, and to take the pledge in his presence. Thus Cork became the Irish Mecca of temperance, and this good priest was the prophet thereof. An apartment of his house on the ground floor was used for a reception room, and there at all hours of the day, and on to eleven o'clock at night, crowds of people might be seen waiting their turn to take the pledge—some of them solemn and reverent, others tipsy and smelling of the "good-bye drink" which they had taken before coming to this teetotal sacrament, as they all seemed to regard it.   Sometimes a big fellow, half drunk, brought to the priest by his anxious wife, would break out in oaths and curses, and declare he would not "demane" himself by signing any pledge ; but just then Father Mathew, seeing the man's danger of backsliding, would catch him by the hand, greet him as a friend, and, taking no notice of his bad manners, would assume that he was ready for the service, which would proceed thus :

"Kneel down now, Patsy," (strong pressure on Patsy's shoulder, under which he sinks on his knees;) "now say the words of the pledge after me."

(Father Mathew recites solemnly, and the poor fellow follows reluctantly.)   "There; now I'll mark ye with the holy sign of the cross, and pray God to save ye from temptation ;"   and so Patsy's name would be added to the long list of teetotalers almost before he knew it.

"Why do you give the pledge to people when they are drunk ?" said one.

"Because I find they keep it," was the priest's reply.

It is not strange that among a superstitious people such a man should, in their eyes, become invested with almost supernatural powers.   Many sick people, it was declared, were cured by taking the pledge of Father Mathew, and receiving his fatherly benediction ; and without stopping to think that it might be the natural results of temperance which had wrought the cure, they began to spread abroad the story of "miracle," till so great was the fame of this temperance apostle that sick and infirm people in great numbers began to throng him, hoping to find health and healing at his hand. He disclaimed any such power over and over again, but the people still believed in him for all that; and thus superstition forwarded the genuine work of temperance reform.

He next began to go from city to city, holding meetings in the cathedrals, and every-where attended by crowds of people anxious to pledge themselves to temperance; the results of which labors are but feebly expressed in the fact that by the year 1840 *two millions* of Irishmen had joined his simple Temperance Society. As a pleasant fact it is mentioned in his memoirs that he visited Maynooth, the seat of his *Alma Mater*, where thirty-five thousand citizens, two hundred and fifty students, the flower of the youth of Ireland, and eight of the college professors, took his temperance pledge.

At one time, as he was passing by stage-coach through the town of Athy, some one caught sight of him, and spread the joyful news, " Father Mathew is here!" Immediately a crowd surrounded the coach so great and so dense that it was impossible for it to move, all clamorous for the pledge at the good father's hand. There was nothing to do but to comply with their request, but it was *five hours* before their numbers had sufficiently decreased to allow the mail-coach to proceed on its journey.

Even in the province of Ulster, that stronghold of the Orangemen, the temperance priest was most kindly received; the chief attempt to rouse the Protestant faction

against him being made by a Roman Catholic liquor-seller, who loved not Rome the less, but business more.

It was the custom for the pledged people to form themselves into local societies, to hold meetings, open reading
rooms, etc., one of these *et cetera* often consisting of a
brass band, without which no great meeting, and especially no society procession, could be a full success. Father
Mathew never could sing a tune in his life; his performance at High Mass, when it was required of the of-
ficiating priest to sing, being a most dismal croak; but
he was the especial patron of the brass band, in which
he greatly delighted, because it helped rouse the enthusiasm, and so forwarded the good cause. These temperance bands were a very notable feature of the great
reform, and cost its chief not a little money. The men
often played with all the more zeal because of their lack
of musical knowledge; but it was a temperance noise, and,
therefore, highly satisfactory to reformer and reformed.

The records of the courts during the progress of this
temperance reformation in Ireland show a falling off of
capital offenses in eight years from sixty-six to fourteen
per year; of sentences of transportation from nine hundred and sixteen to five hundred and four: the consumption of spirits was reduced one half, and the amount
of duties on tobacco decreased by three thousand pounds
in a single year.

His wonderful success among his own nation brought
him a constant stream of invitations to England and
Scotland, among others one from the city of Edinburgh,
signed by two thousand ladies, praying him to commence
a mission in the Scottish capital; to which he replied, " I

must first heal the deep and festering wounds of the Irish people." However, in 1842 he visited Glasgow, where he was received with boundless enthusiasm, as also the following year in the English cities of York, Leeds, and London.

Among those who became his personal friends in the world's metropolis was the "Iron Duke," to whom Father Mathew said, "You must be one of us. You must be a temperance man, or you never could carry that cool head that makes you the Duke of Wellington." Lord Brougham, Dean Stanley, the Bishop of Norwich, the Duke of Norfolk, and others of the nobility and clergy, were his friends and admirers, and his work received the compliment of honorable mention in the English House of Lords.

It was computed that in his campaign in England as many as six hundred thousand persons took the temperance pledge, among them many both from the highest and lowest of London life.

Father Mathew's correspondence was of the most varied and extensive character. Begging letters were legion; appeals for sympathy and advice were numerous; entreaties for visits, addresses, and pledges, almost without number; and occasionally some poor fellow would write, asking his reverence to give him his pledge back again, because he wanted to take a little spirits now and then. All sorts of reform notions were laid before him, and his good offices were sometimes in request to settle legal and family quarrels.

It was given out at one time that he was in possession of enormous wealth, but at that very time he was act

ually in debt to the amount of about seven thousand
pounds sterling, chiefly on account of money borrowed
to give away. " My heart is eaten up by care and solici-
tude of every kind," he said at one of his public meetings at Cork. He was once arrested for debt by the
maker of his medals, while publicly administering the
pledge in Dublin, the bailiff first kneeling before him for
his blessing, and then quietly showing him the writ; but
the good man went on with his pledging as if nothing
had happened; and it was well for the bailiff that he did
so, for if his errand had become known to that crowd he
might have gone the way of a good many other Irish
bailiffs, whose office has rendered their lives very precarious. All the people who took the pledge from him
wanted also a medal, but not more than one in five was
able to buy one, and the good father out of the kindness
of his heart would give away these little tokens by thousands, the cost of which in the aggregate amounted to a
small fortune.

On the occasion of his arrest " Punch " had the following: " Now Mathew the martyr brought his fortune
into the market to buy up vice, to bribe wretchedness
into comfort, to purchase with ready money crime and
passion, that he might destroy them. He laid out all
his means that he might make temperance alluring to an
impulsive, whisky-loving people. He counts his tens of
thousands of proselytes, and then he takes his purse and
counts nothing. He has triumphed, but he is a beggar.
Taught by his temperance lessons, the peasant and the
artificer — aye, thousands of them — have made their
homes worthy of human creatures, and the teacher him-

self is shown the way to a jail. Mathew is arrested for the price of the medals with which he has decorated his army of converts—we know few orders, home or foreign, more honorable, if sincerely worn—and unless Ireland arise as one man the reward of the great preacher is the county prison."

Such an appeal could not fail to bring relief from his financial troubles, but whatever sums were given him, they were sure to be given away.

The Irish famine of 1845-46 brought out the charitable glories of Father Mathew's character still more. He was one of the first to discover that the late crop of potatoes were spoiling in the ground, and to communicate the fact to the authorities, with a view to having measures taken to save the poor from starvation. By letters, by personal efforts to procure some substitute for the potato, the chief food of the Irish poor, and by every possible means of relief, both individual and general, this good man gave still further proof of his heavenly mission. He expended his last shilling in charity, and then made the famine a text from which to preach the doctrine of temperance. Here is an extract from one of his famine sermons :—

"Thousands upon thousands now pine in want and woe because they did not take my advice ; to them the horrors of famine and the evils of blight are aggravated ; while tens of thousands of those who listened to me and adopted my advice are now safe from hunger and privation, because they had the virtue to surrender a filthy sensual gratification, and the wisdom to store up for the

10*

coming of the evil day.   Thousands are now perishing,
who, if they had not the folly to spend their hard-earned
money in drink, in riot, and in debauchery, would now be
safe from danger, and enabled to assist, by their charity,
creatures who are without a friend to comfort or assist them.   The prison and the poor-house are opening
wide their doors for many who have willfully brought ruin
on themselves and their families, and who, had they only
sense, would now be among the wealthy of the land.

" I will ·not upbraid you for the past; I would rather
cheer and console.   I would rather tell you that it is
not too late; 'that no one should despair; that there is
still balm in Gilead, still a physician there.   I would assure you that the oldest and most inveterate habit can
be overcome by a simple effort of moral courage, by one
virtuous resolution.   Habit and custom tyrannize over
men because they want courage to face and oppose their
tyrants; but the strongest chain of passion that ever fettered the soul, and led man's senses captive, can be
broken by a bold, a virtuous effort.   The pledge which I
ask you and others to take does not enslave; it makes
free—free from vice, free from passion, free from an enslaving habit.

" The fewer passions and habits that rule us, the freer
we are; and no man is so free as the man who places
himself beyond and out of the reach of temptation; for,
as the Scripture says, those who court danger shall perish therein.   The freedom which I advocate is one you
can obtain without any sacrifice of health, of pleasure, of
money, or of comfort.   On the contrary, it will add to
your health, your wealth, your pleasure, and your com-

fort. Temperance brings blessings in both hands; bless
ings for time, and blessings for eternity. Let the drinker
of strong drink examine his past life, and he cannot fail
to see that the darkest moments of his life have borrowed
their murky hue from intemperance. I never knew a
young man or young woman to go astray, and walk in
the way of lewdness, whose departure from the path
of virtue was not chiefly from the influence of strong
drink.

*   *   *   *   *   *

"There is no difficulty in taking the pledge. No man
performs his duty better than a teetotaler; no man is
better able to brave the vicissitudes of the season. I am
now in the habit of traveling constantly during the last
nine years, in heat and cold, in rain and snow, by day
and night; and I have never suffered any serious inconvenience from it, because I was a teetotaler; and now,
thank God, I am as active and as full of energy as ever,
and as determined now as I was nine years ago to devote myself to the great cause of reformation, and moral
as well as social advancement. I never knew what true
happiness was until I became a teetotaler; for until I
became so I could never feel that I was free or out of
danger, or could say to myself with confidence that I
would not, at one time or another, be that most degraded
thing, *a drunkard.* Let no man tell me that he is safe
enough, that he has no occasion to take the pledge, that
he is above temptation. There is no one so strong or
firm that he may not fall. I have seen the stars of
the heavens fall, and the cedars of Lebanon laid low. I
have seen the proudest boasters humbled to the dust,

steeped to the very lips in poverty, and sunk in dishonored graves.

    *   *   *   *   *   *

"I am here in the name of the Lord. I am here for your
good. This is a time to try men's souls; and that man or
that woman must be a monster who would drink while a
fellow-creature was dying for want of food. I don't
blame the brewers or the distillers—I blame those who
maintain them. If they could make more money in any
other way, they would; but so long as the people are
mad enough to buy and drink their odious manufacture,
they will continue in the trade. Is it not a terrible thing
to think that so much wholesome grain, that God intended for the support of human life, should be converted
into a maddening poison, for the destruction of man's
body and soul? By a calculation recently made, it is
clearly proved that if all the grain now converted into
poison were devoted to its natural and legitimate use, it
would afford a meal a day to every man, woman, and
child in the land. The man or woman who drinks, drinks
the food of the starving; and is not that man or woman
a monster who drinks the food of the starving?"

It would be difficult to say in what country the most
active sympathy was displayed toward Ireland. The
generosity of the people of England was munificent;
but the practical benevolence of America was in a
special degree cheering and timely. In the great cities
of the United States meetings were held in the early
part of 1847 to raise money for the relief of Ireland, and
these meetings were attended by the most influential

men of the country. Thus, in Philadelphia, the Chief Justice of the Supreme Court presided over a meeting held in that city on the 28th day of January, 1847 ; and the noble charity displayed on that occasion wiped out the last trace of the bloodshed in the riots of 1844. The Vice-President of the United States presided over a meeting held in Washington. In New York and Boston the same sympathy was felt, and the most active exertions were made to afford the description of relief then most required by Ireland. Providence had vouchsafed to America that which it had, for wise reasons, denied to Ireland—an abundant supply of food for man ; and America, in giving from her abundance to her distressed sister, proved how beautiful and holy is that bond of humanity which links nations, the most remote, in one great family, sympathizing with each other's joy and sorrow.

On Monday, the 13th of April, a noble sight might be witnessed in Cork Harbor: the sun shining its welcome on the entrance of the *unarmed* war-ship " Jamestown," sailing in under a cloud of snowy canvass, her great hold laden with bread-stuffs for the starving people of Ireland. It was a sight that brought tears to many an eye, and prayers of gratitude to many a heart. It was one of those things which a nation remembers of another long after the day of sorrow has passed. Upon the warm and generous people, to whom America literally broke bread and sent life, this act of fraternal charity, so gracefully and impressively offered, naturally produced a profound and lasting impression, the influence of which is felt to this moment.

The captain of that unarmed war-ship was thus favorably introduced to Father Mathew :—

BOSTON, U. S. A., March 27, 1847.

DEAR SIR—This will introduce to you the commander of the United States *unarmed* ship, the " Jamestown," Robert B. Forbes, Esq., who has nobly volunteered his services to convey to your shores a cargo of provisions for the relief of the destitute.

It affords me great pleasure to make this philanthropic countryman of ours known to one who is personally known to me, and to millions in both hemispheres, as one of the greatest benefactors of his race.   In Mr. Forbes you will find one of nature's nobles, who, leaving the endearments of home at this boisterous season, crosses the ocean to imitate his and our SAVIOUR, to feed the hungry and raise the desponding.   To you, my excellent friend, I cordially commend him, hoping at no distant day to grasp your hand, and welcome you on our shores, and then assure you that our sympathies and hearts are one, though separated by the ocean and a different faith.

With high esteem, your friend,
JOHN TAPPAN.

The Very Rev. Theobald Mathew.

Father Mathew lost no time in paying his respects to Captain Forbes, who expressed in the strongest terms the pleasure he felt in meeting and knowing the man with whose name he had been so long familiar; and spoke of the impatience of the American people to receive him among them.   Captain Forbes concluded by

offering Father Mathew a passage in the " Jamestown ;"
which offer was gratefully declined, on the ground that
the state of the country required the best exertions of
every one who could in any way assist her, and that it
would be an unpardonable crime to desert her in the
hour of her direst necessity.

Father Mathew's influence upon the wealthier classes
was most valuable at this trying moment, and he did not
fail to exercise it freely in the cause of his clients, the
poor. An instance will happily exemplify the value of
this influence, and the manner in which it was exercised.

Among the industrial schools and work-rooms to
which the famine gave birth was one which a number
of charitable ladies took in charge. Besides providing employment for the destitute girls who worked in
its classes, the patronesses of the school supplied their
pupils with breakfast, thus insuring to them the certainty of one meal in the day—no light boon at such a
time. This breakfast was continued to be given for
several months, and with the best results; but the funds
falling somewhat low, the ladies became alarmed, and,
seeing no immediate prospect of their being replenished,
they determined at least to take into consideration the
expediency of not giving it beyond a certain period. A
day was appointed for the consideration of the proposal;
and the subject being one of very grave importance, a
large attendance was the consequence. The lady who
first expressed her opinion as to the necessity of discontinuing the breakfast now brought the matter forward,
and the other ladies felt that its continuance beyond the
time specified would involve the institution in debt, and

perhaps destroy its usefulness; and the question was
about to be decided according to that view, when Father
Mathew entered.   On being told what had occurred he
seemed greatly moved; and turning to the assembled
ladies, many of whom were his most intimate friends, he
said: "The proposal of discontinuing the breakfast sur-
prises and, indeed, shocks me beyond measure.   When I
was entering the building, I saw a number of handsome
equipages drawn up outside the door, and when I entered
I saw the room crowded with ladies elegantly and even
sumptuously dressed.   Seeing this, I naturally wondered
how any such proposal could find support among persons
surrounded by such appearances of wealth; and I especially wonder how ladies of your position and circumstances could think of refusing a solitary meal to their
poor starving sisters, the virtuous daughters of decent
parents, whom God, for his own wise ends, had afflicted
with an unexpected calamity!   Why, the very ornaments that adorn your persons would provide an
abundant breakfast for these innocent young girls for a
considerable time!"

"O Father Mathew," said the lady by whom the proposal had been brought forward, "forgive me!   It was
I who made the proposal, and I am sorry for it.   I know
I did wrong.   But there is a friend who will give me
£40 to-morrow, and I shall send it to the treasurer.   We
must not give up the breakfast."

The effect was irresistible, and such arrangements were
at once entered into as insured the continuance of the
much-required meal so long as relief of the kind was
necessary.   The £40 from the "friend" was from the

pocket of the lady herself, who was as generous as she was impulsive. Father Mathew was not long without having a personal interview on his own account with the treasurer of the charity.

At no period of his ministry was his preaching more effective than in the very midst of the terrible famine, with misery and sorrow and death on every side. Little time had he to compose an artificial discourse at that moment, when every energy was strained in devising and administering relief. The following passages which are quoted, are certainly not models of style; but such was the earnestness and pathos of the preacher, and the belief in the truth of the pictures which he drew from his daily and hourly experiences, that the eloquence of Massillon or Bourdaloue could not have produced a more thrilling or touching effect. They are given here, not only as being characteristic of the man, and descriptive of the time, but also as they represent the sublime charity which was exhibited by the poor to those more wretched than themselves — the latter being a theme on which, because of his admiration of that marvelous charity, and because of the salutary influence which it produced upon the rich, he loved to dwell. The plaintive tones, the wailing voice, the impassioned earnestness of the orator—rather, indeed, of this apostle of charity—more than atoned for any defects of style in passages such as these :—

"Were I permitted to rouse the men of wealth from their dream of avarice, the ladies of fashion from their silken lethargy, would they permit me to conduct them for one day, where they ought to go every day, and where they should esteem it a high privilege to be allowed to go—to the abodes of pain and sorrow, to the squalid receptacles of the agonized and the dying—I would answer for their hearts. They are surely of flesh and blood; but were they hard as adamant they would not resist the cries of the famishing little creatures, tortured by extreme want and wrung with tormenting pain. There, amid the chilling damp of a dismal hovel, see your famine-stricken fellow-creature; see him extended on his scanty bed of rotten straw; see his once manly frame, that labor had strengthened with vigor, shrunk to a skeleton; see his once ruddy complexion, the gift of temperance, changed by hunger and concomitant disease to a sallow, ghastly hue. See him extend his yellow, withering arm for assistance. Hear how he cries out in agony for food, for since yesterday he has not even moistened his lips! See his affectionate wife, though involved in the same distress, tenderly endeavoring to lighten his sufferings, and during the long and sorrowful night supporting his drooping head. See his little children pressing round him with their wants. He fixes upon them his piercing, dying looks. O, who can conceive the anguish, the exquisite anguish, that now rends the father's heaving breast! Turning his gaze from the killing scene, he lifts his hollow eyes to heaven, and lays before his God his intense grief. O Christian, Christian! is not this wretched man your brother? Is not the great God of all that wretched being's Father? Can you, men of wealth—can you, my female auditors—contemplate such a dismal spectacle, without feeling the warm tide of sensibility rushing to your bosoms? That abject,

that degraded being is not among you, who is not now
resolved to subtract from costly ornaments, jewelry,
and dress, to sacrifice some favorite folly, to retrench
even the ordinary expenses of your families, and be content with the simple necessaries of life, and give this day
into benevolent hands the honorable savings, that they
may buy bread that the poor may eat. The triumph,
the pure feast of soul, which this action would afford,
would leave at an infinite distance behind the selfish
indulgence of vanity or the sordid gratification of sense.

 *   *   *   *   *   *

"Look at this poor child of wretchedness and sin.
She is scarcely sixteen. She was once the only darling
child of fond, indulgent parents. Her father, in early
manhood, was cut off by fever, and the mother was
left alone to provide for her orphan daughter. Disappointed in every struggle for bread, pressed down by the
iron hand of adversity, worn out in the remembrance of
the friends of former days, she is obliged to hide herself
from the light of day in the gloom and damp of a dark
cellar. She soon dies of a broken heart, and leaves her
child to the cold charity of a pitiless world. This poor
forlorn child being left to herself, she soon fell the prey
of the foul seducer. Her black career of sin is soon
ended. See her now extended on that scanty bed of
straw, pale, emaciated, abandoned by all; no friendly
hand to wash away her bloody tears, no pious lips to
pour into her broken heart the balm of religious consolation. Shall she be left a prey to despair, to perish forever? O no, O no! your charity this day, like a summer's sun, will penetrate and cheer her dreary habitation.

Your plenteous charity this day, like dew from heaven, will descend upon her, and this faded flower will bloom again. This poor prodigal will again return, and find here, through Christ, the way to repentance and to heaven.

* * * * * *

"The rich, comparatively speaking, give nothing. That is, there is no proportion between their wealth and their charity. But the poor support the poor; and if there were not a universal destitution among the operatives of our city we would not be branded with the burning shame of being obliged to avow that, in the midst of the blaze of affluence which our city presents, hundreds of our fellow-creatures have perished for want at the very rich man's gates. I could recount instances of heroic charity, among the poorest of the poor, at this very period, that would do honor to—that are worthy of—the apostolic era.

"A desolate widow in my immediate neighborhood, whose sole support is a bed for lodgers, has under her roof, for the last six weeks, an aged stranger, whom nobody knows. She tends him and feeds him as tenderly as if he were her brother.

"There is a lonely plain-work woman advanced in years, who resides in Chamberlain's Alley, in the parish of St. Nicholas, who has for many months supported, out of her scanty earnings, a helpless female; and if she were her mother she could not love her more.

"On last Monday an interesting child was abandoned in the streets by its unnatural parent; and when it was about to be sent to the work-house a poor man, a scavenger, with his broom in his hand, who, with tearful eye, was looking on, came and solicited the child; and when it was given to him his countenance beamed with joy, he clasped the helpless innocent in his arms, and brought it, rejoicing, to his humble dwelling.

"There are, to my own certain knowledge, at this moment, cherished by the very poor in the poorest portion of this city, the parishes of St. Nicholas and Fin Barr, more than thirty children, whose unhappy parents perished during the famine.

"On beholding such charity as this, well may I apply to these blessed poor the words of the Saviour to the widow and her mite—'Amen, I say unto you, She has given more than all.' O ye rich, how your merit fades before charity like this! O, that I could anticipate the glorious welcome that awaits these merciful beings on the great accounting day! O, may my death be the death of the righteous, and may my end be like to theirs! . . ."

In 1847, a vacancy occurring in the office of Bishop of Cork, Father Mathew was nominated as "most worthy" to be his successor, but the Holy See at Rome saw otherwise, and he remained plain Father Mathew to the day of his death. He was, however, honored by Queen Victoria with a royal pension, as an acknowledgment of his "meritorious exertions in combating intemperance."

In 1849 Father Mathew made his long-promised visit to America; and during the long voyage on the ship "Ashburton" devoted himself to benevolent teachings and labors among his poor countrymen in the steerage.

On the second of July he landed in New York, where

he was received as the guest of the city by the Municipal Council, who came out as far as Staten Island in a
small steamer to meet him.

It was considered by those who were present when
Father Mathew entered the Castle Garden that never,
on any occasion, was the multitude of people greater, or
the enthusiasm more intense. New York is, *par excel-
lence*, the city of ovations; but it seemed as if it were resolved to outdo itself in honor of the moral conqueror.
The formal welcome was offered to him by his Honor
Mayor Woodhull, who invited him to accept the hospitalities of the city. The Mayor happily referred to the
special claim which Father Mathew's services to humanity gave him to a public reception on that historic
spot:—

"On this spot we have been accustomed to receive
the most distinguished men of our own and other lands.
The statesman, bearing the highest honors of his much-
loved country, and the victor, fresh from the field of his
proud triumphs, have here been greeted with the saluta-
tions of the most elevated in authority, and with the
general welcome of the citizens of this metropolis. But
you, sir, come among us with a highly different and peculiar distinction. The honors which you wear have
been accorded to you by those who revere you for your
deeds of love and benevolence. Your titles are written
on the hearts of the uncounted masses whom your heroic
perseverance in the humble acts of mercy and good-will
has saved from a fate even more dreadful than the
grave. Your victories are not made up of the dead and
dying left behind in your path, but of living thousands,

whom you have rescued from a fate more remorseless
than the conqueror's march. Your trophies are seen in
the smiling faces and happy homes of the countless multitudes whom you have won from the deepest abyss of
wretchedness and despair. The enemy with whom you
have grappled is one of the direst to the human race.
Frightful are the ravages of plague, and vast the preparations to stay its desolating course ; but the destroying
angel of intemperance has entombed more victims than
any pestilence which has ever afflicted the human family.
All seasons are its own, and no physician can baffle its
downward progress. Quarantines and sanitary precau-
tions cannot check its career. Yet there is one human
power that can subdue this enemy of man. It is the
moral power of a persuasive, earnest, and benevolent
heart, that summons all its affections, and with heroic
sublimity concentrates all its energies to the single work
to be accomplished. It is this power which you have
so successfully exercised, and by which you have attained
such astonishing results."

At eight o'clock in the evening the Common Council
entertained Father Mathew at a public dinner, at which
healths were drunk in glasses of pure " Croton."

" There is as much sincerity," said the temperance
leader, " in water as in wine ; and I beg to give, in a full
bumper of this pure liquid, the health and prosperity of
the Mayor and citizens of New York."

For the next fortnight Father Mathew held levees in
the City Hall, which was daily thronged with visitors of
every class and condition, and representing every sect
and party in the States. So great was the inconvenience

from the crowding on the first two days, that it became necessary to have one day set apart for the reception of ladies, and the next for the reception of gentlemen. And side by side with the belles of New York, or the darker beauties of the Southern States, were the daughters of Erin, from the highest to the humblest—the wives and daughters of the distinguished soldier, the successful physician, the leading lawyer, or the prosperous merchant— or the young girls who had won by honest toil the grand clothes with which they proudly rustled in among the best of them.

Father Mathew was delighted and amused with the appearance and manners of these young servant girls. Their dress was grand in the extreme, the accent a beautiful blending of Irish and American, and the language replete with the salient peculiarities of both countries. Their greeting of the priest of their Church, while it was affectionate and reverential, had a strong dash of independence in its tone; and they who in their old home might have been but too humble, and even servile, now evinced in many ways—in word, in air, in manner, and in carriage—the consciousness of being citizens of a country in which all stood on an equality—at least in the abstract.

"From what part of the old country are you, my dear?" would Father Mathew inquire, as some unmistakably Irish face presented itself; and when he was told the county and the parish whence his visitor had come, he had something to tell her in return which brought the color to her cheek and the tear to her eye, and perhaps a sob to her throat. What visions of bye-

gone happiness or sorrow—alas! generally the latter—
his gentle and familiar words conjured up to the
memory of those exiles, who looked back with tender
regret, even from their hardly-won prosperity and independence, to the humble home and the lowly lot in the
land of their youth!

The month of July was one of incessant labor and excitement; but the excitement, though drawing largely
upon the resources of a constitution grievously impaired,
rendered him insensible to fatigue, and enabled him to
go through his work without faltering for a moment.
Rising at an early hour in the morning, he said mass in
one church or other, and lectured and administered the
pledge; and after breakfast there were visits or visitors,
meetings and pledge-giving, and so on, till a late hour
in the evening.

Thus before he quitted New York for Boston he had
administered the pledge to a vast number, principally
Irish, and had done much, both by exertion and by influence, to add strength and vigor to the temperance organization of the great city by which he had been so
nobly received.

After visiting Boston Father Mathew went to Washington.

As soon as his arrival was made known in the capital,
a resolution was unanimously carried in Congress, admitting him to a seat on the floor of the House—the very
highest distinction which could be conferred upon the
subject of another country by the representatives of this
great republic. When Father Mathew availed himself
of this flattering permission, the members rose to receive
11

him.   Had he been a crowned monarch the respect paid·
to him by that assembly could hardly have been greater.

In the Senate also high eulogium was bestowed upon
the man and his work by such men as William H. Sew-
ard, Lewis Cass, and Henry Clay.   His passage through
the cities of Richmond, Savannah, Charleston, Mobile,
New Orleans, Vicksburgh, St. Louis, etc., was a kind of
triumphal march.   Every-where he gave pledges and
blessings and medals, all of which were held to be both
precious and holy on account of the holy man from
whose hand and heart they came.   More than six hundred thousand persons, mostly Irish Catholics, took his
pledge and his benediction in the United States of
America, and Protestants and Papists vied with each
other in doing him honor.

On the 8th of November he embarked on board the
" Pacific," one of the Collins line of steamers, on his return to Europe.   Previous to his embarkation he published his " Farewell Address to the Citizens of the
United States," from which a passage or two may be appropriately quoted.   It thus begins:—

" My mission among you closes to-day.   I cannot take
my final departure from the shores of your great and
generous country without publicly recording my deep
and grateful appreciation of the generous sympathy, the
delicate attention, and the unremitting kindness which I
have experienced in every section of this vast Union.
The noble reception which you have spontaneously tendered to a stranger, known merely as a humble missionary in the cause of moral reform, proves the devotion of

your people to the interest of humanity, however feebly championed, and has endeared America and her people to me by a thousand ties too sacred for utterance. Though the renewed attacks of a painful and insidious malady have rendered it impossible that I could, without imminent danger to my life, make those public exertions which were never spared by me in the days of my health and of my vigor, I yet thank Heaven I have been instrumental in adding to the ranks of temperance over six hundred thousand disciples in America. I have been much cheered during the past week by the receipt of letters from all parts of the States, bearing unimpeachable testimony to the strict fidelity with which this voluntary obligation is observed. I need scarcely add that virtue, and the duties which religion inculcates, together with peace, plenty, domestic comfort, health, and happiness, every-where followed in its train."

Having borne grateful testimony to the aid which he had received from the public press of America, and the kindness and friendship which had been shown to him by many distinguished individuals, he then addresses his own countrymen:—

" To my own beloved countrymen I most affectionately tender a few words of parting advice. You have, my dearly beloved friends, relinquished the land of your birth, endeared to you by a thousand fond reminiscences, to seek on these distant shores that remuneration for industry and toil too often denied you at home. You are presented here with a boundless field of profitable employment, and every inducement is held out to persevering industry. You are received and welcomed into the great American family with feelings of sympathy, kindness, and friendship. After a few years you become citizens of this great republic, whose vast territorial extent abounds in all the materials of mineral, agricultural, and commercial wealth ; the avenues to honor and fame are liberally thrown open to you and to your children, and no impediment—save of your own creation—exists to prevent you attaining the highest social and civic distinction ; and will you any longer permit those glorious opportunities to pass unimproved? or, rather, will you not, by studying self-respect, and acquiring habits suited to your new position, aspire to reflect honor alike on the land of your birth and of your adoption ? I implore you, as I would with my dying breath, to discard forever those foolish divisions—those insensate quarrels—those factious broils (too often, alas ! the fruits of intemperance) in which your country is disgraced, the peace and order of society violated, and the laws of Heaven trampled on and outraged.

" Friends and fellow-countrymen, I now bid you a reluctant, a final farewell. A few hours more will separate me from the hospitable shores of America forever. I carry with me to the ' poor old country' feelings of respect and attachment for its people that neither time nor distance can obliterate."

He thus eloquently concludes :—

" Citizens of the United States, I fervently pray that the Almighty Disposer of human events, in whose hands are the destinies of nations, may continue those blessings and favors which you have so long enjoyed; that your progress in every private and public virtue may keep pace with your unexampled prosperity; that you and your children's children may be ever true to the great destiny that awaits you, and to the spirit of those institutions under the fostering care of which you have so rapidly progressed. May your country still extend the hand of succor to the helpless exile, afford an asylum to the persecuted, and a home to the oppressed, and thus inseparably connect her future destiny with the interests of universal humanity."

The last days of Father Mathew were spent in much personal suffering. He was afflicted with partial paralysis, brought on, doubtless, by his almost superhuman labors. When remonstrated with by his physicians for taking too little rest, he smilingly replied: " I prefer to die in the harness." To the very last he retained his power of mind, and the same sweet gentleness and benevolence that kept him like his divine Master, going about doing good ; and when, in the sixty-sixth year of his age and the forty-second of his ministry, he passed to his reward, it was with a simple, childlike faith in Him who died on the cross for us all. The date of his death is December 8, 1856.

His statue stands in the city of Cork, where he was mourned by the whole population, many of whom fully believed not only that he was a Christian, but a saint, endowed with miraculous power of healing as well as superhuman self-sacrifice and love.

His biographer, from whose charming pages this sketch is prepared, makes these singular statements:—

"The reader may account for the following, which I give because it is within my own personal knowledge, in any way he thinks best; all I desire to do is to state that which I know to be a fact. A young lady, of position and intelligence, was for years the victim of the most violent headache, which assumed a chronic character. Eminent advice was had, but in vain: the malady became more intense, the agony more excruciating. Starting up one day from the sofa on which she lay in a delirium of pain, she exclaimed, 'I cannot endure this torture any longer; I will go and see what Father Mathew can do for me.' She immediately proceeded to Lehenagh, where Father Mathew was then sick and feeble. Flinging herself on her knees before him, she besought his prayers and blessing. In fact, stung by intolerable suffering, she asked him to cure her.

"'My dear child, you ask me to do what no mortal has power to do. That power rests alone with God.'

"'Then bless me, and pray for me—place your hand on my head,' implored the afflicted lady.

"'I cannot refuse to pray for you, or to bless you, my dear child,' said Father Mathew, who did pray for and bless her, and place his hand on her poor throbbing brow. Was it faith?—was it magnetism?—was it the force of imagination exerted wonderfully? I shall not venture to pronounce which it was; but that lady returned to her home perfectly cured of her distressing malady—more than that, cured completely from that moment forward.

Here is the experience related by a man who was, as
he thinks, cured of blindness by this good temperance
priest: "My eyes got very bad, and I was afraid I was
going to lose my sight entirely, which would have brought
me to ruin. I was obliged to stay away from my business in the market, I became so blind; so I said I would
go over to Cove-street and see his reverence, which I did.
I was so bad that I got a boy to lead me in the streets.
Father Mathew was there before me, and was glad to see
me, and shook hands with me, as he always did; he was
kind to simple and gentle, and there was no sort of pride
in him at all. So I told him how bad I was, and sure he
saw that, for he asked me how did I get so bad. I knelt
down, and he prayed for me, and put his hand on my
head, and made the sign of the cross on my eyes, and he
said it wouldn't signify, and that I would be well shortly;
and sure I was, for I walked home without the boy helping me, and I was as well as ever that day. I brought
my wife to him another day, and he cured her of a sore,
as all the neighbors know." . . .

"Not only were those afflicted with bodily ailments
brought to him, but those likewise who suffered from
mental infirmity. A young man was being taken by his
friends to the Lunatic Asylum of Cork, and the treatment which he received at their hands was not such as
to improve his condition. Bound on a car, his limbs
tied with cords, and his head exposed to the rays of a
fierce sun, he was thus being conveyed to the asylum,
when the conductors conceived the idea of first taking
him to Father Mathew. The idea was fortunately acted
upon, and they turned the horse's head toward Lehenagh.

Father Mathew's heart was filled with compassion at the spectacle of a human being bound like a wild beast, uttering strange cries, and foaming at the mouth. He spoke to him kindly and gently, and thus soothed his chafed spirit; and he then desired his friends to loose the cords that bound him, and to protect his head from the sun. The effect of the kind voice, the gentle words, and the soothing touch, was marvelous upon the patient, who had suffered violent paroxysms shortly before. The poor fellow recognized Father Mathew, in whose power to serve him he seemed to have confidence, and he promised that if he were brought back home he would do every thing that he was asked to do; and upon Father Mathew's intercession he was brought back, instead of being placed in the asylum. In a month afterward a fine, handsome young man, well-dressed and well-mannered, came to Lehenagh, to return him thanks for 'what he had done for him.'

"Another case which I shall mention was that of a young girl from Macroom, who was brought to him by her parents, who were afraid that she would die of starvation, as she had obstinately refused to eat any thing for a number of days, or to utter a single word. Her head was seriously affected, and she could not sleep. She was taken three times to Father Mathew. Through the first visit some good was effected, and after the third visit she was perfectly restored to her natural appetite and sleep. Before she left Lehenagh she ate and drank what was offered to her, and spoke rationally, and without reluctance."

"Another girl, whose hands were tightly clenched, and

the nails of whose fingers were buried in the flesh of her palms, was also brought to him by her parents. For weeks she had been in that condition ; and though the physicians who had been consulted endeavored to open her hands, they tried in vain.

" 'Allow me, my dear,' said Father Mathew, in his winning voice; and, taking her hand in his, and gently unlocking and extending her fingers, he brought it into its natural form."

It is a curious rumor, not set down in his memoirs, that Father Mathew, the Capuchin friar, died a Protestant. This statement has been made to the writer by a prominent gentleman now in the service of a well-known New York book house, who was for years a resident of Cork, was familiar with the good man's life and labors, and who vouches for the assertion that such was widely believed to be the fact at the time of his death. But what matters it? Such a man might easily be claimed as a brother by any or all good people, and whether in the Holy Catholic Church, as Rome understands it—or as the rest of Christendom understand it—doubtless in the Holy Catholic Church Father Mathew lived and died.

After his death the simple, warm-hearted people to whom he had been a minister from heaven held him in memory as a saint. Rome never canonized him; but his tomb became a holy shrine to which pious pilgrimages were made, and his memory is precious to millions whose souls and bodies he helped to save.

The memory of the just is blessed. In this country, as well as in his own, the name of Father Mathew is a favorite one with which to christen Catholic temperance
11*

societies, not because of any special form of organization established by him, for he established none ; but because Ireland is proud of him, as America is proud of Washington, and delights to keep his memory green in this appropriate way.

The similarity of his work from the stand-point of a Romish priest to that of his countryman, Francis Murphy, from the stand-point of a Protestant layman, will, doubtless, strike the reader's attention.   Both movements began with a simple pledge made in the name and strength of God, both pass by all the various arts of social organization, and both urge upon the reformed men a sincere repentance toward God, a sincere faith in the Lord Jesus Christ, and a close and constant fellowship with the Church.

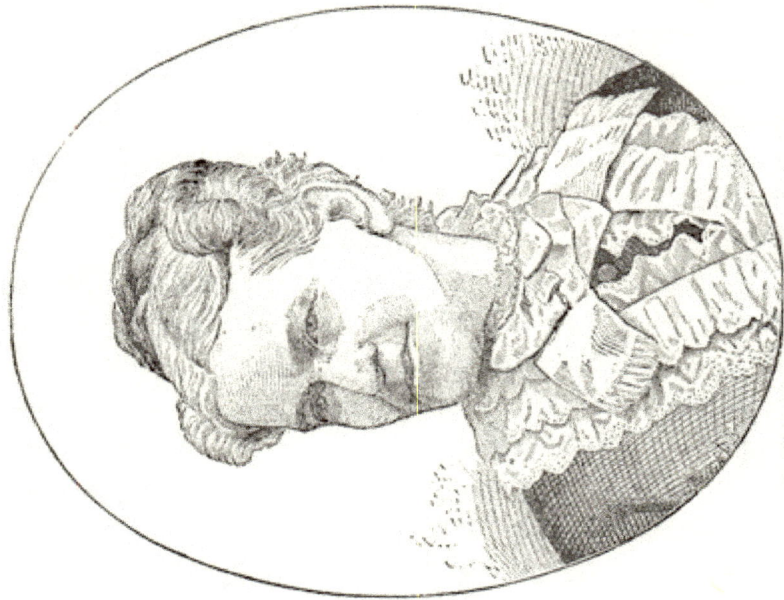

"MOTHER" STEWART.

MRS. JENNIE F. WILLING.

SECTION V.

THE CRUSADES, AND THE WOMAN'S CHRISTIAN TEMPERANCE UNION.

CHAPTER XI.

THE WOMAN'S CRUSADE.

"WHY did the women choose such a strange method of carrying on this reform?" asked one who was amazed to see a company of women kneeling at prayer in front of a saloon.

"They did not choose it," was the reply of one of them; "it was the work of God marked out for us, and we simply did it, according to orders."

"Do you like to see your wife singing Psalms in a saloon?" asked a critic of the temperance movement, of a judge whose wife was one of the most active and influential of the Crusaders.

"No, my friend," he replied, "I cannot say I do; but I would rather see my wife singing hymns in such a place than to see my son there singing bacchanalian songs; and I have seen that."

"But," continued the questioner, "do you like to see your wife kneeling on the dirty sidewalk, in front of a rum-mill, saying her prayers?"

"No, I cannot say that I like to see it; neither do I like to see my son lying in the gutter from the effects of the stuff which he bought at the rum-mill; and I have seen that."

"Well, but, judge, do you like to see your wife marching along in a procession, carrying banners, and making a fuss along the public streets?"

" No," says the judge, " I cannot say I like it ; neither do
I like to see my son marching in a procession of criminals on their way to prison with chains about his hands ;
and I have seen that ! "

This *bona-fide* conversation, as given by the evangelist,
Major Cole, who is himself a reformed man, shows the
great sympathy which this Crusade awakened in the
minds of the best people of the Crusade State ; for rum
does not seek its victims among the lowly and the
ignorant only, but, like the angel of death, the rum fiend
" loves a shining mark."

The credit of projecting the plan of the Woman's Crusade has been given to Dr. Dio. (Diocletian) Lewis, of
Boston, who in his own father's home experienced the
miseries which intemperance brings on the family. His
father was a drunkard, but his mother was a prayerful
woman, whose trials in bringing up her family, and suffering the abuses of her husband, were almost too much
for her endurance.

Many a time she went up to the garret to pray, and
the children would hear her crying out in agony of spirit,
" How long, O Lord ! how long ! how long ! " When
she came down the children would notice that her eyes
were red with weeping, but that her face was shining
with light from the other world.

Under such influences as these it is not strange that
the doctor, who had become famous for his system of
hygienic training, should carry the ideas of love and hope
along the higher plane, and seek for the salvation of men
and women from the disease and death of drunkenness,
which in his boyhood had been such a horror. He

learned to pray of his mother, and grew up with a high estimate of the power and value of such prayers.

These views he set forth in public lectures in various parts of the West, organized temperance bands, drafted and presented appeals to the whisky-sellers, a method somewhat after the fashion of General Putnam himself, facing the wolf in his own den.

As the result of the first week's work along this line in the town of Dixon, Illinois, thirty-nine dram-shops were closed, and for a time it was declared no liquor was sold in the town. At Battle Creek, Michigan, the same plan was tried shortly after, with similar excellent success.

The next places which the doctor visited were Hillsborough, and Washington Court-house, in Ohio, where he gave two evenings to the discussion of women's prayer-meetings in saloons; at the close of which the women present resolved to carry out his plan, which the doctor himself explains in one of his lectures as follows :—

" There have been various methods proposed for lifting the black pall that hangs above us, shutting out the face of God from so many souls. I asked a man the other day, on a railway train, if he had heard any thing about the woman's temperance movement?

" ' Of course I have. I haven't heard of any thing else.'

" ' Well, my friend, what do you think of the method?'

" ' Don't think much of it; don't believe any thing can be done for drunkards in this world.'

" Another reformer was of the opinion ' that it would be well to charge $5 for every drink;' and another was 'for having a law passed that liquor-dealers should not make more than five per cent. on their investments,' while another, who might almost be called fanatical in his advocacy of temperance, declared : ' If a man gets drunk once, send him to State prison! if he get drunk three times, hang him!'

" Now, there are two forms of combating the enemy, by prohibition, and by moral suasion ; and I am afraid that there will be division in the temperance ranks between the advocates of these two methods. The friends of prohibition have always been true and faithful ; but, notwithstanding all that has been said on the advantage of prohibition laws, it is my belief that in the Eastern States prohibitory laws have been a positive harm.

" The Massachusetts law is the most perfect of its kind ; yet there are 3,500 open dram-shops in Boston, selling liquor without attempt at cover or concealment. The trouble is, that prohibitory laws are passed before public sentiment has reached such an elevation as to make them a success, and when one is not enforced it is a stumbling-block in the way of reform.

"Enthusiastic advocates of prohibition will display great energy until the law is passed; then they fold up their hands, and say, Let her work. But she does not always work. Now, I suppose every body will say, Why don't they enforce the law? The difficulty is that the law is in advance of local public sentiment, and cannot be enforced any more than any other law could be which was ahead of the conscience of the people ; therefore I say that a prohibitory law is injurious to the cause of temperance when it diverts the attention from those moral and religious forces which alone can prepare the way for it.

"I hope the time will come, as it has come in Ohio, when prohibitory laws can be made successful, and then I will be in favor of them, but not before. In Mount Vernon, Ohio, for instance, the people have been asking their council to grant them a prohibitory ordinance, which the laws of the State permit, and for twenty years they have asked in vain; but the other night fifty men and thirty women went down to the City Hall, and in forty minutes the law was passed, signed, and put in force. Public sentiment had attained the requisite pitch; and it is as easy there now to punish liquor-selling as it is to punish horse-stealing.

"About twenty years ago I suggested the use of prayer-meetings in rum-shops, and it was tried in some sixty places, in Illinois, Michigan, New Hampshire, and Massachusetts; but only now has the plan found congenial soil and taken root in the State of Ohio.

"Take the town of Washington, for instance. I lectured there one evening on this subject, in the Presbyterian church, and a committee of three women was appointed to draft an appeal to the liquor-dealers, and then a committee of forty women was appointed to circulate it, and ask signatures to what was called the dealer's pledge. In a few hours the appeal was ready, and the women started out, forty or fifty strong, including wives of clergymen, doctors, lawyers, and all the most respectable residents of the town. On reaching a saloon kept by a Mr. Smith one of the ladies knocked at the door, and said :—

"'Have you any objection to the ladies on the side-walk coming in?'

"'No objection, certainly; come right in, ladies.'

"So they all went in.

"'Mr. Smith,' said the leader, 'I want to read an appeal to you; it contains nothing offensive.'

"No objection being made, the appeal was read.

"Then the leader said:—

"'Have you any objection to our kneeling down here and having prayer?'

"The man was too much surprised to object, and so all those women knelt down on the floor of the saloon, and some one led in prayer.

"After prayer they asked if they might sing, and, consent being given, they sang, what has since become the campaign song in Ohio, 'Nearer, my God, to thee!' then, leaving the amazed liquor-seller to his reflections, they went to the next, and the next, until all the thirteen liquor-sellers were visited with petition, prayer, and song. The next day they repeated the process. One dealer said, 'Look here, I can't stand this any longer; if you wont come again I will stop.'

"'We hope we have done nothing offensive,' said the women.

"'No, no; but I really can't stand it. I have thirteen barrels of spirits in my cellar, and if you ladies want to knock in the heads of them I will let you do it.'

"To this proposition they gladly acceded, and, a time being appointed, all the bells in the town began to ring, bringing hundreds of people to the scene. With their own hands the women brought up the barrels from the cellar, and one of them that had suffered most from the liquor traffic seized an ax and dashed in the heads, and the liquor ran over the street amid the wildest enthusiasm!

" 'Some people say women cannot chop,' remarked a spectator, 'but this woman who knocked in the heads of them 'ere barrels seems to be the champion choppist of the town.'

"Another dealer 'came down,' as the phrase then in vogue expressed the closing of the drinking saloons; and in ten days from the time the crusade commenced every saloon was shut up, and the proprietors pledged their honor never to open again.

" Just out of town was one Charley Beck, a German, who kept a fine lager beer garden, and the women determined to visit him. He was in the confidence of some wholesale liquor dealers in Cincinnati, who told him they would give him all the liquor he could sell in a year if he would break down the crusade.

"When he was visited he said, with much impressiveness: 'Go vay, vimmins, go home; shtay at home, and tend to your papies; vhat for you vants to come to my peer garten? Dis is the blace to trink peer; ve don't vant no brayer-meetings in dis garten.' However, the women quietly led a prayer-meeting on his behalf, which, greatly to his surprise, was not such a shocking, howling, fanatical utterance, but a supplication of the throne of divine grace in his behalf, and in a low and gentle manner, as a mother might pray, with her children around her, at the family altar.

" Recognizing this as the last stronghold of the enemy,

a tent was pitched in front of the entrance to the beer garden, and on it was placed a locomotive head-light, which threw its glare full upon the Dutchman's door. The women relieved each other every four hours from six o'clock in the morning until midnight, singing and praying, reading the Scriptures, and keeping account of the persons who went into Charles Beck's garden for three weeks; by which time his business was effectually stopped, and poor Beck, seeing that the hope of his gains was gone, came mournfully over to the prayer tabernacle, and said: 'O, vimmins! I quits, I quits.'

"Shortly after a German in a neighboring town thought he could do a good business by removing his stock of liquors to the town of Washington, thinking that the topers must be very thirsty by this time. He was, however, afraid to use the railway, so he secretly moved his goods one night in a wagon, and the next morning opened out his saloon with the expectation of large and immediate profits. In about half an hour all the bells of the town began to ring, and the Dutchman thought there must be a fire; but presently the head of a procession of over a hundred women came in sight, and the poor fellow was obliged, like the rest, to 'come down' and surrender unconditionally."

When asked whether he thought this plan practicable in cities, the doctor replied that in Columbus and Dayton meetings of that sort had been held, which had not succeeded very well.

"Do the men take part in these meetings?"

"We try not to have them," said the doctor. "We would rather they would keep out. When a man comes up to give his opinion he will extend the palm of one hand as an anvil to hammer on with the forefinger of the other, and say : 'With regard to the archæological relations and the metaphysical proclivities,' etc., etc. The women want none of this. They come to the meeting from their closets of prayer, burning with the love of God, and clinging to him for help. They want power from on high ; but one of the things they don't want is the cool, calculating, speculating theories of the men."

Dr. Lewis was invited to Hillsborough, Ohio, where he spoke on the evening of the twenty-second of December, 1873. On the following night a band of seventy-five ladies enlisted to carry out his plans. Having prepared a pledge for druggists, saloon-keepers, and voters, they bound themselves by this solemn obligation :—

" We, the ladies whose names are hereto appended, agree and resolve that, with God's help, we will stand by each other in this work, and persevere until it is accomplished, and see to it, so far as our influence goes, that the traffic shall never be resumed."

Such a movement of the women, however, could not fail to attract the attention of the men, and at their meeting, in the Presbyterian Church, they were addressed by some of the clergymen of the town before starting out on Christmas morning to visit the saloons.

It was a strange experiment to them, and seemed subversive of all the recognized rules of womanly conduct : these drinking dens, which respectable people abhorred at a distance, they were to enter, and in the presence of the half-drunken crowd of profane and vicious men they were to engage in the solemn act of divine worship.

They shrank from the task, half in doubt and half in
fear; but the thought of the drunkards that would go
reeling home on that Christmas night gave them new
courage, and they went on their way in the spirit of Him
who came not to call the righteous, but sinners, to repentance.

Of this company of eleven women one was Mrs. J. H.
Thomson, daughter of Governor Trimble, and sister of
Rev. Dr. Trimble, of the Ohio Methodist Conference;
who, the record states, offered the first prayer in an Ohio
liquor saloon.

In a few days five of the saloons and three of the drug-
stores surrendered. One druggist stood out, and sued
the ladies for ten thousand dollars for injury to his business; but the decision was in favor of the ladies, who
still kept on with their work. The movement spread,
and was soon the theme of pulpit discussion, prayer-
meeting exhortations, editorials in the newspapers; and
the reports of the progress of the movement were given
with as much minuteness and display as if it had been an
exciting political campaign.

The towns of Gallipolis, Sabina, New Lexington,
New Vienna, Waynesville, New Holland, and others,
were crusaded with success.

One old toper, who was annoyed at the closing of the
saloons in his own town, declared that he would hereafter
do all his trading at Wilmington, but on reaching that
place he found the crusaders had been there before him,
and it, too, was closed against whisky.

The following sketch of the Crusade in Xenia, Ohio, is
taken from "Harper's Weekly," which gave the most

admirable illustrations of the movement, both by pen
and pencil:—

"Observing two ladies entering a church, (United
Presbyterian, I believe,) I followed them, and found myself in the presence of about one thousand people, assembled for prayer, and to discuss the subject of intemperance. The pastors of the several Protestant Churches
were there with their people, and a feeling of humble
dependence upon God, and a deep Christian earnestness
in the work before them, seemed to prevail in the heart
of every one present. After the adjournment of the general meeting, the ladies were called together by Mrs.
Colonel Low, President of the Ladies' Temperance Association, who, after a few remarks, asked:

"'Who will volunteer to lead a visiting party to
Klein's saloon?'

"After a moment's pause a middle-aged lady arose and
signified her willingness to do so. She gathered about
her some eight or ten others, and they started off in
double file to beard Mr. Klein in his den, and I went
with them.

"On arriving at the door of Mr. Klein's confectionery
and toy store, without a moment's hesitation they filed
boldly in and occupied the whole space between the
counters, which ran along three sides of the room.

"On the approach of the ladies the family beat a
hasty retreat, and barricaded themselves in a very mysterious back room, from which issued a very strong odor
of highly flavored XXX whisky, and the cries of a baby
with very strong lungs.

" When the ladies began to sing, 'Shall we gather at the river?' the baby cried a loud and discordant solo, and the effect was not at all pleasing. At the conclusion of the hymn one of the ladies began a most beautiful and touching prayer. No sooner had she commenced, however, than Mrs. Klein, no doubt feeling that her premises had been unlawfully invaded, shot out from the back room in fiery indignation, her bare arms revolving like the sails of a wind-mill, her hair on end, and began to pour forth such a volley of abuse upon the ladies that it seemed as though she carried a mitrailleuse in her mouth.

" The prayer continued, and so did Mrs. Klein and the baby—

"'O Lord, we come not in our own strength'—

"'Shust kit out o' mein shop, every one of ye; ye're a set o' hypocrites; das is zo!'—

"'We would ask Thee to bless this family; enlighten their understanding, that they may be enabled to see the wrong of continuing in this unholy traffic'—

"'I don't vant yer brayers.* Ef I wants to bray, I ko to mein own shursh to bray; I don't pelieve in such dings. O, yes! O, yes! de Lord pless dis family! Veli, dis family kin git along mitout sich brayers; de Lord don't hear dem'—

"'She will not hear our words; but Thou, O God, wilt cause them to enter her heart as arrows of conviction'—

"'Ye're a set o' street valkers. O, I knows dis ting shust as vell as not; it be's like te epysootic; it koes all around, und den koes avay agin!'

" The climax was reached when Klein himself rushed

into the room, bearing aloft a little parcel, and exclaimed at the top of his voice, 'Git out o' mein house immejutly, ye hypocrites! Do ye see dot baper? das red pepper in dere, und I gives you shust five minnits to leave mein shop; ef ye don't I drow dis over ye!' Mr. Klein, however, refrained from carrying his threat into execution, and the ladies concluded their visitation in peace.

"From Mr. Klein's I proceeded at once to Mr. Carroll's grocery and provision store. The ladies were kneeling on the sidewalk in front of the door, engaged in prayer. Two of the party were conversing with Mr. Carroll, who stood in the doorway with a newspaper in his hand, and looking very much annoyed, as he exclaimed, 'Now, I give ye fair warning. I've got the names of ivery one of ye, an' if ye don't lave my primises this instant, I'll push ye till the furthest extint of the law. I'm not a highwayman or a thafe, that ye should come makin' this nonsense in front of my door.'

"The ladies pleaded courteously with him; he was a good-hearted fellow, and evidently got worsted in the argument. He looked convinced, and yet felt he could not abandon a trade which supported him and his family with such ease. After remaining for half an hour, the ladies left him, promising to return again and again, until he would yield to their prayers."

The work of the Crusades in Xenia was all the more remarkable from the fact that this is a stronghold of the United Presbyterian Church, where all religious services were always, of the most correct and dignified style, and where no religious songs were allowed except the Psalms of David. This steady-going town

12

was struck by the wave of the Crusades and fairly
lifted out of its former self. The good women of
that Church had been taught that it was a shame
for a woman to speak or pray in the church—a statement of a fact in the time of the great apostle to the
Gentiles which is a fact no longer—facts and fashions
having changed since his day—a statement which has
been elevated into an orthodox doctrine to the no small
detriment of the Church, and which, with the good Presbyterian ladies of Xenia, was held to be almost as binding
as the Ten Commandments. But now all their former
notions on this subject were reversed ; a great inspiration
came to them, and under its divine direction they, too,
like their Methodist and Quaker sisters, began to pray in
the streets and saloons, with all the more fervor and
unction, that their talents had been buried so long.
Still they would not sing any thing but the good old
Bible Psalms. The modern music, of the Bliss and
Sankey style, was generally supposed to be the only sort
that was adapted to crusading, but the Xenia ladies
marched to the tune of " Dundee," or " Mear," or " St.
Martin's," or " St. Ann's," in which the Psalms of the
old Scotch version have so long been sung, and these
steady harmonies were blessed to the breaking of stubborn hearts and the opening of bleared and blood-
shotten eyes no less than the most stirring gospel songs
of modern revival fame.

Very exciting scenes followed this, in connection with
the surrender of the worst saloon, called the " Shades of
Death," while shortly after almost all the rest closed, and
now, it is said, it is hard to get liquor in Xenia.

In Clyde, Norwalk, Oxford, Warren, and other places, the Crusade was kept up, with varying difficulties but with almost unvarying success. Very obstinate cases were treated with the tabernacle, the same which captured the defenses of Charles Beck. This was the artillery of the movement, and no place could stand a regular approach after this manner.

There was one saloon where the crusaders were responded to upon the sidewalk by fiddling and dancing inside. Hour after hour the women kept guard over this house, singing and praying, until at last the saloon-keeper was ready to exclaim, in the language of the hymn,

"And now I yield, I yield,
I can hold out no more."

Then, amid the ringing of church bells, the songs of thanksgiving, shouts of rejoicing, and tears of gladness, the beer, whisky, brandy, etc., were poured out in the streets, and the place opened as a meat market.

One stubborn publican in Bellefontaine declared that if the crusaders visited him he would receive them with powder and lead; but the unterrified women presently appeared before his door and began to pray.

About a week afterward the dealer made his appearance at a public meeting, signed the pledge, and on the following Sabbath attended church for the first time in five years.

In Clyde an effort was made to drown out the crusaders. When the women kneeled in front of one of the saloons and began to pray, the keeper dashed a pailful of cold water into the face of the one who led in the prayer.

The woman, without stopping for an instant, said, "O Lord, now we are baptized for thy work."

Such an illustration of the perseverance of the saints was too much for the enemy, and it was not long before this saloon-keeper also went to the church and went forward for prayers.

The water treatment was repeated in various places, the water not always being of the cleanest; but the women kept on praying, with more faith and energy than that manifested by the crusaders of old, and with more substantial success attending their movements.

The friends of temperance in Cincinnati watched the progress of the Crusade in the smaller cities of the State with the greatest anxiety. A meeting of women to pray for the success of the movement, and for direction concerning its commencement in the Queen City, was followed by a meeting of men, at which the leading clergymen of the city, Rev. Drs. Hitchcock and Walden, of the Methodist Book Concern, and prominent Christian laymen, discussed the plans and progress of this singular temperance revival, and sought to know how they could encourage their sisters in Christ. The sentiment of this meeting was, God has given this work to the women; let the men keep hands off; we cannot bear arms in this campaign, but we can render good service by our prayers and sympathy.

A call was issued through the daily papers to the women of Cincinnati, and on the 6th of February, 1874, the first meeting was held, in the First Presbyterian Church, Mrs. F. Charles Ferguson, presiding. Soon the hard work of the Crusade was begun, and the first victory is thus described in the "Cincinnati Gazette" fifteen days later :—

"The report was yesterday floating about the city that one of the worst places in Fulton had hung out the white flag, and surrendered to the ladies.   Investigation proved the rumor to be entirely correct.

"A band of women, most of whom were residents of the First Ward, started quite early in the forenoon upon their third round of visitation.   Among the first places visited was the saloon of Dick Manley, on the front street, two doors west of Kemper Lane.   From some incidents in their former visits the ladies were led to believe that the proprietor was not wholly satisfied with his business, but they were not expecting the easy triumph before them.   Benches were carefully arranged by the conscience-stricken saloonist for his fair visitors, and devotional exercises were begun.   The prayers and songs were so earnest, simple, and direct, that at last he could stand it no longer.   As they were about to sing,

'My faith looks up to Thee.'

he broke in with, 'Wait a little; I'll give up.'   He then told the ladies that his stock was at their disposal, and he would himself help pitch the vile stuff into the gutter.

"About this time the scene began to grow exciting. Several ladies burst into tears.   An effort was made to sing,

'Praise God, from whom all blessings flow,'

but the voices of the singers refused to give utterance to the language of their hearts.   Then, when they had somewhat recovered themselves, they set to work with

beaming countenances to pour out every thing about
the premises that could moisten the throat or make glad
the heart of man.   Beer barrels were rolled to the gutter, and while their contents were gurgling out through
the bung-hole, all the bottles on the shelves were brought
out and dashed upon the pavement.   After every thing
had been emptied out the proprietor thought of some
fine old Catawba stowed away in the cellar.   This was
soon hunted up and shared the fate of the rest.   He said
he was bound to make a clean thing of it.

" After the saloon had been pumped thoroughly dry
the ladies went to the place adjoining Manley's, where
another victory was awaiting them.   The proprietor of
the saloon was absent, but his brother, who was in
charge, yielded to the entreaties of the women, signed
the total abstinence pledge, and locked up the concern
forever, as far as he was concerned.   If his brother wanted
to open again when he got back, he might do it.   The
ladies then proceeded to several other places, but met
with no further apparent success.   The gentlemanly
keeper of the Eureka Exchange slammed the door in
their faces, and retired to an upper room, from which he
viewed the proceedings with a sardonic grin.

" In conversation with our reporter to-night, Mr. Manley said he didn't know what he should go into next.
He had a billiard hall connected with his saloon, and he
would carry that on until something better offered.
He seemed resigned at the loss of his stock, and thoroughly glad that he was out of the business.   The jokes
and sneers of his old friends who couldn't see it in that
light seemed to have no effect upon him.   He remarked

to one of them that if he owned all the saloons between
there and Columbia the women might have the whole
of them."

Of the Crusades in Cincinnati, Mrs. Leavitt, who was
one of the leaders in that movement, and now the Vice-
President for Ohio of the Women's Christian Temperance Union, gives the following account :—

"I am often asked to tell the story of the Crusades in
Cincinnati, but I never can do it. The Crusades were
something to be felt, not to be told. The whole idea of
that movement was soul-saving.

"Cincinnati was a hard field, with its three thousand
saloons and its forty millions of dollars invested in the
liquor trade. So strong was this interest that merchants
did not like to have their wives engage in temperance
work for fear of bad results to their business, and at first
we thought we must adopt only mild, old-fashioned
measures. But at last, under the baptism of the Holy
Spirit, we came to the conclusion that the country
method must be our method, and for eight weeks, about
seventy strong, we crusaded the streets and saloons after
the most vigorous fashion.

"The first place we visited was an elegant sample
room. As we came near the place one lady in the band
remarked—

"'I don't know why *I* am here. I have no one in my
family who drinks.' But just as we came to the saloon
she caught sight of one of her own sons in there, wiping
his mustache; evidently just after a drink. The mother
who did not dream that *her* sons were tipplers looked

pale as death. She was the first one to offer prayer in
that place, and ever since she has been active in the temperance work.

"Sometimes the saloon-keepers would invite us in,
and sometimes they would back us out. One German
beer-seller, in view of our probable visit, obtained an old
cannon, and, loading it to the muzzle, he drew it up
before his saloon, and swore he would shoot if those
'temperance fanatics' tried to crusade him. That very
saloon was down in the route of one of our bands, and
when we came to it and saw the ugly-looking machine,
and the Dutchman standing by with a lighted torch in
his hand, we were a little surprised, as you can well believe. But we did not hesitate long; we drew up in line
right in front of the cannon and began to sing, and pretty soon the old fellow threw down the match and began
to cry, declaring that though he 'vas not a bit afraid of
dem voomans, he could not shtand dot singin'.'

"Good Friday of 1874 was one of our great days. We
had a band of about a hundred and twenty of the best
ladies in Cincinnati that day. We started out from the
prayer-meeting at one of the churches, as our custom
was, with orders to take a certain line of march and
visit certain saloons. Our route was to go down to the
esplanade and hold a prayer-meeting on the flag-stones
near the fountain.

"When we came in sight of the place we saw a crowd
of roughs, evidently waiting for us, the leader of which
had sworn a terrible oath that no woman should set her
foot on the esplanade that day. I did not know of it at
the time, so we marched right along, two by two, up to

where the crowd were trying to block up our path, and, going up to this leader, a big burly fellow, half full of whisky, I said :—

"'My brother, you must help us to keep order. We are going to hold a prayer-meeting.'

"A great change seemed to come over him all at once, for he said—

"'Break ranks, boys! These women are coming through!'

"The crowd obeyed him, and allowed us to pass to our station, formed in hollow square around us, and the leader detailed some of them to act as a special police to keep order while we held our meeting, saying, 'We are going to see these ladies through.'

"We began to sing 'Rock of Ages;' next 'Jesus the Water of Life will give,' and then a dear Quaker lady began to exhort those roughs to give their hearts to God. We forgot all about temperance, and held a real gospel meeting, which made a profound impression on the crowd.

"Our orders were, 'South to Esplanade—hold thirty minutes' prayer-meeting—then back to church;' but we heard that the church was full already, so we found out another where we could go, and the crowd of roughs went with us.

"At the church appeals were made to them to seek Christ, and when those were asked to raise their hands who wanted to be Christians, many hands went up; then we asked who would come forward for prayers, and the very first man who came was the ring-leader of the gang; and the poor fellow was saved then and there.

12*

"Another young man came forward, and immediately a woman, seeing him, came and knelt by him, put her arms about him, and began to pray for him—her son.

"You see the Crusades were breaking in so on the liquor business that the dealers and manufacturers were alarmed. Liquors sent out to dealers in the country began to be sent back again because there was no sale for them, so the liquor men besought the mayor to try and stop the work of the women! They made a mistake there: it was not the work of the women but the work of God that troubled them so.

"You know we were arrested and had to go to jail. Just think of it!

"There was a Sidewalk Ordinance which forbade the obstruction of the streets, and under that we were arrested, though we were careful to use only the two feet in width that the law allowed us when we stood in front of a saloon and sung at it, and quoted texts of Scripture at it, and knelt down and prayed against it and for the souls of those who kept it.

"The seven policemen who were detailed to arrest us were crying like whipped children; but they had to do it, and we, like good, law-abiding citizens, submitted, and went in procession to prison—forty-three of us—singing all the way.

"One of your Chicago clergymen, Rev. Dr. Fowler, was in Cincinnati at the time, and he went to prison with us, to see that no harm came to us, and helped us in our work among the poor wretched prisoners we found there.

"We were released after about four hours. Bail was

offered us, but we refused it, on the ground that we had done nothing against the law, and those who arrested us should take the full responsibility of their outrageous act.

"The Crusade prayer-meetings were kept up after that at the churches, and by and by we took the rooms at 200 Vine-street, where we held a constant Crusade. The aggregate attendance at our women's temperance prayer-meeting for the last six months was 14,009; of these 2,932 signed the temperance pledge and sought the prayers of Christians in their behalf. A good many of them—as many as fifty, I am sure—have been soundly converted."

In Columbus, the capital of the State, only seven out of four hundred saloons could be closed, while in the smaller places of Worcester, Cambridge, Akron, and others, where the work was continued, it was estimated that about eighty per cent. of the saloons were permanently closed.

"The New Temperance Era," which was published at Cincinnati during the Crusades, and which was one of the best temperance periodicals ever issued, makes the following statement under date of July 4, 1874:—

"There are three thousand women at work, ably supported by a large number of gentlemen. Over one thousand young ladies have promised not to use wine, and to discourage its use among young gentlemen. There are in the city of Cleveland ten hotels whose proprietors have come forward and announced their intention of keeping strictly temperance houses.

"There are now a thousand indictments for violations of the Adair law, and five hundred cases under the nuisance section, which the temperance lawyers are conducting without fees.

"One wealthy gentleman has pledged himself to give, if necessary, $100,000 to close up the saloons, and some of the dealers say they are not afraid of the prayers of the women, but are very much afraid of the $100,000. Ten thousand names are recorded upon the citizens' pledge; many saloons have been closed; many of the owners of buildings have served upon their tenants notices to quit at an early day. Our wholesale establishments have found their business very greatly reduced, and our saloon-keepers utter piteous lamentations on account of the hard times that have so suddenly come upon them."

A correspondent of the "New York Observer" at Tiffin says : "The assessors and gaugers of the Ninth District of Ohio tell us that, as a result of the temperance movement, not one of the eight distilleries of the district is now in operation. The sale of all kinds of liquors, beer, and ale has fallen off more than sixty per cent."

At Delaware, the seat of the Ohio Wesleyan University, the crusaders were met with a proposition to compromise on beer; but the ladies refused the offer, and continued their work until nineteen saloons had made an unconditional surrender, leaving only four in existence.

In Mount Vernon, Ohio, twenty-three saloons surrendered as the result of a twelve days' campaign.

A correspondent of the "New York Tribune" at Mount Vernon says: "At the hotel I found the landlord actually bragging that he had been the first man to surrender. A commercial traveler was just leaving the hotel, with a bundle of samples under his arm, when the landlord said to him, 'You need not go out at this time of day, sir; you wont find a respectable store in town open now; it's the prayer hour; every day between nine and ten o'clock every body goes to prayer-meeting.'

" From the hotel I went to the Episcopal church. Few places of amusement are ever more crowded. Every seat was filled, and men and women thronged the vestibule, and stood in the aisles, while the inclosure within the altar-rail was occupied by clergymen, every denomination appearing to be represented. Nobody presided; the meeting seemed to run itself. A man rose to speak, giving an account of what had been done at another town; then a woman said, 'Let us pray,' and the congregation followed her with devout air in an impassioned appeal to the throne of grace. When the prayer was ended some one began to sing:—

'Mine eyes have seen the glory of the coming of the Lord;
He is tramping out the vintage where his grapes of wrath are stored,'

the congregation joining mightily in the chorus,

'Glory, glory, halleluiah !
Our God is marching on.'

Then more prayers and more exhortations, until a young man suddenly entered the house, and pushed his way through the crowded aisle to the pulpit.

"'Ladies,' said he, 'I have come to tell you that I cannot hold out any longer; I shall not sell any more liquor, and I want to sign the pledge.'

" Some in the audience forgot where they were, and began to cheer; others shouted, ' Amen,' and then, almost by one impulse, the congregation arose and sang the doxology which every body can sing :—

'Praise God, from whom all blessings flow.'

Before the echo of the song had died away the sexton had hold of the bell rope, and the good news was pealed forth that another stronghold of the enemy had fallen. The bells of the other churches took up the tidings, and for half an hour they chimed away, until it seemed as if every body in Mount Vernon and vicinity must have been aroused.

" The prayer-meeting over, the women sallied out in two sections, each under an appointed leader, to visit the few liquor-stores that still held out. There were several inches of snow on the ground, and the weather was intensely cold, but there was no shrinking from duty."

In Cincinnati a guild of saloon-keepers was formed who were solemnly pledged not to surrender, but to support each other in holding out against the praying women. They also resolved, fearing that some soft-hearted brother might be affected, that the ladies should not be admitted into their saloons.

Similar protective organizations were formed in other cities and towns ; but the saloon-keepers found that the prayer power is something which can get at a man, regardless of the question of whether his saloon be open or closed.

Not less than two hundred cities, towns, and villages were crusaded, and not less than twenty-five thousand women were pledged to labor and pray on behalf of the work of the Crusade.

The name of "Mother" Stewart is a familiar and honored one in the history of the temperance crusades. The following sketch is from the "Good Templars' Watchword," London, on the occasion of her recent visit to England on a mission of temperance :—

Mrs. Stewart, so extensively known in the United States as "Mother Stewart," is a lady of nearly sixty years of age, of medium stature. As indicated by the portrait, she has silvery hair, which is arranged in soft, glossy ringlets, in the manner known by American ladies as the "Martha Washington" style. Her hazel eyes, although no longer young, are very expressive, and flash out thoughts before they find utterance in words, alternately indicating sympathy with suffering, and indignation at wrong and injustice, and constantly recurring humor. The impression she gives and leaves with all who come in contact with her is that she is a genial, kind-hearted woman, who believes in the righteousness of her cause, and is emphatically in earnest in her work.

Mrs. Stewart was born in Ohio, U. S., and was in early life led to consecrate herself to the service of Christ. It will be readily understood that a lady of her temperament, with strong religious convictions of the duty of personal service, would not be slow to find opportunity for active work. In the Church of her choice, of which she has been a member for forty-four years, she has ever been recognized as an efficient laborer. During the civil war, while her husband and sons were in the service of their country, she was busily engaged in pro-curing and sending supplies to the sick and wounded.

Her attention had for years been directed to the great curse of intemperance, and she had been in the habit of delivering lectures on that subject as opportunity offered. And so it would seem that while God was moving the hearts and arousing the consciences of his people in various Christian lands to action against the common enemy, he was also training and preparing Mother Stew-art for the important part she was called to take in the great uprising, and especially in the "whisky war" in her own State, a movement which spread like fire in the broad prairies from State to State, and the fame of which has reached to all parts of the civilized world.

We do not propose, in this brief notice, to enter into the details of the Crusade, or to give a full account of the work. This, we trust, many of our people will have the privilege of hearing from Mother Stewart herself, as she has come to our shores intending to spend a few months with us; "not," as she herself states, "to recom-mend to her sisters here that peculiar form of work," for she believes that that form has had its use and has passed; and, while there were, undoubtedly, many mis-takes—for it is human to err—she is firmly convinced that "God has looked upon the work, has pronounced it good, and has sealed up the book. But out of that form, and the awakening of Christians, has grown an interest and opportunities every-where for work, and she comes to her sisters to counsel, to encourage, and, if possible, to enlist a still greater number of Christian women in the cause."

We heartily welcome such a woman to our shores, and

trust she may succeed in arousing increased attention to the curse we are all pledged, by God's help, to remove. It is scarcely for us to say what means shall be most successful. It is our duty to accept the aid of all helpers, and especially of one who has exerted so mighty an influence in a far-off land. We trust that our brethren every-where will open the way for our earnest and devoted sister; that they will aid and cheer her in her work; and that God may abundantly bless her labors among us.

Another writer has this pen and ink sketch:—

"Along with many others, I passed through a steady downfall of London moisture to see and hear Mother Stewart, at the rooms of the National Temperance League. I had gazed with interest on the artist's presentment of her form and features in the 'Watchword;' the expressive steadfast glance of the eyes looking from under the well-arched, well-marked brows, the finely-chiseled, firmly-closed lips, with a perfect 'Cupid's bow,' the full and rounded, almost dimpled chin, and the ample but proportionate breadth of the lower part of the face, as well as the wide proportions of the chest and bust, so far as displayed in the picture.

"I looked again, and noted the 'artist's lines'—lines that would have delighted Hogarth—of the eyebrows, eyelids, nostrils, and chin; the ear, the throat, the shoul-'der, and the one raised hand. Looking once more, I noticed the width, height, and prominence of portions of the brain—as exhibited by the shape of the 'ivory walls' surrounding it—the large projection forward from the ear, the full development of the forehead generally, and

particularly the width and fullness of the portions over
and between the organs of vision, and the height of the
upper part of the head. The general impression conveyed was that of quick, clear, and searching perceptions,
ready 'mother wit,' breadth and force of character, con-
stancy, hopefulness, dauntless courage, faith, and perseverance to the end, be it sweet or bitter.

"Such were the mental and moral qualities suggested
to me by a perusal of the artist's lights and shadows.
These also led me to expect in Mother Stewart a large
physique; indeed, something masculine was suggested
by the proportions of the chest, and still more so by the
upper lip and lower jaw.

"In these anticipations, however, I was disappointed,
but agreeably so. Mother Stewart is not of more than
average height, and at first sight she strikes one as small
in figure and in features. The lower part of the face is
spare, the complexion fresh.

"Her voice is sweet, and, though not loud, is clear,
and sometimes penetrating. She goes straight to the
point, speaking with all the artlessness, originality, and
verve of one full of the subject and charged with a
mighty mission, yet talking naturally, and expressing
just such thoughts, narrating such facts, and making
such appeals, as occur at the moment, couched in racy
but idiomatic Saxon.

"One's heart goes out to Mother Stewart, standing
there, pleading for help in her righteous cause. If not
large in frame, she has a spirit powerful enough to rouse
and inoculate a vast legion of supporters; her eye
flashes, her ardent feelings and aspirations heighten the

color in her face; now and then the voice will falter just a little, to prove how womanly she is. And O, how well—though it may be briefly—she pleads! Hearing and reading her speeches are very different. A report fails to convey the native raciness, the indefinable charm of her manner, though, in reading, our words seem to come back to us from over the sea, and we can trace how strongly the Northern, Saxon elements of our language flourish in congenial soil, as we look at those sharp, short terms, terse, brief, and pungent.

"As I listened to the speech, there were running in my mind, now the dry, keen, searching east wind, pinching and penetrating what it touched; now the breadth and grandeur of the prairies; and now the mighty rolling rivers, flowing on in resistless volume to their destined waters. Something of these was suggested by the subject, and something by its exponent. With an eagle eye the watchful speaker seems to see the battle-field where intemperance strews the ground with wounded victims— sees where help is to be had, and swoops down upon the plague-spots with infallible certitude; she brings up her corps of angelic praying women, and trusts for the success of their crusade, thinking nothing of the appearance of the thing, but only of the precious souls to be saved from tumbling into hell."

In the State of Indiana, where the Baxter law is in force, the Crusade was carried on with great success. This law provides that no man may keep a saloon, or sell any intoxicating liquors, until he has secured the signature of the majority of the voters in his ward and township to a petition asking for such a saloon. He is required to furnish bondsmen who shall be liable for any violation of the law on his part; and, furthermore, the premises on which the liquor is sold are liable—as under the Adair law in Ohio.

In securing these petitions all kinds of frauds have been resorted to. The directories of other towns, grave-stones, and other foreign resources have furnished names for these petitions. At Valparaiso, Shelbyville, Terre Haute, Richmond, etc., there were great and enthusiastic uprisings, and the work of the Crusade was carried forward with good success.

Indianapolis, the capital, became the center of an earnest work, among whose results may be mentioned, that on the day appointed for the reception of petitions for the keeping of saloons, the lady crusaders, with their lawyers, were present to point out the lying devices of the liquor men to the commissioners, who, in view of the evidences of fraud presented, refused twenty out of twenty-four applications for license.

From Indiana the movement spread into Illinois. In the cities of Springfield, Bloomington, Shelbyville, El-Paso, Jacksonville, etc., the work of the Crusade went on under the auspices both of law and Gospel. In some instances, notably that at Mattoon—which was the scene of a great revival, under the ministry of the Rev. Dr. Goodwin—temperance and religion walked hand in hand. At Urbana, the seat of the State Agricultural College, at Farmer's City, at Bloomington, and at Belvidere, the local elections, which turned on the temperance question, resulted in a victory for " no-license."

The Crusades in the city of Bloomington, Ill., took the form of a municipal election on the question of license or no license. The leadership of this movement fell to the hands of Mrs. Jenny Fowler Willing, a lady already well known in her Church, in which she was a licensed preacher, and an admirable and powerful one. She had recently been elected to the Professorship of English Literature in the Illinois Wesleyan University, and when the crusading spirit appeared among the Bloomington ladies a Woman's Temperance Union was formed, of which Mrs. Willing was elected President.

By the time the spring election came the temperance sentiment had risen to such strength and dignity that the city council ordered the question to be submitted to the voters, " License " or " No License." The temperance workers rested a little from their meetings so as to gather strength for this grand onslaught, and then about two weeks before, the election there was a crowding on of all force to call the attention of the people to the great iniquity. The election was to occur on Monday, and the day before, the pastors, at the request of the Woman's Temperance Union, preached on the subject. The evening was given to mass meetings. Every body who had the gift of tongues was pressed into the service; many who had been timid and conservative were set to presiding or speech making; some who had been on the wrong side found themselves pushed in a corner where they were obliged to declare for or against the great philanthropy. Every body was astonished at the amount of temperance interest suddenly evolved.

The next morning, a raw, drizzling April day, the ladies

met at the First Methodist Episcopal Church, and after much prayer it was voted almost unanimously to go to the polls and work for the "No License" ticket. As usual, there were all manner of bogus tickets in the field—all sorts of cheats with which bad men shape the laws while good men are too busy with their own affairs to ferret them out. The ladies secured the tickets, found out the frauds, cut off the mischievous part of the bad tickets, and then all day, in relays of twos and threes, they went to the voting places, and put the right tickets into the hands of the voters. Mrs. Willing stayed at the church, engineering the affair, with the help of a young lawyer who had had a hand before in political affairs.

As the day passed and the issue seemed doubtful, the pastors of the Churches, the professors of the University, some clerical students who could speak German, and the Roman Catholic priest—all were summoned to the polls to help the ladies.

The outcome, to the astonishment of all concerned, was a complete victory for "No License." Bloomington was the largest city of the Union that was carried by the Crusade. The next summer Mrs. Willing was nominated by the prohibition party for the State Superintendency of Public Instruction, a candidacy which she found it necessary to decline. At the first Chautauqua Sunday-school Assembly this lady's temperance address and subsequent efforts resulted in the organization of the Woman's National Temperance Union. Mrs. Willing was the president, and Mrs. Emily Huntington Miller was secretary, of this preliminary meeting.

In October, 1873, Mrs. Willing was elected President of the Woman's Christian Temperance Union, of Illinois.

In November, at the National Convention, held at Cleveland, Mrs. Willing was chosen to preside. The crusaders were present in force, and many of them were full of fervor and zeal, and with decided opinions in regard to the policy of the new organization; but with quietness and calmness the presiding officer held the meeting during the three days of earnest debate, with a wholesome strictness, to parliamentary decorum. The next year the paper of the Woman's National Christian Temperance Union was planned and launched, under the care of the Publishing Committee. Mrs. Willing was chosen editor, and piloted the paper through the critical period of its establishment, after which, on account of the pressure of other duties, she permitted it to pass into other hands.

In November, 1876, she was appointed by Mr. Moody to the chairmanship of the ladies' work in connection with the evangelistic services held at the Chicago Tabernacle. Large numbers of women were sent out from the meetings to visit among the poor and outcast, to distribute invitations to the tabernacle services. After the close of the Moody meetings she went to Greencastle, Indiana, for a revival service of twenty-one days, which resulted in the conversion of about three hundred, and the helping of a large number into the higher Christian life. That was followed by a meeting of twenty-one days in Indianapolis with large success, all the Methodist Episcopal Churches uniting in services held at Meridian-street, Roberts Park, and Trinity Churches.

At present she is engaged on a work of fiction, embodying her best thoughts on the earnest questions upon which she has been and is still at work; her literary experience and Christian ability eminently qualifying her for such a task.

Chicago, that despair of temperance people, was not neglected by the women crusaders. Encouraged by the success of their sisters elsewhere, a company of Christian women organized themselves into a society for the purpose of holding public temperance meetings in the various churches of the city, establishing daily prayer-meetings at Farwell Hall, and visiting saloons—not after the manner of the crusaders, to sing and pray, but to endeavor to persuade the keepers to sign the temperance pledge, and to close out their business.

The writer of this volume recollects, with distinguished pleasure, the first Sabbath evening temperance meeting held under the auspices of this committee, at the Park Avenue Methodist Episcopal Church, of which he was at that time pastor. The ladies had arranged a programme, but none of them were public speakers, and as the hour for the commencement of the exercises came dangerously near they began to seek for assistance in the services. " No," was the reply, " this is your meeting, and the Lord evidently means that you shall conduct it."

One of the ladies, Mrs. Louise S. Rounds, whose name has become so familiar in connection with the work of the Woman's Christian Temperance Union in Illinois, was appointed chairman, whose duty it was to introduce the speakers, after a brief address of her own. Some tem-

perance hymns had been written for this occasion, and
practiced by the Park Avenue Church choir, to be sung
to such tunes as "Home, Sweet Home," "Auld Lang
Syne," "John Brown's Body," and others, which the
non-church-going people who were expected on that occasion were certain to be able to sing.

After the address by the chairman, a lady rose whose
husband had but recently signed the pledge, and in consequence of which benediction she had devoted herself
to the work of the Crusade. Such an experience as this
could not fail to tell. Following her came Miss Lucia
F. Kimball, now well known to our temperance periodical literature, and as the leader and organizer of the
Christian Temperance Union work among the children
and young people, who that night made her first public
speech on temperance. At the close of the addresses a
couple of pledges at the head of large sheets of blank
paper were produced, and persons were invited forward
to sign, the choir meanwhile singing the temperance
songs. Two long lines of people were presently formed
in the aisles, and for half an hour they pressed eagerly
forward to affix their signatures to the pledge; some of
them with the marks of their evil habits upon them; one
or two evidently just from the saloon.

The success of this meeting gave great encouragement to the crusaders, and, one after another, the Methodist, Congregational, and Presbyterian Churches were
opened for the crusade services. A small sheet was
printed, both in English and German, containing upon
one page some statistics of the fearful results of the
liquor traffic, and upon the other, an appeal to the
13

licensed saloon-keepers to give up their traffic, which produces such misery. The city was districted, and ladies appointed to go out, two by two, to visit saloons and persuade their keepers.

Chicago, as is well known, is controlled by the liquor interest, as is the case with many another great city; but to Chicago belongs the distinguished disgrace of having maltreated the women crusaders in their lawful work. A company of ladies were appointed on one occasion for the purpose of visiting the hall of the City Council, to lay before them a petition for the better enforcement of the laws already on the statute book. There was no reason on earth why this petition should not be granted, but the liquor dealers gathered together a company of lewd fellows of the baser sort, and actually mobbed the committee in their attempts to present the petition, so that it was with difficulty that the ladies could make their way through the crowd of half drunken vagabonds which had gathered about the entrance to the hall, in anticipation of their appearance.

The police were plenty, as they always are at such a place, but no arrests were made, and when the committee, after presenting their petition, came forth again from the hall, trusting in God for their safety, the mob rudely set upon them with evident intention of violence, and the police were actually forced to take the ladies in charge as if they had been prisoners, and conduct them by a private way out of the midst of the crowd.

Being discouraged thus from the hope of attaining any great results by law, they gave themselves up to more earnest use of the Gospel, and established a temperance prayer-meeting, at four o'clock, in the lower Farwell Hall, which meeting has been maintained every day except Sundays for the space of over three years. The work here done in reforming drunkards, and relieving their families, and holding the fort for temperance, has been supplemented by the training of a company of Christian temperance men and women, who, by means of the daily work connected with this Gospel mission, have become acceptable and impressive temperance orators, whose services are in constant demand.

CHAPTER XII.

MORE CRUSADING.

MRS. GEDDES, the wife of the Hon. Norman Geddes, of Adrian, Mich., Vice-President for the State of Michigan of the Woman's National Christian Temperance Union, gives the following account of the crusades in that city, which was the point at which the movement commenced, and from which it extended throughout the State. This lady was already a leader in other philanthropic movements, and naturally and appropriately, as well as by a distinct impression of duty, came to be a leading spirit in this temperance work. Mrs. Geddes is a graduate of the famous Mount Holyoke Female Seminary in Massachusetts, where they teach lessons of self-sacrifice and Christian effort along with the less important matters of literature, science, and art. Of that school she says:—

"I do not know of a graduate from Mount Holyoke Seminary who has not done something for the world, besides merely taking care of herself and family."

"When these Crusades started in Ohio, and reports of them reached us in the papers, something came to me and said, 'That is to be your work in Adrian.' The idea was especially shocking to me. It seemed as if I never could go out as the crusaders were doing in Ohio and elsewhere, and hold meetings in saloons and on the streets; but as I read of the progress of the Crusade the impression repeated itself over and over again, 'This is to be your work,' until I became actually frightened. I could not sleep at night for the dread of this duty, and gave over reading about the Crusades, with the hope of freeing my mind from the disagreeable impression. When the week of prayer came that year I did not attend a single meeting, lest I should hear something about the Crusades.

"Other ladies in the community began to be interested in the work, as the news of the movement began to occupy a large place in the public press, and several of them called upon me to ask me to attend a temperance prayer-meeting in Adrian. I gave various excuses for refusing the invitation, and for three weeks did not go near the meeting, during which time I was so wrought upon by a sense of my duty that I had no rest in my soul, day nor night. Once I took up a paper, and found a notice of Miss Smiley's meetings in Toledo, and went away and stayed as long as possible, to keep out of the way of the temperance work at home. On my return, my husband inquired if I were intending to have any thing to do with those Crusades, whose measures, he thought, were not well chosen, but calculated to lower the dignity of the ladies who engaged in them. I said nothing of my convictions; but the news kept getting more exciting, and the impression of my duty kept growing stronger, until at last it seemed to come to me as a question of life and death: 'Will you do this work, or will you not? You must decide once for all.'

"At this I was so alarmed that I went to the temperance prayer-meeting, which I had shunned all along, and found that a band of crusaders had already been appointed.

"It appeared that the business men of Adrian had been urging the women forward in this movement, saying to them, 'The saloon-keepers expect you; why do you not go?' Public sentiment had already taken sides with the movement; crowded temperance meetings were held in the churches, and it may be truly said that the public conscience and judgment among the business men of Adrian actually drove the women into the work of the Crusade.

"At that first meeting three praying bands were appointed, under three leaders; and what was my amazement to hear my own name read as the leader of Band No. 1.

"The time appointed was two o'clock in the afternoon. It was too late then for me to go home to dinner, so I went with a friend. On my way back to the church I met my husband, who said to me,

"'I hear you have been appointed to go with a committee to the ——— House. I would not go there *first*, for it has been given out that the house has invited the ladies, by way of breaking the force of their visit.'

"This good advice, which also showed the partial conversion of my husband to the movement, was followed; the plan of the afternoon's work was changed. The three clubs united in one, and started out in solemn procession, two by two, from the church, which was left full of people, to pray while we went out to the war. As leader of 'Band No. 1,' the leadership of this first Crusade in our State fell upon me. We marched along the street for half a mile, to the miserable hotel we were first to visit, and as we went along I issued what you may call General Order No. 1 :—

"'Speak not one word, but pray all the time.'

"It seemed as if the day of judgment were come, so great was the solemnity that pervaded our company while the faces of the men who lined the path on either side seemed to indicate a sense of the divinely appointed work upon which we had started out. Even the crowds of boys in the streets were orderly and respectful.

"The first place we visited was the old Sammons Hotel, the landlord of which was an old man, eighty years of age—since dead—who had not been inside of a church, or heard a prayer or a hymn, for many and many a year. When we entered his place he trembled like a leaf in the wind. We talked to him kindly, and he offered all sorts of excuses for the business, which he admitted to be an evil one. There were people present, drinking, but he ordered that silence should be maintained while we sang our hymns and offered prayer, the heavy cross of offering the first prayer of the Michigan Crusades falling upon me.

"Never in all my life before did prayer seem to bring me nearer to God. There was a special baptism of power and love given to me while I prayed in that low drinking place. From that moment all hesitancy and fear departed, and I felt that I was committed to the Crusade for life. Ladies have often told me that the word 'saloon' had lost its disagreeable sound to them after they had passed through a similar experience; and the prayer-meetings which we held in bar-rooms and drinking dens were

among the most interesting and spiritual religious services in which it was ever our privilege to engage.
Never have we felt ourselves nearer heaven than when
kneeling on the floor of a drinking house, praying for the
keeper, and for the success of the Woman's Crusade.   It
may seem strange that a saloon should have any sacred
associations in the mind of any human being; but then,
you know, this sacredness was only to those who went
there, not to drink, but to pray.

"We had at that time a prohibitory law, which had
been standing on the statute books some eighteen or
nineteen years, and under it all the saloons and drinking
places in Adrian were shut up so closely that for six
weeks there was no open drinking in the town.   During
those six weeks the sum of fifty dollars covered all the
expense of the criminal business of the city.

"The whole community was pervaded with a spirit of
religious temperance enthusiasm; and from Adrian the
movement spread, until the whole State was alive with
crusaders.

"But in an evil day pride began to creep in.   We had
done great things; we had won a great victory.   Certain
ambitious ones began to take a little glory to themselves,
and insisted upon carrying on the movement begun under
the Gospel by the help of the appliances of the law.   We
had shut up all the front doors of the drinking places,
and now it was proposed to shut up all the back doors,
so that there could be no private drinking; and for this
purpose it was proposed to bring detectives from Chicago,
who should watch for evidences of drinking on the sly,
and thus bring prosecutions against the places that were

still secretly selling liquor. A good many of us, who had been more interested in praying than in prosecution, opposed this new movement; but it was advocated with so much spirit that, rather than have a division in our ranks, we yielded a reluctant consent. Detectives were brought from Chicago, who hunted up evidence of secret liquor-selling, and on this evidence legal action was brought against the offenders. The lawsuits brought on anger and ill-feeling; and whenever you get angry your praying is done. With the beginning of this law-movement the religious work fell off, and the good that was confidently expected to be accomplished by legal means was never realized. We did, indeed, gain our cases before the courts, but our cases before the court of Heaven seemed to languish; and, what was more, some of those who had not joined in the praying Crusades, and who had been most active in advocating the legal one, fell away from their interest in the cause when difficulties began to thicken, and the lawsuits were left at last on the praying women's hands.

"We had some curious experience in those days. There were some places where we were received courteously, and others which we were forbidden to enter. There was one place in particular from which we had been turned away that we were determined to visit. So, starting out with a band of crusaders, at an unusual hour of the afternoon, the first two of the procession reached the place somewhat in advance of the others, and entered almost before the keeper knew we were coming. But when he looked out and saw the procession he locked the door against us, making prisoners of the two leaders of our

13*

band. This, of course, looked serious, but we determined on no account to abandon those who had been taken captive by the enemy. So we gathered around the place, and began to sing and pray on the sidewalk, waiting until the keeper of the saloon should release his captives. The prayer-meeting being over and the door still fast, we held a speaking meeting; relating our experiences and cheering one another in the work. In the meantime quite a company of gentlemen had gathered around, and, seeing that we were besieging the place with prayer and song and temperance discourses, and had been at it long enough to be weary, they kindly brought out chairs and benches, and we continued our meeting with much comfort, except that we were anxious for our sisters, who were inside.

"Night came on, and still the prisoners were not released. Then our husbands and brothers and sons went away and brought us hot coffee and sandwiches, and we, thus further refreshed, went on with the singing and praying and speaking. A great crowd of people gathered, and some of them, seeing the situation, cheered us on, and seemed to be deeply impressed with the religious exercises that we were engaged in. About ten o'clock at night the keeper of the saloon released the captive crusaders, who had improved their captivity by exhorting him to repentance, being in nowise molested, but becoming somewhat anxious at their long detention. This saloon presently closed for good. The keeper of it took his departure, and the place was used for another line of business.

"Our last crusading was on a place kept by a Dutch-woman, who attempted to use similar tactics upon the whole company, locking them in, and abusing them with sharp words, and, what was worse, keeping them in the dark as night came on; shutting up the place so that they might be suffocated with bad air, to which was also added the fumes from the pipes of a company of men, who in the next room were endeavoring to 'smoke them out,' as they say, when they haze a freshman at college. The ladies were, indeed, in danger of violence, and it was ten o'clock at night before they were rescued from the captivity of the old Dutch-woman and her customers, who had worked themselves up to such a state of fury that for a while it was doubtful whether murder would not come of it.

"Like all other excitements, even in a good cause, the interest in the Crusades died away, but there was left the organization known as the Woman's Christian Temperance Union, which, through all discouragements, has maintained itself, and has now a healthy and active existence."

The Temperance Union of Christian Women of the city of Brooklyn is one of the best specimens of those organizations to be found either East or West. Its history is so full of spiritual life and practical power and wisdom that it is worthy of special mention in the annals of the great reform.

In the winter of 1873-74 a remarkable temperance interest appeared in a Union Bible-class of ladies, which held weekly afternoon sessions in the Friends' Meeting-house. The tidings of the Crusades in Ohio came to

them as a new revelation, some of them being ladies of
the most wealthy and elegant circles of society, and always accustomed to the use of wine among their other
luxuries.   But as the news became more exciting these
Christian ladies found themselves strangely moved to
pray in secret for the success of their sisters who were
waging this new warfare, and at length they began to
confess their unusual experience to one another; the
first result of which was a prayer-meeting, where the
divine Spirit was marvelously poured out upon them, and
they were led to consecrate themselves renewedly to
God, though they had not the most remote idea that
they should ever be called upon to do so inelegant a
thing as go to a saloon and sing and pray.

"I always thought," said one of them to the writer
of these pages, "that drunkenness was to be found only
among low people, and, such being the case, it was a
matter that did not concern us; but since we began this
work I have found sad and heart-breaking proofs that in
the highest walks of life, as well as in the lowest, this
great curse and crime is terribly common.

"At one of our temperance prayer-meetings a young
man came to me and said: 'I am lost, I am lost! pray
for me!'

"I looked at him in surprise.   He was a son of one
of the leading families of Brooklyn.

"'Why do you not ask your mother to pray for you?'

"'Ah!' said he, with indescribable sadness, 'I never
heard my mother pray.'

"The broken-hearted wife of the pastor of a leading
Church once came to beg me to join her in prayer for

her wretched husband, who had been for years drinking in secret, and who at that time had been lying for three days in a state of senseless intoxication.

"I had always drank wine at my own table, and at the fashionable hotels at watering-places, but I began to see that a Christian had no business to set such a dangerous example."

The prayer-meeting above mentioned led to the call for a women's temperance meeting at the hall of the Young Men's Christian Association, which, to the surprise of the ladies, was attended by such numbers that hundreds were obliged to go away for want of room. An organization was formed, with Mrs. Mary C. Johnson as President, whose portrait appears at the head of Chapter XIV, and Miss E. W. Greenwood as Secretary—under whose direction the Gospel Temperance Prayer-meetings were carried on, though even then it was thought their duties would be along the usual lines of dignified Christian effort. These temperance prayer-meetings all at once became a wonder. Crowds attended; victims of strong drink presented themselves for prayer of their own accord; all the New York and Brooklyn newspapers gave full reports thereof, and the whole community was awakened, as never before, to work and speak and pray against the evil that is all the time making such havoc of bodies and souls.

Presently, as if to open the way for real crusading tactics, a saloon-keeper, under conviction of the Spirit of God, sent an invitation to the temperance women to hold a meeting in his saloon. This came like a shock to those elegant and orderly people, who felt that even to speak or pray in a public meeting in the house of the Lord was a wide departure from the lessons of a lifetime, and almost unpardonable in a lady, unless in most exceptional cases, of which the temperance prayer-meeting was the only one they had ever met; but to go down to a house of the devil and bear this unaccustomed cross was too much for their sort of human nature to bear. But all at once the memory of that first meeting came over them. "We promised to obey the Lord without reserve," said the President, "and we dare not falter now."

Accordingly, a committee of twelve ladies, with Mrs. Johnson at their head, marched to the saloon, and, drawing up in a circle in the room, with a card-table for a reading desk, and a crowd of some three thousand spectators, representing every description of low and vicious life, for a congregation, they held their first Crusade prayer-meeting in Charles Meyer's gambling-house and saloon.

"Once when I was sick, a number of years ago," says Mrs. Johnson, "a strange vision came to me, of a vast crowd of people, in whose presence I was standing—a wild, wicked crowd, of all ages and in all grades of sin and misery; and just before me was a precipice, toward which they were moving and over which they were falling. I was thought to be even then in the very arms of death. I heard the watchers say, 'She cannot live but a few hours;' but from that vision I knew that I was to recover, and that God had some work in store for me. I had vainly tried, over and over again, to find the meaning of this vision, but until I began this Crusade work my life had been all the time among lilies and roses; now it began to be among thorns and briers.

" From the time we entered the saloon till near the end of the meeting I did not dare to look up, being oppressed with a sense of the strangeness of our situation; but after a dear Quaker sister had finished speaking I ventured to lift my eyes, and — there they were: the very crowd I had seen in that vision years and years ago. I knew them at once, and understood the meaning of the precipice over which they were falling."

Of · her address in that strange place others have spoken in admiration. She says of it: " I could speak then, for I saw the precipice and they did not."

At the close of the meeting thirteen men of their own accord came up to the ladies, and offered to sign the pledge, and a few days after the proprietor of the saloon closed his business and gave the key of his saloon into the hands of the crusaders.

The work of saloon-visiting, thus providentially opened, has, unlike its history in most other places been steadily and persistently kept up; the Union has become a well recognized agency for truth and righteousness; its daily prayer-meeting, whose first sessions were so marked with the divine presence, have been maintained at the rooms of the Young Men's Christian Association; a Reformed Men's Meeting has been organized; a Friendly Inn, a Temperance Restaurant, established, and a wide-spread work of temperance evangelization has grown upon its hands.

The results of two years' work by the Brooklyn Temperance Union, so far as such results can be shown by mere letters and figures, are thus given by its President in a communication to the editor of this volume :—

"It may be said of the work in this city that 'the Lord hath magnified his name.'

"When the Union was formed less than a score of Churches were open to Christian women. Now almost all the Protestant church doors throughout the entire city are open, and ministers and people bid them cordial welcome and God-speed; and are no longer afraid the 'women's movement will lead into extremes.' One hundred and sixty-five Churches have thus been visited and addressed by the ladies of the Union, among whom may be mentioned Miss Albina Hamilton, Mrs. Caroline E. Ladd, Mrs. Mary A. Wilder, Mrs. Jacob Chase, Mrs Ellen C. L. Conklin, and others, whose names do and do not elsewhere appear in this volume.

"When the work began, in 1874, the doors of 3,000 saloons were open on the Sabbath, bidding defiance to the Sunday closing law, as well as the sacred day. Now there is no open selling on the Sabbath, and whatever there is, is done by stealth, the doors of these places being closed, as in other business houses. There were, also, 6,810 fewer arrests in 1875 than in the previous year. Nearly one half of the saloons of the city are gone from the streets, and property holders refuse a rental of buildings for such purposes.

"It is a matter of special gratefulness to God that the ladies observe that every saloon, without exception, in which they held saloon prayer-meetings, is entirely closed, and the buildings are devoted to other purposes.

"Scores of reformed men are members of Churches, and have taken their places as useful 'and respectable citizens, and favorable accounts are heard from them by letters. Among these reference is made with special thanksgiving to the labor of Mr. Hallenbeck, whom God has called into his great harvest-field as a most successful temperance evangelist. He has been during the last year (accompanied by his friend, Mr. Cassidy) the instrument in a great revival work in Southern Indiana, Illinois, and other states. The meetings have been enthusiastic, and so crowded in many towns that the rush for admittance exceeded any thing ever seen in those parts before. The signers to the pledge numbered thousands, and hundreds were inquirers of the way of Christ.

"Another of the Brooklyn reformed men, who left a band of minstrels three years ago, has been for several months preaching with great acceptance, in connection with others, in out-door Gospel meetings, in the streets of New York city, where the degraded and fallen most frequent.

"The untiring and successful labor in a legal direction, bearing upon Sunday closing, of Captain Oliver Cotter, is well known throughout the whole State and adjacent States, and the demand for his time and services is beyond that to which he can respond.

"The Brooklyn Union in the three and a half years of its existence has held four hundred and fifteen meetings in towns and cities outside the city of Brooklyn, and has done much in setting in motion the good work in many places on Long Island and Staten Island.

" No more licenses will be granted to women in Brooklyn.

" In two years our Union has made two thousand five hundred visits to public houses, held one hundred and thirty meetings in churches, kept up two daily prayer-meetings, and five regular Sabbath meetings, at which one thousand three hundred and twenty-five persons have asked for prayers; held public meetings in sixty-two different cities and villages; and during those two years, not altogether as the direct result of our efforts, but, as we believe, in answer to our prayers, one thousand three hundred and eighty saloons have been permanently closed."

When Mr. Moody began his evangelistic services in Brooklyn, he had not yet attained that full faith in woman's work, as a distinct department of the kingdom of Christ, which he has since experienced and turned to such good account. It was while he was absent in England and Scotland that the gift of prophecy had been so richly given to the " daughters " and " handmaids," and, finding him still wanting in sympathy with the woman's movement, some of the Brooklyn brethren labored with him in word and doctrine, till the evangelist consented to appoint a women's meeting, and allow it to be organized as a separate section of the revival system. Mrs. Johnson was appointed by him as the permanent leader of the meeting, and under her admirable leadership, with the assistance of other devoted Christian ladies of Brooklyn, a class of work was accomplished in the parlors of the rich and the hovels of the poor which at once gave this department a distinct and honored place in the list of revival means and methods.

When Mr. Moody went to Boston he sent for Mrs. Johnson to come and take charge of the parlor meetings, in which line of effort she had already been so successful ; and her admirable conduct of these meetings in the elegant homes of that city was every way worthy to share the highest honors with the public meetings for women conducted by Miss Frances E. Willard. For three months these two accomplished Christian ladies, by public addresses and drawing-room *conversazioni*, led the religious thought of the Christian women of Boston, and gave such scriptural expositions and such practical directions as have added greatly to the spirituality and usefulness of the ladies of that city and vicinity.

In 1875 Mrs. Johnson was invited to England to hold similar drawing-room meetings, where her services were most highly appreciated among the upper classes of London society. Many were the sorrows that wealthy and titled wives, mothers, and sisters poured into her ear ; for among that class are to be found a sad proportion of dissipated and reckless young men; and they listened most eagerly while she told of the Gospel temperance work of the women in America, by which so much salvation had been wrought both among the rich and the poor. This is a department of Christian effort the reports of which do not find their way into the public prints, but which has been, under the divine blessing, one of the most effective means of grace brought into use by the wonderful evangelism of our times.

A brief personal sketch of this lady, which appeared

in the "Chicago Post" during the recent annual meeting of the Woman's National Christian Temperance Union, will appropriately close this part of our record:—

"Mrs. Mary C. Johnson, of Brooklyn, Recording Secretary, a woman of the best social standing, a blonde in features and a lady in manner, the daughter of a public-spirited Christian banker, has given the past three years most heartily to the temperance cause. After many years of gayety and worldliness she became actively engaged in Sunday-school work, and had charge of 300 little girls. She had also been President of the Home for the Friendless, and was the first contributor to the infant department of the 'Sunday-school Times.' She is president of the Woman's Temperance Union of Brooklyn, where over 1,000 saloons have been closed during the past year, and where she is greatly beloved by all classes. Until the temperance crusade her work was emphatically for women. She was led into this latter work because she believed it a call from God to save souls. She has labored abroad most effectively, having spoken in 121 drawing-rooms by private invitation, and to London audiences of 3,000. Her father was a warm friend of the family of Elizabeth Fry, and the mantle of the gifted and beautiful preacher in the prisons of Northern Europe seems to have fallen upon her."

The Crusade also extended its work throughout the States of Michigan and Wisconsin—that paradise of beer-makers and beer-drinkers—also in Iowa and Minnesota; in certain portions of Nebraska, Missouri, Kansas, Colorado, and the Pacific States. In these latter States the

Crusade movement was comparatively brief, but, instead of disappearing like the summer's cloud, as was prophesied, there has arisen out of it a movement whose permanency, peculiar organization, loyalty to Christian principles, and determined perseverance in fighting this great enemy, give promise of a measure of success which hitherto has never been seen in connection with any organization of the temperance movement.

From among many thrilling incidents of the Crusades these will serve as specimens:

A letter from Boston to the Corresponding Secretary of the Cincinnati Woman's National Christian Temperance Union contains the following:—

"Last week there came into our temperance prayer-meeting, on North-street, a young man who said he once drank whisky to excess. He acquired the habit by taking whisky and quinine for fever and ague.

" 'In the streets of Cincinnati,' he said, 'I found myself alone, sick, and without friend. Wandering about the city, I came upon a band of women kneeling before a saloon and praying. I stopped to listen, and never before had I heard such prayers.

" 'I was sent to the hospital, and there I thought of it all, and now I trust in God as my strength and my Redeemer. I have given up whisky forever.

" 'I never saw one of those ladies to know them; I do not even now know their names, but shall throughout all eternity bless God for their prayers.' When asked to write his name upon the pledge book, he said, 'I will if you wish; my pledge is stronger than that; it is with Jesus.'

" Is not this word of the Lord true, 'They that sow in

tears shall reap in joy. He that goeth forth and weepeth, bearing precious seed, shall doubtless come again with rejoicing, bringing his sheaves with him.'"

Mrs. Leavitt, of Cincinnati, relates the following :—

One of the Conferences of the Methodist Episcopal Church, in Kentucky, was held in Louisville some months ago. During its session there was a ladies' meeting in the lecture-room of the church, in the interests of the Woman's Foreign Missionary Society. Soon after the opening of the exercises two men came into the room and quietly took their seats. Just before the meeting closed one of them arose and asked permission to speak.

Said he : " I can't express my feelings this afternoon. I've been for two years hungry to hear a woman pray. I've been a very wicked man. I was a drunkard for fifteen years. I neglected my family; my children died; then my poor wife's heart broke, and the town buried her. Two years ago I found myself in Cincinnati. I hadn't drawn a sober breath in months; I spent my days in saloons, my nights in the station-house. I didn't care for myself, and nobody cared for me.

" One day a band of the praying temperance women came into a saloon where a lot of us were drinking. Standing in front of the counter, they sang,

'There is a fountain filled with blood '—

a hymn my mother used to sing; then they all kneeled, and one after another prayed. O, I can never forget those prayers as long as I live. I couldn't keep the tears

back. For the first time in years there came into my
heart a great desire to be a man once more.

"When they left the saloon I followed them to the
church. There I signed the pledge, and took my first
step toward a better life. As I wrote my name, my
hand trembling and unsteady, a lady said to me, ' Jesus
can help you; O, can't you trust him, brother?'

"I could not say one word; but all that afternoon I
kept saying to myself:

"'She called me "brother." I'm somebody's brother
—I'm somebody's *brother!*' At the close of the
meeting she came to me, her eyes full of tears, and said,

"'All this afternoon I've been praying for you. O,
you are in great danger! Jesus wants you, and Satan
wants you; which are you going to serve?' Then I
broke down, all to pieces, and I sobbed out, 'I do want
Jesus to help me; but O, I am such a wretched sinner,
there can be no help for me! I've sinned away my day
of grace. I've murdered my wife. I've murdered my
children. I've broke my poor old mother's heart. I've
committed every crime; there can be no mercy for me.
I don't deserve mercy; but O, my heart is breaking!'

"Somehow I went right on my knees. All I could
say was, 'Have mercy on me, Lord—have mercy on me,
Lord!'

"How those women talked to me! They told me
Jesus didn't come to call the righteous, but sinners, to
repentance; that he would save even to the uttermost;
then I laid hold of Christ, and peace came.

"I can never tell you how happy I was then, and have
been ever since. I want to tell every body what a dear

Saviour I have found.   I want every one to love Jesus.
If any of you live in Cincinnati, tell the temperance
women I've been true ; tell them God has given me over
fifty souls here ; glory be to his blessed name !

"Sometimes I feel I must go back.   I went on my knees
to thank those dear women for dragging me from the
mouth of hell, and leading me to Christ.   O, dear friends,
it was woman's prayers and woman's tears that saved me ;
that's why I came into your meeting.   I thought perhaps you had met to pray for the drunkard.   I'm glad
you are praying for the heathen ; but O, don't forget
the heathen at home !   There are drinking men in Louisville to-day by the hundred, hungry for the bread of life ;
they don't know it—but women's prayers can save them
—they'll all go to hell if something isn't done.   Wont
you go to them and tell them, ' No drunkard can enter
heaven ?'   They'll believe you ; they will reform if you'll
plead with them.   Every drunkard's heart can be touched.
All are not hardened ; they have many bitter hours ;
they get down-hearted, and then Satan leads them off.

"O, pray for me, and pray for the drunkards of our
city before you go."

None who were present will ever forget the closing
moments of that missionary meeting.   As prayer after
prayer was offered for that man, and the class for whom
he had been so earnestly pleading, the sobs and tears
from the kneeling audience told how deeply their hearts
had been touched.

MISS FRANCES E. WILLARD.

MRS. ANNIE WITTENMYER.

CHAPTER XIII.

WOMAN'S NATIONAL CHRISTIAN TEMPERANCE UNION.

THIS organization is the form into which the Woman's Crusade has crystallized. That great movement, whose chief element was a divine enthusiasm, afterward took the form of a permanent and efficient organization.

The Christian women who went forth moved and sustained by an impulse irresistible, divine, to pray in the saloons, became at length convinced that theirs was no victory to be easily or speedily won. The enemy was rich beyond computation; he had upon his side the forms of law and the knavery of politics—with the leagued strength of that almost invincible pair, avarice and appetite. He was as persistent as fate, and determined to fight the battle out to the last dollar of his enormous treasure-house, and the last ounce of his power. But these women of the Crusade believed in God, and in themselves as among his appointed instruments to destroy the rum power in America. In the name of Christ, whom they loved and trusted, and for the sake of their sweet and sacred homes, they went forth, first as scouts and skirmishers, then at length they formed into line of battle, and the little praying bands were organized into Women's Temperance Unions. Under that leadership which followed the law of " the survival of the fittest," they were regularly officered in the usual way; with a

14

constitution and by-laws and an order of business—which machinery, however, constituted a much smaller proportion of the whole movement than has been the case with some of the most elaborate temperance organizations.

In the spring of 1874 the women who had been crusading in half a dozen States, notably in Ohio, Indiana, and Pennsylvania, called a convention for consultation, which resulted in State Temperance *Leagues.* The name was, however, soon changed to " Union," the latter word better emphasizing the non-sectarian spirit of the Crusade.

In November, 1874, a Woman's National Temperance Convention was held in Cleveland, Ohio, at which Mrs. Jennie F. Willing, of Chicago, presided, and to whose efforts this national organization is chiefly due, though of late the claims of strictly evangelistic work have left her little time for this line of Christian effort. At this convention a constitution was adopted, and a plan of organization projected, which was to reach every city, town, and hamlet in the land. Appeals to the women and girls of America, a letter to lands beyond the sea, and a memorial to Congress, were in order; a national temperance paper, to be edited and published by women, was projected, whose financial basis was one cent per week, to be given by all the members of the Union; and last, but not least, a special committee was appointed on temperance work, among the children.

The permanent officers of the society then organized were, Mrs. Annie Wittenmyer, of Philadelphia, President; Miss Frances E. Willard, of Chicago, Corresponding Secretary; Mrs. Mary C. Johnson, of Brooklyn, Recording

Secretary; Mrs. Mary A Ingham, of Cleveland, Treasurer; with one vice-president from each of the States represented in the convention.

The spirit of this assembly is shown in the closing resolutions adopted, as follows :—

" *Resolved*, That, recognizing the fact that our cause is, and is to be, combated by mighty, determined, and relentless forces, we will, while trusting in Him who is the Prince of peace, meet argument with argument, misjudgment with patience, denunciation with kindness, and all our difficulties and dangers with prayer."

In accordance with the action of this convention a monthly newspaper, called the " Woman's Temperance Union," was established in Philadelphia, published by Mrs. Wittenmyer, edited by Mrs. Willing, with Mrs. Johnson and Miss Willard as corresponding editors.

At the first annual meeting of the Union, held in the First Methodist Episcopal Church in Cincinnati, November 18 and 19, 1875, there were delegates from twenty-two States of the Union.

The Union has been busy in producing and circulating fresh, vigorous, Christian, temperance literature, organizing opposition to license laws, etc.

The following recommendations were made in the President's address, along the lines of which the Union has been faithfully, devoutly, and successfully at work :—

" 1. To establish a Lyceum Bureau, which should furnish organizers, speakers, singers, etc., to those wishing to form local reform clubs.

" 2. To arrange a definite plan by which young women may actively engage in our work.

" 3. To appoint a medical commission to investigate the medical uses of alcohol, its effect upon the health of the country, etc.

" 4. To appoint a commission of women on Bible wines, since doctors of divinity seem to reach no conclusion.

" 5. A committee on presenting our cause to ministerial, Sunday-school, educational, medical, and other Associations, urging them to declare their intentions in regard to it.

" 6. A committee on international conventions of women.

" 7. A committee on finance, and the incorporation of the Woman's National Christian Temperance Union."

It was under the auspices of the Woman's Christian Union that Dr. Henry A. Reynolds, the distinguished temperance reformer, was instrumental in the reformation of sixty thousand men in Massachusetts and other parts of New England, while during the last year, as will appear in another portion of this volume, his labors in the State of Michigan, under similar auspices, have resulted in the pledging to total abstinence of eighty thousand men, all of whom had been more or less addicted to the use of intoxicating drinks.

Daily gospel temperance meetings have been conducted by women in all parts of the country, and new life and new power have appeared in the progress of this reform, which now, first under the blessing of Almighty God and the Christian faith of women, has taken its proper place as a part of the Christian religion.

Thus the Woman's National Christian Temperance

Union, which has been aptly characterized as the sober second thought of the crusaders, and the affiliated Reform Clubs which have come into existence as the result of its labors, constitute the rallying line for the forces of God's people who feel themselves specially inspired to contend against sin in this particular form.

Their watch-word is not prohibition, but salvation; not the pledge, but piety.

Their work is no less a temperance crusade, though the peculiarities of that movement have disappeared. It is now the steady onset in the name of Christ, under the inspiration of the same vision which Constantine saw in the heavens, when there appeared above him a shining cross, and above it these words: " By this, conquer!"

MRS. ANNIE WITTENMYER.

"Some of us," says Miss Frances E. Willard, "have not forgotten that 'Volume I, No. 1,' of that journalistic venture, 'Our Union,' was edited and published by Mrs. Wittenmyer, whose courage and faith were equal to the test of starting a paper without a cent in its treasury, or a subscriber's name upon its books. This proceeding was quite 'in character,' as is shown by the following account of our friend's active and beneficent career, from the pen of a New York journalist:—

" Mrs. Wittenmyer's maiden name was Turner. She was born in Ohio, but her early home was Kentucky. Her grandfather was a graduate of Princeton College and an officer in the war of 1812. Her father was a native of the State of Maryland, her mother of Kentucky, so that she inherits the warm, fervid temperament

of the South, united with the cool, calculating reason of
the North. She attended for several years a seminary
in Ohio, where her education was carried much farther
than was usual for young ladies at that time. She was
married in her twenty-first year, and enjoyed many years
of happy married life. She was very prominent in the
Church in consequence of her religious zeal and enthusiasm, and also for her great activity in all charitable
enterprises.

"At the beginning of the War of the Rebellion Mrs.
Wittenmyer was appointed Sanitary Agent for the State
of Iowa by the Legislature. Secretary Stanton, of the
War Department, gave passes for herself and supplies
through the army lines, and a letter of instruction to army
officers to co-operate in her enterprise for the relief of
the soldiers. In this worthy endeavor she continued
throughout the entire war, changing her relation to it,
however, by resigning her position as Sanitary Agent for
Iowa to enter the service of the Christian Commission.
Here she had the oversight of two hundred ladies, and
she developed in this work her plan of Special Diet
Kitchen, to the great advantage of the health of our
soldiers. The first kitchen was opened at Nashville,
Tenn. In it was prepared food for eighteen hundred of
the worst cases of sick and wounded soldiers. These
kitchens were superintended by the ladies under her
direction. In this work she had the assistance of the
Surgeon-General, Assistant-Surgeon, and all the army
officers, both military and medical. General Grant was
a personal friend, and did all in his power to facilitate
her efforts. By invitation of the Surgeon-General she

met the Medical Commission appointed to review the special diet cooking of the army. The work of this Commission led to a thorough change in the hospital cooking of the army, which was lifted to a grade of hygienic perfection far above any thing before known in military affairs, and from which it is not likely to fall again to the old standard. It is simple justice to add, what is a matter of history in the United States Christian Commission, that these improvements in the diet kitchens of the army were the means of saving thousands of valuable lives, and of restoring many noble men to health and usefulness.

"About the close of the war Mrs. Wittenmyer set in motion the idea of a 'Home for Soldiers' Orphans,' and became herself the founder of the institution bearing this name in Iowa. It is not generally known that this enterprise originated with the brave woman who had cared for the husbands and fathers through the perils of camp and hospital life. When the fact that such an institution was to be opened in Iowa was generally known, hundreds of soldiers' orphans became the wards of the State. By request of the Board of Managers of the Iowa Home she went to Washington City, and obtained from Secretary Stanton (other departments co-operating) the beautiful barracks at Davenport, which cost the Government forty-six thousand dollars, and hospital supplies amounting to five or six thousand more, subject to the approval of Congress, which was afterward obtained. The institution thus founded and equipped has accommodated over five hundred children at one time, and it still maintains a flourishing condition under the care of the State.

" Mrs. Wittenmyer next conceived the idea that the vast amount of talent and energy brought into activity by the philanthropies of the war should be maintained on a Christian basis in the Church. Bishop Simpson, always ready to aid in any movement promising greater usefulness for women, entered heartily into the plan, and the Methodist Episcopal Church established a Home Missionary Society of women, organized for the express purpose of ministering to the temporal and spiritual needs of the strangers and poor. This organization was made a General Conference Society at the session of 1872, and Mrs. Wittenmyer was elected its Corresponding Secretary. During the year 1876 over fifty thousand families were visited under its auspices.

" At the commencement of this new work Mrs. Wittenmyer removed to Philadelphia and founded her paper known as ' The Christian Woman,' an individual enterprise, which has proved exceptionally successful. She has more recently established a juvenile paper, called ' The Christian Child,' which is rapidly winning its way to public favor. In addition to this large publishing work she has carried forward all the enterprises of the society above described, and known as ' The Ladies and Pastors' Christian Union,' traveling in its interest thousands of miles, and speaking in every State from Maine to California.

" When, as an outgrowth of the Crusade, the temperance women met in their first National Convention, it was but natural that they should choose as a leader one whose name already exhaled the perfume of a life of heroism on the field, and whose praises were spoken

daily in thousands of homes. Her achievements in the
past were a guarantee of success for the future. The
record of the temperance work during the past three
years fully proves the wisdom of their choice. Twenty-
three States have been organized as auxiliary to the National Union, and a paper has been founded as its organ.
Mrs. Wittenmyer has also labored tirelessly in the lecture field, speaking sometimes six evenings in the week,
besides traveling hundreds of miles. She has attended
all the large Conventions, of which forty-six were held
in 1875. At the second annual meeting of the Woman's
National Christian Temperance Union, held in Cincinnati, November, 1875, she presided with marked ability,
and was re-elected President for the Centennial year by
a unanimous vote of the delegates.

"One of the most notable acts which has characterized
her administration was the presentation to Congress (in
February, 1875) of a huge petition on behalf of our
Local, State, and National Unions, asking for the prohibition of the liquor traffic, on which occasion a 'hearing'
was granted by the Congressional Judiciary Committee.
Another act, even more important, was the sending of
a letter of inquiry to the International Medical Association, which met in Philadelphia in the summer of
the Centennial year. This led to another hearing before
a committee of celebrated physicians of Europe and our
own country, and resulted in the well-known 'resolutions' expressive of the most important medical opinion against intoxicants on record, when we consider the
representative character of those who gave it. The latest official act of our President was holding a 'Woman's

14*

National Camp-Meeting,' at Ocean Grove, which, conducted wholly and addressed largely by women, commanded the earnest attention of the thousands present
to the close, and was equally remarkable for spiritual and
intellectual power.   We believe the first woman's camp-
meeting on record was held in Iowa last year, and it was
quite in keeping that one whose public work began in
that noble young State should have conducted the first
east of the Alleghanies.

"At the annual meeting in Newark, 1876, Mrs. Wittenmyer was elected a third time to the chief office in
the gift of the temperance women of America, and by a
unanimous vote.

"It is a pleasant sight to see our friend, in her cheery
Philadelphia home, with her efficient secretaries, Miss
Fisher and Miss Merchant, and her exemplary son,
Charlie, around her, all of them blithe and busy as so
many bees.   In addition to the care of her two papers
and the duties of her office as our President, this inde-
fatigable worker is writing a ' History of the Woman's
Temperance Crusade.'

"Mrs. Wittenmyer is devoted to the advancement of
her sex in usefulness and opportunity.   First, last, and
always she is ' a *woman's* woman.'   Her editorials ' cry
and spare not ' against the tyranny of prejudice and
custom.   She tilts a free lance, and deals blows worthy
of a more stalwart arm.   ' The See Trial' (' None so
blind as those who *wont* ') was the occasion of several
cogent arguments from her pen, to prove that women
' have a right to preach or speak in the pulpit,' and she
has recently added to the larger of the two editions of

her paper a department headed, 'Pulpit of The Christian Woman,' in which a 'sermon' appears monthly from the pen of some one of the rapidly growing sisterhood of evangelists.

"The Crusade spirit abides with Mrs. Wittenmyer; the Gospel work is her delight, and her hymn of 'Victory,' written for our convention at Newark, embodies her declaration of faith as a temperance reformer. The first verse of this hymn forms a fitting close to this imperfect sketch :—

"The Lord is our refuge and strength ;
    His promises never can fail ;
We've learned the sweet lesson at length,
    His grace over sin can prevail.

"In the sweet by and by
    We will conquer the demon of rum ;
In the sweet by and by
    The kingdom of heaven will come."

OUR HOPE AND OUR REASONS FOR IT.

At the National Convention of the Woman's Christian Temperance Union in Chicago Mrs. Wittenmyer was for the third time elected its President.

The following address by this forcible, straightforward female orator, at a convention of the National Christian Temperance Union will not fail to be read with interest :

"I have been trying to abridge my remarks, to formulate my creed on the temperance question in a brief sentence. I very carefully and prayerfully read the 'Liquor-Dealers' Gazette' every week, and I have made up my mind that I am in favor, on general principles, of every thing that liquor-dealers are opposed to.

I am in favor of local option. It seems to be a very

democratic thing. I can hardly understand how an American man can be so mean as to sell liquor in the face of law and the express public sentiment of the community. I am in favor of civil damage laws. I think that when men rob the community and destroy property and life they ought to pay for it, and pay well for it, and if they kill people they ought to be hung for it. I am opposed to license, and in favor of prohibition. I never could understand, though I have given much thought to the subject, and I do not still understand, how the mere putting a thing that is wrong on the statute-books makes it right.

Because men, as I have seen them, put their feet upon the back of their desks in legislative halls, and smoke their cigars till the whole ceiling is almost hid with a cloud of tobacco-smoke, and vote for license laws, that does not make it right. Then I am in favor of the Crusade. I think that it is well understood that women compose about one half of the inhabitants of this Republic; that we have an interest, and ought to have a say, in this matter. None have suffered so much as women, and they are suffering still. I am glad that I have been climbing these last years the hills of hope. I have got up where these sweet singers [the Hutchinsons] are; for I can see the good time coming in the near future.

I had the privilege a few weeks ago of saying this to the Governor of Pennsylvania—and he is a very fine-looking man, I ought to say as I pass along. He knew that a hundred of the first ladies in the State of Pennsylvania were going to visit him.. He stood by

the mantel-piece in his great parlor, supporting himself, and looking like a bit of statuary. He had braced
himself up against the mantel-piece for the shock. Well,
it was a shock. I am not going to enter on the course
of argument that took twenty-five minutes of the best
speaking that I ever did in my life or ever expect to do
again. But I said to him this: 'If you take from us
local-option—for we were there to protest against the
repeal of the local-option law—we will give you within
the next political decade prohibition.' I said to him,
and I may throw out the hint here, 'We hold the balance
of power.' The boys are just about what their mothers
make them, and the men are only boys of larger growth.

"The Woman's National Christian Temperance Union
—which is a co-laborer in this field, and reaches out both
hands to co-operate with this organization (as the secretary of this Society knows very well)—is taking hold of
the children with a purpose to save the next generation,
and bring them up to be more temperate, more truthful,
and more honorable, if they should happen to be sent to
our legislative halls, than the present incumbents.

"Well, I can give some reason to-night for the hope that
is within me; for I look very hopefully on this national
movement of the women.

> "Though woman's hands are weak to fight,
>   Their voices are strong to pray,
> And with fingers of faith they'll open the gate
>   To a brighter, better day.

"I can give you some reason, it seems to me, why
the Lord has called this mighty force into the field
for more active work now than in the past, because

it seems to me that this is a movement under divine direction.

"The first reason is because God chooses the weak things of the world to confound the mighty. You know we have always been called weak. We did not like it very much; we want to be strong like our brothers, and when they called us the weaker vessels we did not exactly understand it. But the weakest ware that we have on our tables is the finest and most costly. We are looking into those passages of Scripture with enlightened eyes. We did not understand that all the great movements in nature, all the great moving powers, are the silent forces, the little things; and as we come to think about it, it is not the great clumsy instruments that can do the best execution, after all.

"Now, these men—and all honor to these temperance workers—have been using the plow. They have been plowing around this tree of evil, while we women (and you know we go right at a thing) come up with the ax in our hands, and lay it at the root of this tree. We intend to cut and slash, woman-fashion, until there is not a root or branch left. We are so weak that we are forced to trust God and to lean upon his almighty arm, from whence cometh our strength. A great many women in this land during the last year have come near enough to Jesus to touch the hem of his garment, and feel the mighty outflow of power that comes from divine contact. It seems to me that the women during this last year have followed more closely in the footsteps of the blessed Christ than ever women did since the Maries followed him up Calvary. Women of all denominations are clasping hands around the cross, with one prayer going up to God, as from one heart. The Quakers are singing beautifully. At the Massachusetts State Convention, the other day, the Quaker President started all the tunes. Our Presbyterian ladies are waxing eloquent in the presentation of this subject; and so, forgetting our denominational differences, we join hands and hearts for glorious work in this contest. But there are other reasons.

"You know it has been said that woman's work was never done, and we thought that it was an insinuation that we were not very industrious; but we have come to understand it better now. I have been led to ask, Why is it that woman's work is never done? I see that men work about so many hours, and then they quit; they do not work any more, not because all the work of the world has been done up, but because, I suppose, they grow weary. But women never grow weary; they work on and on; they are tireless in their energies. Then, you know, it has been said that when a woman will she will, and when she wont she wont. Well, now, there is deep meaning in these old sayings, and they mean just about this to us now: that women never weary in good works; that if a thing can be done, if it is within the range of human possibilities, they will do it; and they have such will in great moral movements that they cannot be intimidated, or discouraged, or bribed.

"In all the contests of last winter, when Congress and our State Legislatures were in session, and our women were going up to appeal to the law-makers — for our blows are not aimed at the drunkards, but at the rum-sellers and the manufacturers, and the law-makers who shield them—when they have been going up to present their case, I have never yet heard of a bribe being offered. The liquor men are wise.

"But there is another reason. They have the moral courage. It is perfectly wonderful to me how these women talk. They talk right out in meeting, and tell about their pastor, about their Church, and about the members of the Church; and the things that were covered and hid away are being uncovered. They have the moral courage to say what they think. Now, perhaps I cannot better explain this than by telling a little incident. Some of you know what it is to stand in the presence of the enemy's guns—what it is to stand where the shot and the shell come over. That is physical courage. I know all about that kind of courage, for I have come near being shot more than a hundred times, and know the ring of all sorts of destructive missiles. That is one kind of courage. But I have come to know, within the last eighteen months, that there is a higher style of courage than that.

"A few months ago some ladies were visiting saloons —(and I tell you it takes more courage to go into these saloons, and stand in the presence of the liquor dealers, and protest, in the spirit of the Gospel, against the traffic, than it does to stand up and take the chance of a random shot and shell)—they were visiting saloons in Jacksonville, Illinois. They had visited all the saloons but one, and the good, kind brethren advised them not to visit that saloon, as the dealer was a very violent man, and would, perhaps, do violence to them.

"They thought and prayed about it, and one day, when they were in the church praying, there came down upon them the mighty constraining influences of the divine Spirit, and they rose up as one to go out and visit that saloon. Well, the liquor-dealer had been expecting them for several days, and when he saw them coming he threw his door wide open, and stood in the door, with a pistol in his hand. He held it out; they marched right on, and as they approached very near he said—

"'Ladies, if you undertake to come into my saloon I will shoot the first woman who undertakes it.'

"Well, they never knew exactly how it was, but a young lady of the company, as if constrained by a divine impulse, sprang up and stood beside him, singing,

"'Never be afraid to work for Jesus,
Never be afraid.'

"Somehow his arm got weak; the pistol hung by his side; tears came into his eyes; he stepped back, and took a seat in the saloon. They went in and sung and prayed to their hearts' content. That is what I call the highest style of courage; and it is being displayed throughout the length and breadth of the land.

"I do not believe that it is within the range of our language to portray the evils that grow out of the liquor traffic. If any body can do that, it is Mr. Gough, and I am going to give way to him pretty soon.

"O, I remember as I stand here to-night that there are women hid away in the palaces of this great wicked city, whose hearts are breaking under silks, and there are other women who are hid away in garrets and cellars, whose hearts are breaking under rags. There is not a mother before me who has not, at times, a sinking of heart lest this evil may come nigh her dwelling. And who shall measure a mother's love or a mother's anxiety? It is the one pure, true thing on earth. It did not go down in Eden. It was the master-gift that came with motherhood; and when the mother has her child in her arms, and it reaches up its dimpled fingers to touch her cheek with its velvet touch of love, like the rod of Moses, it opens a fountain that will never cease to flow.

"My boy that stands by my side is mine to-day, and he will be mine forever. The children that went out to follow the Lamb whithersoever he goeth, and join the song of the redeemed like the sound of many waters, are mine, and will be mine forever. O, what anxiety and interest the mothers of this land feel lest their sons, so beloved, should be overcome by this evil! And there are mothers lingering to-day about the jails. Why, our jails are filled with the victims of this vile traffic.

"I was speaking in Wheeling not many months ago, and I understood before I commenced speaking that there were a good many liquor-dealers in the audience. I was so glad; it always helps me so much. After the meeting was over a gentleman came to me and said:—

"'Madam, if you go on and have success, you will break up my business.'

"I said, 'I hope I will, if you are a liquor-dealer.'

"'No, I am not a liquor-dealer, but I keep the jail, and that is about the same thing.'

"Our jails would be empty but for this traffic. Not long ago I was in a jail. I am not going to detain you

with a description of a jail; but if you want to feel more
interest in the temperance cause than ever you did, just
visit your police courts and your jails, and you will have
something to quicken your interest. I was in a jail in
Ohio. There were, perhaps, twenty men in the outer
court, and as many in the inner prison — little dark
places with narrow walls, where they were confined in
dungeons worse than Barnum keeps his wildest animals
in. As I went up to speak to them, I was obliged to
thrust my two fingers (I could not get the three fingers
through) between the iron bars. I wanted to shake
hands with them. I found, as I looked into those dark
cells, that they were all young men, and learned that
every one (except one) of them was there because of
crimes committed under the influence of liquor, and
some of them were very young. I pushed my fingers
through the iron bars, and pressed my face against them
to look in. I felt my two fingers clasped with a tight
grasp, and, looking closely, I saw a boy there not seventeen years old. As he held on to my finger-tip I said,
'You are very young to be here!' and his lip quivered.
He had such an innocent face my heart was moved. I
said, 'Have you got a mother?' He said—

"'No, ma'am; my mother died when I was a baby.'

"O! what a story of heart-hunger, neglect, and temptation that little sentence revealed to me. I said—

"'Have you got a father?' and he answered:—

"'Well, I might just as well have had no father; he
did not care for any thing but whisky. I don't know
where he is; I expect he is dead.'

"O, what a sad story! and yet it is repeated all over

this land.   I need not take you out of your own city for
instances of crime and cruelty.   Only last Sunday morning a drunkard's wife walked the streets of Jersey City
for more than two hours, unfit to appear in it, without
proper clothing, with two little children clinging to her
skirts, having no home, and without a friend in the wide
world.   Rum had robbed her of every thing, and left
her wandering a castaway in the streets; and she carried a dead baby in her arms only three weeks old.   And
these things are so common that we forget or lose the
sense of their horribleness.

"I ought to have said, by way of showing the amount
of courage a woman can have, that my very presence
here is the biggest argument that I ever heard of.   That
I should be speaking in the hearing of the eloquent man
who is to address you in a few minutes is a perfect wonder to me; for I have sat in the audience many times,
when he has been speaking, and thought he was the
prince of orators.

"I just want to say, in conclusion, that the Woman's
National Christian Temperance Union have organized in
all the Northern States of the Union except four, and
they are now arranging for that.   All this side of the
Missouri River we are organizing, more thoroughly than
any set of politicians ever organized, by States and congressional districts, down to little school districts.   We
are not in politics, we want you to understand; but we
are determined, whatever party goes up or goes down,
that the rum power shall go down.

We are not trusting in our own strength.   Some of us
have stood where the Revelator stood when he saw the

golden censer before the throne ; and the voice of prayer, from the Atlantic to the Pacific, is going up every day from the women of our Union. We are encouraged to believe that our prayers will be heard.

"We have wonderful encouragement in the work. Jesus has made it very plain. I only want to call attention to one of his beautiful lessons—about the unjust judge. It seems to me he went down just as low in the scale of human depravity as he could go to bring up that unjust judge ; because, if there is one man meaner than another, it is the man who undertakes to weigh out justice, and then takes bribes and deals unjustly. He was not only an unjust man, but he was an infidel and did not believe in God. He was not only an infidel, but he was a reckless fellow, who did not care for his fellow-men. He had sunk so low that he did not care what men thought of him. Well, to this man came a woman. She was poor; she had no money to give him ; she had not any friends to help her. She had no great, eloquent words or arguments on her lips when she came, but she said, 'Avenge me of mine enemy.' She cried after him and followed him ; and yet, although he cared not for God, neither regarded man, yet because this woman cried unto him and troubled him, he said he would avenge her. And will not God, our just God, avenge his own elect, who are crying unto him day and night ? Verily, he will. So we are lifting our cry ; and we remember that we have an Advocate with the Father that never lost a case."

MISS FRANCES E. WILLARD.

The following sketch of Miss Willard, who is so well and widely known as the late Secretary of the Woman's National Christian Temperance Union, and extracts from her addresses as reported in the " Boston Globe " will show something of the record, style and success of this accomplished and devoted woman, both on the temperance platform and in the pulpit.

" Much of the success which has attended the women's meetings which are held daily at the Berkeley-street Church is due to the modest and effective leadership of Miss Frances E. Willard. As Miss Willard is comparatively a stranger in Boston, all attainable particulars regarding her life and work will be of interest. She has for some years been a leader in the temperance work among the women of the West, and, judging from her success thus far in Boston, her influence for good will be as marked here as where her life-work hitherto has been wrought.

" Miss Frances E. Willard was born near Rochester, N. Y., and was graduated at the North-western Female College, near Chicago, in 1853. She is of New England parentage, and is descended from a race of teachers, being herself possessed of no common talent for the instruction of the young. Her Alma Mater commanded her services for some time, and in 1867 Miss Willard was chosen Preceptress of Genesee Wesleyan Seminary, at Lima, N. Y. This responsible position she held for four years. In 1861 she was called to the presidency of the College for Women, established in connection with the North-western University, near Chicago.

She was the first woman elected in this country to be the president of a college, and her work has demonstrated the fitness of the choice beyond all cavil. In 1869 Miss Willard, in company with her life-long friend, Miss Kate A. Jackson, of Paterson, N. J., made an extended foreign tour, being abroad nearly two years, and visiting Europe, Syria, and Egypt. Since 1874 Miss Willard has frequently spoken in public on educational and temperance topics, and always with success. Besides numerous contributions to the press, she published in 1864 a book called 'Nineteen Beautiful Years,' a tribute to a deceased sister, which was warmly commended. Of Miss Willard's earnest labor in connection' with the revival work of Messrs. Moody and Sankey it is unnecessary to speak. Its results speak for themselves, and the promise for a continuance of the divine blessing in the woman's meeting is very bright."

A BIBLE LESSON BY MISS WILLARD.

"Let us turn to the tenth chapter of Luke, and the twenty-fifth verse:

"'And, behold, a certain lawyer stood up, and tempted him, saying, Master, what shall I do to inherit eternal life? He said unto him, What is written in the law? how readest thou? And he answering said, Thou shalt love the Lord thy God with all thy heart, and with all thy soul, and with all thy strength, and with all thy mind; and thy neighbor as thyself. And he said unto him, Thou hast answered right: this do, and thou shalt live. But he, willing to justify himself, said unto Jesus, And who is my neighbor? And Jesus answering said, A certain *man* went down from Jerusalem to Jericho, and fell among thieves, which stripped him of his raiment, and wounded *him*, and departed, leaving *him* half dead; and by chance there came down a certain priest that way; and when he saw him, he passed by on the other side. And likewise a Levite, when he was at the place, came and looked *on him*, and passed by on the other side. But a certain Samaritan, as he journeyed, came where he was, and when he saw him, he had compassion *on him*. And went to *him*, and bound up his wounds, pouring in oil and wine, and set him on his own beast, and brought him to an inn, and took care of him. And on the morrow, when he departed, he took out two pence, and gave *them* to the host, and said unto him, Take care of him: and whatsoever thou spendest more, when I come again, I will repay thee. Which now of these three, thinkest thou, was neighbor unto him that fell among the thieves? And he said, He that showed mercy on him. Then said Jesus unto him, Go, and do thou likewise.'

"There is no commentary that gives at all the clearness of the glory and beauty of the law of God so well as does this parable; but I thought to-day, perhaps, to have a commentary of the actual experiences of something that has been done in these later times, analogous to what was done in that parable; something that has been done in these temperance meetings, and which has been such a help to many of us—I hope to all of us—would be as well. Not much has been said to young women of the beauty, or privilege perhaps I should say, which there is for them in this word. I have wished that from the lips of young women we might hear of the blessedness of carrying this temperance gospel to those who drink and to those who sell. The girls bore a grand part in that crusade work. The part they bore has not been much heralded; it was just the outgrowth of the sentiment of that time. In Cleveland I heard of three young ladies who went with three young gentlemen, and they were in the habit of taking wine. They went out into the country one day to spend one afternoon, something like a picnic, and when they were preparing for lunch, the gentlemen brought on wine, to place upon the table. But these ladies looked with new eyes and new feelings upon this wine now, and they said, 'We cannot sit down at a table where there is wine; wont you please put it away?' And they said, 'Certainly, we will put it away if you wish it, and we will not take any ourselves.' Thus, standing there true, they won their victory.

"I was in the Palmer House after one of our evening meetings, with a friend, and I saw there a party of half a dozen ladies and gentlemen, and I saw the waiter bringing wine, and one of the young girls blushed, and it required some courage to say as she did: 'Gentlemen, I am sure you will be willing that we should have something else not quite so strong.' Courtesy, gallantry, and kindliness forbade their refusing, and these girls, preaching there their sermon and standing firm, won their victory.

"In Delaware other things have happened which I might relate to you. A young lady, educated in a French conservatory of music and cultured to the

15

highest possible point of expression, went out upon the
street in this holy work, and her sweet voice found entrance where otherwise the doors would have been shut.
And her friends said to her, ' Don't do so much ; you
will use your voice all up. Just rest and wait awhile.'
But she said : ' My voice, and any thing that culture
can add, is none too good to lay upon the shrine of such
labor.'

"A Christian young lady in Cincinnati told me that
she never spent such delightful days in her life as
'going from rum-shop to rum-shop with grandmother.'
She was very wealthy and very cultured. And in one of
the rum-shops she met some of her tenants, and as
she asked them to sign over to Him, and to put their
names down upon this pledge in significance of their
surrender to God, one of them said : ' I think, Miss
Jessie, you have never signed the pledge.' He said this
in a sneering way. The man was infinitely below her in
what we call the social scale. She said, ' True ; I never
thought of that. Give me the pencil. We never have
wine at our table, and I never tasted it, but if it will help
you to sign, I will sign,' and her autograph went down
upon that dirty paper along with the names of those
rough men.

"In one place—the only place, I believe, where they
met with such opposition—a gruff man held a pistol in
his hand and pointed it at them. Some of them had not
sufficient moral courage, but this young lady quite knew
what to do. She went right up to his side, singing,
' Never be afraid to speak for Jesus.' And that band
of noble women went in and held a meeting in that

place, and that man bowed before God and gave his heart to Him.

"The key-note in all this work, in all these girls' hearts, was Jesus. I borrow the words from one of these dear sisters of Israel. When her aristocratic friends importuned her to go to fashionable dances and parties instead of going to these drinking saloons, she would answer: 'Anywhere that my dear and only brother, now ruined, can go to drink, there I will go to pray.'"

On another occasion Miss Willard spoke of the worldly and careless criticisms which are constantly being made of Christianity and its converts, and then said :—

"We wish that every body would get converted. It is the only true life—to be born of God. The world is not all converted yet, though Christianity is the simplest problem that man has to encounter. There is no government so grand and so incalculably satisfactory to the Lord God as the reign of temperance. Within the sacred influence of school and Church there nestle in this broad land of ours, protected and covered by the star-spangled banner, 250,000 rum-shops. To carry out the business of these groggeries requires 550,000 of America's citizens. The net revenue is $650,000,000. But that is not all. Seventy-five per cent. of all the murders in the country are committed through the influence of rum ; fifty per cent. of all the insanity in the country is the result of drinking ; eighty-six per cent. of all the criminals in the land become such while staggering under a load of liquor ; ninety-six per cent. of all the drunken youths leave a fond but agonized mother's arms to go to the black perdition of strong drink. Every year 100,000 of our best and brightest men reel into eternity and a drunkard's grave. Every year the statistics tell us of 500,000 steady drinkers and a million moderate drinkers, and, last of all, there are millions of handsome, intelligent lads going tramp, tramp, tramp to a drunkard's destiny. The bar-room is but the school of American politics. Each year 100,000 drunkards go staggering up to the ballot-box to deposit the vote which shall elect to the responsible government of this mighty republic the candidate whom their drunken intelligence taught them to be the proper person. What a sad reflection this is for us to-night!"

Miss Willard made a very eloquent appeal to her hearers to arouse themselves, and by their Christian endeavors free society and politics from this curse.

" What has each one of you done? Who has saved one human soul from the pit of the blackest darkness? You have taken from $50 to $500 per year from the liquor-dealers ; you have given to industry the strong arm and well-developed muscles of mature manhood ; you have replaced the key-stone in the broken arch of home ; you have given to the commonwealth a conscientious ballot, and you have given to Christ's Church another member. Dear brother, you can have those shackles that bind you broken off if you will. No matter what your sin, Christ can break the shackles. I tell you, young men, that drunkenness is the ripe fruit of moderate drinking. Give yourselves, then, on the side of total abstinence. If there are any here who do not feel the need of taking the step, I beseech them to do it, that they may set an example to their weaker brother. May you, one and all, know in your hearts the importance of total abstinence. I wish we could act as unitedly as our forefathers did. Men and women of New England, see the heritage your forefathers and foremothers have given you! How true it is that 'now is the accepted time!' There is a time for every purpose and every work in this world. The time has reached us. The time to work has come. How many in this assembly are pledged on the side of total abstinence? I ask those who are not, in the name of God, to place themselves there. Sometimes, they say, a woman's fingers can undo bars and bolts in the human heart which men cannot move. I think this is so, and if it. is, sisters, why can't we do all that our influence will enable us to overcome this terrible tide of horror? Many of you have heard the story of the confession a murderer made in his cell to a Christian minister. He said: 'If people had only come to me before, and told me these things when my heart was young, my life might have been spared.' At last his sullen, tigerish, cold and heardened heart was broken by a woman, who by some little kindness found the door to his heart and the flood-gate to his tears. God help us, one and all, in Christ's dear name to participate in this glorious work!"

Miss Willard's farewell address at the close of the Moody meetings in Boston is thus reported in the "Globe":—

"I remember that Abraham Lincoln, in that address of his which we have heard so often in other years, tells a story of the Orient.   Once there was a young monarch, and upon his ascension to the throne he called all his wise men to come before him, his sages and his learned ones.   And he said to them, ' I want you, between this sunset and the next, to bring me some form of expression into which you shall condense the sum of your knowledge ; and I want you to bring to me another sentence which shall be applicable to every form of human expression ; which shall always be true, when, where, how, or by whom uttered.'   And after he had said this he reminded them how swift and sure is the flash of the Damascus blade, and he made a gesture across the bowed necks of the sages, and they knew what was coming if they failed. They gathered together their old manuscripts and books, and they sat down in great distress and perturbation, but to study hard ; and by the time the morning had dawned, one of them, a young man, bright and keen, said, ' This is the sum of all knowledge—" perhaps." ' And they took this to the king, and he accepted this. But the hardest task was yet to come.   Not one of them could answer it the first hour, and they feared and trembled.   But one of the oldest of them, who had looked out upon human life, and who had learned its secrets and its sorrows, gave this sentence, and he found it, as you will find it, applicable to every possible circumstance : ' This, too, shall pass away.'   We know that that is true, be it of great things or of little things.   Now, let us turn to a very different book, and look into Daniel, the seventh chapter and the fourteenth verse :—

" ' And there was given him dominion, and glory, and a kingdom, that all people, nations and languages, should serve him : his dominion *is* an everlasting dominion, which shall not pass away, and his kingdom that which shall not be destroyed.'

" And now look at the thirteenth verse :—

" ' I saw in the night visions, and, behold, one like the Son of man came with the clouds of heaven, and came to the Ancient of days, and they brought him near before him.'

" How I have wished that he might come near to me ! And again, turn to Hebrews, twelfth chapter and the last verses :—

" ' Wherefore we, receiving a kingdom which cannot be moved, let us have grace, whereby we may serve God acceptably, with reverence and godly fear: for our God is a consuming fire.'

" That pronoun ' we ' seems to bring it right home to us.

" ' The kingdom of God is within you.'

" It is not some sweet persuading of the imagination ; it is that ' God was made manifest in the flesh.' Then there is something in Matthew xxiv, 35 :—

" ' Heaven and earth shall pass away, but my words shall not pass away.'

" This is reiterated in Mark xiii, 31.

" In the twenty-third chapter of Luke he impresses this upon us for the third time. No matter who stops, no matter who comes or goes away, these words ' shall not pass away.' May God put it into your hearts and minds to be studious of that which is able to save your souls from death. There are many other passages that it would be well for us to look at and talk about, in these last few days that are left us of this great reawakening. Christ is the end of it. In Romans x, 4 we read this :—

"'For Christ is the end of the law for righteousness to every one that believeth.'

"A great many people are saying that they are trying to act as well as they can; they are trying to do all they know that is right; but this is not what Christ says. He says he is 'the end of the law for righteousness to every one that believeth.' Do you believe on the Lord Jesus Christ as your Redeemer and Master? Some of us are thinking of the things that pass away; others of the things that will never pass away. O, may God help us to study those things that do not pass away!

"It is thirteen weeks since I began this work, and eleven weeks since I came to you a stranger. I want to say something to you of what it has been to me to be here with you. I know that I am speaking to my friends, to sisters in the dear name of Christ, to those whom I love for their works' sake, and who love me for my works' sake; and for that sweeter, but not holier or higher motive—I love you for your own sake. When Mr. Moody first spoke to me about coming to Boston, to see what I could do here, it was a great surprise to me. I had been in Brooklyn, organizing temperance unions; I had work there to do, and I did not know whether I ought to come. And when one whom I had honored and trusted, but had never seen but twice, said, 'Let us ask God about it,' if I have known an earthly inspiration of sympathy, it has been the prayer that he offered then. He asked God to show me whether I ought to go or not, and that if there was any word that I could speak that would benefit any one, it would be made known to me. When I went to my little cottage home I asked my mother, as I always do, and have done since my lips could form words, 'What do you think about it, and would you like to have it so?' My mother is seventy-three years of age, and I am her only daughter, but her first words were, 'My child, do as the Lord says.'

"And so, with my mother's blessing, and with that good man's prayer, and with my own belief, I came, and we have labored lovingly together, and I believe and hope that God's blessing has come down upon our work. Dear friends, Mr. Moody said something else to me then. He said, 'I cannot help thinking of the great magazine power there is in the hearts and consciences of the New England women. If they could only get hold of the word of God, what a power they would be?' There is no brain and heart so susceptible of God as the brain and heart that is full of God's word. This, then, is my farewell message, even the words of the blessed Master himself. Search the Scriptures; learn how tc trust them for your own safety. They are an ark in which to sail over the mountains of sin and sorrow on the floods of God's mercy as the ark of Noah sailed on the flood of his wrath. And then learn to use them to rescue the perishing; for, unlike that day of doom, this is the day of grace."

15*

CHAPTER XIV.

WOMAN'S CHRISTIAN TEMPERANCE UNION.—STATISTICS, REPORTS, ETC.

THE last report of the Chicago Woman's Christian Temperance Union, of which Mrs. T. B. Carse is the President, and Mrs. Louise S. Rounds is Secretary, contains the following spirited sketch of its organization :—

On the sixteenth of March, 1874, at six o'clock in the afternoon, a little company of about sixty women might have been seen passing slowly—two by two—down the broad stairs of the Clark-street Methodist Episcopal Church, and quietly turning their steps toward the Council Chamber of this great city. It was at an hour when Chicago's busy thousands crowd her streets, and amid the hurrying throng this little band passed unnoticed until they stood within the shadows of the corridors of the City Hall. The massive doors of the dim chamber where gather our City Fathers swung open to admit them, then closed again—and were bolted. Alone, in the gathering darkness of that March evening, sitting in silence with bowed heads—what brought those women to that strange and unfamiliar place? Some foolish fancy of the brain? mere idle curiosity? Nay!—they were a chosen band from out the hundreds who had gathered that day in God's holy temple to pray for the deliverance of our city from the rum power.

MRS. MARY C. JOHNSON.

MRS. MARY T. BURT.

They went from that sacred room, from the atmosphere of prayer and song, from the very presence of God, into the presence of those who claimed to be our city guardians, and, with respectful and deferential attitude, asked that the sanctity of our Sabbath might be preserved from desolation by that fiend—the liquor traffic. The sequel is known. Ridiculed by members of that Council, their petition rejected, they left that hall only to be met by one of the largest and most ruffianly mobs that ever disgraced our streets. During the hours those heroic women sat within that chamber the news of their presence there had spread like wildfire, and from out the saloons and dens of vice all over the city came the representatives of the liquor interests — a howling, blaspheming mob : and through this seething, reeking mass of humanity passed this little band of brave hearts—through jeers and insults—back to that " upper room," to spread before God the petition rejected by man !

Then came the deep and settled purpose of a conflict with rum ; and in that solemn hour, with hand clasped in hand and heart beating responsive to heart, the Chicago Woman's Temperance Union was born.

The following is the report of the current work and its results for one year, Sept., 1876, to Sept., 1877 :—

SUMMARY.

Condensed we present the following :—

1. Business meeting weekly at head-quarters, Room 3, Farwell Hall.

2. Consecration meeting daily, at head-quarters, Room 3. Farwell Hall.

3. Gospel Temperance Meeting daily (Sundays excepted,) in Lower Farwell Hall.

4. Bethel Home Gospel Temperance Meeting, weekly.

5. Burr Mission Gospel Temperance Meeting, weekly.

6. Portland Avenue and Twenty-fifth-street Gospel Temperance Meeting, weekly.

7. No. 97 South Desplaines-street, Gospel Temperance Meeting, weekly.

8. Open Air Gospel Temperance Meeting—now closed for the season.

9. Forty-seventh-street Gospel Temperance Meeting, semi-weekly.

Total—Thirteen public Gospel Temperance Meetings held every week during a large portion of the year under the auspices of the Union, and led by *known Christian workers.* Total signatures to the pledge for the year, about 1,800.

To Him who called us into the work, who has led us thus far, and to whom we look for direction and strength for the future, BE ALL THE GLORY.

MRS. LOUISE S. ROUNDS,
Cor. Sec. of Woman's Christian Temperance Union.

TEMPERANCE FRIENDLY INNS.

The work of the Woman's Christian Temperance Union includes, besides the usual methods, a class of cheap eating houses called Friendly Inns, managed on gospel as well as temperance principles. The above words placed conspicuously on a building have an attractive look to a poor fellow who has lost all his old friends through the degradation of drunkenness, and is impelled to look for

new ones among the temperance people. The old answer to the question, "Where can one always find
sympathy?" is "In the dictionary." To this must now
evidently be added—At a Temperance Friendly Inn.

The Central Place Friendly Inn, at Cleveland, will be
something of a curiosity to those who have never seen
the working of any other means of grace than those
which imply stained glass, steeples, broadcloth, velvet,
and feathers. Down in the midst of the roughest part
of the City of Cleveland is one of the good Samaritan
hotels, where, besides the things requisite and necessary
for the body, are provided some that are good for the soul.
It has a reading-room, in which there are sometimes to
be found as many as twenty-five men and boys, who thus
are using, instead of wasting, their time. But the chief
feature of the work here carried on is the religious services, in which a revival is constantly going on. During
the last year the lady in charge reports three hundred
and eighty-one meetings of various kinds, with an aggregate attendance of 28,302 persons. There is an adult
Bible class of over a hundred men and women, some of
whom cannot read, but may profit by hearing; others
have been well educated. Here is a German woman who
knows hardly a word of English, sitting next her friend,
who in a low voice translates for her what is said; there
is a deaf mute, who has his silent interpreter.

At the Inn there have been nearly three hundred persons seeking Christ, about one hundred of whom have
already believed unto life. These have been organized
into a Christian communion or Church, over which the accomplished and devoted Miss F. Janet Duty, is the pastor.

Of this lady, a Cleveland girl by birth and education, one of her co-workers says :—

" She is wholly a product of the West, though one would take her for the traditional ' Boston girl.' She is as smart as if she were not pretty, as good as if she were not smart, and as humble-minded as if she were neither of the three."

When the Crusades began in Cleveland, Miss Duty, then a teacher in the public-schools, was one of the leaders in that work, and when the movement crystallized into the Woman's Christian Temperance Union she forsook all, to follow its fortunes and help on its Christly mission. Her sermons, Bible-class work, and personal instruction, have gathered in these hundreds of lost sheep, and in their opinion, whatever others may think, she is the divinely ordered, if not ordained, successor of the apostles, to whom the care of this little flock has been committed.

Among the helpers whom she has found is a man who was for forty-five years a drunkard, and who had not been inside of a church for twenty years. He had served out several sentences in the workhouse, had kept a saloon on Canal-street, and was at one period drunk for nine months together, without one sober day in all that time. When he came to the Inn he was hatless, coatless, shoeless, and had the look of a maniac, but gave evidence of being in his right mind, for he wanted to sign the pledge. He was permitted to do so ; being at the same time pointed to Jesus Christ as the only Saviour of sinners, and the one who could not only save his soul, but his body, also, even to the extent of taking away his appetite for strong drink. The poor wretch believed, and was saved, converted, almost transfigured, indeed, from what he had been in his ruin; and now, though he cannot read, he is able, by means of his wonderful memory, to preach the word to his old associates; bringing out the promises which he has treasured up in his heart as well as in his head, and using them to save others as he himself was saved.

The "parish" about this Inn is thoroughly explored from time to time; over twelve hundred visits have been made to families and saloons, a part of the programme being a Scripture reading and usually a prayer. Thus the Gospel is preached "from house to house" in true apostolic fashion, and no wonder the results are glorious. There is evidently more actual salvation in progress down among those by-streets and alleys than among any region of equal population in the most aristocratic parts of the city.

So hopeful is the outlook that a church edifice is under way, the design of which is given herewith.

Of this churchly movement the pastor says:—

"Those who have been reformed at the Inn cherish a very warm attachment for it, and regard it as their spiritual home; hence it has seemed to us impracticable and unwise to take the majority of these persons into the Churches, while those who might be received are so identified with our work that they can be illy spared. For many reasons we have felt that God has led us to form a religious association, which should give to its members the privileges of baptism and the Lord's Supper; the former to be administered in the manner the

candidate might choose.   Those who are admitted to
this association must give good evidence of conversion,
sign the temperance pledge, and subscribe to simple articles of belief, so scriptural and undenominational that
they can be assented to by every one of the Christian
women engaged in this work, notwithstanding we represent in our Church membership five different denominations.

"We regard our company of believers as a part of
Christ's Church on earth, and believe we have fellowship
with all who are in Christ."

The sacraments are celebrated by the different pastors
of the city, and the internal affairs of this " Women's
Church" are administered by a committee of seven
women—shall we call them deaconesses? why not?

In this Women's Church there is a Sunday-school, with
an average attendance of 118.

The other two Friendly Inns of the city are also doing
good work, each under the direction of a committee of
ladies appointed by the Woman's Christian Temperance
Union.

Similar to these Friendly Inns are the Temperance
Coffee Houses, which have been established in some of
the larger cities   chief among which are the Model Coffee Houses of Philadelphia, established by the active,
enterprising, philanthropic Mr. J. W. Bailey, a Christian
merchant of the Quaker City, who already rejoices in
their large and growing usefulness and success.

The Fourth Annual Convention of the Woman's National Christian Temperance Union was held in Farwell

Hall, Chicago, commencing Oct. 25, 1877. The following from the address of welcome given by Miss Frances E. Willard, the Secretary of the National Society, as reported by the "Christian Cynosure," contains some of the boldest and most hopeful utterances on national as well as Christian temperance which that reform has ever called forth.

Our thanks are due to the "Christian Cynosure" for the report:—

Mrs. President and Delegates ; Beloved Co-workers, one and all :
In the name of the great North-west, of the peerless Prairie State, of wide-awake Chicago and its Woman's Temperance Union, so dear to me, I bid you welcome to our hearts, our homes, our Farwell Hall.

Many other conventions have assembled in this city to discuss questions relating to public weal. There have been great meetings · of missionary boards, general conferences, synods, associations, under different banners, civil and ecclesiastical. Most notable of all was the convention held in our famous old wigwam (now destroyed) which gave Lincoln to the Union, and, through Lincoln, freedom to the slave.

But this convention of ours has no status, military, political, ecclesiastic ; and I am glad that it has not. Forever in the progress of ideas and principles, truth pours itself into new molds and channels, and the old ones are left behind as empty, outward shells. Forever sounds the voice of Him who sitteth on the throne : " Behold, I make all things new." It is the genius of Christ's Gospel. Let no man tell us he has ascertained and measured its final evolution. So, when we speak about this Gospel temperance movement of the women— born from the Pentecost of the Crusade—we speak, perhaps unwittingly, yet none the less surely, about the germ of a regenerated home, built on the principle of total abstinence, and purity for two instead of one ; we speak about the germ of a new Church, in which, as Christ declared, there shall be neither male nor female, and in which the signing of the pledge shall be a prerequisite of membership.

We speak, too, about the germ of a new political party, based on the fact that what is physically wrong can never be morally right, and what is morally wrong can never be legally right.

We speak about a better Indian policy, wherein dwelleth righteousness, and from which fire-water is eliminated: about a wiser civil service reform, inaugurated even now by the President, given to America in answer to the crusaders' prayers—a man who is thumping the heads of political parties together until you can no longer tell one from the other, and clearing the deck of our old ship of State from dead issues, that the people may bring on their live ones.

For our parties are like a dog that has lost its bone. They have dwindled to a mere personal difficulty between the ins and outs, a scramble for the loaves and fishes. In Pennsylvania the resolutions of Democrats are the same as those of the Republicans in Indiana. The people can no longer tell the uniforms of the opposing camps apart. In vain the party leaders spur the steeds of a personal ambition along the lines, and try to marshal the rank and file by beating on the tomtom of hard money, waving aloft the poor old rag dollar as an ensign, and stoutly contending that "They'll fight till they die."

But there, between the lines, at last, firm, patient, and uncompromising, stands forth the living issue, the Temperance Reform, with all that it involves for woman in the State and in the home; and this issue will not down for all the noisy incantations of its foes.

That's "pure fanaticism," is it? So they said of the abolition speeches till the seceders fired on Sumter's flag, and then such utterances became pure patriotism. Who knows but a few more railroad riots may make even temperance popular?

You cannot know as we do, who have so earnestly desired your presence here, all that our welcome means. Shall I attempt to show you why we assure you with so much heartiness, not only that you are welcome, but also that you are *well come?* Then let me speak about our marvelous young city, enthroned between the prairies and the lake.

There are men in our streets to-day who are older than Chicago. Men who heard the cow-bell tinkle in the pasture now transformed into our Court-house Square. Others will tell you of all that stout hearts and strong arms have wrought upon this marshy flat between the pastoral bell of other days and the stroke of the Chamber of Commerce clock on that same Court-house Square to-day. Others will tell you of Chicago's rank as the greatest market on the round earth for beef and pork, for grain and fruit and lumber. Others will point you to its spacious harbor, and tell you that six millions represent the tonnage of the port; will tell you, too, of its twenty-five converging railroad lines, its thirty miles of wharf, of its innumerable warehouses, of its huge grain elevators, (the liveliest reminders our New England friends will find "out West" of "hills for which they sigh.") Others will speak of our surprising water-works, which pump up through the tunnel under the lake one million two hundred and fifty gallons of water per hour; by no means enough, however, to satisfy the city's thirst, as I shall show you later on. Others will tell you how ingeniously we have manipulated our abused Chicago river, turning its current out of Lake Michigan toward the Mississippi for purposes of better drainage, setting our bridges on a pivot for the convenience of our shipping, and boring tunnels under it for the accommodation of our teamsters and pedestrians.

You will see for yourselves our parks and boulevards, the palaces in which our travelers are lodged and our business transacted, the costly churches in which we worship, and the costly mansions in which our money kings are wont to eat and sleep. As you drive along our streets a vacant lot, a heap of shattered stones, a bit of charred wooden pavement here and there, will be shown to you as the only traces of the greatest fire of modern times—one that burned more than two thousand four hundred acres out of the city's heart, and destroyed $200,000,000 worth of property, turned one hundred thousand people out of doors, and happened but six years ago. Along many of the streets thus ravaged you will see rows of great trees transplanted at untold expense, as if our citizens would coerce nature into covering up the ghastly wounds which nature's most terrific element had made on the fair city of their pride.

But in my endeavor to explain why it is well that you have come, I would not speak to you about the outward seeming, but the inward reality; not of Chicago's body, Antæus-like in strength and vigor, and dauntless as a young Apollo, but of Chicago's soul—nay of 400,000 souls; not of the fire before whose awful breath our blocks of granite and of marble crumbled like children's toys, but of the lurid flames that burn right on through the years, consuming the tissues of our noblest brain, shriveling the fibers of our kindest hearts— that burn right on, enkindled by our lawmakers, fed from our homes, protected by a public sentiment strong as gravitation and relentless as fate.

We have three thousand saloons whence this fire is constantly replenished, and twenty-three powder magazines, called distilleries and breweries. They are all burning brightly while I speak. Upon the Sabbath day their flame is of peculiar brilliancy and largely increased volume, for their worm dieth not and their fire is not quenched. Each person who goes within the fascinating circle of these perpetual bonfires (and every seventh man does this, besides women and children) begins to burn, and in course of time becomes a walking torch. Upon thousands of cheeks is set the brand of the drink demon, and every-where you will be sickened by breaths that a lighted match would set on fire. Looking into these faces, where flickers the flame that burns with horrid impartiality bodies and souls, you will not need that I should tell you how frightful are the ravages of Chicago's great and unquenchable fire! Alas for the living faces behind which are dead souls, on these Chicago streets! for

> "When faith is lost, when honor dies,
> The man is dead."

Nearly all the large cities of Europe and America have passed before my eyes in the motley panorama of the traveler, but in none on this side of the sea, and in very few beyond it, have I seen more faces on the street of which I felt afraid. Let me give you a few figures, quite unlike those usually set before company in our self-confident young city. They are mainly statistics of the great fire of which I am now speaking. There were 27,292 arrests in our city last year, 847 assaults, and each week a murder or a suicide. Justice Scully is authority for the statement that seven eighths of these grew out of strong drink. "Do away with whisky" (these are his words) "and our prisons would be closed." One person in every fourteen of our inhabitants was arrested last year; and one in every seven and a half was an applicant for public charity.

But in Illinois our drink bill was forty-two millions of dollars. Chicago has six millions invested in the liquor traffic, while the sum of its annual bill for drink would give a homestead, worth five thousand dollars, to each family of four, assuming that all the people of our city were set in families.

Do not grow weary; most of you are strangers to our city, and I am but acting as a guide to show you the landmarks, progress, and results of our great fire, now at the height of its fury. Here let me say, the daily papers are excellent guide-books to the "burnt district," if you wish to follow up this branch of sight-seeing. Note their records concerning the wild escapades of the scores of mad men daily turned loose from the saloons on our defenseless population. Read of the random knife-stroke, the promiscuous bullet, the incendiary's torch, the slaughter of the innocents, the beating of wives, the outrage of defenseless virtue.

Since that other fire, which we at last succeeded in putting out, our city fathers have made a law that within the fire limits no wooden buildings shall henceforth be erected. They have coolly interfered with a man's ancient, inalienable right to build himself such a home as he pleases. It is a regular iron-clad "sumptuary law," of course, but nobody complains; for bitter experience has taught us that it's a law framed for the greatest number's greatest good. Civilization makes its laws, as a general rule, upon this basis, leaving Piute Indians, South Sea cannibals, and politicians to act upon their favorite principle, "Every man for himself, and his Satanic Majesty may take the hindmost."

Sisters, beloved, do you recall the story of the relief of Lucknow? Do you remember poor Jessie, who, with ear preternaturally sharpened by pain, distinguished in the distance the faint, familiar notes of an old Scottish song dear to her heart in childhood? "Dinna, ye hear the pibroch?" she said to those around her as she leaned forward with face inspired. But they could not make it out. "Dinna ye hear the slogan?" again exclaimed the girl, faint with hunger and yet radiant with hope. Bending forward the devoted band now caught the sweet notes of the old Scotch song,

> " The Campbells are coming,
> Hurrah, hurrah ! "

We draw a vail over that scene. No words may measure its pathos or its joy. Dear friends, let us take courage. Hungry for the bread of life many a sad and sinful heart to-day listens for the music to which our marching army of relief keeps time, and murmurs with unutterable joy, "The Christians are coming, thank God, thank God!"

To this address of welcome appropriate response was made by the Assistant Secretary, Mrs. May F. Burt, of Brooklyn. The secretary's annual report gave the following statistics by States :—

"Number of Unions in Maine, 9; (many others not auxiliary as yet; Juvenile Unions, 35; Reform Clubs, 250. New Hampshire, Unions, 8; Reform Clubs, 125. Vermont, Unions, 14; Juvenile, 8; Reform Clubs, 50. Massachusetts, Unions, 122; Juvenile, 22; Reform Clubs, 60. Connecticut, Unions, 23; Reform Clubs, 8. Rhode Island, Unions, 4; 23,000 pledges taken. New York,

Unions, 34; Juvenile, 150; Reform Clubs, 18; Friendly
Inns, 2. New Jersey, Unions, 43; Juvenile, 13; Reform
Clubs, 12. Pennsylvania, Unions, 17; Juvenile, 16.
Tennessee, Unions, 2. Maryland, Unions, 6. Ohio,
Unions, 130; Juvenile, 50. Friendly Inns, 5. Indiana,
Unions, 150. Iowa, Unions, 75; Juvenile, 30; Friendly
Inns, 1. Minnesota, Unions, 11; 17,000 pledged chil-
dren. Nebraska, Unions, 10. Wisconsin, Unions, 15.
Whole number of Unions in the United States, 820;
Juvenile Unions, 383."

The following interesting comparative statistics were
also presented :—

"Indiana has the largest number of auxiliary Unions.
Maine has raised $15,000, and expended it in temperance
work. New Hampshire is temperance 'all the way
through,' one fifth of the entire population, or one third
of her voters, being pledged to total abstinence. Pennsylvania rejoices in fifty-two yards of petition. Minnesota has an army of temperance juveniles 17,000 strong.
Ohio has the most Friendly Inns, and a flourishing
Woman's Church. Maine has the largest number of
Reform Clubs—250—with a membership of 90,000; (Dr.
Reynolds hails from there.) New Hampshire offers sixty-three free reading rooms. The little District of Columbia has circulated 300 petitions during the past year.
New York has 150 juvenile Unions, the largest number
auxiliary to the Woman's Christian Temperance Union
of any State. New Jersey has doubled the number of
her Unions each year of their existence within her borders. If she keeps on at that rate, every daughter of
the soil will be 'taken in' within twelve or fifteen years.

Iowa has yielded the largest yearly increase, 26 new Unions and 900 new members having been added during 1877."

One remarkable feature of this convention was the report of the committee on Sunday services in the churches, after the manner of a Methodist Conference, a Presbyterian Synod, or a Congregationalist Association; no less than nineteen Churches having applied for the ministry of these Christian temperance women.

Miss Lucia F. Kimball reported that a great victory had been achieved by the women of Boston lately. When Mrs. Livermore and other ladies asked that no liquors should be furnished by the city for the presidential banquet, the mayor refused. A week ago last Monday night the council of that city passed a resolution deciding that henceforth neither wine, liquor, nor cigars shall be purchased for any banquet given by the city.

The officers elected for the current year were, President, Mrs. Annie Wittenmyer, of Philadelphia; Corresponding Secretary, Mrs. Mary T. Burt, of Brooklyn; Recording Secretary, Mrs. Mary C. Johnson, of Brooklyn; Treasurer, Mrs. S. K. Leavitt, of Cincinnati.

The "Chicago Post" contained the following pleasant personal sketches of "notable women" in attendance at this Temperance Convention, evidently from the pen of a lady familiar with the whole *personnel* of the movement. The sketches of Mrs. Wittenmyer, Miss Willard, Mrs. Johnson, Mrs. Geddes, and Mrs. Lathrop are omitted, since their portraits, both by pen and pencil, appear elsewhere in this volume.

Mrs. Mary T. Burt, of Brooklyn, last year Assistant Recording Secretary, now Corresponding Secretary, formerly a Western woman, of attractive face and dignified manners, is likewise a lady whose home and social circle have been among the highest.   An Episcopalian by Church membership, she never did public work until the days of the temperance Crusade.   She first lectured on temperance in her own city, Auburn, N. Y., and was immediately elected President of the Union.   Since that time she has been untiring in her duties as publisher of " Our Union," giving to it her strength, time and devotion.   She will fill her new position with honor and ability to the National Union, and speak effectively for the cause.

Mrs. Sarah K. Bolton, of New York, Assistant Corresponding Secretary, formerly of Cleveland, O., is a New England woman by birth and education.   Has given her time to literary pursuits and study, aside from active labors in Church work, evangelistic and temperance work. When quite young a book of her poems was published by the Appletons ; later, a temperance story, entitled " The Present Problem."   She has written regularly for the *Advance* for some years, besides many religious and secular papers, East and West.   She was actively engaged in the crusade work of Cleveland, and the first woman to lead a band in Northern Ohio at Berea, after the good news spread from Hillsborough.   Mrs. Bolton has a happy home and family.   She was nominated for Corresponding Secretary at the late convention, but declined on account of going on a proposed visit abroad.

Mrs. J. Ellen Foster, of Iowa, is an able and accomplished Christian lawyer. Was a New England girl, daughter of a minister who became almost ostracised for abolition principles. She married a lawyer, read Blackstone with her baby in her arms, and was induced to take up the profession of law, at her husband's earnest solicitation. She believes she was called of God into this work, especially to help her own sex who need redress in their sufferings through the liquor traffic. She has practiced in every court, even before the Supreme, a thing not done by any other woman. At first she was greatly opposed to public speaking by women. She has a very happy home, several children; is a most lovely and sympathetic woman as well as an eloquent speaker. She is very popular among the men and women of her own State. She is Corresponding Secretary of the Woman's International Temperance Union.

Mrs. Elizabeth K. Churchill, of Rhode Island, is a lyceum lecturer, and well known as a journalist through the Providence " Journal," to which she is an editorial contributor, the " New Century," the paper published last year by the Woman's Centennial Commission in Philadelphia, and the " Woman's Journal." She is Vice-President of the Rhode Island Association for the Advancement of Women, and the Social Science organization of women, which held its annual congress three years ago, in Chicago, and lately in Cleveland. She is a clear thinker and an able speaker. She is identified with all reforms especially designed to help women, and with many of general interest.

Miss Margaret E. Winslow, of Brooklyn, editor of " Our Union," the organ of the Woman's National
16

Christian Temperance Union, was for some years teacher in Packer Institute, Brooklyn. She has written for the "New York Tribune," "Observer," "Evangelist," "Witness," Hartford "Churchman," "Christian at Work," and has published two temperance books, "Barford Mills" and "A More Excellent Way," as well as many beautiful poems, which have found their way into the leading papers of the country.

Miss Julia Colman, now of New York, Chairman of the Committee for the Dissemination of Temperance Literature, has done valuable service in the temperance cause in the Juvenile Department of "Our Union," her "Catechism on Alcohol," her scientific articles on temperance, her "Leaflets" scattered all through the country, and her "Young People's Comrade," a temperance paper especially attractive to young people. She was for a long time in the editorial department of the "Sunday-School Advocate;" is a Western woman, and sister of Rev. H. Colman, one of the leading Methodist clergymen of Wisconsin, now located in Milwaukee.

Miss F. Jennie Duty, of Cleveland, Ohio, *petite* in form and pretty in face, is, perhaps, the youngest of any of the active workers in the Union. She is finely educated, of good family, and was preceptress for two years of the Ohio Female College at Cincinnati, and Principal of Wheeling Female College, an earnest worker in jails, prisons, and among the destitute, before the Crusade. When *that* came she gave up her lucrative position as teacher, devoting her time wholly to the reformation of men and women. No person was braver in visiting drinking saloons, or was more courteously received.

For the past three years she has given her time entirely to the Gospel temperance work of the Friendly Inns. Large numbers have attended her excellent Bible-readings, Sunday services, Sabbath-schools at the inns, and meetings for mothers. A revival of religion has crowned her efforts, and two hundred or more have been converted through her instrumentality, and formed themselves into a "Temperance Union Church," a committee of seven women constituting the officers, and the ministers of the city administering the sacraments. She is their honored and beloved pastor in all save name.

Mrs. L. H. Washington, of Iowa, is the wife of a minister, and has four children. She has for years been a contributor to the press, is a highly educated woman, an earnest Christian, and an able lecturer. Not suffering from intemperance in any members of her own family, her warm heart found a field for untiring labor among her less fortunate sisters, who had borne their sorrows in silence. She led the work earnestly in the Crusade, and is a brave, cheerful, and true-hearted woman.

The Vice-Presidents of the National Union here present are as follows:—

Mrs. S. J. Steele, of Appleton, Wis., is the wife of a minister who has been President of Lawrence University, Appleton, Wis., for twelve years. She is a woman of superior education, *physique*, and address, and has had supervision of woman's foreign missionary work in her State for years; was president of State temperance work for four years, superintendent of a large Sunday-school in her own Church for several years, and has had the advantages of foreign travel. Mrs. Steele has ten in her well-ordered family, and one of the happiest of homes.

Mrs. M. A. Stone, of Connecticut, is an unassuming, motherly women, and has been a leading educator. Has had a family of her own, besides caring for four other children for eleven years. She has conducted a large and flourishing boarding-school for young ladies for thirty-nine years, and has been an officer in the National Educational Society longer than any other woman, and was president of the meeting held last year at Baltimore; was president for twelve years of the Ladies' Department of the Connecticut Agricultural Society. Mrs. Stone was one of the National Teachers' party appointed to visit the schools and colleges of Europe, and was with them entertained by royalty itself. She has been an active worker in the cause of missions, and loves temperance as one of the agencies for bettering humanity.

Mrs. Allen Butler, of Syracuse, New York, is a middle-aged lady of most gentle and agreeable manners, whose means have enabled her to give her time heartily to all good works. She is President of the Presbyterian Woman's Society of her city, of the Old Ladies' Home Association, of the Foreign Missionary Society, State President of the Temperance Work in her State, and Chairman of the Juvenile Work for the National Union. She has had a large infant class in Sunday-school for twenty years, is thoroughly domestic, while at the same time, with the hearty co-operation of her husband, she gives her time to public work.

Mrs. J. M. Haven, of Vermont, is an educated, wealthy woman, and gives generously. She is a Congregationalist, President of the Auxiliary Board of Missions, and president for her State in the temperance work. She is a faithful and capable worker, and a woman of great social influence.

Mrs. R. T. Brown, of Indiana, is a noble Christian woman. Her husband is Professor of the Indianapolis Medical College, was also Professor of Literature in the North-western University, chief chemist in the Department of Agriculture at Washington, and author of a valuable Physiology, which brings in the temperance question, and has been gladly adopted by the public schools of Indiana. Mrs. Brown has two sons who are ministers, and one a teacher. She has done good work in her Church, in foreign missions, and in temperance. In her capacity as State president she has carefully organized the State for active work.

Mrs. M. R. Denman, of New Jersey, a lady past middle life, is a most devoted Christian worker. She has always been actively engaged in Church work, and is President of a Home for the Friendless. She and Mrs. Wittenmyer have been laboring through the Southern States for the temperance cause. She was the first to begin the work in New Jersey, and, with Mother Hill, she has had but one ambition—to win souls.

Mrs. Stevens, of Iowa, is an elderly lady, wife of a clergyman, a devoted Christian, yet full of the humor that makes a public speaker attractive. No good work languishes where she is.

Mrs. A. P. Kelley, of Chicago, is a lady of fine manners and excellent executive ability, whose elegant home, full of evidences of the culture of foreign travel, was freely offered to all the delegates to the National Convention. Her hospitality will give her a warm place in the hearts of temperance workers all over the country. Her wealth, time, and heart have been given heartily to the temperance cause.

Mrs. Julia M. Church, of Washington, is a white-haired though not elderly lady, of great refinement and gentleness, but of persistent purpose in all right doing. Her excellent common sense, and the general respect accorded her, have made her able to do in Washington a good work that few others could have accomplished.

Mrs. Myra J. Hackett, of Minnesota, formerly a New England woman, a modest, cultivated lady, always interested in Sunday-school work, has been enabled to do more for the children in temperance work in her State than, perhaps, any other woman. She wrote to earnest women in all the counties, and they to the towns. She has three hundred women working on her plan in the Sunday-school. They visit the superintendent and obtain, if possible, on one Sunday of each three months, fifteen minutes' temperance talk, get the children to sign a pledge, and take books and papers. By this plan she has bought and distributed over one thousand copies of the "Youth's Temperance Banner," and given fifteen thousand certificates to as many pledged children.

"In the grand army of women that was marshaled by the drum-beat of the Crusades, there are at least two hundred scattered over the twenty-three organized States, who are entitled to the rank of regimental leaders. Among these may be named such notable temperance workers as Mrs. Prentiss, Crossman, Stevens, and Miss Crosby, of Maine; Mrs. Sturdevant, of Vermont; Mrs. Scott and Miss M'Intire, of New Hampshire; Mrs. Gifford, Amsden, and Talbot, of Mass.; Mrs. Buell and Moody, of Conn.; Mrs. Barney and Holmes, of R. I.; Mrs. Martindale and Miss Coates, of Delaware; Mrs. Crook and M'Leod, of Maryland; Mrs. Church and Mrs. Linville, of Washington, D. C.; Mrs. Butler, Kenyon, Hartt, Decker, and M'Clees, of New York; 'Mother Hill,' Mrs. Clark, Nobles, Crane, Haines, and Miss Barker, of New Jersey; Mrs. Chase, French, and Misses Davis, Jennings, and Remington, of Pa.; Mrs. Carpenter, Leiter, Sumner, Pugh, and Woodbridge, of Ohio; Mrs. Wait, Carse, Henry, Manny, and Villars, of Illinois; Mrs. Brown, Denny, Jarrett, and Vining, of Indiana; Mrs. Comstock, Hudson, Boise, and Smith, of Michigan; Mrs. Stevens, Wheeler, Washington, Aldrich, and Moore, of Iowa; Mrs. Cooly and Pinkham, of Wisconsin; Mrs. Hackett, of Minnesota; Mrs. Hardy, of Nebraska.

"Of women conspicuous in temperance literature are Mrs. Mary A. Livermore, Mrs. L. D. Barrett, Mrs. Sarah K. Bolton, and Miss Winslow; Miss Julia Colman, the medical writer, whose tracts are high authority in her department; Mrs. Hackett, Mrs. Beale, Miss Kimball, and Mrs. Griffith, the Juvenile Work Quartette; Mrs. Elizabeth Comstock, Mrs. Robinson, and Elizabeth Greenwood, pulpit speakers; Miss M'Cartney, the young lady whose mission is to 'Our Girls;' Elizabeth K. Churchhill, whose specialty is 'Strong Foundations, described in her lecture of that name, on the influence of ancestral habits, food, early training and home surroundings on the development of the appetite for intoxicating drink. Some sections of the army workers, a few of whose leaders we have named, move forward only on the line of prayer, Bible exposition, and the temperance pledge; others combine with these the supplementary work of petitioning municipal authorities and legislatures, circulating temperance literature, and opening reading-rooms, Friendly Inns, and such like."

The above roll of honor, by no means complete—to present such a one would fill a volume—has been furnished the editor by the kindness of one of the ladies, whose name if given would be every-where recognized as high authority on the *personnel* of the woman's temperance work.

These sketches and reports are presented simply as some of the best specimens of the workers and their work, and not by any means as the complete record thereof.

If the Crusaaes were a sudden flash of heavenly illumination, the work of the Woman's Christian Temperance Union is like the steady and perpetual glow of the altar flame; and may we not say with reverence, in many cases it has been to lost wayfarers in the wilderness of sin like the shining of the pillar of fire to lead them to sobriety and salvation?

Whatever may be said of the peculiarities of other methods of temperance work, surely sensible men and godly women need have for the simple gospel methods of this society only words of encouragement and praise.

DR. HENRY A. REYNOLDS.

SECTION VI.

DR. REYNOLDS AND THE RED RIBBON REFORM CLUBS.

16*

CHAPTER XV.

DR. REYNOLDS AND THE RED RIBBON REFORM CLUBS.

"DARE to do right." The movement of which this stirring phrase is the motto and watch-word is among the latest and most important in the history of temperance reforms, and may be defined as a rebellion among the subjects of King Alcohol against his tyrannical government. Like the Washingtonian movement, which began in a drinking club in a Baltimore hotel, the Reform Clubs had their origin in the awakening and conviction of certain victims of strong drink to a sense of their danger and sin.

Unlike the early total abstinence meetings, from which religious exercises were carefully excluded, lest somehow temperance and religion should get mixed, this movement avows its dependence upon God, and finds its greatest stronghold in prayer. In this it is kindred to the Woman's Crusade, of which it is, in some sense, the outgrowth. It teaches men who are too weak to reform themselves to ask of God the strength which they require, not only to save them, but to keep them.

In January, 1872, Mr. J. K. Osgood, of Gardiner, Maine, himself a reformed man, who from a high position in society had in fifteen years reduced himself to the lowest grade of drunkenness, inaugurated a reform movement among drinking men of his own town.

In August, of the previous year, he had found himself

out of business, without friends, and absolutely without money.   Returning home late one night he saw his wife through the window, waiting for him, and her sorrowful condition touched his heart, and caused him such grief that then and there he resolved, God being his helper, he would never drink again.   That resolution, by the grace of God, he was enabled to keep, and a few months later he commenced to work as a temperance reformer. Having been reinforced by the reformation of an old chum, a lawyer, who had been as much demoralized by liquor as himself, Mr. Osgood drew up a call for a meeting, which both the friends signed, and which read as follows :—

" REFORMERS' MEETING.—There will be a meeting of reformed drinkers at City Hall, Gardiner, Friday evening, January 19th, at seven o'clock.

" A cordial invitation is extended to all occasional drinkers, constant drinkers, hard drinkers, and young men who are tempted to drink, to come and hear what rum has done for us."

The meeting was a great success; the two reformed men speaking with all the power and eloquence of suffering and deliverance, and producing the deepest impression upon the crowds which flocked to hear them.

As a result of these meetings the "Gardiner Temperance Reform Club" was organized, which very soon numbered one hundred men, every one of whom had been to a greater or less extent addicted to the use of strong drink.

The movement spread like wild-fire, and in a few

months clubs had multiplied until their membership was numbered by thousands.

From Maine Mr. Osgood proceeded to Massachusetts, where he labored under the auspices of the Massachusetts Temperance Alliance, in which State about forty clubs were organized.

The Constitution and By-laws adopted by the Reform Clubs provides that " All male persons of the age of eighteen years who have been in the habit of using intoxicating liquor to a greater or less extent are eligible to membership, and if any objection is offered against the reception of a brother, the affirmative vote of two thirds of all the members present shall be necessary to elect such candidate."

The club exercises a watch-care over its members, as will be seen by Article twenty :—

" It shall be the duty of the president, upon receiving reliable information that any member has broken his pledge, to report the same to the Executive Committee, who shall investigate the case, and report the same to the club at the next meeting."

Article twenty-six provides :—

" That any member of the club in good standing who shall wish to withdraw from the club shall, upon a vote in the affirmative, be entitled to an honorable discharge."

The Reform Clubs differ in their mode of organization ; some of them admitting women to their business meetings, and discussing political and religious topics, as relating indirectly to temperance, others restricting the active membership to men, and ruling out all questions except those of a strictly temperance character.

As the Washingtonian movement has for its chief personal distinction the name of John B. Gough, so the Reform Club movement has its leading figure in the person of Dr. Henry A. Reynolds.

This scholarly Christian gentleman—who is also a reformed drunkard—whose name is a word of blessing in half a dozen States of this Union—was born in the city of Bangor, Maine, November 9, 1839.

He enjoyed the advantages of wealth, and, having a taste for the medical profession, was sent to the Medical College of Harvard University, from which he graduated in 1863.

The use of wines and liquors was a matter of course in the circles in which he moved, and, as is so often the case with young men of genius and spirit when left to the influences of fashionable life, he fell into habits of dissipation, from which he was not rescued till he had sounded the awful depths of drunkenness and despair.

After his graduation he entered the army, as assistant surgeon in the First Maine Regiment of Heavy Artillery, served during the two last years of the War of the Rebellion, and at its close was honorably discharged, and returned to practice his profession in his native city. His skill as a medical man would have made his fame and fortune had it not been for his slavery to drink. One of the leading physicians of Bangor says: " Dr. Reynolds's practice, if attended to, would have been worth at least five thousand dollars a year." He was, for a time, city physician ; but his downward course was rapid, and, in spite of all the pride of his noble nature, the claims of friends and family, the allurements of professional, ambition, and the voice of an educated conscience, Dr. Reynolds sank lower and lower, till he became the slave of his appetite and a blasphemer of God. Of his former habits the doctor says:—

"I am one of the unfortunate men who inherited an appetite for strong drink. I love liquor as well as a baby loves milk. When I was but a child of less than eight years of age I began to strengthen that appetite first by drinking cider. Cider I call the devil's kindling-wood. Next I used to drink native wines, then ale and lager bier, and the stronger drinks. I drank at parties, weddings, dances, etc.; I had liquors on my table while keeping house, and treated all friends who called on me in my office or at home, for this I thought necessary to their proper entertainment. I have really been a drinking man, to a greater or less extent, for twenty years, the last six of these years to a greater rather than a less extent. I was a periodical drinker from necessity, as I could not drink all the time; but a periodical drunk with me usually lasted six weeks. I have had the *delirium tremens*, and suffered the torments of the lost; but, for all that, I brought myself to the verge of the same suffering a hundred times afterward, knowing that I could not, in all probability, live through another attack. I was a slave to my appetite, and actually did not know how to rid myself of it.

"I am compelled to give the same painful testimony that so many do, that no one asked me to turn over a new leaf, or said an encouraging word to me in the way of urging me to try and live a sober life. Had some kind friend shown me the way out of it, and whispered in my ear that I could be a better man, I might have been so. I attribute my salvation from a drunkard's grave to the Woman's Temperance Crusade; or, rather, I consider myself as a brand plucked from the burning through the prayers of the Christian women of America."

The following account of his reformation is from one of his own public addresses before the National Temperance Convention :—

"I claim to be one of God's feeblest instrumentalities, raised up by his grace, and trying to do something for him and for those who have suffered as I have suffered through rum. It has cost me three thousand dollars for what I know about drinking intoxicants, and I consider my life previous to two years ago ten thousand times worse than thrown away. I have walked my father's house night after night for seven nights and days, a raving, crazy madman, as the result of intoxicating beverages.

"At the time that I was suffering, and on the verge of *delirium tremens*, I resolved to do something I had never done before, in order to rid myself of this infernal curse. I had 'drunk my last drink;' I had broken my bottle; I had sworn off 'before a justice of the peace;' I had tried to 'taper off;' I had done every thing men ordinarily do to rid themselves of the habit of drinking—all to no purpose. My resolutions all went for nothing. Again I was on the verge of the *tremens*, where I could look over and see the serpents and devils, and hear them hiss and howl at me; and it was evident I must do something different from what I had done before, if I was ever to be rid of this infernal appetite. I knew but

very little about the Bible—drinking men don't read the
Bible much—but I knew God had promised to assist
those who ask in faith believing, and I threw myself
on my knees in my office, and asked of my God to
save me, and promised him that if he would save
me from such sufferings as I had once been through,
with his assistance I would be true to myself and to
him, and do what I could for the salvation of others.

" At that time a little band of noble women who had
caught the inspiration from the West were praying in
my native city in a public place.   Some of these women
had been educated in Churches where they did not believe in women's praying or talking in public.   Some of
them had suffered very much, as the result of having
drunken husbands and sons.   They had received no assistance from the pulpit, the law, or the press, and were
compelled to do something different from what they had
ever done before.   So they threw themselves on their
knees at the foot of the cross, and asked God to give
them relief from their suffering; and I stand here to-
night, believing myself to be a monument of God's grace,
saved through the prayers of the noble women of America.   I feel myself to be a beacon light, erected on the
breakers upon which I have been shipwrecked, to warn
off others from those breakers and shoals.   Since I
signed the pledge I have become a happy man.   I used
to be an unhappy man.   I did not want to live.   I
dragged out a miserable existence, and I would have cut
my throat or blown out my brains, but I did not dare to.
Now I am one of the happiest men in the world.   Instead of going about the streets cursing and swearing, I

am going from Dan to Beersheba doing what I can to make other people happy, singing, 'Nearer, my God, to thee,' 'Rock of Ages,' 'All hail the power of Jesus' name!' and looking upon the world as my country, and all mankind as my countrymen."

That temperance meeting held by the crusaders, at which Dr. Reynolds signed the temperance pledge, was a memorable one. To it he went, being the wonder of the whole assembly, and at length pressed his way through the crowd to the front, and affixed his name to the pledge. The ladies were shocked at what they regarded as an act of impiety; for they presumed, from their knowledge of the man, that he was signing the pledge in diversion. They were not long, however, in finding out their mistake, for the doctor not only kept his pledge, but became active in inducing other persons to reform. He began to talk to his acquaintances, make little speeches in the meetings, and in this work he was so acceptable that he soon began to receive invitations to speak in the neighboring towns.

On another occasion he said, concerning his almost miraculous deliverance from another snare of the devil :—

"I was also a slave to tobacco, and used it for months after I left off drinking. But it occurred to me that it was not consistent for a man who was looked on as a leader in such a cause to smoke and chew tobacco, and that my influence was not as great over those I wished to persuade from drinking as it would be if I were more nearly a clean man. 'Cleanliness is next to godliness.' So I concluded to leave it off at whatever sacrifice, for the sake of being able to do more for the dear fellows whom I was trying to rescue. But I deferred it from time to time, for *I did love it*. I would leave the table hungry to get my pipe. I used to get up in the night and smoke. I took a cigar before breakfast; in fact, I smoked about seventeen hours out of the twenty-four.

"Well, besides this I wanted to be a Christian, and was trying, as best I knew how, to be one; but did not become clear until I went to the National Temperance Camp-Meeting, at Old Orchard Beach, in August, 1875. Mrs. Helen A. Brown, President of the Woman's Temperance Union of New York, asked me that day to leave off, and to ask God to take the appetite away from me."

"Don't you remember," he writes to a friend, "that we all kneeled down—two ministers, four temperance women, Frank Murphy, and I—and you all prayed for me, and I asked God to take away the appetite for tobacco, that I might become a stronger workman in his service? *And he did it instantly, then and there;* since which time I have never known what it was to *want* tobacco; nor have I missed it any more than if I had never used it.

"More than that, I, at that time, passed out into the 'peace which passeth all understanding.' And I have remained there, only getting happier and happier all the time, until now I am the happiest man in the world. God has wonderfully blessed me in every way since then, and what has been accomplished has been done by him, through one of his most insignificant instruments."

Concerning his method of work, the doctor says: " I

organize Reform Clubs made up wholly of men who
have been moderate drinkers; for I believe there is a
sympathy existing between two men who have been
drinkers that cannot exist between one who has and
one who has not been a drinking man; and much of the
success of the movement is, doubtless, to be attributed
to the recognition of this principle. I begin and talk to
the audiences made up of all kinds of people, get signers
to the general pledge, and at the close of a series of
meetings I get together what of the above-named material I can, and organize a club. These men really become self-constituted missionaries and go to work, which
helps to save themselves as well as others."

Dr. Reynolds insists on the religion of Christ as the
only salvation of the inebriate. His own experience has
taught him that the "will power" of which so much has
been said is not a safe reliance in the case of a man
whose appetite has grown strong by years of indulgence;
hence, very little is heard about this "will power" in the
societies which he forms. It is his habit to come before
his audiences with an open Bible in his hand. He mag-
nifies the power of God, and establishes himself in the
word of God.

The work in Maine, which was commenced in Bangor
nearly three years ago, continued in that State until the
number of reformed men was reported to be forty-six
thousand. These the doctor gathered together, and organized into clubs for mutual protection, encouragement,
and missionary work, under a constitution similar to that
already in use by the Reform Clubs formed by Mr. Osgood and others.

These clubs are social and moral fraternities, in which there is a greater or less amount of religious services, according to the composition of the clubs. Dr. Reynolds himself is not accustomed to open the club with prayer, confining his religious services to reading the Scriptures and the singing of hymns. He has been brought up in the Protestant Episcopal Church, and has, therefore, enjoyed no training in those extemporaneous services of devotion which form so large a part of the religious services of other bodies of Christians. Nevertheless, his work is done in a religious spirit, and is carried forward in the fear and strength of God.

The doctor once received an offer from a gentleman who was interested in his success in reaching men; saying, " I will give you fifty dollars if you will tell me how you do this temperance work."

Dr. Reynolds replied, " It is not I, but God, who does the work. I am one of the foolish things of this world that has been raised up to confound the wise. I have sympathy for the drunkard. I love him as my brother; and as the result of going out and doing good for my Leader I have come to be what I believe to be a practical Christian. I have the honor and privilege of saying, that during the past twenty-one months fifty-one thousand men have been reclaimed from drunkenness, and planted on the rock of total abstinence, looking to God for his assistance to enable them to keep their feet there. Hundreds and hundreds of them have also become full-souled Christians. They have not been saved by cuffs and curses, and the cold shoulder, but by reaching out to them the hand of brotherly love ; not by standing up

somewhere and beckoning to them to come up ; but by
going down to them, as Christ did, and giving them a
hand through which they feel the electric thrill of sympathy which impregnates their whole being, and makes
them feel that they have at least one friend in the
world."

In another of his addresses Dr. Reynolds says :—

" This reform movement is not very high-toned. Some
people find fault with it because it is not high-toned
enough. But the difficulty with these high-toned people
is, they wont come down. They don't 'dare to do
right,' and so they don't do right. This reform commenced and has been carried on, like other reforms,
among the humbler classes in society.

" It was so with Christianity. Christ was the reputed
son of a poor carpenter, and for the most of his time
he was in the highways and hedges. He did not stand
up in high places and beckon men to come up, nor judge
of men by their property, or nationality, or color, or
any thing else except by the principle of love that was
in him. He mingled with the most debased, and vile,
and unfortunate, and wretched ; led them along and
worked with them, and saved them by kindness, and
sympathy, and brotherly love."

The deliberate manner of Dr. Reynolds' speeches is
well expressed in his own remark, " It takes me about
an hour and a quarter to make a twenty-five minute
speech." It is his way to bring out others who can
speak better than he, while to himself he reserves the
quiet, but more efficient, work of organization and securing signatures to the pledges.

The following is the form of Dr. Reynolds' pledge, and the basis of all the Red Ribbon Clubs :—

> ## "DARE TO DO RIGHT."
>
> We, the undersigned, for our own good, and for the good of the world in which we live, do hereby promise and engage, with the help of Almighty God, to abstain from buying, selling, or using Alcoholic or Malt Beverages, Wine and Cider included.

The Red Ribbon idea originated as follows: Some months after his reform Dr. Reynolds had called a convention of reformed drunkards to meet in Bangor, Maine ; and while sitting in his office the thought struck him that it would be a good idea if the delegates coming in that night—September 10, 1874—had some badge whereby they might know each other.   After cogitating over the matter for a few moments he sent his office boy across the street to a dry-goods store for several yards of red ribbon, which he cut up into six-inch pieces, tied one in the lapel of his coat, and tied one into the lapel of the coat of each one of the delegates who were supposed to be reformed drunkards.   There was another convention in June of the next year, at which delegates wore the ribbon in memory of the former convention.

When the doctor started out for his campaign in Massachusetts he made the red ribbon a badge of membership of the Reform Club ; but the ribbon did not by any means play the part in the work in Massachusetts that it afterward did in Michigan, where it became almost a sacred thing, signifying to the reformed men who wore it their solemn life-pledge to total abstinence.

Not only do those who wear the ribbon respect it, but

it is said that in some of the Michigan saloons, if a man wearing a red ribbon should come in and order a glass of liquor he would be refused. An instance of this kind lately occurred in the city of Jackson, when a reformed man with a red ribbon in his button-hole was overcome by his appetite for strong drink, went into a saloon, and called for liquor.

"No," said the saloon-keeper, who had known the man as a miserable drunkard for many years, "I will not give you any thing to drink. A man who has been damaged by liquor as much as you have, and who has been helped by letting it alone as much as you have, ought to know better than to touch it again. Your family are happy, too, and I will not be the man to destroy you and them."

Mrs. S. M. I. Henry, the well-known and successful missionary of Rockford, Ill., whose own work in the temperance cause has been so largely blessed, thus speaks of Dr. Reynolds in the temperance column of the Rockford "Register," of which she is editor :—

"Dr. Reynolds is a man all by himself. He continually provokes the inquiry, What is the source of his power? In personal appearance the doctor is rather commanding, measuring six feet, well proportioned, straight as an arrow, moves with energy and grace. His complexion is a little of the florid order. He wears a sandy mustache, and in address and general appearance he is a gentleman. He makes no pretensions to oratory. His words are few ; his style, pleasing and smooth. He never lifts his voice above the conversational tone, never makes any effort to play on the emotions, but deals in stern, naked truth, using his own experience and that of others simply as illustrations. His appeals are to the common sense and manhood of his hearers, and to their moral feelings. When he tells of his life he uses terms that a half-drunken man would understand. He says 'drunkard' instead of 'inebriate,' and calls himself 'a reformed drunkard.' He seems to look at this question of drunkenness and reformation from the stand-point of those who have suffered from the one, and who are in need of the other; and the first thought which seems to take possession of the unfortunate men who hear him is 'Well, now, he was such a man as I; may be I could be saved if I try the same way he did. *I'll try.*'

"The secret of his success is the absolute absence of every thing like pretense, and in the inspiration of *work* which he carries with him, while his own sole reliance is upon the support of God. 'Old Business' he is frequently called; and the thoroughness of his methods of organization warrant the title.

"His creed, which he announces whenever there is occasion for it, is this: 'I believe in God; I believe in prayer; I believe in every thing between the two lids of the Bible, whether I understand it or not'; and I believe I am a saved man to-day, through the instrumentality of the prayers and work of the women of my country."

With respect to the various political questions arising in temperance the doctor says: "Let every thing else alone. You reformed men have enough business on your hands to take care of yourselves, without being made cat's-paws for politicians to pull their chestnuts out of the fire."

17

CHAPTER XVI.

DR. REYNOLDS IN MASSACHUSETTS.

AT the old Orchard Beach Camp-meeting, in 1875, Dr. Reynolds received an invitation from Mrs. Mary L. Ward, Secretary of the Woman's Christian Temperance Union of Salem, Massachusetts, a lady whose record of usefulness in the cause of temperance is something the like of which good men and women everywhere might covet. In response to this invitation the doctor made his first appearance in Massachusetts in March, 1876. Of his labors and successes in this field he thus speaks, as reported in the " Boston Traveler ":—

" A few months ago I came to Salem by the invitation of the Woman's Christian Union, for the first time. Then by their aid and through their prayers commenced this grand awakening, whereby thousands of homes have been made happy, and thousands of men have been turned to God. Not to me is due the praise, but to our Father in heaven, who has chosen me to do this work.

" I believe that women do more for fallen men than men will or can do for themselves ; and I thank God that the women of the United States had commenced their crusade, and the wave had spread eastward till it reached my home in Bangor.

" We organized a little club of eleven reformed drunkards in Bangor, for the purpose of encouraging one another to dare to do right ; and from that the movement spread. Once we went to St. John, New Brunswick, where a small Reform Club was started. It proved to be the little leaven which leavened the whole lump, for this club of a few has become a club of very many, and its influence has extended through the British Provinces.

"The reform movement seems to me sometimes like the crusade of John the Baptist, and if any thing can be found to do more good I should like to know it. I am in sympathy with all kinds of temperance movements and with all branches of the Church of God, but this is the work to which God has called *me*, a work like the mission of our blessed Saviour himself, to go out into the highways and byways, hedges and ditches, and raise up the fallen ones.

"Two years ago I was rescued from the verge of a drunkard's grave by the Christian women of Bangor. I joined the Young Men's Crusade Club. It was composed of men who had led a sober life, of those who had been moderate drinkers, and of those who had been common drunkards. The result was continual quarreling and strife. The organization died. It then occurred to me to form a society composed entirely of reformed men. There is a bond of sympathy between reformed men which binds them together. Such a club was formed in Bangor: it increased to an unprecedented number. I then resolved henceforth to form such clubs, and do all I could for the cause of temperance."

At the close of his labors in Salem a complimentary benefit was tendered to Dr. Reynolds, which proved to be an enthusiastic temperance ovation. Honors enough have been paid to him by the clergy and leading citizens of places in which he has labored to turn the head of a vain man or a small man; but Dr. Reynolds is manifestly the opposite of both of these, and the praise he receives does not seem to hurt him in the least.

For about thirteen months he labored in Massachusetts, occasionally extending his work into Connecticut, New Hampshire, and Rhode Island; the center of his line being in the counties of Essex and Middlesex, though he was occasionally called to the interior of the State.

In Gloucester, which was one of the first towns visited, the Red Ribbon reform was so successful that a list of twenty-two vessels sailing from that port was published, whose entire crews were temperance men, and most of them members of the Reynolds Reform Club. In Salem a club was formed of two hundred and twenty-five members; at Marblehead, one of two hundred members; in Lynn, one of forty members; in Peabody, one of eighty members. Every-where he went the doctor was cordially aided by the pastors of the Churches, more especially the Methodists, Congregationalists, and Baptists. The Young Men's Christian Associations also recognized the power of the movement led by this reformer, and joined hands with him, to carry on the good work.

Of this movement the "Congregationalist," of Boston, under the date of March 29, 1876, says:—

"The work of Dr. H. A. Reynolds is little short of a miracle. For example, upon Saturday, March 25, he went, in a furious storm, to the town of Ashland, by a night train, met a hundred men at the town hall, and talked with them an hour, in a free, conversational way,

then met a hundred in the same place on Sunday afternoon, mostly drinking men. He organized a Reform
Club of forty. In the evening he obtained sixty more
members to the club, and left town Monday morning,
leaving a temperance organization which within a few
weeks has gathered in drinking-men by the score. This
work is repeated in three towns and cities every week,
and in every place with substantially the same success.
Within eighteen weeks thirteen thousand reformed men
have been organized by Dr. Reynolds in Eastern Massachusetts.

"His club plan is such that the men hold each other
up. Eighty-five per cent. of the thirty-four thousand
reformed men who have taken the pledge within nineteen months are holding to it to this day.

"At Waltham the work has been a most remarkable
one. On Thursday of last week, on his return to that
town again, Dr. Reynolds was met at the depot by an
array of three hundred reformed men, and escorted
through the principal streets, to the vestry of the Congregational Church, where a collation had been provided by the ladies of the Christian Union. In the
afternoon and evening there was a grand mass-meeting,
and the reform already accomplished in the town corre-
sponds with that in Gloucester. This grand temperance
wave is already reaching the men in the towns in the
region of Boston."

The great manufacturing city of Lowell was the scene
of one of his temperance triumphs.

The following is an extract from one of his addresses
there, which is of especial interest, not only as giving a

glimpse at Dr. Reynolds' own history, but also as setting forth his views on the question of the proper attitude of the temperance reform toward drunkards and rum-sellers :—

" I am a graduate of Harvard College, and received a thorough medical education ; but I have been drunk four times a day in my office, and if there is any worse hell than I have suffered I don't want to be there. No nobler class of men walk the earth than some who are drinking men. They are naturally generous, whole-souled, genial, jolly ; but by intemperance their minds become diseased. They become scorned and degraded outcasts in the ditch, kept there by thoughtless people, less generous and honorable by nature than themselves. But for rum, these might be on the throne instead of in the gutter.

" Drunkards are not all fools, as some people believe ; but every man who drinks is living a life of self-condemnation.

"I never insult men who sell liquor. Some men can sell it conscientiously, in some cases, because they are educated to it. At Gloucester, where I was last year, two rum-sellers have left the business and signed the pledge. The only difference between the respectable rum-shop and the low groggery is that the one finishes up the work the other has commenced. The drunken pauper is better than the drunken aristocrat.

" My sympathies are with the poor men in this temperance work, and I wish to reach as many of them as possible ; and for this reason, as well as for others, I wish to carry on this work not in connection with aristocratic

Churches, but in non-sectarian, non-political, public halls.
I represent no organization, and am under the pay of
none.

"At Gloucester the interest in the Reform Club last
week increased until this morning members of the Temperance Reform Club of that place, numbering three
hundred and fifty men, marched in procession to the
depot with a band of music to escort me.

"On my departure thousands assembled at the depot,
and many were the expressions of sympathy and friendship I received. The wives of former drunkards were
there, with their little children in their arms, to bid me
God-speed. When the train moved off the band played
'Auld Lang Syne,' and there was singing and cheering
by the crowd. Now, that don't set me up. I want to
create the same interest here as at Gloucester, and hope
to have the united assistance of all who claim to be good
people.

"If there are any drinking men here to-night, I want
them to commence now to dare to do right. It is easier
to stop drinking now than it will be three weeks from
now. Sending a drinking man to jail will not make him
sober. When he comes out the first thing he will do
will be to take a drink if he can get it. But of those
who take this pledge eighty-five per cent. have thus far
kept it."

At the close of the meeting Major Emery, of Lowell,
came forward and indorsed the remarks of the doctor,
and the meetings resulted in the formation of a Reform
Club of fifteen hundred members.

After his great success in Lowell and Gloucester

Dr. Reynolds was invited by the Boston Methodist Episcopal Preachers' Meeting to appear before them and give some account of the work. He was received by this large and influential body of ministers with great cordiality. The Rev. Frank Wagner, pastor of the leading Methodist Episcopal Church of Lowell, Rev. Albert Gould, of Gloucester, and others who had been associated with him in the work, bore testimony to its divine and saving efficacy.

At one of the reform meetings in Lowell Rev. Mr. Gould gave the following account of the movement in his own city:—

"The liquor traffic in Gloucester was fearful beyond description. The ministers of the city first consulted together and decided on a series of meetings. After a few meetings had been held Dr. Reynolds's success at Salem induced me to secure his services. The work opened there with smaller audiences than it had in Lowell; but the interest so increased that the City Hall was engaged for the meetings, and it was crowded with vast audiences for four nights. The Reform Club first organized consisted of sixteen; it now numbers five hundred and twenty-nine, nearly all reformed men, who five weeks ago were drunkards, some of them gutter drunkards.

"The liquor traffic is almost stopped. One dealer has hung crape on the door of his saloon. The business men of the city stand behind the movement with their money; and the red ribbons, worn as the badge of the club, are immensely popular. The best feature of the work is its religious element. The pledge signed recognizes God as a helper, and the reformed men believe that they need his help. No man in Gloucester is so popular to-day as Dr. Reynolds."

The Stoneham Club, which commenced with a membership of thirty-three, was rapidly increased to two hundred and five. One of the pleasant peculiarities of the club is its liberal provision in money for the expense of of the club and its missionary work.

The Lawrence Club was organized early in April, 1876. In this great manufacturing center of New England it was to be expected that the liquor interest would have one of its strongholds. When Dr. Reynolds went to this place he was informed by one of the ministers that he was coming into the jaws of hell; but still he was ready to come, saying, "I have declared my purpose to be to save men of whatever race, color, sect, or party. I have nothing to do with men's opinions or prejudices. Lawrence is, doubtless, a cold place to begin, but by proper work great good will be done here."

The good sense of the doctor's methods, and his straightforward earnestness of purpose, gave him favor in this unfavorable locality, and as a result of his labors a Reform Club was organized, of three thousand members.

At one of the meetings in Lawrence a youth, scarcely fifteen years of age, was introduced, who had been a drunkard. This lad was too young to be a member of the Reform Club, but the boys took hold of the work, and organized a Reform Club of their own. The women of the city were also greatly interested in the reform work, as appears by the fact that nineteen hundred of the leading ladies of the city signed a petition to the

17*

local authorities against the granting of licenses to sell liquor.

On May 12, 1876, a State Convention of the Reform Clubs was called to meet at Lurline Hall, in Boston, for the purpose of giving greater unity and efficiency to the movement. In his opening speech Dr. Reynolds said :—

" This meeting is to be called in the interest of no faction, no party, and of no individual, but for the good of our unfortunate brothers. We have no ax to grind, but we meet to talk of mutual interest. The season has arrived when it will be necessary for us to put forth our united efforts to keep up the interest in the movement for the next three months; after that the child will be able to stand alone."

The reports of delegates from all points were in the highest degree encouraging, and from their meeting they went down to their houses and local clubs with a larger faith in God, and in the success of the movement represented by his servant, Dr. Reynolds.

Certain temperance politicians were much displeased at the doctor's rigid determination to keep his clubs out of politics, but the determination was supported by the best people of the State. The " Springfield Republican," whose judgment in such matters is usually valuable, says : " The decision of the Reform Clubs not to mix teetotalism with politics is, probably, a settler for the prohibitory party in this State, at least as far as this year's canvass is concerned. These clubs are by far the most vital temperance associations going at present. They have the dew of their youth yet on them, believe in themselves and their work, and the prohibitory party.

with these clubs standing aloof, is the merest shadow of a shade that ever flitted across politics. Some fifty of them were represented at the Lurline Hall, in Boston, day before yesterday. The number of delegates elected, including self-elected ones, is variously stated at from two hundred to four hundred. The meeting became turbulent, got beyond the control of the chairman, and stayed there. There was a minority element which had no sympathy with the purposes of the gathering, and no notion of being suppressed. They vigorously contended that it was the duty of temperance men to vote as they prayed, while Brothers Ford, of Boston, Knight, of Cambridge, and Scott, of Lowell, were the principal spokesmen in the steer-clear-of-politics party. Personalities were exchanged in any thing but a temperate manner, and a large number of delegates left the hall in disgust ; but enough stayed to pass the resolution declaring, 'That we emphatically condemn the introduction, discussion, or agitation of politics in our meetings.'

"We make our compliments to the Reform Clubs on their good sense."

Not satisfied with this utterance of their first convention, a proposition was made to hold a State convention on the eve of the presidential election, in the city of Fitchburgh, where the Red Ribbon movement had been very successful, resulting in seventeen hundred signatures to the general pledge, and the organization of a Reform Club of over a hundred men. The date fixed for this political temperance-convention was Sept. 20, but Dr. Reynolds, being consulted thereon, wrote as follows :—

" Put me down squarely against that Fitchburgh convention, or any other method by which it is proposed to divert the Reform Clubs from their legitimate purpose of saving men, or cause them to become the tools of politicians. Reformed men have enough to do to take care of their own business."

In spite of his protest the convention was held, but very few Red Ribbon Clubs were represented at it, and the political brethren, finding that their efforts to commit the convention to the support of the candidates of the prohibitory party had excited a storm of indignation all over the State, prudently adopted a policy of silence, and the result was a very pleasant temperance meeting.

One of the most interesting temperance events of the Summer of 1876 in New England was the International Temperance Camp-meeting, at Old Orchard Beach, in Maine. At this meeting Dr. Reynolds was elected President of the National Temperance Association, with ex-Governor Perham, of Maine, Mrs. Wittenmyer, of Philadelphia, and Francis Murphy, as Vice-Presidents.

It was at this meeting, as we shall see, that Dr. Reynolds was first induced to extend his labors to the West, where such glorious successes were awaiting him.

Of the reform movement in Worcester a correspondent says: "Probably never before has the heart of the old Commonwealth been so warm in the cause of temperance as it is at this time. Our Reform Club has held meetings in all the principal churches Sunday evenings all winter, and at each and every meeting hundreds have turned away, not being able to gain admittance. The club recognizes and develops the moral side of the movement, and many members have become professing Christians since their reformation. The club has nearly eleven hundred enrolled men, all of whom have been addicted to the use of alcoholics as a beverage, to a greater or less extent, and their influence has reached as many more. The club has grown at about the rate of a hundred a month, and at its last business meeting added nearly a hundred members.

" This club was organized by Dr. Henry A. Reynolds Jan. 16, 1876, and the work has been carried on by the president of the club, Mr. William H. Blanchard, who gives all his time and talents to the cause. The club is practically and emphatically Red Ribbon in all its movements and machinery. It has the idea of letting severely alone both politics and religious dogmas, and working for the reformation of men. It has been called the ' Banner Club ' of the State, not because of its numbers, but because of the unanimity and practical working of its members. They have just moved to elegant rooms on Maine-street, near the Old South Church."

An interesting feature of the work of the Worcester Reform Club is a course of literary and scientific lectures by its president, Mr. Blanchard, the first topic being, "South America;" thus adding the important element of intellectual training and culture to the other valuable work of the club.

At Stoneham, where a very successful campaign was held, the doctor's remarks are reported in the " Boston Traveller," as follows : —

" Dr. Reynolds commenced by lamenting the absence of clergymen at the meeting, which was held at the hour of the usual Sunday evening service. He said the time of meeting must be changed.

" Men have got to be saved ; and if there is any place where clergymen ought to be represented it is actively in the temperance movement. Rum is an obstacle at entrance to the church-door. Our ministers, instead of preaching to little vestries half full of people, should preach to full houses, and they will do so if they can feel that the temperance work is only the forerunner of something better and higher.

" It is this sort of practical work which is to be, and must be, done. Drunkards would form the best class in the community, were it not for the curse of rum. As a rule they have no passion except rum, and it is that which causes them to commit crime. Rid your community of intoxicating drinks, and you will see how quickly crime will decrease among your people. Now they receive scoffs and kicks because they drink, when really they are a great deal better men than some who never drank a drop of liquor in their lives.

" You can't fail to see by my talk that I am a friend of the drunkard. The men who sit in this Reform Club to-night would not be here if they had been ridiculed and abused as scalawags. Take them as they are, not as they were once. I would not turn a cold shoulder to a discharged convict if I thought he had become a good citizen.'

The doctor then exhibited the faucet through which the last drop of liquor in Lockport had passed into the public street and gutter, saying he would like to have such a faucet from every town in the Union.

"Now," continued the doctor, "I want to inform
he rumsellers that this movement means business, not
or you, but for us.   I have driven my stake for sixty
housand men in Massachusetts, and I am going to have
hem, too.   We despise your business, and we despise
ou while you are at it; but if you will only sign the
ledge and try to get out of it we will shake hands with
ou."

Of the opening of the campaign in Springfield, in June
876, the "Republican," of that city, says:—

"Dr. Reynolds regards the club as a very promising
ne, (it was only a club of thirty-seven members,) but
till thinks Springfield rather fallow ground for temper-
nce work; which tallies with the testimony of the
iquor dealers and makers, that this city has more nu-
nerous and more elegant bar-rooms, and consumes more
eer and liquor, than any other city of its size in the
State.   The club does not include any very prominent
itizens, but its members, of course, are in earnest, and
ope to increase its numbers rapidly."

A subsequent letter from Springfield gives the intelli-
ence that this club of thirty-seven members had grown
o a membership of over four hundred, and that the
neetings held under its auspices sometimes filled three
arge halls in different parts of the city.   At three o'clock
Sunday afternoons and in the evenings, mass meetings
ave been held in the Protestant Churches, all of which
ave given the Reform Clubs and reformed men a warm
nd hearty welcome.

To the members of the East Boston Reform Club
he doctor gave this sound advice: "You are to blame

for not having a larger and more effective club. You ought to be self-constituted missionaries. Out of gratitude to God for your deliverance you ought to be the first to go out into the byways and hedges, and compel others to come in. I know what it is to have a pleasant home and a lucrative practice; but I have abandoned both that I may be the means, under God, of saving others from the depth of sorrow and suffering from which I have been extricated. I could not rest. Don't leave a stone unturned to reform others. Work for this, and you will succeed.

"It don't make any difference to God whether it is a boot-black or a millionaire that you are instrumental in saving. Members of the East Boston Reform Club, start out every one of you, as a committee of one, and you will revolutionize the whole island. The Reform Club is a life-boat. It restores men to a good name, and happiness. It brings joy to the whole household; it makes men feel that they can be just what they most desire. Let a man struggling to reform feel that he has a friend.

"If there is a moderate drinker in the house, and I have no doubt there are many, let me tell them that they are on the road to destruction. Do not flatter yourselves that you are stronger than others who now fill drunkards' graves.

"Men of the Reform Club, wear the Red Ribbon. I would as soon go without my shirt as without my Red Ribbon. I don't have to change my ribbon when I change my vest, for I have one in every vest. I once was not ashamed to get drunk; why should I be ashamed to acknowledge that I don't drink, and am consequently free from the curse? I want to be known as a man who dares to do right ; and if every man who reforms wears a Red Ribbon, it wont be long before the absence of the ribbon will be noticeable.

"It will keep men from drinking. A man with any decency in his make-up would want to take off his ribbon if he was tempted to drink; but while he was taking it off God would be at work at his conscience to save him from falling.

"I thought two years ago that I had some sympathy for my fellow-men, but I find now that I have ten times more love for them than ever.   Now, my friends, urge on this Reform Movement.   There is necessity for it ; but don't forget that its platform is non-political, non-sectarian, and non-legal."

On the 22d of May, during the progress of the Red Ribbon movement in Massachusetts, the Rev. Joseph Cook, at the Monday lecture in the Tremont Temple, moved the following resolutions, which were adopted by a rising vote :—

"*Resolved*, by the audience at the Monday Lectures, embracing representative clergymen and laymen of all denominations,

"First. That the Churches ought to draw forward the tidal wave of just reform, and never be dragged in its wake.

"Second. That the two leading principles of the Reynolds Reform Clubs in the recent New England Temperance Movement are known to us to be in practice really what they are announced by a recent convention, in Lowell, to be in theory : first, that reformed men should aid each other; second, that religion and temperance should go together.

"Third. That these principles deserve financial, social, moral, and intellectual support from the pulpits and congregations of all denominations.

"Fourth. That Providence has specially blessed the nation in the New England temperance prayer-meetings, and other distinctively Church gatherings and discussions for the reclaiming of intemperate men, and teaching the community its duty in respect to the sale and use of intoxicating drinks.

"Fifth. That the interests of every factory child and all the perishing and dangerous classes in cities, and especially of the rich and fashionable, imperatively call on the Churches to follow with comely zeal this indication of Providence.

"Sixth. That the renting by Church members of buildings or property to be used for the liquor traffic is inconsistent with the teachings of Him who purged the temple with a whip of small cords."

From Massachusetts Dr. Reynolds extended his work into Connecticut, at Bridgeport, Middletown, and New Haven. He also visited Providence, R. I., with distinguished success.

Of the reform movement in Providence it was said:—

"The Temperance movement in Providence is something remarkable. It is less than three months since the Red Ribbon Reform Club was started by Dr. Reynolds, and the signers of the pledge number over two thousand. The effect is wonderful. The principles they advocate take strong hold on the minds of men. The women workers are engaged· in the same cause, and the politicians and the press are also beginning to turn in the direction of this great movement. Provision has been made for entertainment outside of the saloons, by having reading rooms for use in the day and evening, and measures are taken for the permanent lifting up of all who are down.

" The movement, from the first, is one of moral conviction. It is the belief of its leader that men cannot keep their pledges unless the mind, the heart, and the will, are engaged in the work.

" The Reform Club was started under unfavorable auspices, and at least one of its officers was actually intoxicated when he signed the pledge. Every body but the doctor prophesied his fall; but, instead of falling, he has worked so successfully for the cause that he has increased the membership of the club sevenfold, and it now stands one of the most prosperous in all New England, having a membership of eleven hundred, who have been drinking men. There is also an auxiliary society of over six thousand, which is a good working organization in the temperance interest, and whose Sunday evening meetings call out immense audiences."

In all his speeches the doctor insists upon the need of divine assistance in the prosecuting of temperance work. He believes in prayer, but yet he says prayer alone is insufficient.

" I believe in prayer, but I believe in work, too. It is useless to pray with a man or woman who is starving or perishing with cold. The first thing to be done is to feed them and clothe them. Thus they will be in a condition to listen to your prayers and receive permanent benefit.

"The other day, as I was down in the Eastern Railroad Depot, in Boston, I saw a finely dressed man, who came up and asked if I knew him. When I told him I did not, he said, 'I am the man who took your pledge in Barre, Mass., when I was too drunk to stand alone. They held me up while I signed it. I never used to go to church or care any thing for religion, but, by the help of God, I have kept my pledge. Now I have good work and good pay, and I and my family are as happy as we can be.'"

Later in the Massachusetts campaign the "Congregationalist," of Boston, says:—

"The enthusiasm of its early stages has settled down into solid purpose of regular work; Reform Clubs spring up in every direction, and seem certain of accomplishing great good. The politicians and professionals have no hand in this work. It belongs to the people, and, belonging to them, it will succeed. Was there ever a time when the Churches could labor in the cause so profitably as now?"

Dr. Reynolds' work also attracted attention in the Massachusetts Legislature, as appears by the statement of Mr. Fuller, of Boston, in his place on the floor of the House, where he declared that "The reform has done more good than all the laws enacted during the last forty years." This statement of Mr. Fuller is more significant from the fact that he was the chairman of the House Special Committee on the Liquor Law.

These are only specimen facts from the history of the Reform Clubs of New England — specimens, however, which bring out most, if not all, the leading features of this great temperance movement. Of the general results of Dr. Reynolds' thirteen months' labor in Massachusetts, and other parts of New England, it is safe to sum up by recording the fact that, large as was his hope and faith, even more than his coveted "sixty thousand" drinking men have signed the pledge and joined the Red Ribbon Reform Clubs, besides uncounted thousands more who have "dared to do right," and consecrated themselves to lives of sobriety and helpfulness in the name of Him who is the Father of us all.

CHAPTER XVII.

DR. REYNOLDS IN MICHIGAN.

A T Adrian, Michigan, on the 24th of November, 1876, Dr. Reynolds, by invitation of the State Vice-President of the National Christian Temperance Union, Mrs. Judge Geddes, of Adrian—whose name has already been mentioned as the leader of the first Crusade in Michigan—held his first meeting in that State.

His coming appears to have been one of those events which people are accustomed to describe as "providential," as if only those affairs whose results for good are most clearly seen were under the immediate and personal direction of the power above.

The excitement caused by the Crusades had died away, but the Woman's Christian Temperance Unions still remained, whose life and power were shown, if in no other way, by their regular weekly temperance prayer-meetings, which were organized in the time of the temperance Crusades, and which, even in the most discouraging times, were faithfully maintained—although on one Thursday afternoon Mrs. Geddes relates that the Adrian meeting consisted of only herself and such heavenly presence as may be supposed to be always met with in the place of prayer. In the summer of 1876, while this lady was on a tour to the sea-coast, her attention was attracted by a notice of a Temperance Camp-meeting to be held at Old Orchard Beach. Changing her intended route, she devoted a week to this camp-meeting, during which time she became convinced that the admirable system of organization which characterized the Reynolds reform movement was just the thing required in the temperance work at the West.

At this time the reaction of the Crusade movement was painfully apparent in Michigan. The prohibitory law, which for nineteen years had stood on the statute books, was, by a special effort of the anti-temperance people, repealed, and a Local Tax law, which was nothing more nor less than a license law, enacted in its place, under which liquor-selling increased alarmingly, and the friends of temperance were correspondingly disheartened.

During these days the anti-temperance people used to say to the Crusaders sneeringly:—

"What are you doing *now?* What has become of your Crusade? You are holding prayer-meetings, are you? What do you expect to do by means of them?"

This temporary triumph of the liquor interest made the State of Michigan an attractive field of labor to one who desired to devote his time and strength where it would do the most good, and it may have been this consideration that induced Dr. Reynolds to agree to make a temperance campaign in Michigan at the close of the engagements which he then had before him. During the summer and autumn of that year the doctor was constantly reminded of his promise to come to Michigan, and at length a letter was received, stating that he would commence his work in that State the last of November.

No pledge had been made to him of even so much

money as would pay the expenses of himself and his family; but he had been offered the hospitality of the mansion of Judge Geddes, where he might leave his family during his travels through the State, and Mrs. Geddes had promised to arrange, through the pastors of the Churches and the local Woman's Temperance Unions, for appointments which the doctor should fill; relying on the blessing of God and the liberality of the people for all the expenses of the campaign, including rents of halls, printing, traveling expenses, and salary of lecturer.

The city of Adrian, which was the initial point of the Michigan Temperance Crusades, is also distinguished as the point from which the Reynolds reform movement radiated throughout the State of Michigan. The sudden arrival of Dr. Reynolds, unheralded except by a few days' notice, gave no opportunity for a general system of appointments. There was, also, the underlying difficulty arising out of the general discouragement of the temperance people, and the bad feeling which had been engendered by the legal temperance prosecutions already mentioned. It was, moreover, in the midst of the great excitement over the presidential election. However, Dr. Reynolds was on the ground, and the campaign must be begun, and Adrian was the place at which he must commence, since there was no other place open.

At this time the family of Judge Geddes were shut up with a case of scarlet fever, and the doctor was obliged to go out and make his own arrangements. He secured a hall of moderate size, and held a public meeting, which was not very largely attended. The second meeting was still more discouraging; but on Sunday afternoon the tide began to turn; the men's meeting was attended by about three hundred persons, many of them drinkers, if not drunkards; and after addresses by Dr. Reynolds and several of the Adrian pastors, twenty-eight drinking men signed the total abstinence pledge. The news of this success spread rapidly, and in the evening the mass meeting at the Opera House, in which the Methodist, Baptist, Congregational, and Presbyterian Churches united, was large and enthusiastic. At this meeting the signatures to the pledge reached the number of fifty-five, and on Monday it went up to eighty, every one of the signers having been more or less in the habit of using intoxicating drinks.

By way of helping on the good work Judge Geddes and his wife held a reception in the name of Dr. and Mrs. Reynolds for these eighty members of this first Reform Club in Michigan, at which they were right hospitably entertained.

"You have done a good thing, Judge," was the salutation of several eminent citizens, when they heard of this invitation of the Reform Club to his house; "you have done a good thing, and by and by we will do likewise:" but the Geddes temperance reception has been thus far the only event of that kind in Adrian.

From this time the interest increased, until the whole community was aroused. The Opera House was crowded, and it became needful to hold overflow meetings in the neighboring churches. The prayer-meetings, which still survived the falling away that was experienced after the crusading zeal had abated, became the

18

center of the religious element of the reform ; from a weekly meeting, attended by a few faithful women, it became a daily meeting, with crowds of people pressing into it. Women who had been known as crusaders were sent for to go to different parts of the State to help in similar meetings; and it was, doubtless, the baptism of power which descended upon the temperance crusaders that became the means whereby the interest in this new temperance reform was fanned into a flame.

This suprising success at Adrian opened the doctor's way to the hearts of the people of the neighboring towns of Tecumseh, Hillsdale, Cold Water and Monroe. There had been many hands reached out and reached down to help reform the drunkard, but this was the first uprising of the drunkards themselves in favor of total abstinence that had ever been seen in those parts. The old fable was becoming a reality: the sheep were organizing for defense against the wolves.

The next Sunday the doctor held a meeting in the city of Jackson, where still greater success attended him. A strong club was organized, spacious rooms were fitted up for it, presided over by a secretary, who is one of the brands plucked from the burning ; and not only has the work been steadily and successfully maintained in Jackson, but that city soon became a temperance missionary center from which the reform has been carried in all directions.

In one instance two of the brethren, Messrs. Linter and Meseroll, of the Jackson Club, were sent for to open the Red Ribbon work in the Canadian city of London. On their return they reported, as the result of their work for four and a half weeks, seven clubs organized in London, (one of which is composed of colored men, and one of the best working clubs in Canada,) three in Strathroy, and three thousand three hundred and sixty signers to the pledge.   Their work was indorsed and fellowshiped by prominent gentlemen in the order of Good Templars ; also by the venerable Dr. Evans, a Presbyterian minister, who organized the first Temperance Society in British America, over forty years ago.

Mr. Edmund Baynes Reed, the Grand Worthy Chief Templar of Canada, said, on the occasion of a call from Messrs. Linter and Meseroll, " I feel myself honored at receiving this visit from you, and heartily indorse your work.   I believe it to be one of the best works ever brought before the public, and take great pleasure in signing your pledge, and if you wish me to do so I will sign it officially ; as I am satisfied that you are reaching a class of men whom no other work has ever succeeded in reaching."

The visit of Dr. Reynolds to the cities of the Saginaw Valley was attended with such wonderful success that the temperance people, ministers, and Churches throughout the State caught the divine enthusiasm, and thenceforth the doctor had the whole State of Michigan on his hands.

DETROIT.—During the autumn of 1876 Rev. Dr. Eddy, of Detroit, was a guest at the house of Judge Geddes, and hearing from his hostess that Dr. Reynolds was expected to come some time to Michigan, he expressed his delight thereat, saying that he had heard accounts of the doctor's work in Maine and Massachusetts, and wished, as Mrs. Geddes was the appointing power, that she would write down the city of Detroit as the place where the temperance campaign should begin. On the doctor's arrival, therefore, a letter was dispatched, offering his services at Detroit, but it was three weeks before an answer was received, and that answer was quite discouraging.

It appears that the ministers had called a meeting to discuss the matter, at which highly conservative counsels had prevailed. No one doubted the usefulness of Dr. Reynolds in Maine and Massachusetts, but no one was prepared to take the responsibility of bringing him to Detroit.

There would also be considerable expense attending the meeting, and who was to furnish the money? The ministers' meeting attempted to give the matter over to the care of the Young Men's Christian Association, but this body, either through lack of faith in the movement, or lack of knowledge of what might be expected from it, or through lack of funds to sustain it, declined to take it in charge, and the door must have been shut in the doctor's face but for the Christian Temperance Union, a little company of Christian women, who, with a faith and courage equal to any which was manifested in the best crusading days, undertook the management of the Reynolds meetings in Detroit. They hired the Opera House at an expense of seventy-five dollars a day, sent out notices and posters, received the doctor on his arrival, and managed the whole affair, which resulted in a most astonishing success.

The first meeting filled the Opera House, and when

the general pledge was circulated large numbers of signatures were received. The interest increased hour by hour, until the city was thoroughly filled with temperance enthusiasm, and at the Sunday afternoon meeting for men, held in the Opera House, there was a crowd waiting before the doors long before they were opened, which filled the audience room to suffocation; and from among them, at the close of the meeting, five hundred men signed the temperance pledge, every one of whom was, to a greater or less extent, addicted to the use of intoxicating drinks. The evening meeting carried the number of signatures up to nine hundred, which afterward reached over a thousand—among them some of the most influential and prominent citizens of Detroit. D. Bethune Duffield, Esq., a prominent lawyer, was one of the signers of the total abstinence pledge, and on the organization of the Reform Club he was made its first president.

This great success was due, as we have seen, to the courageous work of the Christian Temperance Women. When once this great club had taken on its proper form the work of the women was forgotten, at which some among them were not a little grieved; nevertheless, having so much to rejoice over in the way of substantial results they could well afford to be a little while left out of sight, and to comfort themselves with the thought that God had used them at the critical moment to turn defeat into victory.

Hon. Sylvester Larned, of Detroit, whose income as a criminal lawyer previous to the Reynolds movement was not less than six thousand dollars a year, says that the criminal business has so fallen off, as a result of the labors of the Reform Club, that his income from it is scarcely one hundred dollars a month: and what is true in his case is true in the case of all leading criminal lawyers of Detroit.

As further proof of the beneficent result of the Red Ribbon movement it is stated that in the city of Detroit, where formerly there had been nearly a hundred arrests per month for drunkenness, the number had fallen off nearly one half during the last three months. Later on, the *Press* of that city reports that while, for the nine days preceding the Red Ribbon movement there were sixty arrests for drunkenness and disturbing the peace, for the nine days following it there were only eleven arrests for those causes; and during four of the last mentioned nine days no arrests had been made either for drunkenness or disturbing the peace.

Justice Harbough says: "The Red Ribbon seems to be doing good. Not a single person was under arrest yesterday morning in the police station for drunkenness or disorderly conduct."

An interesting feature of the movement is a Red Ribbon Club organized among the members of the police force, who wear their Red Ribbon along with their silver star.

The Detroit Club now numbers three thousand seven hundred members, and is the largest association of the kind in existence. Its Sunday evening meetings at the Opera House are large and enthusiastic, and its membership is constantly increasing.

Pontiac, with three thousand six hundred and fifty inhabitants, has over seven hundred in its club.

The Red Ribbon clubs of the three cities of the Saginaw Valley, Saginaw, East Saginaw, and Bay City, number over seven thousand members.

The Grand Haven Club was raised to four hundred and twenty-five members in four days; the one hundred and fortieth signer of its pledge being U. S. Senator Thomas W. Ferry.

At the village of Mt. Clemens, with but sixteen hundred inhabitants, a club of over one hundred members was organized at one meeting. The keeper of the most profitable bar in the place poured his liquors on the ground; and within one week there were two hundred and sixty-five names on the roll. Not a few vessels float "Dare to do right" pennants, and their crews are all members of Reform Clubs.

Kalamazoo reports a Reform Club of seven hundred and seventy-eight members.

Flint, with eight thousand two hundred inhabitants, has about two hundred on the roll of its club.

The Muskegon Club numbers fourteen hundred members, in a city of eight thousand inhabitants.

The following correspondence from one of the Muskegon pastors is a fair showing of the hesitancy of many committees in reference to the doctor's temperance work at first—as well as its overwhelming success when heartily entered upon.

The pastors of the Churches of Muskegon having been written to by the manager of the doctor's appointments, offering him for a series of meetings in that town, replied in substance that personally it would be very gratifying to them to have the doctor labor in their town, but there were many difficulties in the way. Among others, revivals of religion were in progress, and it was feared that the temperance movement would interfere with them.

Later, one of these pastors writes :—

"MUSKEGON, *January* 18, 1877.

"*Mrs. J. M. Geddes—Dear Madam :* You remember I wrote you that, on account of revival work in this city, I did not know that arrangements had better be made to have Dr. Reynolds come here. This revival still continues. But I am inclined to think, judging by the favorable reports I hear, that if Dr. Reynolds should come it would not only incline many intemperate men to a better life, but also help in the glorious work of saving souls. Our city is cursed terribly with intemperance ; we have nearly ten thousand inhabitants, and saloons by the score."

After the close of the doctor's labors, this same pastor writes again :—

"MUSKEGON, *March* 7, 1877.

" Dr. Reynolds has been the humble instrument in the hands of God of a great deal of good in this city. The Christian people here had carefully prepared the way by preliminary work and earnest prayer. His first audience numbered nearly one thousand; the Saturday evening meeting was larger than that of Friday evening. The meeting on Sunday afternoon was for men only, and was attended by nearly one thousand. Two hundred and fifty-five men joined the Reform Club that afternoon. In the evening a very large public meeting was held, and many more accessions were secured to the club.

"Monday afternoon a meeting for women was held in the audience room of the Methodist Episcopal Church. Over three hundred ladies joined the Woman's Christian Temperance Union. On Monday evening another very large meeting, for men, was held in Union Hall. It was attended with great enthusiasm, the men sometimes being fairly wild with excitement, and breaking out into deafening cheers. The club was increased to more than five hundred and seventy.

"This morning the Reform Club, led by a fine brass band, and attended by our city pastors, escorted Dr. Reynolds to the depot, and he departed for Big Rapids. His departure left, as results, a Reform Club, of six hundred and three men; a Woman's Christian Temperance Union, of three hundred and sixty ladies; and one thousand signers to the total abstinence pledge.

"Yours truly,   C. L. BARNHARDT,
Pastor M. E. Church."

In order that the arrangement might be in all cases as nearly perfect as possible, forms for notes were sent from the head-quarters of the movement at Adrian, to the places where meetings were to be held. But the doctor would not permit himself to be advertised to give an "address," or deliver an "oration," or any thing of that sort, and when by mistake some editor or committeeman refers to him as a temperance lecturer the doctor laughs and says:—

"I never delivered a lecture in my life. I only *talk* to these men."

Lansing, the capital of Michigan, was the scene of one
18*

of the doctor's triumphs, where, with the assistance of
Dr. Duffield, and Messrs. Crosby and Pruden, a most
successful campaign was held. It is said that no such
excitement had been known since war times. A Reform Club was organized, which enrolled drinking men
over a thousand, among whom were the members of the
Lansing Common Council, and quite a number of the
members of the Legislature. This number was afterward
increased to about twelve hundred; and that in a city
which has only eighteen hundred and fifty voters!

At a meeting of the Woman's Christian Temperance
Union, in connection with this campaign, a "White
Ribbon Club," of four hundred and sixty-three members,
was organized; so called from the badge, a knot of
white ribbon worn on the right shoulder.

In one of his "talks" at one of the Lansing meetings
the doctor said:—

"I stand before this audience a reformed drunkard.
I was born a drunkard, and I have suffered in every way
that a man could suffer by strong drink. At thirty-six
years old I was a drunkard and a pauper. I had earned
thirty thousand dollars by my profession, and the whole
of it had gone in sprees. I was the unhappiest man in
the world: I wished for death, but I had not the courage
to take my own life. I have drawn the charges from my
pistol, burned my razors, and thrown poisons from my
window lest I should use them for my death in some insane moment.

"When the Woman's Crusade rose in the West I
cursed it. The great wave rolled to the East until it

reached my native State. Women who had prayed in private, and had besought and agonized over a drunken husband, or son, or brother, driven to desperation, united their prayers in public for the lifting of the curse which was crushing them. Still I cursed them. I felt indignant enough to kill my own sister if she should join such a movement. But at last, as I was walking my office one day, on the verge of *delirium tremens*, I bethought me in this last extremity to appeal to God. And then this poor, ragged, trembling wreck of humanity fell on his knees, and alone, in the presence of his Maker, poured out his soul, and raised a last despairing cry for that relief which God alone could give.

"I rose up another man. I promised God that I would publicly renounce the thralldom of alcohol, and a few days afterward I went to the woman's meeting in my native city of Bangor, and publicly signed the pledge of total abstinence. Then I went to work among my friends. But before I knew it I had kicked my practice overboard, and stood fully committed to this work—the work of saving drunkards by the power of love.

"The first Red Ribbon worn in Congress will go into the House of Representatives on the coat of Edwin Willetts, of Monroe, Mich.

"You want to know why we have a Red Ribbon? Well, I will tell you. A few years ago a lot of good, big-hearted, whole-souled fellows, who had been in the habit of drinking, got together and resolved that they would rather wear a Red Ribbon than a red nose. And they acted accordingly. The Ribbon is tied in a hard knot, you see, for the reason that no man would like to go into a saloon and ask for a drink with that badge on; and while he was stopping to untie it the Lord would come in, and cast the devil of appetite out of him, and save him."

When pledges were offered for signers, four hundred and fifty persons came forward and affixed their names One young lady, whose escort was about to pass by on the other side, informed him, in firm but quiet tones, that he must sign that pledge or bid her good-night right there. He looked the girl in the face, and, seeing that she meant just what she said, his admiration for the little woman conquered his false pride.

"Well," said he, "I'm in for it; here goes!" and he boldly stepped forward and signed his name, and, tucking the arm of the little maid under his own, he marched off with the air of a conqueror, more than repaid by the winning smile upon the lovely face lifted toward his.

At the next meeting the doctor is described as "cutting and slashing in a Moodyish style," which was quite amusing to some of the audience, but must have been unpleasant to those on whose backs the well-meant blows were inflicted. The doctor thought it was in vain to attempt to reform a drunkard till Christian people could divest themselves of their pride, and go down into the slums and gutters to those unfortunates; not to treat them as outcasts, but as unfortunate men and women who had souls to be saved—and by the power of love lift them on their feet, and pilot their uncertain footsteps to the Rock of safety.

At Saginaw the lumbermen engaged their men for the spring drive of logs wholly from the club rooms.

It is officially reported from Ludington, on the Lake Michigan shore, that not a single keg of beer has been shipped into that town since this movement began.

The civilized Indians in the Lower Peninsula have also felt the influence of the work, and there is a flourishing club, of this race exclusively, at Indian Town, in Autumn County.

At Ypsilanti, Battle Creek, Port Huron, Benton Harbor, and in most of the other cities of Michigan, flourishing Reform Clubs have been organized; while, not to leave any stone unturned, Dr. Reynolds spent the last four weeks of his work in Michigan among the frontier settlements of the Upper Peninsula.

From the officers of the law in all parts of the State reports come of a marked diminution in arrests and police business. One of the circuit judges wrote to a legislative committee, which was considering the matter of a redistribution of circuits, that if the Red Ribbon movement continued, his district could easily be increased two counties. The effect of lessening crime is so apparent that it has been made the ground of a joint resolution of thanks to Dr. Reynolds, which has been passed with substantial unanimity by both branches of the Legislature, as follows :—

"*Resolved*, The Senate concurring, That in the recent work introduced into the State by Dr. Henry A. Reynolds we recognize a reform so beneficent in its aims and so wise in its measures as to have won public confidence in an unprecedented degree, not only achieving marvelous results in its effects on individuals, families, and communities, but promising to be so far-reaching in its influence as to lessen a. d greatly diminish poverty and crime, the expense of alms-houses, police courts, and prisons, as well as the demand upon public charity, and promising also to solve the vexed problem of tramps, vagrants, paupers, and convicts, striking, as it does, at the root of pauperism and crime.

"*Resolved*, That to Dr. Henry A. Reynolds, the originator and prosecutor of this reform as developed in this State, we tender grateful appreciation and thanks.

"Approved May 3, 1877.

> (Signed)   "ALONZO SESSION,
> > "*President of the Senate.*

(SEAL.) (Signed)   "JOHN R. RICE,
> > "*Speaker of the House of Representatives.*

> (Signed)   "CHARLES M. CROSWELL,
> > "*Gov. of the State of Mich.*"

These resolutions, handsomely engrossed, signed by the presiding officers of both Houses and the Governor, with the State seal affixed thereto, was presented as a testimonial to Dr. Reynolds.

The following resolutions were passed by the State Congregational Association, which closed its session at Ann Arbor on the eighteenth of May, 1877. Rev. Ira C. Billman, chairman of the Committee on Temperance, offered the following report and resolutions, which were adopted :—

"*Whereas*, The cause of temperance, one of the most practical workings of Christianity, embracing many of the dearest interests of humanity, social and religious, has received a great and far-reaching impetus in our State within the last few months, especially under the forms of what are popularly known as the Red Ribbon Movement, the Woman's Temperance Union, and the Children's Band;

"*Resolved*, That we have devout cause of thanksgiving to God and encouragement for still more untiring devotion to this arm of the Master's service, and that, as ministers and Churches, we lend our influence to promote their utilization.

"*Resolved*, That special mention be made of Dr. H. A. Reynolds, who has been confessedly, under God, the efficient instrument in this great work, and we recommend him, from personal knowledge, to the confidence of all to whom this may reach. We also express, in this connection, our appreciation of the services of Mrs. Norman Geddes, of Plymouth Society, Adrian, through whose efforts he was secured at first, and who has by continued, inspiring assistance, planned and encouraged the great campaign."

Thus from all quarters, secular, legislative, and religious, comes the testimony which has been expressed in a newspaper heading of one of the Michigan papers as follows:—

" The Lord hath done great things for us, whereof we are glad. The sword of the Lord and of Dr. Reynolds is conquering man's most formidable foe."

On July 9–16, 1877, Dr. Reynolds conducted a Temperance Camp-meeting on the grounds of the Lake Bluff Camp-meeting Association, of Illinois, at which were gathered many of the most prominent Temperance workers, both men and women, from different parts of the Union and Canada. At this meeting the number of reformed men in the Red Ribbon Clubs of the State of Michigan was reported at *eighty thousand;* besides about two hundred thousand other men, women, and children, who had then signed the total abstinence pledge.

During this meeting the doctor modestly kept himself in the background, putting forward such temperance orators as Francis Murphy; the Rev. Dr. Foster, of Fredericton, New Brunswick; Jack Warburton; Miss Frances E. Willard; Mrs. Lathrop, of Jackson, Mich.; Mrs. S. J. Rounds, the efficient Secretary of the Chicago Temperance Union; Mrs. Youmans, from the Province of Ontario; Mrs. Jenny F. Willing; and Mrs. M'Gowan, since deceased, the voluntary chaplain of the Cook Co. Jail, in which, as she said, she had been able to induce seven hundred men and boys to sign the Temperance Pledge.

At this meeting it was arranged that Dr. Reynolds, after finishing his labors in Michigan, should devote the year 1877–78 to temperance work in Illinois; his first appointment being Cairo, at the southernmost point from which the temperance people have the comfortable assurance that the wave of reform will sweep through the State up to Lake Michigan and the Wisconsin line. As in Michigan the doctor's appointments were made by a woman, so in Illinois a woman, Mrs. S. M. I. Henry, of Rockford, herself a widely known and successful Christian temperance worker, is assigned to take charge of the campaign.

On the occasion above mentioned Dr. Reynolds stated his views concerning the success of the Maine Liquor Law. When asked if the law was enforced, he replied, "Yes, sir. A man who sells rum in any form is there deemed as disreputable as a horse-thief, even if he does wear diamonds on his shirt-front, or drive around in a gilded carriage. Public opinion in favor of cold water has been so strengthened that the election resulted in filling up the Legislature last winter with teetotalers, all except ten, and now wine and cider have been added to the prohibited drinks. The law is a grand success, and all statements to the contrary are worse than nonsense. Still, this law business is not my best hold. Till you can reform public opinion, and get men to hate rum, it is of no use to try to get prohibitory laws passed. As long as at the polls ballots are cast by men who enjoy their morning cocktails and their evening night-caps we can't have any great temperance reform by law.

"When public feeling sends strong temperance men up to the legislative houses, then temperance laws will be enforced to the letter."

The doctor also expressed himself strongly against the proposed tapering off of the public appetite by the use of lager beer, light wine, etc.

"It is with these drinks, in my opinion," said he, "that drunkenness commences. Men do not begin with fiery, throat-burning whisky, but with cider, ale, and beer. Beer is leading men to the drunkard's grave. It takes longer for a man to get drunk on beer than on rum, but it is a worse sort of drunk when it does come. I know by experience. I have been drunk on every kind of intoxicant that was ever mixed."

At the camp-meeting encouraging reports were brought from Wisconsin, the great lager beer State of the West. The Rev. Mr. Clough, of Lacrosse, stated the fact that the majority of saloonists in the western part of Wisconsin were so badly in debt that they could not keep up business much longer.

"I was recently in attendance at a county court in that part of the State," said he, "when I was informed by the prosecuting attorney that he had in his pocket writs against nine tenths of the saloon-keepers in the county; the sale of beer and other liquors having so fallen off through the efforts of the Temperance Reform, chiefly the Good Templars, the Woman's Christian Temperance Unions, and the Reform Clubs, that their creditors, the brewers and distillers, were obliged to sell them out."

Very earnest persuasion was used on the doctor to induce him to labor the coming year in the State of Wisconsin; and this may, perhaps, be the next scene of his labors, after his work in Illinois.

An interesting feature of the Red Ribbon movement in Michigan is the boys' clubs, which had their beginning in Adrian.

The following letter to the editor of this volume tells the story of the first Juvenile Reform Club :—

"ADRIAN, *December* 18, 1877.

"*Dear Sir:* I belong to the Reform Club of Adrian, and thought that my little boy, nine years old, might be benefited by attending the meetings with me. When the pledge was read he came to me, and asked if he couldn't sign. I told him no; he was not old enough yet; that he must be eighteen years old before he could become a member of the society. He replied that nine years was a long time to wait: and I thought it was, with all the influences that tend to draw our boys from virtue and from God. Nine years hence he might be any thing but a fit subject for a temperance society. It troubled me, and I told him that I would write him out a pledge, and he and his little sister and play-fellows could sign it, and have a little society of their own, which pleased him very much.

"Thanksgiving morning I wrote this pledge :—

"'We promise that we will not use any cider, wine, beer, ale, or other intoxicating liquor.

"'We promise that we will neither smoke, chew, nor use tobacco in any form.'

"He wrote his name, Charley T. Boyd, on the pledge, and said he would have his play-fellows come and sign. Shortly six or eight came in with him, and, after reading the pledge carefully to them, they put their names to it. I gave them a red ribbon for not drinking, and a blue one for not smoking or chewing, and tied the badges in their button-holes. These few went out after more, and they kept me busy almost the whole of Thanksgiving day, and at night I had on the roll about five hundred boys who wore the badge, and dared to do right.

"The fathers and mothers became interested in the work, and gave the boys a grand reception, in the Opera

House, where over five hundred boys marched, with drums and banners and flags, to such a table as they had never before seen. The musicians gave the boys a short concert, we had a little speaking, and then supper.

" I have had the pledge always open for signers here in the city, and have visited and helped to organize, in almost every town in the county, clubs of both old and young persons, to the number of over fourteen hundred boys and girls, and hundreds of men and women. It is a good work to lift degraded ones out of the ditch, and help them to be sober men and women ; but I love to take these pure children, and lead them up into manhood without the sufferings which the drunkard undergoes— for in the children is our country's hope.

" I remain, sir, respectfully yours,

" R. W. BOYD."

P. S.—On the eve of sending this volume to press the intelligence is received that the work of Dr. Reynolds in Cairo, Illinois, has opened with all the tokens of power and blessing which marked its history in ·Michigan and Massachusetts. The Red Ribbon Club of reformed men and the White Ribbon Club of Christian temperance women in Cairo already number six hundred members ; the surrounding towns are joining in the movement. The able assistants of the doctor are in demand to hold re- form meetings in many places, and there is great hope in the hearts of the temperance people of Illinois that the day of their triumph is drawing nigh.

FRANCIS MURPHY.

SECTION VII.

THE MURPHY MOVEMENT.

CHAPTER XVIII.

FRANCIS MURPHY AND HIS WORK.

A REFORM movement which has gained millions of signers to the temperance pledge, which has a national organization, and hundreds of active local societies scattered through twenty-eight States of this Union, and these under a leader who has been rescued from the very verge of perdition, to which depths the grace of God has stooped to save him, and whose testimony has been blessed to the reformation of multitudes of criminals and outcasts from both sides of the bar and the gambling table—such a movement and such a man must have a prominent place in the history of the temperance reform and its great reformers.

Francis Murphy, the temperance evangelist, the hero of the Blue Ribbon, the advocate of " Malice toward none and charity for all," the powerful, warm-hearted Irishman, the brilliant genius without education, the orator without art, is one of the miracles of our times. That this man, with ruined fortune, ruined reputation, ruined home, and ruined hope, should have come forth from the prison-house where his body was caged with bars of iron and his soul with bars of fire, to stand before the world, a free man, beckoning his lost brethren to liberty in the name of the Lord, is one of the greatest evidences in our times that nothing is too hard for God's almighty love and grace.

Francis Murphy, the youngest of a family of seven children was born in the County of Wexford, in the south of Ireland, April 24, 1836. He was the heir of two great misfortunes, poverty and orphanage: the family having lost their old homestead through debt, and been compelled to remove to a little cottage by the sea, where, a little time before the birth of this boy, the father and five of the children died of that fearful disease, the scarlet fever.

The mother, who was a sensible Christian woman, and a devout Catholic withal, struggled bravely with her double load of care and sorrow, and when the remaining children were old enough they lent willing hands to her assistance. In his lectures Mr. Murphy draws a charming picture of his little cottage home, inside as neat as wax, outside half covered with woodbine and ivy, in which the tiny wrens used to build their nests; a little garden in front, full of bright flowers, while away above on the smooth green. hill-top stood the old homestead, with its green elms waving in ceaseless adoration, as if to answer back the everlasting psalm of the sea.

"I never heard from my mother a single improper word," is the sweet testimony he bears to her memory; "She was a beautiful little woman. I thought she was the handsomest woman in the world. In her white, broad-bordered cap, her snowy kerchief crossed upon her bosom, and her great Irish cloak, she looked as much like a little nun as a woman could possibly look and not be one."

For awhile the inmates of the little cottage saw sorry times. The mother toiled early and late, while the boys

would go out into the harvest-field to glean after the
reapers, and then come home with their sheaves, which
they had gathered straw by straw, and thresh out the
grain on the little cottage floor.   But after a while their
fortunes improved again, though not enough to allow
the boys to be sent to the higher schools.

The lad learned, as a matter of course, to love the
taste of whisky.   Of the beginnings of this appetite,
which so nearly brought him to death and destruction,
he says :—

" Throughout the section of Ireland in which we lived
the giving of dinners was extremely popular, and though
we could not very well afford them, our friends would be
invited to partake of our hospitality, because my dear
old mother thought that she would be considered mean
if she did not make a feast like other people.

Ah ! well do I remember those days, when the friends
came to be feasted at the humble little home.   The table, so deftly covered with nice white linen, whiter even
than the driven snow, groaned beneath the great pile of
tempting luxuries which were so lavishly heaped upon
it ; but unless there was liquor upon it there seemed to
be something wanting.   Unfortunately, it has been the
fashion in my country, from time immemorial, to have
liquor on the table ; and it is thus that a great many
young men have been brought into the habit of drinking, which, in the course of time, has resulted in their
disgrace and shame.

" I remember, when the table was spread, how I was
allowed to come into the room and look at it.   The little china tea-cups, with a beautiful goold rim around
19

them, looked too delicate for my fingers to touch : and I
remember, too, that when I ventured to touch one of
them it would seem to sing like a little bird, so it would.
Then there was a great big cake, heaped full of raisins—
the nicest and biggest of raisins. I could see them all,
and how tempting they were! It was with great difficulty that I could keep my fingers from wandering to
them, though I knew, of course, that if I ventured to
disturb them my mother would stir me up.

"When you have a feast in this country the children
are brought into the room and introduced to the friends
who are assembled. This is not so in the ' ould country.' There the youngsters are gathered together, and
all huddled out into the kitchen. When every thing was
ready, my mother would call me to one side and say,
' Frankie, come here now; be a good boy; keep perfectly still; go straight out of this room, and make no
noise. Mind that, now.'

"Thus I remember being unceremoniously turned out
into the kitchen when the strangers were visiting us; and
how my little fingers doubled up in perfect indignation
at the treatment which I received! I can yet feel the
scalding tears coursing down my feverish cheeks at this
cruel treatment.

"Now, let me say this to you : Don't ask your friends
to come to your homes at the expense of your children.

"But in this country it is far different from what it is
in Ireland. There the wee folks have to go into retire-
ment while the guests are feasting and reveling; but here
in America young Dobbin is the first to be introduced
by his proud and loving mother. He is there to be ad

mired. Great deference must be paid him. He comes
to the table with his nicely-arranged bib, and there he
sits like a king, and the company must not be unmindful
of his august presence.

"On the occasions I referred to I kept walking back
and forth in great restlessness. Often was it that I came
to the door, and put my ear to the great crack, that I
might in some way hear the conversation and enjoy the
fun-making of the merry guests. A little latch was
swung across the crevice, and the least touch would
cause it to fly up, and the great oaken door to swing and
creak on its heavy, rusty hinges. I waited and waited;
finally, patience ceased to be a virtue, and, slyly touching the latch, the door swung open. At this, one of the
friends noticed me, and beckoned me to come into the
room. I was greatly pleased, and entered very cautious-
ly, for if my mother had observed me she would have
sent me back. At this time the friends had gotten
through their eating, and were quite merry over their
drink.

"My friend, who had beckoned me from the kitchen,
drew me to his side, and, feeling pretty good under the
generous food and drink, patted me upon the head, and
talked to me quite familiarly. He was a dear friend of
the family, and he petted me quite extensively. Taking
up his glass of punch, he added a little sugar and water
to the steaming beverage, and, placing it in my hand, he
urged me to taste it. He took a bright silver teaspoon,
and let me sip from it the tempting liquid. I can now
well remember how palatable it was, and how it tingled
all through my body, even down to the tips of my tiny

fingers. Thus it was I first learned to love the taste of liquor, and it was there that the appetite was formed. Yes, it was there that the seeds of intemperance were sown within me, and which made a wreck of me thousands of miles away from my native land.

"In 'ould Ireland,' if a half dozen friends meet together they must have 'a wee dhrap of the crather, av coorse.' They couldn't get along without it, at least they think so, such being the custom of the country; and it is a very pernicious and debasing custom. Nobody likes liquor better than an Irishman; I know it, for I'm one of them. The whisky unloosens his generous nature. A glass or two tingles through his veins and makes him talk a great deal, and very often it is patriotic talk, for the Irishmen are full of patriotism. But the whisky soon flies to his head, and Pat is himself no longer. Drink is a most dangerous thing for any body, but more especially for an Irishman.

"In the 'ould country,' however, a man would be considered mean unless he had liquors on his table on special occasions; and no man likes to be called mean or stingy. To an Irishman there is something fascinating in the thought that he is a liberal man, and that his friends will say, 'I would like to visit him again; what beautiful whisky and what splendid wine he has! it is glorious—and what a good fellow he is!' It is this social drinking that leads to so much intemperance in Ireland. It is the bane of that beautiful country, and so it is of yours."

There was a lord who lived in his castle not far away, and to him young Francis was sent to be a servant in the house. When this man was sober he was stern and dignified, but when he was drunk, which was pretty often, he would take his servants into his confidence, drink and carouse with them, and make himself the veriest clown of them all.   In such a place the young lad was not long in learning to drink in the style of a gentleman, and also to be quite proud of the accomplishment.   Still, the position of a servant was galling to his spirit, and he begged of his mother to let him go to America : as'there, according to his boyish fancy, he could quickly become a wealthy man himself, and then return in great magnificence, to make his mother a lady of leisure, and carry his head as high as any other man in the Emerald Isle.

The ways of God are past finding out.   From the depths of destruction and despair, a saved and happy man, Francis Murphy may, indeed, return to his dear old home across the sea, with a name and fame equal to that of his sainted countryman, Father Mathew; but the mother, whose eyes he hoped might behold him in all his earthly glory, will not see him, unless, indeed, God should kindly draw aside the celestial curtains, and let her look down upon her son from the upper world.

Of the last week he spent at home, and of the last night before his parting with his mother, he speaks as follows, in his address on Real Life :—

" I was only sixteen years of age then ; yet, blessed be God ! the memory of that home, that face, and that voice, is still fresh and sweet in my heart.   And the last night before I was to leave that hallowed home, O, well do I remember it !

"There was a custom existing in Ireland, when a man was passing his last night at home, to send for his friends and have a jollification; but my mother said to me, 'Frank, my son, I should like to be alone with you to-night; it is your last night with me,' and then the great tears flowed.

"Nobody was invited. My trunk was partly packed, but there were some clothes upon the bureau, remaining to be put into it. Gazing intently into my eyes, she said, 'Frank, get your chair, and sit alongside of me to-night.' Then she took her seat by the table, with her head resting upon her hand. At times she would lift up her head and look intently into my face, then she would drop her chin upon her breast and place her hands across her bosom, and struggle to control her great grief.

"We sat there in silence until it was one o'clock, and I don't think there were twenty words spoken between us.

"When I was ready to start, mother stood with her back to me, and I could see the dear soul trembling. I had not yet received her blessing, and that was about all that she could give me. Rising from my seat I walked up to where she was, and, putting my arms tenderly around her neck, I said to her, 'Mother, now give me your blessing before I go.' I knelt at her feet, and then, placing her loving hand gently upon my head, she said,

"'May the blessing of God go with you! Remember, my dear boy, that the same sun which shines on you shines on me; that the same God who is watching over us in our humble home will care for you in a foreign country. And O—may you not forget your mother!'"

On board the ship young Murphy made the acquaint-

ance of some other young Irish adventurers, and when
they arrived in New York the boys all went on a grand
jollification together, till their money was all gone, and
then the landlord of their hotel, who had been exceedingly polite, suddenly grew very cool in his regard for
the young emigrants, and without further ceremony
turned them out of doors. Then followed two years of
mingled misery and toil, looking for employment, and
losing it through drunkenness whenever it was found
—till at length a canny Scotchman, himself a drinking
man, and since dead from drunkenness, took a sort of
fatherly interest in the poor waif, and, as the only chance
for his salvation, actually drove him away from the city,
to seek employment with some farmer in the country.

Of farming according to the American fashion the
young man knew nothing, and many a hearty laugh has
he given his audiences, as he has described his early efforts in the service of a Yankee farmer in York State, to
drive the oxen and milk the cows; to which stories he
gives a moral turn at the end, after this fashion—now
and then dropping into the broadest Irish brogue, and
acting the scene to the very life :—

"I wasn't very well up in the ways of Yankee farming,
but then I was determined to learn. The farmer who
hired me was on good terms with all the live stock
about the place, and could make them do just what he
wanted them to do. One day, when he had the oxen
yoked to a stone-boat, he put the stick into my hand
and said,

"'Here, youngster, let me see you drive them 'ere
cattle.'

"So I took the gad, and began to talk to the oxen as I heard him talk. 'Whish, haw! Buck! come here now!' brandishing the stick in a highly professional style. But the oxen shook their heads, and kicked up their heels, and started off on a run across the meadows. Then I ran around them to head them off, giving them a crack every time I got near enough, and shouting, 'Whoa! whish! haw! jee! get up! what's the matter with ye?' the oxen all the time on the full jump, the stone-boat leaping and flying through the air, and the Yankee man bent up double with laughing at me.

"Then I began to study into the matter, and took notice that when the farmer went round among the cattle he would often carry the big pockets of his frock full of corn nubbins, which they used to eat out of his hand; and I said to myself, 'Why can't I get on good terms with them in the same way?'

"There was a long row of ears of corn hanging up along one side of the barn; so one day, when the man wasn't looking, I stuffed my pocket full of them, and went into the yard where the oxen were, and held out a great handsome yellow ear of corn to old Buck. He gave me a queer look out of his great soft eyes, as much as to say he hadn't forgotten about the race we had the other day; but I kept creeping up closer and closer, and holding out the corn till I felt sure I had got his attention, and then I stopped.

"He turned his head a little on one side, gave a shake of his ears, rattled the hoof of one hind leg, and inquired, with something of doubt in his countenance,

"'Is that for me?'

" ' It is,' says I.

" Then he came a step toward me, reached out his great red tongue, half as long as your arm, and I reached out the ear of corn—and after that I never had any more trouble with the oxen.

" Now, my friend, if kindness works so with oxen, why not try it on *men?*"

For six years the young Irish farmer led a sober life. At the age of eighteen he married a worthy young woman, not quite as old as himself, and during the next four years they lived quietly and contentedly.   But at length Frank began to grow restless and ambitious.   His brother had come out to America, and the two determined to remove to the city of Portland, Maine, and try their fortunes at keeping a hotel.

This was not at all to the liking of Mrs. Murphy, who foresaw the evils of such a business.   Her husband tried to quiet her fears by renewing his pledge to her, that, though he must keep liquors for his guests, he would not drink them himself.

"Ah, but some one will drink them!" was the sorrowful reply.

At first fortune favored the two Murphys; then the older brother withdrew, leaving Francis the sole proprietor, with good prospects ahead; but at length he began to yield to the invitations of his guests to drink with them at his own bar, and it was not long before he became a drunkard again.   Lower and lower he sank, until his house had been stripped of its popularity, its good character, its decent furniture, and every other token of its former prosperity; then he took a poorer

19*

place, and kept a low groggery and lodging-house, where cheap liquor and rough society were always to be found.

The besotted landlord, when not under the influence of liquor, still retained his genial spirits, and many of his tipsy countrymen still clung to him in real Irish friendship; but the police had his name on their black list.

Through all his fallen fortunes his faithful wife clung to him, crying out to God in the anguish of her broken heart for grace to reclaim her husband, to save her children from becoming like him, and to help her to bear up under the crushing weight of sorrow and disgrace which was bowing her loving heart to the borders of the grave.

These were the times of the famous Maine Law; of which, as a saloonist, the Francis Murphy of those days had a supreme dislike; and even to this day he confesses himself to be under the influence of those same opinions to a considerable extent; which fact, along with the kind interest he still takes in his former brethren of the liquor bar, has brought him into disfavor with those temperance people whose chief hope and dependence is in temperance according to law. In one of his addresses he brings out his views on this point, weaving in a personal fact or two, which belong to this portion of his history:—

"There are some people so intent on saving one portion of the human family that they will let the other be lost. They do not realize the power of divine love, which is so far-reaching, and infinitely greater than mere human love. There is a great difference of opinion as to the way of obtaining total abstinence. This movement in which we are engaged proposes to save *all*, and there is no doubt but that it will be a grand success in this country.

"We must not condemn any one. We can succeed better with love and kindness, according to our motto, 'With malice toward none, and charity for all.' It will be better for us to present it in such a way that all men will fall in love with temperance, rather than to try to compel them to adopt it.

"The moment you begin to fight men, that moment you will find opposition. As long as four fifths of the population drink, so long will men engage in selling rum, and it cannot be stopped unless the men can be induced to stop drinking. You can't drive them; they will find ways of getting it. The stringent law they had in Portland couldn't stop it. One day I saw there an old lady in the market selling eggs at a dollar and a half a dozen! What wonderful pullets to lay such eggs! But the eggs had been emptied of their original contents, filled with whisky, and sealed up again.

"I never fought the prohibitory law. When I was engaged in selling liquor in Portland, and the officers seized my stock, I never attempted to get it back by false swearing. There were men who were regular false swearers, and there were those who were ever ready to get them to swear for them. But these professional swearers, who could be obtained whenever they were wanted, were never of any use to me."

On one occasion, while addressing a large audience in the Annex, at Philadelphia, to which thousands of liquor-dealers had been personally invited, Mr. Murphy said:—

"My dear friends, I ask for your prayers while I am

speaking. Long and earnestly have I prayed for the privilege of speaking to the liquor-sellers. I have no hard words for you ; I did not bring any stones to throw at you. I don't know how many liquor-sellers are present, and I shall not ask you to hold up your hands. I believe in my heart that there are as good and true men in the liquor traffic as there are on the face of the earth. I know if the poor call upon them for aid they are not turned away empty. I know that if the country needed defenders the liquor-dealers would not be called on in vain. I know that we are all men and brothers, and that God loves us all.

"There are men here to-night who if they would come forward and sign the pledge the city would be shaken. Unfortunately many of us drift into the liquor business unconsciously, without knowing what we are doing, and when I speak to you of temperance you shake your heads and say: 'What's the use of talking about it? I have my family to support, and I can't get out of it.' Now, my brother, I don't blame you for talking that way, for I have said the same thing myself.'

"There are so few who have ever joined the ranks of temperance from the ranks of the liquor-sellers, that, as a class, these men have been regarded as public enemies, criminals, pests of society, whom it is the duty of all good teetotalers to execrate and shun ; they are called 'drunkard makers,' and the heaviest share of the blame for the measureless curse of drunkenness is heaped upon their heads; their hands—often, alas ! with blood upon them—are supposed to be against every man, and it is generally thought to be the duty of every man to raise his hand, or, at least, his voice, against them. Stemming this tide of righteous indignation, Francis Murphy seeks to meet it with the doctrine of "Love your enemies:" an old doctrine enough, it is true, but one which few temperance reformers ever before attempted to apply to liquorsellers. Hence it is not strange that this new departure should, at first, outstrip not only the faith, but also the patience, of many good men and godly women, and bring its advocate no little opposition even from those who were at work in the same good cause.

It may not be true that Mr. Murphy has more of the spirit of the Gospel than those temperance reformers who have gone before him, but he has an experience which they have not: he has been a rumseller himself, has passed through all the grades from the gentlemanly and popular landlord down to the drunken keeper of a common saloon; and it is out of the depths of this experience that he draws his sympathy and kindness toward the men who sell liquor, just as others, out of the depths of their experience on the other side of the counter have drawn their sympathy and kindness for the men who buy it.

Of the fearful history which ended in a prison cell these pages may not now speak. Mr. Murphy has pledged himself in due time to open more fully that terrible chapter of his life. The solemn judgment of the law has been passed upon him; a lenient and merciful judgment, too, as of one whose hand went further than his thought.

And more than this: by the action of legal and Christian' officers this wretched prisoner, dying with sorrow and remorse, which gave place at length, through God's mercy, to heart-broken penitence and believing prayer—

this stout, burly man, driven almost mad by his own sins and the sorrows of his literally starving wife and children—was set free, and came forth from his prison cell a poor, weak, emaciated creature, the merest skeleton of a man (he had fallen from one hundred and eighty to a weight of about ninety pounds) but with a new life and a new hope in his soul, which spoke of pardon for the past and power for the future.   No wonder that, ascending out of such an abyss, Francis Murphy has a heart of sympathy even for those lost men, who, by his own experience, he knows are not beyond the power of God's saving grace.

At the recent session of the National Christian Temperance Union in Cleveland, Ohio, of which he is the honored President, a scene transpired which showed how fresh is his memory of those terrible days, and how slightly healed even yet is that great wound in his heart —the like of which it is not often given mortal eyes to see.   At one of the prayer-meetings, which were a prominent feature of the convention, Mr. Murphy's son Edward, now eighteen years of age, who accompanies his father as private secretary, offered prayer, in the course of which he prayed for his father, thanking God for the blessed salvation which had come to him, and asking for still more grace to help him to save others.   A flood of memories came sweeping over the father's soul, memories of sin and sorrow and death, and of life from the dead, too strong for him to withstand : and the strong man bowed himself in an agony of penitence and thankfulness, and, fainting with emotion, had to be carried from the room.

Some uncharitable people said it was "all a piece of acting;" but no such theory is necessary in order to account for it in the case of a man who stands in the midst of such heights and depths as does Francis Murphy. "He to whom much is forgiven, the same loveth much."

"None of you are more surprised to see me doing this work than I am," said Mr. Murphy, in one of his addresses, "and the temperance is the smallest part of it. I have suffered, it seems to me, more than any other man in all the world; but to-night I am a saved man by the grace of God, and I want you to do as I have done, in this respect. I want every drinking man to find the Lord Jesus Christ behind his total abstinence pledge. You may think you are lost, but you can't be worse off than I was, and if you will only give yourself to God he will tune the jangled chords of your nature, and at his touch you will send forth sweet music in his praise.

"Now, I have found that there is a good deal of mystery in the minds of some men about this conversion. They don't understand how they are to get new hearts. Well, I'll tell you about that. If I was going to give you a present I suppose you would let me do it in my own way. Just so with salvation. It is the gift of God; so don't you worry about how he gives it, for he will give it to you just in his own way.

"It was on the 30th of July, 1870, that I was arrested and taken to jail, and when I entered that little cell I looked down at the stone floor and up at the iron grating, and I said to myself, ' I am lost.' But there was still the mercy of God for me.

"There was a man in Portland to whom, under God, I

owe every thing—a man whose religion takes him among
the poor and the unfortunate, among the prisoners and
the paupers. His name is Captain Cyrus Sturdevant,
the manager of a line of coasting steamers which sail
from the harbor of Portland. It was this man who obtained permission to hold some meetings for the prisoners, and to his meeting the keeper invited me. I did not
want to go, but finally I went out with the rest; and
what was my surprise to see my wife and children there,
among the people who had come in to hold the meeting
with us! The first words of Captain Sturdevant came
home to me: 'There is hope, in God, for you all.'"

"After the meeting was over I was hurrying to my
cell to think over what he had said, when I heard the
Captain coming after me, and, laying his hand on my
shoulder, he said kindly:—

"'I am very sorry to see you here, Mr. Murphy.
Would you not like to be sober, as you once were, and
stop the business of selling liquor, and be at home with
your wife and children?'

"'Yes,' I answered, 'I would like to be respected,
but I am afraid there is no hope for me.'

"Then Captain Sturdevant, from the fullness of his
noble heart, responded by saying:—

"'Yes, there is hope for you, and if you'll only make
an effort to help yourself we'll help you, and God will
help you.'

"O, how sweetly those words came to my heart! I
shall never forget them. As I looked up into his face,
and saw the great tears coursing thick and fast down his
cheeks, I said to myself, 'God helping me, I'll make an

effort to become a sober man;' and I can say that I secured the victory over intemperance through the kindly grasp and encouraging words of this good, noble, Christian man.

"The next Sunday there was another prisoners' meeting. The captain was there, and so were my wife and children. As the meeting went on my eldest daughter, Mary, stole away from her mother, and crept up to her father's side, bringing a beautiful bouquet of flowers. Then she threw her arms about my neck, and said, 'Father, we have been so lonesome for you,' and I answered her, 'Daughter, I have been lonesome for you; and, God helping me, I shall make an effort to be a sober man.'

"When the meeting was over Captain Sturdevant came to my cell, and there we had a little prayer-meeting. The captain knelt close by me, and, placing his arm lovingly round my neck, he said :—

"'Mr. Murphy, give your heart to Christ, and all will be well with you.'

"In a little while my family came in.

"I hardly dared to look to heaven, for I had been such a sinner; but a ray of hope came to my poor aching heart, and then, with my poor suffering wife and children, we all knelt down together upon the cold, dark, prison floor, and prayed to God for mercy and grace. The work was there done, and I arose from my knees with an evidence of God's acceptance of me. Blessed be his name!

"In all our married life my dear Christian wife never gave me a malicious word. I was a bankrupt, and had nothing in the world; but she kept up a good heart, and tried to save the children, if she could do nothing for me. But want began to stare them in the face—there were seven of them altogether—and my patient, suffering wife was for a long time their only helper, except the great Father above.

"One day the two eldest boys came to her and said, 'Mother, we want to do something to help you till father comes home again. Let us stop going to school and try to earn a little money!' So she gave them leave, and the little fellows began to tramp the streets of Portland to find little odd jobs. There was a great heap of cinders down on the steamboat wharf, and they used to go down there to sift out coal for mother's fire, until somebody sent them away. After that they often had to go without a fire.

"My wife denied herself bread to feed the children, as a good mother always will; she would even send me a bite when they came to see me. Finally the children could not come to the prison to see me any more. It was a long way, and they had no money to pay their car fare.

"On the thirtieth of October, 1870, I received a letter from my dear wife, the last one that I received from her. It appears that they had no regular meals that day; there was nothing in the house to cook. Johnny, the youngest, came up to her and said, 'Mother, haven't you got a piece of bread for me?' She opened the cupboard, and searched in vain. For the first time there was actually not even a crust or crumb for the pet, for whom she had previously been able to save at least something.   The mother's heart failed her, and then she sat down and wrote me this letter:—

"'DEAR HUSBAND—I have had a week of bitter trial. My strength is failing me.   I cannot live long, but don't be discouraged.   My trust is in God.'

"It was night, dark and dismal, when I received this heart-rending letter.   There was no lamp in my cell, and I could not read it there; but, by peering through the iron gratings of the iron-barred door, I managed to pick it out by the dim light of the gas jets in the corridor.

"That was an awful night: my brain reeled.   I thought I should go mad.   I resolved to show the letter to the keeper in the morning, and if he did not take pity on us I determined to die.   There was a Bible in the cell, and I took it and opened it, and the place to which I opened was the fourteenth chapter of the Gospel by John: 'Let not your heart be troubled; ye believe in God, believe also in me.'   Just then the rising moon sent a stray beam in through the grated prison window, and it lighted on the floor of my little cell like a benediction fresh from Heaven.   I looked at it, and hope revived.   All night long I paced back and forth between those narrow walls, watching that little spot of light while it lasted.   God was in it, and I did not once set my foot upon it: it was a sacred thing to me.

"The keeper was a man of iron to all appearance, but, like a good many other hard-looking men, he was only iron-clad; under his ribs he had a heart as warm and as soft as a woman.   When I showed him the letter the big tears came in his eyes, and he said, 'I'll see you released to-day.'"

It would appear from this that a movement was already on foot to secure this result, and that the final steps were within the power of the jailer.

"Is the man really saved?" was the question asked of Mr. Perry, the "man of iron."

"Yes," was the reply; "I think he is saved by the way he prays."

On the 31st of October, 1870, the prison door opened, and Francis Murphy walked forth a free man. No one but himself can do justice to the scene of his arrival at the wretched place his family called their home. Almost all the furniture had been sold for bread, and only a few of the commonest and poorest articles remained. The devoted wife, too, was worn down with work and want, till she, like her wretched husband, was only little more than the ghost of her former self.

The reunion of this stricken household was sanctified with prayer. His good friend, Capt. Sturdevant, and a house full of other friends, came at his invitation to help him set up his family altar, and to signify their joy at the upward, heavenward turn of his affairs.

But the climax of sorrow still awaited him. His faithful, patient wife was wounded unto death. She tried to bear up under the effects of past sorrows and the weight of present joys; but her heart was broken, and in December, less than three months after her husband's release, she went home to her Father's house, where there is neither death, nor want, nor tears.

CHAPTER XIX.

MR. MURPHY AS A TEMPERANCE EVANGELIST.

"AND now," says Mr. Murphy, in his account of these days, "The time had come for me to vindicate my honor and keep my total abstinence pledge. I had no money and no trade, but I had a pair of willing hands, and a heart that was not ashamed to use them.

"I have passed through all the grades of labor. I can use a spade ; faith, I'm a beautiful digger, av ye plaze ; I used to own a saw and buck, and go around the streets of Portland looking for a big wood-pile ; I used to help the wife of that Yankee farmer in the kitchen—shure, there's a hape of things I can do nate and foine. I have seen a man tramping along the streets with his hands in his pockets, while his poor tired little wife was tugging along with a big fat baby in her arms—more shame to him, the lazy spalpeen !

"This theme of honest labor is a hobby of mine. I believe in that spirit which will not submit to want and poverty, but will conquer it by honest labor. Sometimes I have been met by your fine gentlemen who look down on the Irish people because they are laborers. Look at the iron horse, with his hoofs aching to go ! What a splendid thing ! All aboard ! How we fly along the iron track, at forty miles an hour ! Well, my boys, you Irishmen have made it possible for that iron horse to run that glorious race, and if you did not drink too much whisky you might all be able to ride like gentlemen behind him.

"Don't be ashamed of honest labor; it makes the crooked places straight, and the rough places plain. I stand here remembering that I came to this land an Irish peasant boy; and, now that I am a free man, saved by the grace of God, I pledge to this free land the best and most loyal service of my heart and hand."

At the invitation of some citizens of Portland Francis Murphy, the released prisoner, the reformed liquor-seller and drunkard, consented to give some account of himself in one of the public halls. The effect of his words was what might have been expected from one who, like all the fortunate sons of the Emerald Isle, is a rhetorician by nature as well as by practice, and out of whose heart he could bring forth such arguments and sorrows as would fill the hearts of listeners with emotion and overflow their eyes with tears. A number of his old drinking companions signed the pledge at the close of the meeting, and a Reform Club was organized, of which he became the leading spirit.

Presently invitations began to come for him to speak in the neighboring towns. On one occasion he rode forty miles in cold winter weather, thinly clad, because he was too poor to dress according to the season, and gave an address, at a little out-of-the-way schoolhouse, to an audience of six persons, receiving for his services the sum of forty cents—which the speaker modestly declares "was every bit it was worth."

At the farm-house where he was entertained he noticed

the good woman tenderly wrapping her house plants in a warm flannel blanket, which little circumstance he turned to good account thus:—

"That woman was very fond of her flowers, and took a great deal of pains to keep them from the cold, and to make them healthy and beautiful. What a fine thing it would be if helpless, wretched men and women, and poor little children, could have such love and care; and how they would blossom out in health and happiness and virtue!"

It was not long before Mr. Murphy found himself so occupied with temperance meetings that he had no time for the use of his saw and buck, and it is doubtful if he now knows where he left them when he used them last. · He has not hid them, however, and they might be worked up for him by heraldic art into a family crest or coat of arms, along with a spade, rampant on a green "field;" for, with all his honors, this man does not despise the toil which helped to save his soul as well as his body in those dark and dreadful days; nor does he give his brotherly hand less cordially to a man who is a laborer than to one who is a merchant prince.

The following outline of the early work of Mr. Murphy as a temperance advocate appeared in the first number of "The Temperance Ensign," a paper that was started to float on the tide of the Murphy movement in Pittsburg, and which has done good service in the cause.

Being endowed with a natural gift of earnest oratory, he was easily induced to essay a public lecture by those Christian gentlemen who took an interest in his reformation, notable among whom was Captain Cyrus Sturdevant; and in the City-hall in Portland, on the 3d of April, 1871, Francis Murphy delivered his first temperance lecture, to an audience of his old friends and neighbors, who looked upon the man as a miracle of grace.

As he had a host of acquaintances in the city, the mere announcement that he was to deliver a lecture was sufficient to attract a large crowd, and he had a full house before which to make his *début* as a lecturer. He was somewhat dismayed by the sea of upturned faces which met his gaze; but, speaking with his native energy and peculiar earnestness, from the stand-point of a bitter personal experience, his maiden effort made a profound impression upon his audience. Probably the only dissatisfied person there was Mr. Murphy himself, who thought he had made a most inglorious failure, and he left the platform and started to go out through the audience feeling that he could never succeed in his new field. But before leaving the hall he had more than fifty applications for his services as a temperance lecturer.

Receiving such kind and hearty encouragement as this, he went on with his noble work, and delivered some thirty-eight or forty consecutive lectures in that city, with most gratifying success, concluding by the formation of a "Reform Club." Subsequently he delivered several lectures at various points in Maine, embracing nearly the entire State.

After concluding his labors in that State Mr. Murphy went to Rhode Island, wherein he lectured at various places for about four months, always meeting with astonishing success. Here he induced hundreds of fallen men to sign the pledge and start on the journey of life anew.

Mr. Murphy then concluded to try what could be done among the people of the "Granite State," and spent about a year in lecturing in its principal cities.

While engaged in this work in New Hampshire a National Temperance Camp-meeting was convened at his instance at Old Orchard Beach, in September, 1874. Over fifteen thousand persons were present, and to this vast audience Mr. Murphy delivered his now famous lecture, entitled "Real Life." Dio. Lewis was announced to follow him, but he declined, saying, " I cannot make a speech after Mr. Murphy. I have heard speeches for forty years : have been on the rostrum myself for over twenty-five years, but I have never heard such a speech as his to-day. In God's name, keep that man telling his story all over the land, every night, as long as his breath and strength are spared."

The fame Mr. Murphy acquired at this great gathering soon spread far beyond the confines of New England, and the story of his grand success was repeated in the far West. His first invitation to transfer the scene of his labors from the East to the West came from Miss Frances E. Willard, President of the Woman's Temperance Union of Chicago. Mr. Murphy accepted this invitation, and on the 5th of November, 1874, he delivered the first of a series of thirty-two lectures in that city, which were given in various churches, and always to immense audiences. Large numbers of depraved men were reclaimed by him, and ere he left Chicago no less than eleven different Reform Clubs were organized, and prayers were frequently offered up in the churches for the success of his noble mission.

20

The next scene of his labors was Monmouth, Ill., where, in the short space of fifteen days, he received no fewer than fifteen hundred signatures to his pledge. Within the succeeding year he visited many important towns and cities in the State, and spoke almost every night. The strain upon both his mental and physical organization was very great, and no one but a man with an iron constitution could have withstood it; but he had a noble work to do, and no obstacles could prevent him, no difficulties were insurmountable, no mere personal privations could deter him from performing it. And yet the demand for his services was far greater than he could possibly fill, no less than thirteen hundred applications for his services having been received within that year.

At the town of Sterling, wherein he delivered eight lectures, fifteen saloons were found in full blast, every one of which was voluntarily closed in a few days by the proprietors.

Mr. Murphy seems to have formed a very close attachment for the people of this town, and has sent four of his children there to be educated.

In the early part of July, 1875, Mr. Murphy returned to the State in which he had commenced his labors, to attend another Temperance Camp-Meeting at Old Orchard Beach. While there he received a pressing invitation from the President of the Woman's Temperance Union of Iowa, Mrs. E. A. Wheeler, to come to that State. Deeming it his duty to do so, he accepted this invitation, and so on the fifteenth of September he delivered his first lecture in the Opera House at Cedar

Rapids. After holding a series of meetings here, he commenced a general tour of the State, which he continued until the latter part of February, 1875, when he was again induced to go East, to labor in Brooklyn, under the auspices of the Christian Brotherhood. Having fulfilled this engagement, which was not very successful, he again went West, and continued his ministrations in Iowa and Illinois, until within about a month of his coming to Pittsburgh, and in every instance with the same wonderful results.

A sincere love for God, and a broad and deep love for his fellow-men, a kind word and a glad smile for every one—these are the secrets of his success.

The central theme of all his discourses—and they are generally brief — is personal salvation through Christ. He preaches the gospel of temperance from his own saved soul, warm, intense, loving, rich and free, and the multitudes of common people hear him gladly.

It was in view of these wonderful successes that he was invited, at the instance of Rev. George Woods, LL.D., Chancellor of the University of Western Pennsylvania, to lead a temperance campaign in Pittsburgh. The Chancellor is a philanthropist as well as a Christian scholar, a native of the State of Maine; a man who believes in the Maine Law, and in every other practical and practicable method of lessening the amount of evil produced by intemperance; and, though his professional duties seem to imply a cloistered life, into which the strifes and questions of the outer world do not enter, he is an enthusiastic and aggressive reformer.

The Young Men's Temperance Union of the city of

Pittsburgh, under the counsel of Dr. Wood, arranged with Mr. Murphy to come and deliver a series of addresses, in the hope of making some marked impression on that peculiar community, in which the two extremes of wealthy elegance and vicious degradation so often dwell side by side. But the overwhelming success of

"THE OLD HOME."

this Murphy movement was an unlooked-for joy and triumph: its measures were somewhat new and striking; while its free use of sacred themes in such a "common" way as offering salvation, by the grace of God, from the appetite for liquor, tobacco, and other low pleasures, was almost shocking to those who had never seen any other revival work except such as was carried on, in reverent order and with pious surroundings, in some well appointed house of worship.

Mr. Murphy's first lecture in Pittsburgh, before an immense audience, was delivered at the Opera House on Sunday evening, November 26, 1876. During the first week the meetings were held at the Second United Presbyterian and the Third Presbyterian Churches, after which they were permanently established at the First Methodist Protestant Church, which has become so famous among the friends of the Murphy movement as "The Old Home."

The official report of the Executive Committee of The Young Men's Temperance Union has the following :—

"Mr Murphy was originally engaged for eight lectures, at twenty-five dollars a lecture. Subsequently, when his engagement proved such a success that it was found advisable to retain him for an indefinite period, he was proffered a salary of $125 per week and expenses. The Young Men's Temperance Union had just eighty dollars in their treasury when they secured the lecturer's service. Since then they have been entirely dependent upon the receipts of the Sunday evening lectures in Library Hall for financial support. These receipts amount to something like $3,000, and out of this amount has been paid the entire expenses of the movement. Those expenses include a salary to Mr. Murphy, and also to Mr. and Mrs. Lincoln, as organist and vocal soloists ; rent of halls, services of janitors, printing expenses, etc., besides money loaned in small amounts to assist poor men, and board paid for a number of impecunious men whom the Society has reformed and afterward taken care of until they could procure work. Rarely has so much been done with so small an amount of money. The pledge, now so familiar to all, is as follows :—

YOUNG MEN'S TEMPERANCE UNION.

"With Malice Toward None and Charity for All."

I, the undersigned, do pledge my word and honor, God helping me, to abstain from All Intoxicating Liquors as a beverage, and that I will, by all honorable means, encourage others to abstain.

Francis Murphy.

" This heading has since been changed to NATIONAL CHRISTIAN TEMPERANCE UNION.

" Among the first signers were Ed. Timmony, George Hall, David Hall, John Irwin, Col. Hetherington, S. T. Paisley, Frank X. Burns, and Capt. Barbour.

" These were principally young men, and had been known in the city as ' hard drinkers.' They signed at a time when signing was an effort, and boldly placed themselves forward as targets for the shafts of ridicule and animadversions that were freely hurled at them by old associates. They now have the pleasure of reflecting that through the breach they made have poured the forty thousand, and round the banner they reared as a forlorn hope gathers the hearts of over one hundred thousand people of Pittsburgh. Mr. Murphy developed a new feature in the lecture field. He made orators of converts, and no sooner were their names on the roll than they were mustered into active service. At first the city smiled, and expressed but little interest in the movement. The 'heavy-weights' of the community stood back, until the humble foot-soldiers should have cleared away. If the rank and file opened a pathway for them they would use it; if the rank and file failed they could complacently stand on the solid ground of 'I told you so,' and 'We never mixed ourselves up with these things,' unsoiled by contact with the disgraced conflict. But the rank and file had no intention of failing, and in after days, when they had hewed their way to honor and success, they still held the van, and the 'heavy-weights' were pleased to come in and partake of the victory.

"The movement grew. People came to hear Mr. Murphy and his converts actuated by curiosity, and departed imbued with a spirit of hope and faith. In the beginning it was proclaimed that the movement was for the reclamation of men addicted to drink, and not for the amusement of sober people. The glove was pulled off, and the naked, warm hand of help, charity, and fraternity extended to all. No sectarianism cast a shadow upon it; no illiberality rotted in its core; no personal assault was made upon legalized traffic; no mask was worn on its face; no fustian on its limbs. Naked, open-faced, and clear-eyed, in all the brawny strength of truth, honor, justice, and love, the movement seized the populace by the ears, and carried into captivity their hearts—a lesson for the present, an example for the future.

"There is not at this day, probably, as familiar a spot

to Pittsburghers as that homely, but very dear old structure on Fifth Avenue called the 'Old Home.' It certainly has been the birthplace and cradle of many a new
existence. Some of the church trustees objected, after a
few meetings had been held, that considerable damage
was being done to the church edifice. The reform crowd
broke windows, spit tobacco juice on the floor, disordered
the pews, and did various other obnoxious things. But,
with a spirit that is recognized here and will be acknowledged in the hereafter, the Church people determined that, so long as the work was for the glory of God
and temperance, it could go on if the entire structure
lost every pane of glass in it, and was inundated with
tobacco. Not only this, but the basement of the church
was thrown open for charitable purposes of every description, and Mr. Murray, the pastor, has never tired in
giving his own services. It is hardly necessary to remark that down in the hearts of the people this old
church on Fifth Avenue, and those who so kindly gave
its use, are held in high esteem.

"In the fourth week of its progress 'the cause' had
five thousand names enrolled. At this date (ten weeks
after) it has forty thousand. The meetings are peculiarly
original in their character. Mr. Murphy generally has
them opened with prayer by some minister present.
A few weeks ago he had some trouble in securing a
clergyman for this purpose, the writer having frequently
seen him gaze around his vast audience and ask,
'If there's any minister of the Gospel present, I wish
he'd come up here and pray for us;' and when no
response was made, he would undertake the prayer him-

self. Of late he has had no difficulty in securing prayers, however, as the pastors are constantly and actively engaged in the good work.

"After prayer the regular business of the evening commences. A volunteer choir is constantly on hand, and the best congregational singing that Pittsburgh has ever heard takes place at the 'Old Home.' The congregation is not so very particular about time or tune, but they open their mouths and sing with such a hearty earnestness that every thing but the theme of the song becomes forgotten, and there is a fascination about it that appeals to the hearer, not as melody of the ear, but as music of the soul. The songs consist principally of the campaign slogans of Bliss and Sankey, 'Hold the Fort,' 'What Shall the Harvest Be?' 'Let the Lower Lights be Burning,' and 'I Hear Thy Welcome Voice.' This last is Mr. Murphy's favorite, and generally his first request to the choir is, 'Now let's have a verse of "I Hear Thy Welcome Voice."' At its conclusion, 'Now, another verse, if you please.' These songs have found their way into all classes. They are played on pianos in elegant homes and whistled by boot-blacks on the streets. Even down among the wrecks of our social world, the ribald song and vulgar distitch are laid aside for 'Let the Lower Lights be Burning,' or 'What Shall the Harvest Be?' and a softer feeling comes as a balm to crushed hearts, and the soul once more finds expression in the eye, as the lovely melody floats around even in an atmosphere of sin.

"As before stated, Mr. Murphy immediately puts his converts to work. Without regard to class distinctions,

20*

abilities, or prepossessing appearances, he brings them forward and bids them tell their tale. There is nothing solemn or formal about the meetings. Murphy's introductions are of a genial nature, and place the convert who is about to make his maiden speech, and the audience who are about to listen to it, in the best of accord. 'Brother George Magoffin will now tell us how good he feels. Brother George, tell the people how happy your wife and little ones are since you signed the pledge.' And forthwith ' Brother George ' will unfold the secrets of his hearthstone to two thousand strangers as though he had known them all his life, and the two thousand strangers will listen, and joy with him in his joys, and weep with him in his sorrows. A studied effort on the part of a speaker meets with but little approbation, whereas the free, impromptu outpourings of the heart, however rudely dressed in uncultured verbiage, claim their close attention and win their sympathy. Men who have never addressed a congregation of ten persons in their lives get up before the vast audiences, and tell the story of their lives with an ease and freedom that is remarkable.

" Occasionally some weak brother turns pale, and trembles with that nervousness known as 'stage-fright;' but Mr. Murphy's strong hand is always ready to support him through the ordeal, and it is doubtful if a ' break-down ' has ever occurred with a speaker since the meetings began. Among many well known Pittsburghers who have joined the reform and spoken at the meetings are the Hon. J. K. Moorhead, James Parks, Jun., Joseph Dilworth, Josiah Copely, Chancellor Woods,

Rev. Travelli, Dr. Scovel, Marshal Swartzwelder, Colonel Richard Realf, William C. Moreland, S. T. Paisley, Gilbert M'Masters, George Garber, George and David Hall, F. Johns, George Potter, Chief of Police Ross, Frank Burns, Robert Pollock, Dr. Mundorff, Dr. M'Clarren, Joe Cupples, Daniel Burk, Harry M'Gregor, Felix R. Brunot, Captain Barbour, Thomas M'Clellan, and a host of others. These gentlemen have come boldly to the front at the 'Old Home,' and the incomplete list does not include the hundreds of prominent men who have both signed the pledge and spoken in their own church overflows.

"The speeches are of every kind, from grave to humorous. Some touching, pathetic recital of past struggles and sorrows, with the names of loved ones, of wife, mother or children, connected with it, elicits tears ; while following this may come some quaint reminiscences of services in the tanglefoot battalion, which causes a broad smile, which frequently deepens into a ripple of laughter, among the audience. Applause is also frequent and unstinted. There is a sociability about the whole affair that is singular and attractive. Chatting, so long as it does not interfere with the proceedings, is by no means considered indecorous, and rarely is there seen a sea of happier faces than fills the 'Old Home.'

"Many very pathetic incidents occur. At the Smithfield-street M. E. Church—worthy old ' brimstone corner '—one evening a young man stepped up and signed the pledge. Scarcely had he done so, when a young woman with a babe in her arms came forward, and, falling upon his neck, kissed him and wept. Drink had separated the young couple; and as, with pledge in pocket, and the baby on one arm, and his wife on the other, the husband walked through the crowd, and received the congratulations of every body, it is safe to say Pittsburgh held not a happier man. All social barriers and cold conventionalities of society are ignored at the meetings, and people speak as familiarly to one another as though licensed by an acquaintanceship of years.

" At one of the noon meetings a gentleman was walking up to sign the pledge, when a curly-headed little fellow who had been nestling under a lady's arm, jumped up on the cushions of the pew they were seated in, and, clapping his hands in childish glee, exclaimed ' O, auntie! auntie! there goes papa to sign the pledge. Now let's go and tell mamma! ' and his childish haste to ' go and tell mamma ' brought tears to the eyes of many who witnessed his boyish raptures.

" Sometimes a son whose feet have wandered from the paths of rectitude will, after signing, return to his mother's side, and then, in some sheltered corner, mother and son, pressed to each other's breasts, will mingle their tears of love, hope and happiness together, while the audience draws around them the respect of privacy. Women, both old and young, have become most enthusiastic crusaders. It frequently happens that a bevy of young ladies will surround some gentleman friend, and perforce, of necessity, he in a short time finds himself with a pledge in his pocket. Whatever may be the result, that these pledges are taken in truth and earnestness no one who has ever watched the signing of them can for a moment doubt. There is a grave determination visible in the faces of those who come forward that discovers the solemnity and magnitude of the feelings actuating them. Strong men take the little piece of pasteboard, and looking reverently at it, as though it were a sentient thing, full of fate, put it in their pocket, and, turning about, receive the congratulations of friends with a heart too full for utterance. Many a tear drops on the pledges from eyes that have long been unfamiliar with such emotions, and hands tremble that have seldom trembled before.

"Sometimes, all alone, a ragged-looking stranger will approach. He feels quite sure that no one cares for him. Undemonstratively he takes up the pen, and with tight-drawn lips strikes a death-blow at the enemy that has made him an outcast among his fellow-men. Though surrounded with humanity, he is apparently solitary and alone. Not so, however. There are hearts listening to his. An undefined fellowship suddenly surrounds him. His case seems intuitively understood by those about. Hands are extended in warm and friendly grasp; endearing and encouraging words pour into his ear. Life is born anew, and in the new birth he sees a world worth living for. By one it has been likened to the dark hour before the dawn, when the earth seems dead, not sleeping, and the lone stars, their vigils keeping, gaze faintly through the cloud wrapped around it like a shroud. Then comes the gray of early morn, then the opal hues that tint the horizon, and then the sea-shell painting of rose and violet upon the somber border of night, until at last God's warm sunrise streams in upon awakening

Nature, and the very earth lifts up its heart and claps its hands in joy and gladness.

> 'Grim clouds precede the brightest morn ;
> The darkest hour's before the dawn.'

"Many instances of what Mr. Murphy has been pleased to term weddings have taken place. Family ties that have been broken by the rude hand of dissipation have been mended, and estrangements between husbands and wives brought to a happy conclusion.

"Occasionally some long-winded or vapid-tongued orator essays an effort on the platform. After patiently listening, with frequent 'glories' and 'amens,' Mr. Murphy will pleadingly say, 'Somebody please say, Amen,' followed by 'A verse, if you please, Brother Lincoln,' and the talkative brother will retire, in the best of humor with himself and with every body else.

"Many objected to allowing drunken men to sign the pledge. But it is a notable fact that hundreds who have signed while under the influence of liquor have returned the next night, perfectly sober, 'clothed, in their right minds,' and given their testimony in favor of the pledge as a most valuable agent in 'sobering up.' "

The meetings, originally confined to the "Old Home," have widely extended, and are now held each evening in fully thirty churches in the city and vicinity. Temperance Clubs are organizing on all sides, and, in the vernacular of the river men, the cause is "booming."

Many of the Churches of Pittsburgh have taken a more or less active part in the movement, and thrown open their doors to it. Among those that have done so may be cited Wesley M. E. Chapel, Smithfield-street M. E., Emory M. E.; Arch-street M. E., Alleghany; North Avenue M. E., Alleghany; South Common M. E., Alleghany; Centenary M. E., Walton M. E., South Side, Union M. E., First Methodist, Fifth Methodist, Soho, Second Methodist, South Side, Sharpsburgh Methodist, Birmingham Methodist, Second Presbyterian, Temperanceville Presbyterian, Central Presbyterian, Cumberland Presbyterian, and a number of others. Among the pastors who have entered zealously into the good work may be mentioned Rev. Messrs. Clark, Templeton, Thomas, Frazier, Gill, Donohoo, Senour, Shields, Scovel, Murray, Cowl, Wallace, Siviter, Hamilton, Smith, Vernor, M'Guire, Snyder, Cox, Baker, Ferguson, and others.

This spirited and admirable report has the following on temperance poetry :—

"Mr. Murphy has no use for temperance poetry, looking upon the subject as too severe for doggerel, and of too practical and common-sense a nature to be treated of in rhyme. The poetasters have inundated him with their effusions, but not only has he consigned them to the waste-basket, but he has emphatically expressed a desire that cold-water odes and teetotal rhapsodies may find no place in the choir's *repertoire* at the meetings."

It was not long before the whole of Western Pennsylvania was aglow with temperance enthusiasm. From all quarters came requests that Mr. Murphy would send them some Gospel temperance workers—not mere lecturers, but men of experience, that is, experience in salvation from the power of strong drink ; and in response a large number of the reformed men were pressed into the service. Many of these became acceptable and powerful missionaries. Not only were there overflow meetings in Pittsburgh itself, but the revival there overflowed in every direction. Along the Alleghany valley, and the oil country, up as far as Erie, where one third of the entire population signed the pledge under the direction of one of the Pittsburgh reformed men; along the southern line of counties of the State of New York, under the leadership of Col. Luther Colwell, of Elmira, an old-time editor, landlord, and politician transformed into a powerful temperance advocate; down into Kentucky, under the labors of Charles Wendell, formerly keeper of a fashionable drinking and gambling saloon in Pittsburgh, assisted by his old friend, George Leavenworth, who used to follow the same business in Cleveland and elsewhere, but now converted by the grace of God into a stalwart temperance worker—every-where with the same enthusiasm and every-where with the same success.

The personal history of some of these reformed and reforming men is full of interest, as showing that nothing is too hard for divine power and grace.

Among the earliest adherents of the present temperance movement was Mr. George I. Hall and his brother, David Hall. They have come into a new world of associations and influences, and made thorough work of it. The parents of these brothers settled in Pittsburgh nearly fifty years ago. They were good Christian people; but while the younger ones of the family of eight were only little children the mother died, and two years afterward the father, leaving the orphan children with characters yet to mature. The rough world was hard to trust, and

its temptations crowded close about the forsaken ones.
The oldest child was a sister, who assumed the responsibilities of the home; but the effort to keep together was
too great, and the brothers were soon scattered. The
sisters clung together, and to this day their names are
honored by all who remember them.

George began to support himself by selling apples and
oranges, and was soon thrown into evil company. He
was not vicious, but susceptible to bad influences. There
was no one to advise or protect him. He soon became
rough in words and manners, was known in his teens as
a fighter, and the next step was intemperance. To
this habit he attributes all his subsequent misfortunes.

George Hall was never mean and malicious; but his
besetting sin lured him into danger and crime, and he
suffered. He says he has spent nearly one quarter of his
lifetime in prison! All this while, when the world held
him a culprit, his wife never forsook him, and his chief
regret through all his incarceration was the suffering imposed upon her.

His testimony now, in his deliverance not only from
prison, but from the enemy of souls, is tender and beautiful with tributes of affection to his companion. During his
long imprisonment that noble woman wrote him frequent
letters to comfort and encourage him; and when his time
was served she met him at the prison door with a carriage
of her own, purchased by the earnings of her own hands at
hard work, and he was taken home in that, with emotions
such as no words can express.

The prayers of his mother, together with the prayers
of his wife, are now answered in his conversion. He is

free and happy in Christ, and a member of "Murphy's band." He says: "I bless the day that God guided Francis Murphy's footsteps to our city."

At one of the large and enthusiastic meetings presided over by Dr. James Orr, President of the "Old Home" Union of Pittsburgh, quite a number of the "boys" made addresses; but the notable event of the occasion, says the "Temperance Ensign," was the signing of the pledge by James Onslow, a local politician and writer of some note, and a very hard drinker. Jim had been given up by all but a few Murphyites, who still had hopes of his reformation. The following is his experience:—

"Ladies and gentlemen: Those of you who have known me for the last ten, fifteen, or twenty years (and that number is by no means small) will doubtless be surprised to see me here to-night, and many of you will say, 'Jim Onslow has drank whisky too long, and loves it too well, to ever be able to keep his pledge or become a sober man.'

"For entertaining this opinion, my friends, you are not to blame; my past life justifies you, perhaps, in thinking and saying just what I have indicated, (although I never signed the pledge and broke it;) but, believing in the idea 'that while the lamp of life holds out to burn, the vilest sinner (or drunkard) may return,' I resolved last night, in bed, all alone, with God's help, aided by your prayers, and sustained and encouraged by your friendship, to make a strong effort in that direction.

"Last night, about twelve o'clock, awakening from an uneasy slumber, a voice seemed to say, 'O, my son, remember, no drunkard can enter the kingdom of heaven.

If you persist in living as you have been doing you can never see those who love you well, and whom you loved so dearly while we were all together on the earth below.'

"Without believing in dreams, ghosts, or hobgoblins, I must admit that this semi-vision appeared like a call or warning from above to halt in my career of dissipation, if I would escape the wrath to come. I have slept none since, and this morning my mind was fully made up that whisky and I would part company forever.

"And just here let me say that those that expect me to abuse and rail against my old friends, the saloon-keepers, will be mistaken; also to remark, for the benefit of several of those old friends, that while they will not be called upon to score up any more drinks against a former customer, they shall all of them be paid every cent now chalked down against him; but here, with the help of Him that rules and reigns above, whose attributes are mercy, peace, and love, the account will close. Fully indorsing the idea of that great apostle of temperance, my eloquent and enthusiastic countyman, Francis Murphy, that abusing people is not the way to reform them, no harsh or unkind word shall ever escape my lips either about him who sells or him who drinks the life and soul destroying liquid. If I can save myself from filling a drunkard's grave, as many of my former associates are now doing, and can keep some other poor devil like myself from doing the same thing, it will in my humble judgment be far better than abusing any one.

"And now, in conclusion, let me say a word to the ladies here present, noble representatives of those who are going about like angels of mercy, continually doing good; representatives of those who were last at the cross and first at the sepulcher. May God, in his infinite goodness and mercy, watch over, bless, and protect you now and forever. May your pathway through this life be strewn with flowers of the brightest hue, and finally, when you have passed the dark valley and shadow of death, may He take you to himself, where you will enjoy the society of those whom you most resemble—is the earnest prayer of your humble servant."

On Christmas day, 1876, twelve hundred homeless men were fed at the First Methodist Church, on Fifth Avenue, (Pastor Murray's.) Late on Saturday it was proposed to give Mr. Murphy's temperance signers a free lunch on Monday, and the ladies responded at once by entering heartily into the work. The lecture-room was made a dining-hall, and the poor fellows, entering by tickets, went down in squads of fifty at a time, thus avoiding confusion and crowd. This was just the gospel that many of them needed. They could understand a Christianity which took their bodies as well as their souls into consideration, and, being warmed and fed, they went up stairs, where a meeting was held the entire day, in a much more receptive condition than they could have been if cold and hungry.

"The Recorder," organ of the Methodist Protestant Church, published in Pittsburgh, has the following interesting and reliable words, under date of January 13, 1877, concerning the Murphy reform movement, which it calls "The Temperance Pentecost:"—

"We might mention a score of churches all filled nightly by people who rejoice together in this grand work. It is a temperance Pentecost. Best of all, God is in it. It is the Gospel of Christ, reaching the multitudes, and blessing them in soul and body.

"Brother Francis Murphy itinerates from one meeting to another during each evening, tarries a half hour, speaks, leaves his blessing, and so toils on for souls as no man in this field has ever done before. His speeches are always short, pointed, practical, and full of spiritual power. He preaches Christ as the deliverer. He urges immediate and full surrender to him. And the uniform testimony of the converts to temperance is that of praise to Christ, who opens the prison doors and breaks the captive's chains.

"Very rarely has the harmony of the meetings been disturbed by rowdyism, notwithstanding the motley multitudes that are packed together. The speeches of the 'boys' are remarkable for appropriateness, honesty, humility, and tenderness. There is little boasting in self-strength. In such a harvest it would be strange if a few tares were not reaped in the swaths with the wheat. No doubt there are some mistaken ones. A few may be in the crowd from wrong motives. But surely the Lord is in the movement. Nothing less than the divine power could produce such results. The right objects are reached, and they are touched at the right point— the heart. These are the very subjects of gospel grace. The lowest down men and women, the outcast, the broken-hearted, the prisoner, the lost soul—what else but the power of God could reach them and lift them up? But the great salvation has come to this very class, and the effect is marvelous in our eyes.

' The substantial citizens, as well as the leading ministers of the city, are interested in the work. Bankers and
millionaires have been in the meetings in the same pews
with tramps and drunkards. Tears have flowed from all
their eyes at hearing the same testimonies. The common heart of all has been thrilled by the sweet songs
and the eloquent words of every meeting. The expression which involuntarily leaps from the lips of all
who attempt an expression of opinion, touching the
sights and sounds of every day, is, ' It is wonderful!'

" Brother Murphy seems more anxious to get the new
converts to work than to speak himself. He is an admirable manager, and as sincere and open as the sunshine of summer. He wins men to the truth. The
grace of God is preached as the only really saving power
from sin. It is distinctly a religious movement. The
First Methodist Episcopal Church (Brother Murray's) is
crowded twice every day of the week, the noonday
prayer-meeting being one of the chief agencies employed
in this great reformatory movement. These marvelous
results have come about by faith and prayer. God is in
the work. The tears, the broken sobs, the uttered experiences, of scores and hundreds who but a few days ago
were slaves to strong drink, are the witnesses of the divine power in this crusade against Satan and sin.

" The temperance work in Pittsburgh is quite as wonderful as the Moody and Sankey work in Chicago. God
is stirring the hearts of the masses, and calling to a better
life. We hope that the blessed work may intensify until
not one large church only, but a dozen such edifices, shall
be crowded every day by the people. Let the aisles of

all sanctuaries be trodden by the feet of returning prodigals. These are welcome indeed. This is the Church's work.

"As the movement is now general, let every Church follow it up by vigilant oversight, and every pastor be ready to lend a hand to these dear young men who are escaping from thralldom and death. When the prodigal son came home, in the beautiful Gospel story, the father ran out to meet him, and fell upon his neck and kissed him. That was the welcome the young man received who had wasted his substance in debauchery and crime. The prodigal came home in rags, but the father, seeing his poverty, and pitying his condition, said to the servants, 'Bring forth the best robe, and put it on him, and put a ring on his hand; for this my son was lost and is found.' But the elder son, the respectable stay-at-home fellow, was not quite pleased with such enthusiasm. And to-day there are the 'elder brothers,' the sober, staid, unpitying stand-bys, who never knew the tempting wiles of the destroyer of hearts, who gaze upon this temperance revival, wondering how many will hold out, whether it is not a mere fanaticism, hesitating to incur the expense of a fatted calf, or ring, or robe, frowning upon the uncouth multitude that throngs the velvety pews and tramps the carpeted aisles? O the precious calf—don't let it be killed!

"How rather we take to the father's enthusiasm! Let the fatted calf be killed! Bring the best robe! Fetch the ring of gold! Let these hundreds of saved men in Pittsburgh be cared for by the Churches."

It is estimated that in Western Pennsylvania sixty

thousand persons signed the total abstinence pledge under the labors of Mr. Murphy and his co-workers, and that about five hundred saloons were obliged to close in consequence of the falling off of their business.

It is said that in Tioga County, Pa., with only about thirty-five thousand inhabitants, twenty-one thousand signed the Murphy temperance pledge. Oil City, Titusville, and other towns in the oil regions were quite revolutionized. In New York the town of Corning gave three thousand signers to the pledge; Elmira, eight thousand; a very large number in Hornellsville; while in Trumansburgh, with only eighteen hundred inhabitants, there were twenty-five hundred pledges taken! the numbers being made up by visitors who came in from the regions round about. In Rhinebeck three fourths of the entire population signed the pledge. In Sherburne a thousand signed. Mr. C. E. Folsom, one of the Murphy workers, reported fifteen hundred pledges as the result of twenty-one days' work in New Berlin, N. J.

Many other towns in the State of New Jersey have already been reached by this tidal wave, and there are now about twenty reformers at work there along this Gospel temperance line.

CHAPTER XX.

PHILADELPHIA—THE NATIONAL CONVENTION—TROY, ETC.

" MR. MURPHY was launched at Pittsburgh," remarked the Rev. Dr. Cuyler, in his bright sen-
satious way. He was now fairly afloat and ready for
battle: not with any of his fellow-men, however sinful
they might be in heart or hand, but with the sin that is
in them, from which he hopes to separate them by
means of righteousness and temperance ; waiting for his
vindication from the blame which his unusual methods
of work have brought down upon him till the awards of
the judgment to come.

Early in the spring of 1877 Mr. Murphy was invited
to Philadelphia, where he opened his temperance campaign at the rooms of Mr. John Wannamaker's Sunday-
school.

For some time a series of Gospel temperance meetings
had been in progress under the auspices of the Woman's
Christian Temperance Union, and, on Mr. Murphy's arrival, the forces were ready to join in a simultaneous advance. It was a common saying among the workers—

"These men go to Mr. Murphy's meetings and sign
the pledge, and become convicted by the Holy Spirit.
and then go to the ladies' meeting and get salvation."
Mr. Murphy calls these daily afternoon meetings the
" inquiry room " for his own work.

A spirited call was issued for workers, and the women

of Philadelphia came up nobly to the front, where God greatly used them in polishing his jewels.

"At one of these women's meetings," says the "Christian Woman," "two testimonies were given, one by a man who had played in every leading theater in this country, the other by one of the most talented of his profession, who had been for five years incarcerated in the Ohio Penitentiary. He gave a recital of a burglary he and one of his associates were about to commit, and told how his heart had been so touched when, looking through the key-hole, they saw a beautiful girl kneeling and praying to Jesus to save her father, that the prayer was answered by his leaving the house undisturbed. Now this man is converted, and rejoicing in a Saviour's love.

"A bar-tender, reading in a daily paper of Mr. Murphy's meetings, felt for the first time that he would have to stop selling liquor to barefoot children and scantily dressed, half-starved women, and that very day left the nefarious business, signed the pledge, and went into an overflow meeting, led by one of the ladies, who read Ezekiel's prophecy of the dry bones. As he walked down the aisle she read, 'Shall these dry bones live?' These words, with the comments following, and a touching, pleading prayer for the stranger, fastened the power of conviction upon him. He prayed all night, and as the day dawned light broke into his soul, and now, instead of standing behind a bar, dealing out death to his fellow-man, he is lifting up Christ by offering the water of salvation and the bread of life. For eight weeks this has been going on, and about four hundred souls have been washed in the blood of the Lamb.

"Many other interesting cases of reform are reported. One was that of a young man who at first refused to sign the pledge, but was at last induced by a lady to pledge himself to abstain for ten days. He was on the verge of *delirium tremens*, and had almost at once to be shut up in his room and put under medical treatment. Many prayers were offered up for him, and he recovered, and was converted."

The following curious incident from the work at Wheeling, Va., is from the same paper :—

"There was a large meeting in the Opera House. Francis Murphy had spoken and left for the train. How could the crowd be held and the cause advanced?

"A prayer was breathed to God for help. Just then there was a stir—a parting of the crowd, and a stalwart man in Indian costume came forward, and, with a wild Indian war-whoop, that made the blood fairly curdle in one's veins, signed the pledge. Facing the audience and holding up the pen, he challenged ' Buffalo Bill,' another wild scout of the mountains, turned actor, to do the same:

"' Come on and sign, Bill, you know you ought to; you know you drink more whisky than is good for you. You and all your company ought to come forward and sign this pledge.

"' I don't sign it because I drink—I never drank a drop in my life. My mother died when I was only a child, and she said to me just before she died, "Little Jack, I want you to promise me that you will never drink a drop of intoxicating drinks;" and I promised her, and I have kept sacred the promise I made to my mother.'

" Then, turning to the audience, he made a thrilling
address, full of original thought.   The audience was elec-
trified.   Mrs. Riley talked with him, urging him at once
to abandon the stage and give himself to Christ and his
work.   He was almost persuaded, but he pleaded previous engagements.   He said that he was to pilot a company through the wilds of the Rocky Mountains this
summer, and then he would throw himself into the temperance cause.

" Mr. Murphy is full of sympathy—has a kind word
for the poorest beggar that approaches him.   ' You dear
child, God bless you !' is the greeting the ragged,
wretched, bloated victims of rum receive, as he grasps
their hands with a hearty Irish cordiality.   ' Be men !'
' Dare to do right as God gives you to see the right.'
If he succeeds in teaching professing Christians the lesson of the brotherhood of man in *Christ* his mission will
be a blessed one.

" There has been more hand-shaking in this city since
Mr. Murphy came than ever before in the same length
of time.   He is never taken by surprise, or in the least
embarrassed.   If a man speaks too long he pats him lovingly on the shoulder and tells him, ' Now you must stop
—God bless you, brother,' and, grasping his hand, leads
him off to a seat, while Mr. and Mrs. Lincoln, who are
always ready with an appropriate song, make melody.
An appeal is made by Mr. Murphy at the close of each
meeting for all who have not done so to come forward
and sign the pledge.   ' Come forward, men, and sign the
pledge ! Now, Brother Lincoln, sing us into the kingdom !'
And while the music rolls like the chimes of silver bells

hundreds crowd forward to sign the pledge. The three
tables on which the pledge books lie are soon surrounded
by an eager throng, awaiting their turn to sign the Murphy pledge, a duplicate of which they carry away with
them on a card. An hour or more is thus passed in securing pledges, the choir, led by Mr. and Mrs. Lincoln,
keeping up the music as long as the crowd throng the
tables to sign the pledge.

"It is estimated that over twelve thousand have already taken the vows of total abstinence upon themselves. And still the good work goes on."

Mr. Murphy does not propose to take to himself the
glory that belongs to God, though he is often found
fault with for insisting on having what he thinks rightly
belongs to himself. In one of his addresses he says:—

"The speakers who preceded me have been pleased to
call this movement a 'Murphy' movement. To look
upon this vast audience you would think that a pretty
good crop of 'Murphies' has been raised this year.

"I have not had a good night's rest in a week, for I
have been traveling constantly during that time to speak
at temperance meetings, and it is a work of love with
me to do what I can do to stop men from drinking rum.
But it is not my work to save them. That must be done
by the grace of God.

"You belong to the Murphy movement, do you? I
don't amount to any thing. This is not Murphyism, but
Godism. If there were nothing in the movement but
my name it never would have reached your city."

For the last two or three months the Philadelphia meetings were held in the Annex, on the ground of the Cen-

tennial Exhibition, where great crowds were constantly in attendance, and there he was assisted by some of the best temperance talent in the country. The farewell meeting was held there on the 18th of June : but after Mr. Murphy's departure the work was still carried on by the Woman's Christian Temperance Union ; which seems every-where to be the ultimate dependence, after all, for steady, persistent, persevering temperance effort.

Of the reform movement in Ohio Mr. James C. Dunn, Corresponding Secretary of the National Christian Temperance Union, contributes the following interesting account for this volume. It is by no means a full record of the reform in that State, but serves to indicate its spirit and something of its wonderful success :—

COLUMBUS, *December* 1, 1877.

DEAR BROTHER : The Temperance wave struck Columbus about the 27th of March, 1877. A meeting was held in the rooms of the Young Men's Christian Association, and an address was made by a Mr. Weber, from Pittsburgh. The meeting was sparsely attended, and, although but " thirty-five " signed the pledge, it got the Christian people to thinking that it was time to be up and doing, and the result of the meeting was that a committee was appointed to confer with the pastors to get their co-operation. All the pastors except *three* agreed to use their influence, and the committee, backed by the pastors and the Christian people, set to work to have the Murphy movement inaugurated in our city.

Prof. Cook, Principal of the High School, and O. B. Stockwell, Secretary of the R. R. branch of the Y. M. C. A., went to Pittsburgh to select the workers to start the work in earnest. Their choice fell on three men, Gilbert M'Master, Robert Lowe, and David Hall. M'Master was a lawyer by profession, Robert Lowe, an ex-Mayor of Steubenville, Ohio, and David Hall, a reformed saloon-keeper. These men had all seen and felt the evil effect of strong drink, and they proved to be the right men in the right place. They came to Columbus on the 5th of April, and went to work in earnest. A meeting was held in Wesley Chapel on the evening of the 6th of April, and one hundred and fifty-one signed the pledge; on the 7th, one hundred and forty-one; on the 8th seventy-five signers were obtained. The work had begun in earnest; the people were aroused, and, after a few meetings held in the above place, it was thought best to seek more commodious quarters. The Opera House and the City-hall were engaged, and were filled with the curious crowd. The roll began to get larger, and during the time that meetings were held in the City-hall signers were obtained at the rate of two hundred to three hundred per night.

In the early part of the movement the Christian people were the principal signers. But it was not long before the boys, as we call them, were captured, one by one at first, and then by dozens. The saloons began to show signs of dull trade, and I have it from the proprietors themselves that business had fallen off from $100 per day down to $20 and $25 per day. The largest saloon in our city was compelled to close its doors, and several of the smaller ones gave up. After nine weeks' work Mr. M'Master and Mr. Lowe left us for other fields of labor.

They had done their work well, and will ever be remembered by the temperance people of our city. On the 30th of April a meeting was called for men only. Over twelve hundred men gathered together at the City-hall, and organized the Columbus Christian Temperance Union.

After the organization had been completed calls came from the towns around us for help, and as we had brought out some good talent we were in good trim to send out speakers through the country.

Meetings were started in Delaware, Circleville, Xenia, London, Logan, Winchester, Lancaster, and in almost every town within fifty miles of Columbus.

The work was started in Cincinnati by Gilbert M'Master and James C. Dunn, and I leave it to others to tell of the good work that was done in that city. In all the towns where we were instrumental in beginning the work organizations were formed, and the work was carried on till in most of the smaller towns every saloon was closed and most of the citizens had signed the pledge. During all this time we had many speakers, from Pittsburgh and other places, among whom J. Mentini, Mr. Swartzwelder, of Pittsburgh, Geo. Hall, Charles Wenzell, and many others, who did a good work while with us. Francis Murphy was with us June 7, 8, 9, and none heard him but acknowledged that there is but one Francis Murphy. As the warm weather crept upon us the interest began to fall off. But the meetings were kept up, and new names were added to the roll.

Out-door meetings in the Park and in front of the State House were a grand success, and were kept up during the warm weather.

This brings me up to the first of October, with fourteen thousand signers. As we look back and see the good work that has been done, we cannot but acknowledge that this work is the work of God. The movement was begun in prayer, and it will end in glory. It has been estimated by those who have kept their eyes open that not two per cent. of those who have signed the pledge in our city have gone back. Many have joined the Church, and are clinging to the cross. I mention a few cases of those who have been saved. Fred Kent, well known to the theatrical profession, was a rather remarkable case. He had fallen so low that he was shunned by every one. Stripped of all his money and all his friends, he seemed lost, indeed. But he was induced to sign the pledge. His record since he came out for temperance has been a good one. He has proved himself to be a *man*, and has done good work for the Murphy cause.

Isaac Tucker's case was another rather remarkable one. A man of about forty-five years of age; most of his life had been spent in debauchery, and, to use his own words, he had not drawn a sober breath for a year previous to signing the pledge. He has proved himself to be one of our best workers, as well as a tip-top speaker.

I will mention one more case, one of our colored brothers, Ned Brown, as he is always called. Ned was a hard case. It was not thought possible that Ned could keep the pledge. His whole life had been spent in debauchery and sin. No one would trust him; his word was good for nothing, and it seemed impossible for a man to get lower than he was. But Ned signed and

21*

has kept the pledge. He has joined the Church, and has done a noble work. It is Ned Brown no longer, but Mr. Brown.

All the officers of the Union, with the exception of two, are reformed men, and one of them was elected Corresponding Secretary of the National Christian Temperance Union, at the late Convention held at Cleveland, October 17. Many other cases could be mentioned would time admit. Here is a partial summary of what has been done: we have sent out one hundred and four speakers, all reformed men; we have closed two hundred saloons in Franklin County; one hundred and seventy thousand have signed the pledge within a circuit of seventy miles of Columbus; up to this date we have sent out over two hundred thousand pledges; we have relieved the wants of many, clothed the naked, and fed the hungry.

Our organization is now in good working order; meetings are being held four times a week, and signers are obtained every day. Hoping and trusting that the good work may go on, I am yours,

JAMES C. DUNN,

Cor. Sec., National Christian Temperance Union.

Mr. Murphy spent the summer of 1877 in vain attempts to rest. Wherever he went he was discovered, and prevailed upon to speak. Invitations came from various camp-meetings to come there and rest, and talk a little on temperance, to many of which he responded, thereby adding to his wide and growing popularity. The camp-meeting at Sea Cliff, under his direction, was one of the notable temperance events of the year. He was also in great request for "lectures" under the Lyceum system, and filled a number of such engagements at one hundred and two hundred dollars a night. For this he was severely criticised, as making merchandise of temperance, not only by certain good temperance people, but by some of the secular newspapers.

Whether these criticisms were the inevitable penalty of success in public life, or whether they were of the nature of that friendly and righteous rebuke which is like an excellent oil instead of a head-breaking cudgel, does not yet appear; but, after making a number of such engagements, Mr. Murphy became convinced that this was out of the line of his divine calling, and, therefore, canceled them, falling back upon such support as might come from his regular Gospel temperance missions

TROY.

On Sunday, the eighteenth of November, 1877, Mr. Murphy opened his temperance campaign in the city of Troy, N. Y. His coming was in response to a call in which the Ministerial Association, the Methodist Preachers' Meeting, and twenty-five leading citizens of Troy united. The correspondence was conducted by the Rev. George C. Baldwin, D.D., who for thirty-three years has been the pastor of the Third-street Baptist Church of that city, and who was the first man to suggest and advocate this measure for promoting a temperance revival.

The well-known motto of Mr. Murphy, " With malice toward none, with charity for all," as well as the non-

sectarian, non-political character of the movement, dis-
armed all opposition in advance. The city government
voted the reformer the free use of the new and elegant
City-hall for his meetings; the press gave him a hearty
reception; and thus, under the most favorable auspices,
this great revival effort opened, which was destined not
only to prove a means of temperance and other grace to
the city itself, but to spread its saving influence over the
whole surrounding region of country.

The plan of the work was the same as that in Pittsburgh—first, public evening meetings, opened with devotional services, and aimed at securing signers to the
total abstinence pledge; second, noonday prayer-meetings at some church, where God's blessing should be
statedly and steadily implored upon the work, the
workers, and the reformed men; third, overflow and
branch meetings in various parts of the city; and last,
but not least, personal interviews held by Mr. Murphy
and his assistants, for the purpose of giving religious instruction to those who, having taken the first step toward God by throwing away their cups, were desirous of
knowing what was the next thing to do to be saved.

One pleasing feature of the work in Troy is the cordial co-operation of the clergy, the press, the city government, and the citizens of all classes.

Dr. Baldwin, of the Baptist Church; Rev. Mr. Farrar,
of the Methodist Episcopal Church; Rev. Mr. Robinson,
of the Presbyterian Church, have been among the leaders
and helpers; "The Times," "Press," "Trojan," and other
daily and weekly newspapers, have aided the movement
with admirable reports of the great meetings, while from

Albany, West Troy, Fort Edward, and many other places, have come in pressing calls for the services of this temperance evangelist, or some of his able corps of assistants.

A feature of pleasing and powerful interest in the Troy meetings is the singing of Mr. and Mrs. Wilson, the latter a sister of the sainted P. P. Bliss, whose Gospel songs, inspired from heaven, and lovingly written and published, may now be heard around the world. Colonel Colwell, of Elmira, already mentioned, is the Nestor of the troupe. "We all go by the colonel," says Mr. Murphy, showing his kind and generous appreciation of this gentleman, considerably his senior, who, having been converted under the Gospel temperance preaching of Mr. Eccles Robinson, one of "Murphy's men," at Elmira, has closed his connection with business and politics, and devoted himself to the work of saving men, especially drinking-men.

In the address of this ex-landlord, at West Troy, where, at the invitation of the Rev. Mr. Alderman, of the Methodist Episcopal Church, a branch meeting was established on the day after Thanksgiving, the colonel said :—

" I have drank all sorts of liquors in all sorts of society. My knees have been under the Governor's mahogany, where I have hob-nobbed with senators and assembly men, and I have drank cheap whisky in corner groceries which were in our political interest. I have taken the wine-cup from the jeweled hand of elegance and beauty, and had a drink shoved at me over a sloppy groggery bar. I know all about this business. I have drank liquor and sold liquor, and I tell you it is a bad business both for drinker and seller.

"Our doctrine is 'With malice toward none, with charity for all.' Now when you go a-fishing, you put on a bait such as you think the fish will like, and this Gospel bait of love and kindness is what caught me up at Elmira last year. You might have bobbed for me for a life-time with a hook baited with hard words, and prohibitory laws, and temperance politics, and I never should have done more than look at it; but when Brother Robinson dropped this charity down before me I swallowed it—hook, line, bob, sinker, and all.

"Depend upon it, there are plenty of other just such fish as I was, behind the bar as well as in front of it; and what is to hinder you from catching them, just as they caught me?"

Then, after relating the story of his conversion, first to teetotalism and then to Gospel grace, in answer to the prayers of his wife and daughter, he announced that he and Mr. E. T. Murphy, a worthy son of his father, who, though but eighteen years of age, is beginning to develop a high order of talent for temperance work, had come to West Troy to stay—how long he did not know, but he hoped till the last drunkard in that section of this city had been persuaded to sign the pledge and give his heart to God.

The noonday prayer-meetings in Dr. Baldwin's Church are a reliable feature of this Gospel temperance revival. Here, as elsewhere, religion is in the foreground.

It is related that a couple of men who claimed to be "Murphyites" because they were reformed inebriates, went out to hold temperance meetings in a Virginia town, boldly announcing that they "wouldn't have any religion in theirs;" but their efforts resulted in conspicuous failure, and one of them remarked to his comrade: "I say, Jim, we can't do a thing at this temperance if we don't have a prayer-meeting:" thus irreverently bearing testimony to the supernatural source of this great temperance movement.

As a specimen of those noonday prayer-meetings, take the last which it was the privilege of the writer of these pages to attend :—

On the day before Mr. Murphy had caught sight of three or four ragged fellows who had lately signed the pledge, sitting in one of the rear pews; and straightway he left the pulpit, went to them, insisted that they should take seats in front, and then at a proper time actually pressed them into speaking a word, as his custom is, by way of committing themselves more fully to their new way of life, and of gaining the blessing from the Lord which is reserved for those who confess him.

"I have signed the pledge," said one of them, "but I want something more. Pray for my salvation through and through."

"We will, my brother," replied the leader. "Come up to me after meeting." Then, turning to the congregation, he said, "Our Saviour tells us, 'I am not sent but to the *lost sheep* of the house of Israel.' Now I want to know if these Christian people are ready to stand by that doctrine?"

"We will! We will!" was the response; the audience

catching the speaker's meaning at once, without stopping to think of the rational bearing of these words, but remembering only the *lostness* of the sheep, which the great Shepherd came to find.

"Well, then, take a look into your wardrobes, and see if father or husband hasn't a coat he doesn't need. It is coming cold weather, and there is a great deal of grace as well as comfort in a warm coat given to a poor fellow who is cold."

Then at the close of the meeting he said: "Here is Brother Ellis, one of our reformed men. He can do up your painting for you. Any body who wants a room touched up, just let me know, and I'll send you round a man to do it in genuine teetotal style."

The "Troy Times," in its ample and spirited reports on the Murphy movement, has this little sketch of this same man and his speech at one of the City-hall meetings:—

"With his characteristic good nature Mr. Murphy turned to Henry Ellis, a 'bummer,' converted but a few days ago, and said: 'Come along, Brother Ellis, and tell us how your head aches to-night.' He (Ellis) remarked that he supposed he was the proudest man in the city of Troy last night, and wished he was as good-looking as he felt. 'And why shouldn't I feel well?' he exclaimed. 'Why is it that people who would not speak to me two weeks ago shake hands with me now, and give me kind words of encouragement? What a difference between my position now, and as it was only a few weeks ago, when I was locked up in the jail, walking the hard floor of my cell, and longing for the morning light to come. ['God help him!' from a voice in the audience.]

Thank God, to-night I am a temperance man, sincere in my purpose, and propose to stick to every vow.'

"On another occasion Mr. Murphy announced that he had the pleasure of introducing to the audience an inmate of the jail, whom Ellis had succeeded, with the permission of the keeper, in inducing to accompany him to the hall and sign the pledge. Martin Peelor was led to the platform, and spoke as follows:—

"'Allow me, my kind friends, to speak to you a few minutes. This evening at six o'clock my friend, Mr. Ellis, came to the Troy jail, and invited me to come and hear Francis Murphy, and take the pledge. Just now the thought flashes across my mind that the last glass of liquor I drank was on my way to the jail, given me by this same man Ellis. While in this hall my mind has been wandering back over my past life. Ten years ago I took my position in society, and was a man among men. Language cannot adequately express my feelings when I think of those days; memory almost breaks a bursting heart. To-night I shall sleep in yonder jail, but, my friends, I feel like a brand plucked from a burning pile, and I am happy to say, God helping me, I shall in the future lead a life of virtue and sobriety.

"' For the past ten years I have been whipped through the world with the lash of scorn. I see before me familiar faces, and I warn them all to take a lesson from my experience. The habit of drinking strengthens itself until the appetite for liquor becomes ungovernable. God helping me, I would not take another drop of liquor for the wealth of a continent.' Mr. Murphy declared the man should not sleep in the jail that night—that it would be a shame for them to allow him to go there; that he had trodden the floor of the cell for the last time. This was the signal for loud and prolonged applause from the audience, which had been very much affected by the ex-drunkard's remarks."

On this day of which we are now to speak Mr. Murphy came in, shaking hands all along the aisle, mounted the pulpit in a reverent manner, and knelt in prayer behind the desk, getting down almost out of sight in a manner which seemed to say how marvelous a thing it was that in the great mercy of God he should be there at all. Then, rising, he opened his Bible to the twelfth chapter of Romans, and began to read, explaining a little as he went along. This Bible study and explanation is coming to be one of Mr. Murphy's strong points, and many a deep and lasting impression does he make by some luminous opening up of a common truth, shining with light from God's holy word. Thus, when he came to the fifth verse he said :—

" I wish we could find out the true spirit of that text. We are apt to think that *we* are doing about all the really pure things that are done, but the truth is we are all doing business on other people's capital. This great river, that rolls past your city so grandly, has forgotten all about the little brooks and springs up among the hills without which it could not be a river at all. Just so with ourselves: we think we have done some great thing, when, quite likely, we caught the inspiration of it from some little word from another's tongue, or some tear in another's eye. Paul would have us remember that we all belong together. Just hear what he says:

' So we, being many, are one body in Christ, and every one members one of another.' That is, we are all knit together, like a stocking."

That beautiful song, " The Ninety and Nine," was now sung, arranged as a duett by " Brother and Sister Wilson," as he always calls them, and then Mr. Murphy asked those who desired the prayers of God's people to help them keep the pledge and to save them from all their sins, to stand up. Three rough-looking men arose, and Rev. Dr. Robinson offered a most tender and loving petition in their behalf.

And now up rises an old gentleman, and breaks into the line of exercises to tell of a drunkard's wife and the mother of six children, whose husband has just signed the pledge, and who has sent a request by him to the meeting to join her in the thanksgiving to God.

" Shall I give you the second verse of that chapter?" said Rev. Mr. Farrar. " A poor woman rang my door-bell early this morning, and when I went to open it she said,

" ' I want you to see my husband's pledge,' and then she held up one of these little cards, with her husband's name on it, saying, ' I am so happy? so happy.'

Col. Collwell next arose and said, " I can give the third verse. A woman came to me at our meeting in West Troy last night, with a face shining with joy, and said, ' My husband, my son, and my father, have all signed the pledge to-day.' "

This brought Dr. Baldwin to his feet:

" We had an old-fashioned Baptist covenant meeting

at our Church last night," said he, "where every one of the deacons had on a blue ribbon, (the Murphy badge,) and forty-five people signed the pledge."

After prayer by Brother Wilson, he and his wife, perhaps the most effective Gospel singers in America, sang, with indescribable effect, the sweet song entitled,

"That will be heaven for me?"

Then, while a divine tenderness seemed to have touched all hearts in the great congregation, and many were wiping away the tears, Mr. Murphy called up a man who had been imprisoned for drunkenness again and again, and who had recently signed the pledge, sought the Saviour, and found a new life, but who had never opened his voice in public prayer:

"Come up here, Brother Ellis, come up here on the platform besides us, and lead us all in prayer."

It was no small cross for such a man to do such a thing in such presence, but the leader took him by the hand, helped him to his place, and knelt beside him at the front of the platform, while in a few penitent, earnest, simple words this reformed, regenerated drunkard uttered his first public prayer.

The scene can be better imagined than described. But the climax of the meeting was reached when Mr. Murphy offered prayer for himself, for his work, and for the poor shivering and hungry bodies, the broken hearts, and the tempted souls of the victims of strong drink. Taking up the thought of the fatherhood of God, he claimed to be like a little child who had started from its cradle, and with tottering steps, clinging to chairs and tables and stools, was trying to get to its father's knee and climb up into his arms.

When the prayer was ended, one of the brethren on the platform, who had heard a great many severe remarks against this reformer, some of them even questioning his sincerity, leaned over to his next neighbor, who, like himself, was in tears, and said:—

"No man could pray like that except God were with him."

Before the meeting closed Mr. Murphy gave some good advice to "the boys" about going to Church.

"Too many other temperance reforms," said he, "have led men away from the Churches, but this reform is to bring them into the Church. Fill up the Churches, boys. The Church is your mother.

"When I was a raw emigrant, wandering up and down in this strange country, looking for something to do to keep myself from starving, how I longed to get back to that little cottage by the sea, where my dear mother was! Ah, she is gone away from the cottage now! I may go to the dear old spot some time, but it will not be 'home' any more, for my mother has moved away—up yonder. Boys, the Church is your mother; come home to her!"

"You say, perhaps, that the Church doesn't care for you, and so you go off and complain of her. Now, that isn't fair. When the shepherd goes out into the mountains after the lost sheep, the sheep ought not to hide away from him. Show yourselves, boys; put yourselves in the way of those who are looking for you; come to the house of God, and you will find warm hearts and brotherly hands among his people."

As this volume goes to press the Gospel temperance revival at Troy, and in the surrounding sections of country, is deepening and spreading. The first two weeks showed thirty-five hundred signatures to the total abstinence pledge, crowds in attendance at the City-hall meetings, with frequent overflow meetings at churches near by; a general awakening among the Churches to new life and activity, a cordial union among the clergy in the good work, and the evident blessing of Heaven, which was manifest in the increasing number of reformed men who were asking what they should do to be saved from all the rest of their sins.

THE NATIONAL CHRISTIAN TEMPERANCE UNION is the name adopted by the affiliated societies of the United States which have sprung up under the labors of Francis Murphy and his helpers. It was organized at Pittsburgh, Feb. 22, 1877. Its spirit will appear from the following preamble to its Constitution :—

"*Whereas*, The evil effects of intemperance upon individuals and communities have become so very apparent that it is now the duty of all well-disposed persons to join in united effort to reclaim those already fallen, or in danger of becoming habituated to the use of stimulants, and by every honorable method to stay its further progress; therefore, recognizing our dependence on almighty God, and desiring the assistance of divine·grace in our efforts in this behalf, we hereby organize ourselves into an association for the purpose of preventing the further progress of the evil, having as our motto the ever-memorable words of Abraham Lincoln, ' With malice toward none, and charity for all.' We agree to be governed by the following Constitution and By-laws."

Its first officers were, President, Francis Murphy; First Vice-President, Marshall Swartzwelder; Second Vice-President, W. C. Moreland; Recording Secretary, F. X. Burns; Corresponding Secretary, J. H. Miller; Treasurer, Joseph Dilworth; Executive Committee, Jas. Parks, Jun., Capt. J. K. Barbour, Jos. R. Hunter, W. Mason Evans, S. H. Baird—most, if not all, of them reformed inebriates, and some of them life-long victims of strong drink.

The Constitution provides for holding County, State and National Temperance Conventions, as well as local unions. The second session of the National Convention was held at Cleveland, Ohio, October 17-19, at which an interesting report of the first year's work was read by Capt. Barbour, Secretary to the Executive Committee.

From this report the following extracts are made:—

" From all the information received fully 3,000,000 of people have signed the total abstinence pledge ; and we can safely say that not over two per cent. have broken their pledge ; and we have discovered that when individuals, no matter how degraded through the effects of strong drink, have placed their trust and reliance on divine aid and commenced an entirely new life, they have been enabled to stand up faithfully, and are to-day among the front rank, battling nobly in the cause of Christ and suffering humanity."

After reference to the work in Ohio, which has been given elsewhere, the report continues:—

" In the State of New York the work was inaugurated

only last March, in Elmira and Dunkirk, and since that time the southern tiers of counties of the Empire State have been ablaze, and on the tenth of last September they organized a State association, with a firm determination that, with God's help, they will strive to continue and push the work so nobly begun.

"The benign influence of the work has permeated the whole State of Indiana, although we have no report of a State organization in that State.

"Kentucky has also felt the influence of its healing balm, and thousands of her people have been redeemed from the thralldom of intemperance. On the tenth of this month she organized a State association.

"Tennessee has applied for help.

"We hear the glad tidings from Missouri, that since last July over twenty thousand of her people have signed the pledge. On the tenth of this month she held her State Convention, and will also add her voice in this Convention in favor of total abstinence.

"Illinois, Kansas, and Nebraska are now reaping the benefit of the work, but as yet we have no official report from these States.

"We also hear from the far-off State of Colorado, which rolls up some twenty or thirty thousand signers of the pledge. On the tenth of this month she also held her State Convention, and will, no doubt, be largely represented in this Convention.

"Your committee have had several inquiries from the extreme Southern States for aid, but as yet no definite arrangements have been made to commence the work.

"We would also report that proper caution has not been exercised by the auxiliary unions in receiving and employing speakers to assist in carrying on the work. Men of no character, or men who are not in sympathy with the movement, have been secured, and when it was too late they have discovered that they had obtained more than they had bargained for. Your committee asked the last Convention to instruct them how to avoid this, and a resolution was passed instructing the committee not to give open credentials to any person, and only to give letters of introduction to the place when asked for, and as soon as they get through in that locality they should get fresh letters to the next place where their services are required. We then thought that was a sufficient protection to the cause. But the people were so anxious that the movement should be inaugurated in their midst that they received any one who cried Murphy, or could say a word for temperance, no matter under what auspices. In consequence, the work has been injured, and in some instances it would have been better if it had never begun.

"Now, your committee would ask that a resolution be passed that no speaker or worker be secured by an auxiliary, unless furnished with credantials as to character, influence, and knowledge of the work, signed by the secretary of the organization to which he belongs, if he labors in his own county. If his labors are out of the county, it must be indorsed by the Secretary of his State organization and by the Secretary of the national organization.

"This recommendation was adopted.
22

" The officers of the National Christian Temperance Union elected at this Annual Convention were :—

" President, Francis Murphy, Pittsburgh.

" Vice-Presidents, A. P. Herriford, Colorado ; James A. Beaver, Pennsylvania ; Rev. E. W. Archer, Ohio ; John Barry, New York ; Rev. A. Fanney, Indiana ; E. E. De-Garmo, Missouri ; Rev. J. E. Gilbert, Kentucky.

" Corresponding Secretary, James C. Dunn, Columbus, Ohio.

" Recording Secretary, Rev. J. E. Letton, of Nicholsville, Kentucky.

" Treasurer, John M'Clymonds, of Cleveland.

" W. H. Doan, of Cleveland, Joseph Dillworth, of Pittsburgh, John M. Dunlap, of Missouri, R. F. Smith and William Bowler, of Cleveland, Board of Managers."

DWIGHT L. MOODY.

SECTION VIII.

EVANGELISTIC OR "GOSPEL" TEMPERANCE.

CHAPTER XXI.

GOSPEL TEMPERANCE.—MR. MOODY.

THE climax of the temperance reform is the doctrine, which is supported by multitudes of personal testimonies, that through faith in Jesus Christ, and by the power of the Holy Spirit of God exercised upon the submissive, obedient believer, the power of the alcohol appetite over him may be immediately and absolutely broken, so that the drunkard of yesterday, lost to society, family, honor, and hope, may become the reconstructed Christian of to-day, happy in his deliverance from the bondage of a lifetime, and safe, divinely safe, from its old irresistible enticement.

It is a well-known fact that the effects of alcohol upon the stomach, and, through it, upon the whole nervous system, are such that they often bring a drunkard into that wretched state where his own will, though roused to action by the strongest motives which can be found in heaven, earth, or hell, is powerless to resist the craving for strong drink. "*I must have it*," is the desperate cry, before which every thing else is of no account. Under the earlier dispensations of the temperance movement such slaves of appetite were given over to perish, just as the doctors give over to certain and speedy death those patients whose diseases are wholly beyond the reach of the healing art. They were mournfully useful as awful examples; their lost condition being used as the rich man in hell wanted his case to be used, that is, as a warning to his brethren lest they also should come to the same torments; but that such a drunkard could be saved was what no one ventured to hope, unless it might be his broken-hearted wife or his praying mother.

Love, with something of omnipotence about it, can sometimes create a hope out of nothing, just as God creates worlds; and, alas! how often the hopes thus made of nothing have come to nothing again!

But in these last days men have learned that there is such communication between heaven and earth that the powers of the one may be invoked to cure the ills of the other. "Why should it be thought a thing incredible that God should raise the dead?" and why should it be thought a thing incredible that the love of God, and the grace of our Lord Jesus Christ, and the communion of the Holy Ghost, should save and keep a drunkard from his appetite for strong drink?

"But that would be a straight-out miracle," some one will reply, "and the days of miracles are past."

Alas for us! Some theological doctor sometime took it into his head that the days of miracles were past, because he had never happened to witness any miracles and in an evil day, he wrote down his opinion in a book which came to be an "authority," just as that other falsehood came to be an authority, namely, "The velocity of falling bodies is in proportion to their weight." Aristotle taught that theory, and the world accepted it on his authority; but one day Galileo bethought him to prove the thing. So he got him two balls of lead, one weighing one pound and the other two, and, having invited some of the chief admirers of the dead "authority" to witness his experiment, he went up to the top of the leaning tower at Pisa, dropped the two balls at the same instant, and, of course, they struck the ground together: for we have learned that the velocity of falling bodies is in proportion to their specific gravity, or density, and not according to their weight.

But the medieval doctors who witnessed Galileo's test were exceeding mad, and said, " He must be possessed of the devil to be able to do such a thing contrary to nature," whereas it was contrary to nothing except their own ignorance, prejudice, and pride.

In just this way that old false doctrine, " The day of miracles is past," which neither appears in the word of God, nor yet in the experience of mankind, has shut the door of hope against all men who were so far gone in the sin of drunkenness, either by the use of alcohol or opium, that their appetites could neither be reached by medicine nor controlled by their will. But of late years, especially in connection with religious awakenings under the labors of the great evangelists, both in Europe and America, here and there a man has testified that he has been saved at once and entirely not only from the sin of drunkenness, but *from the appetite for strong drink.*

" Impossible!" cried the believers in antiquated " authorities." But the number of such cases began to multiply; Christian workers began to think that " perhaps there was something in it:" by and by, in connection with the revivals under the labors of Mr. Hammond, Mr. Moody, Francis Murphy, Major Cole, Mrs. Lathrop,

Charles Morton, and at the meetings of the Christian temperance women all over the country, it began to be a frequent occurrence for men to rise from the gutter, come into the prayer and inquiry rooms, or kneel at the altar; and in a little while, during which time they had been taught how to lay hold on the hope set before them in the Gospel, they declared themselves saved from the curse of alcohol, appetite and all.   By the same power men and women rose up here and there to bear testimony that, through faith in His name by whom the lame man walked they also had been delivered from the subtle slavery of opium.

At the close of this section ample testimony will be produced to establish the fact that the Lord Jesus Christ, the Saviour of sinners, has placed his infinite grace within reach of the lost and hopeless inebriate, and that on condition of his consecrating himself to God, even in his wretchedness and ruin, the divine power laid up in store to meet his case will be given to him, and the man may experience a complete deliverance from this miserable " body of death "—a liberty which will continue as long as he clings to his Saviour's hand.

D. L. MOODY.

Mr. Moody's connection with the Temperance Reform Movement is incidental.   Temperance is one of the Christian virtues, and, as such, this great evangelist feels it his duty to teach it.   He does not regard the sin of drunkenness as any worse than the sin of lying, or Sabbath-breaking; but when the Gospel Temperance Movement had become so noticeable and so successful he found it well to give up one regular service each week to the work of saving sinners from this particular sin.

He does not teach that drunkards are in any greater need of salvation than other sinners, or that they are to be saved in any different way. Worldly mindedness, pride, the lust of the flesh, and the lust of the eyes, are all as certain to destroy men's souls as the vice of drunkenness; and this view of the case, which is somewhat unusual, is sometimes a ray of hope to those who have by common consent been given over to destruction because they were in the power of strong drink.

Mr. Moody has seen instances in which people have been saved not only from the habit of drunkenness, but, also, from the desire for drink; accordingly, he has changed his former opinions, as he himself declares; and now a large proportion of the lost ones for whom he labors are men and women of this class.

With his usual radicalism and impetuosity Mr. Moody has taken a firm hold of this " Gospel Temperance," and preaches the power of divine grace as the *only* salvation from this sin. He even refuses to co-operate with those who rely upon such human means as signing the pledge, reform clubs, mutual benefit associations, and the like.

He declares that there is no power in man to save himself; that he is totally lost, and that, whether he be a drunkard or any other kind of sinner, if he is saved at all, it must be by the sovereign grace of God.

Mr. Moody is in this, as in other things, entirely consistent with himself. He accepts the conclusions which, as he thinks, these doctrines force upon him, to the no small regret of many excellent Christian men and wom-

22*

en, who see no harm, but rather help, in leading drunkards even so far out of the old ways as to resolve to reform, and signify that resolve by signing the temperance
pledge. But Mr. Moody's temperance work is strictly
Gospel work. Every thing else he holds to be simply a
waste of time.

At one of the Gospel Temperance meetings in Boston,
which were held every Friday, Mr. Moody read the first
six verses of the Fortieth Psalm: "I waited patiently for
the Lord; and he inclined unto me, and heard my
cry," etc.

"In these six verses we find five precious things:
first, ' He heard my cry.' That is what God always does;
if a man cries from the heart, God always hears him.
Next, ' He brought me up, also, out of a horrible pit,
out of the miry clay.' The margin says the ' noisy pit,'
and that is just the pit the drunkards are in. There are
some old pits in England that go away down to the
roots of the mountains. Now, you set a man down into
one of the coal-pits, fifteen hundred or two thousand feet
deep, and he cannot get out without some one to help
him; but he could get out of that pit easier than he
could out of the pit Adam put us into. Only Christ can
lift us out of that.

"Next, ' He hath put a new song in my mouth.' You
sometimes hear drunkards singing in the saloons, but
their songs are lewd and blasphemous. Now, with the
new heart a man has a new song: a song of the praise
of God; a song of victory over self and sin; a song of
redemption by Jesus Christ. Here, in the sixth verse, he

says: 'Mine ears hast thou opened.' O, may God unstop every deaf ear to-day to hear the joyful song of the Gospel! And what great things the Lord hath done for those who have trusted in him! Then he says, 'Many shall see it, and fear;' and when God comes right into the congregation, and begins to save the people, and the young converts begin to tell what God has done for them—that brings God pretty near, so that we can see what he is doing, and people who prefer to have God a long way off sometimes get frightened.

MR. MOODY'S DISCOURSE ON THE MARRIAGE FEAST OF CANA OF GALILEE.

"In this second chapter of John we have an account of Christ's miracle of turning water into wine.

"When Moses began his miracles down in Egypt he turned the water into blood, that is, into death; but when Christ began his miracles he turned the water into wine, that is, into life and joy. That is the difference between the law and the Gospel. The law says, 'Thou shalt die,' and the Gospel says, 'Believe and live.'

"Now, there is the class of people who tell us that there are no miracles which cannot be explained by natural causes; they do not believe in any thing supernatural, and they try to prove that all these miracles of Christ were nothing but sleight-of-hand performances. I should like to have such a man explain how this water was turned into wine; and when he gets through with that, let him take some of the miracles that are performed in connection with our meetings in the saving of men from their appetites for strong drink.

"I heard, in a little meeting after the prayer-meeting yesterday, a man who said that he had been a confirmed drunkard for thirty years; but he came here a week ago to-day, and the God of heaven took away his appetite for strong drink; and his face shone with joy as he told what God had done for him, soul and body. Now, that, I think, is supernatural. I should like to have any one explain how such a thing can be done by natural causes.

"I know that there are a great many who doubt these witnesses; and if a man had told me five years ago that a man could be a drunkard for twenty or forty years, and then have his appetite for liquor suddenly taken away, I should not have believed him. I have always believed that God could save a drunkard, but I supposed that he would have to carry that appetite down to the grave— fighting against it all the time. But I find that God is able to destroy the works of the devil thoroughly, and this appetite is surely one of the works of the devil.

"Hear what the mother of our Lord says when the wine had given out: 'Whatsoever he saith unto you, do it.' If men will do what God says he will give them power to resist temptation and to overcome the tempter I should like to give you this sentence as a key-note of these meetings, 'Whatsoever he saith unto you, do it.'

"Well, what does he say? If there is a man out of Christ he says to him: 'He that cometh to me I will in no wise cast out.' Your heart may be as black as hell, but come to Christ; bring your black heart along with you; he will cleanse it and purify it; that was just what he came for.

"I was very much interested last Friday in a man

who sat near the reporters' desk. He was so drunk that he fell asleep before the meeting began. I was glad to see him here, because this is the class of men that we want to get hold of; and after the meeting was over some one tried to get him into the second meeting, but he would not go; afterward he came in and presented himself for prayers.

" Now, I suppose a good many Christian people would say, 'It is no use praying for such a man as that, he is too drunk;' but the brethren gathered round him and prayed for him, and last night I found him in the inquiry room, and he had a very strange story to tell. He said that while he was on his team some of the boys said to him, 'Moses, go into that Tabernacle,' and he came in, and again and again, thinking that he was too great a sinner to be saved; but Jesus Christ came for him, and I am thankful that he is here to-day.

" Now, I want it understood that these meetings are for just such men.

" This man is saved, and his appetite for strong drink is taken away. That I call the power of God; nothing else than the power of God could have got hold of the man's heart and life and turned its whole current from sin toward righteousness. You may call that supernatural; every conversion is supernatural, I believe. This telling men to work their way into the kingdom of God is one of the devil's own delusions; nobody can get into the kingdom of God by himself. Paul says, 'You are not to be saved by works, but by faith.' Now, 'Whatsoever he saith unto you, do it.' Do your part, and see if Christ does not do his. Submit your will to his, and accept of him for your Saviour, and see if you do not get a new heart and a new life.

" ' Whatsoever ' you desire, ask it of Christ.   Are you weary?   He says, ' Come unto me, all ye that labor and are heavy laden, and I will give you rest.'   Are you blind? Come to him with your blindness, and he will open your eyes   Is your heart hard?   Take it to him ; let him soften it, and then Christ will not appear to you ' as a root out of dry ground, without form or comeliness,' but he will be 'the chiefest among ten thousand, the one altogether lovely ;' he will be to you like ' the lily of the valley,' like the 'rose of Sharon,' 'the bright and morning star.'

" I remember a man in Chicago who was the greatest drunkard I ever knew ; he was in the habit of drinking ten or a dozen glasses of lager beer every day.   But while we were holding meetings there one cold day in the winter he came into the Tabernacle, and the spirit of God touched his heart, and he resolved to reform.   He had no home ; he used to spend his time hanging about the saloons, where he spent what little money he man-aged to get   But now his heart was touched, and he re-solved to keep away from the tempter; so he went to a cheap lodging-house.   They gave him a bed there in a great room, with a good many other rough, wild, wicked people, who were talking and laughing and swearing until late into the night.

" This used not to trouble him, but now his ears were troubled by these vile words.   He endured it for awhile, and then arose from his bed in the middle of the night, put on what clothes he had, (the poor man was so far gone that he had no overcoat, and his boots were quite worn through, so that they let in the snow,) and in this condition walked the streets of Chicago all the rest of the night rather than spend it in that wicked place.

"He came to us the next morning, and told us about it. 'I was a walking prayer all night,' said he. Such prayer as that was sure to come into the ears of the Lord, and the man who was once hopeless is to-day a happy Christian.

"That is just what the Gospel says: 'If any man be in Christ, he is a new creature: old things are passed away; behold, all things are become new.' There is more difference between the new heart and the old heart than there is between the wine and the water out of which it was made. We believe in these great miracles; can we not believe in that smaller one?

"I received a letter the other day from a man who had been brought up to drink from a child, and who never saw any harm in it until he had ruined himself, and driven away his family, and become a wreck. He came into our meetings in New York one night, and he looked so bad that we thought it was hardly worth while to do any thing for him. But some of the young converts took hold of him, and began to pray with him, and when he rose up from prayer he said, 'I feel like a new man in old clothes.' His appetite for liquor was all gone, and he was a new man, indeed.

"Now, that is just what the new birth does; it not only takes away the sin, but it takes away the desire for it. There is not a day but some poor captive comes in here, bound hand and foot with the chains of drink. Some

of them say, ' I am all right,' or, ' I will come round
right by and by.'

"Others say, ' There is no use taking the pledge; I
have taken it ever so many times, and broken it.   There
is no hope for me now.'   But, thanks be unto God! I
can give you good news.   Christ is able to save you
from your sins, no matter what they are.   It is just as
easy for him to save a drunkard as to save any other
kind of sinner."

From Mr. Moody's address at the last anniversary of
the National Temperance Society :—

" I have always found enough in New York, Philadelphia, Chicago, and Boston to get up a prayer-meeting,
and we want to hold right on.   I believe that if the
Churches of New England would take hold of this matter as they ought to, and pray God that these men may
not only be reformed but regenerated, it would close up
more than half the saloons in New England in six months.
The Church of God has been asleep long enough.   We
do not want any more whitewashing; we want men re-
created, and then they will have power to overcome this
terrible appetite, to hurl the cup from them, and live as
God would have them live.   I want to throw this out as
a suggestion, and if the praying men and women in this
audience think they would like such a meeting let them
do what I suggest.

" It is easy to come up to this anniversary and clap
your hands, but we want those who are willing to work
three hundred and sixty-five days in the year.   It is a
long, steady pull, but we want it.   It seems to me this

work is in the very air. I believe we are going to put
this terrible curse away, and I trust there is a time coming when, if there is a minister of the Gospel that stands
in the pulpit and advocates a moderate use of liquor, the
men and women will get out of the Church as Lot did
out of Sodom.

"I tell you, get a man that encourages this traffic out
of your Churches. We want clean hands to carry the
pure Gospel from the Churches. We want the Church
right, and then we will have power with God and man.
I like this organization because it is stirring up the
Church. We have the Church so pure and holy, and
when the Church takes hold of this matter and reaches
a helping hand to the drunkards, and tells them that
there is hope for them, they will come flocking in. That
has been demonstrated in New York and Philadelphia.
During the past few weeks we have heard tidings from
those cities that are wonderful, and we hear them from
Pittsburgh and Ohio. The Bible wave is rising in the
West, and I hope it will sweep over the land. Let that
be our prayer and that be our work."

CHARLES W. SAWYER.

Soon after Mr. Moody began his revival work in
Chicago he sent for Mr. Charles W. Sawyer, of New
York, a "reconstructed man," as he calls himself, to
take charge of the special department of Gospel Temperance. Throughout that four months' campaign there
was a continued succession of remarkable conversions of
drunkards, some of whom have themselves become
useful temperance reformers.

Before his connection with Mr. Moody he was a well-known leader in New York city; was for awhile editor of the temperance paper called the "Living Issue;" and since he has joined that most successful of all modern evangelists his own success has been greatly increased.

In the following report of one of those Gospel Temperance meetings will be found a brief sketch of his own experience, as well as a glimpse into the manner and spirit of his work:—

"I want to call your attention to-day," said Mr. Sawyer, "to the eleventh chapter of Luke, the twenty-fourth verse;" and he forthwith proceeded to read about the unclean spirit which walked through dry places, seeking rest and finding none, and afterward returning to the house, accompanied by seven other spirits more wicked than himself.

"I thought I'd take for a key-note to-day the will of God," said Mr. Sawyer. "We have met here in the simplicity and honesty of our hearts to do his will, and it must be his will that we hold up the light of Christianity to the poor souls that are wandering in the outer darkness of sin. Let us save the souls that are struggling. What is the will of God? To believe in Him. O, I feel for those young men who are striving, and who held up their hands yesterday, and said they wanted to believe."

In concluding he said that the sisters wanted to have more praying at the meeting, so he would not make any long remarks. They had better devote the greater part of the hour to prayer, but they should each be brief. If there was a prayer fifteen minutes long, probably the person making it would omit the very things that they wanted to have remembered, whereas, if there were numerous short petitions they would very likely include every thing needful. The brethren and sisters had been toiling, and striving, and praying, and they had met with a blessing from God. It was true that they had been imposed upon frequently, but though the wicked ones might deceive men, they could not deceive God. "Now go right along with your short prayers."

There was no hesitation about responding to this invitation. Half a dozen brethren and sisters followed each other with petitions to the throne of grace for the souls of those that were bound by the chains of drunkenness.

The hymn, " Did Christ o'er sinners weep ? " was then sung.

" Our key-note is to do the will of God," said Mr. Sawyer, "and the will of God is that we indulge in prayer and thanksgiving. We have had prayer, now let us have thanksgiving. I have been sheltered behind his blood for years.

" One day when I had been up the Hudson on a drinking-spree, and had come to be one mass of corruption, I stumbled into a lawyer's office in Poughkeepsie, threw myself into a chair, and dropped to sleep. Why I was there I do not know, unless it was God's providence to bring me under the voice of the Gospel, but when I awoke a gentleman spoke kindly to me, and said: 'I understand all about your situation.'

" ' Don't talk to me,' said I ; ' I am altogether lost. There is no hope in the world for me.' Then he told me that he had lost every thing he had in the world, and actually fallen into the ditch on account of strong drink, but that God had saved him, and given him back every thing that he had lost. Then he cited to me the case of Naaman, the leper, and I saw that the way was very simple ; it was only to 'wash and be clean.'

" My friends, we have come up through great tribulations. When I became a Christian the bar-room people pointed the finger of scorn at me, and the Churches were all afraid of me. So I was between two fires, and could do nothing but cry to God for mercy. You, also, if you come to Christ, will be between two fires. God may not take away the trial from you, but he will give you grace to bear it.

" The first thing I do in the morning is to go to God in prayer, and then I try to keep praying all day long. It is not we who are saving ourselves, but the grace of God that is saving us.

" There are praying fathers and mothers, who come to these meetings, and break the precious ointment in silence. They speak no words, but God hears the cry of their hearts, and he has sent his Son that their sons might be saved. I am so glad temperance has assumed a Gospel shape. We don't preach any pledge or society, but we preach Christ. I have been approached by several drunkards, since I came here, for help, but I have said unto them, ' Gold and silver I have none.' What you want first of all is to come to Christ. If you seek for Christ and money both together you will lose both. Settle it in your minds, if you are to die in the poorhouse, you will die believing in Christ, and then, if you seek first the kingdom of God and his righteousness the other things will be added.

"After I gave my wretched self to Christ I began to look around for work. At last I met an old tanner, who asked me if I knew how to do any thing. I said I had never been brought up to work, but was ready to do any thing I could. I worked for him for nine weeks, for $4 a week, and paid $5 for my board; and when the spring opened I went into a brick-yard, doing the best I could, hoping that God would take me out of that as he did out of the tannery, and presently God set me to preaching the Gospel of temperance. After a while, having great success in reaching special cases, and being all the time happy in Christ, I thought I would go back to money-making again. So I hired myself out at a good big salary to a dry-goods man, but he died in a few weeks after, and so I was thrust back again into this Gospel temperance work, and a blessed work it is.

"Now let us have some more thanksgiving."

"I thank the Lord," said a man with a slight German accent, "that I am saved. I brought a man into these meetings a few days ago, and he was saved. Last Sunday he went to church, and went to bed rejoicing at twelve o'clock. At two o'clock he passed away. Is there any one here who will accept the Lord?"

A song.

A man in very plain clothes, and a voice that was not so plain, rose up and said: "My Christian friends, I have been a great sinner. When I consider what I was a week ago, and what I am now, I thank God. As I expect to leave town to-morrow, I ask your prayers."

"This brother has found salvation here," said Brother Sawyer.

"I thank God that I've been saved at Brother Moody's meetings," exclaimed a young man, and sat down.

"I've been saved from a drunkard's grave," remarked a well-dressed man, "and intend to go to my Father's house rejoicing."

"I've had a great blessing from your meetings," said the Rev. Mr. Wyckoff, on the platform, "and I felt that I must tell you so."

"Now tell them what they must do to be saved," said Brother Sawyer.

"Well, I will," replied Mr. Wyckoff, and, taking a Bible, he read about the leper who met Jesus coming down from the mountain. "And here is what that leper said, 'Lord, if thou wilt, thou canst make me clean.'"

"There are a good many lepers here to-day," said Brother Sawyer. "There is a poor leper right here in front of me—God help him!"

"Now, here is a little hymn," continued Mr. Wyckoff, after a lady in the audience had narrated her experience, "and I want to sing it to you, if you will listen :—

> "'Oft I hear the Saviour say,
>   Lean on me, lean on me ;
> I will smooth thy rugged way ;
>   Lean, my child, on me.
> Mine's a love that cannot fail,
> More than all that friends unfold,
> I have found by every song,
>   Lean, my child, on me.
>
> "'Thou art weak, I know it all,
>   Lean on me, lean on me ;
> Trust, and thou shalt never fall,
>   Lean, my child, on me.
> Thou dost need my constant care,
> I will hear and answer prayer,
> Teach thee how the cross to bear ;
>   Lean, my child, on me.'

"Now, are there any souls here that want to lean on Him ?" exclaimed Mr. Sawyer feelingly, at the close of the song. "If so, let them hold up their hands. God bless you, dear friends ! I see many hands up over there. There's a dozen right through there. Any off here that want to lean on him ? Any along yonder ? I tell you these are solemn times. Is there another one to be delivered from sin before we close ? We'll wait a minute longer. Another soul ? Hold up your hands, you that want light."

"I want to travel with Christ across Jordan," shouted an old man in the rear of the hall, waving his cap enthusiastically.

"That brother has been in bondage fifty years," said Mr. Sawyer.

Mrs. Rounds offered a prayer, and was followed by several other ladies. A request was read from a sister in Monmouth, Illinois, who said that that town was on the eve of a local election, at which the issue was license or no license, and she desired prayers for the success of the latter ticket.

"How singular it is," said Brother Delight, the Portuguese barber, who, since his salvation from the life of a "fast man" and a good deal given to drink, is about the happiest man in Chicago "how singular it is to think how Jesus wants to get us all to him, and we don't come. Three years ago I was a hard case, and many people have wondered how I reformed. I told them to read the Bible every morning. 'The moment you go back on God,' said I, 'you are liable to fall.' As long as one prays in his closet he is all right."

"I want to say," said a lady, stepping forward, "that the influence of these daily meetings is felt throughout the North-west. I have testimonials from Wisconsin, Iowa, Indiana, and Michigan, from people who have been converted here, or who have heard of the meetings. I talked with a man some time ago who had been forty years a drunken sot. I asked him to reform. 'You know not what you ask when you ask me to reform,' said he. I said, 'Jesus can help you. Looking me in the eye, he said, 'I am bound by the chains of the devil.' I said, 'Jesus alone can save you.' Three days ago I found him a penitent man, and there was a light in his eye, and he told me that his motto was, 'Jesus can save you.'"

A sister asked prayers for young women who were about to marry young men fond of liquor.

"Now," said Mr. Sawyer, "if there are any more requests for prayers, let them be quickly made."

"I have a request," said a lady. "I want you to pray for a busi ness man who is located near here. I asked him yesterday to come to Moody's meeting, and he said there was too much of a crowd."

"My heart goes out for those young men whom I see going into saloons," said an old lady with white curls, "and I don't know what to do; so I ask you to pray for them."

"A young man in my neighborhood," said a young man, "is going down to the very dregs of sin, although he has a sister who has worn herself out in his behalf. There seems to be no hope for him, as he has lost all respect for himself and for others. Pray for him!"

Several prayers were offered.

"Three hundred prisoners stood up in the Bridewell yesterday," exclaimed a man with a loud voice, "and asked for prayers. I was saved by a woman's prayer."

A lady requested prayers for a young man who had been a professor of Christianity, but who had backslidden. A young man asked for prayers for himself. A gentleman from Detroit wanted prayers for a Roman Catholic family. A drunkard wanted prayers for himself.

"Every trembling soul who wants prayers hold up his hand," said the leader. "One, two, three, four, five—I can't stop to count them. We'll pray for you, young sister, and for you, dear young brother. We want—the Church wants—young men; and now Sister Rounds is going to bind up all these requests in a sheaf to send it up to Heaven."

MRS. JANE M. GEDDES.

MRS. MARY T. LATHROP.

MRS. MARY T. LATHROP.

This lady evangelist, whose portrait appears on the preceding page, is a resident of Jackson, Michigan. Of her general religious work in many portions of the country, both East and West, though it has been wonderfully blessed of God, it is not the province of this volume to speak, except so far as to show the right which her ability and success have given her to speak, with some claim to public confidence, on the subject of Gospel Temperance. For several years Mrs. Lathrop has been a revivalist, taking an active part in all Christian enterprises of the Church, and devoting no small share of time and labor to the work of saving drunkards.

At the Lake Bluff Temperance Camp-Meeting last summer, under the management of Dr. Reynolds, who was then near the close of his wonderful year's work in Michigan, in which he had been considerably assisted by Mrs. Lathrop, that lady gave an address which was remarkable alike for practical good sense, genuine rhetoric, and spiritual power. At its close Francis Murphy was called to the platform, and in his opening remarks said:—

"Dr. Reynolds tells us that he is slow of speech, though we do not find him slow of work, as witness the eighty thousand signers of the pledge in Michigan this year. Eighty thousand, my boy! Think of it!

"Well, we read that Moses was slow of speech, and the Lord gave him Aaron to speak for him; and after listening to the eloquent words of the lady who has preceded me, I find that the Lord has done the same for my brother here that he did for Moses. And is not Mrs. Lathrop a most admirable Aaron to Dr. Reynolds's Moses?"

In response to a request for incidents of temperance salvation for this volume, the following letter has been received, whose facts will be read with interest, as specimens of many which have come under this Gospel Temperance evangelist's observation :—

NEWARK, N. J., *Nov.* 26, 1877.

DEAR BROTHER—I was a temperance worker before I was a preacher, but my experience in reforming drunkards was not encouraging. Early in my public Gospel work I heard two men in the meeting at our Book Rooms, in Philadelphia, tell how *Jesus* saves from appetite. I rejoiced with trembling, not half believing, yet longing to preach such a salvation to drinking men if true. I prayed over it, and finally said, "It is no more than raising the dead and healing lepers, and our Jesus is *Jesus* still," so I began to tell a story for drunkards in all my meetings. God blessed me, and I have never held a revival in which some of this class have not been gloriously saved. They have come to the altar half intoxicated sometimes ; but I never fear ; I know what Christ can do.

One poor fellow came that way in Ann Arbor. I did not say much to him until meeting was over ; then I took his hand and said to him, "Not a drop of whisky to-morrow, brother, and come to the four o'clock meeting." He promised—I prayed. The next day he was there *sober*. That night God converted him, and he was free the last I knew.

Last winter a drunkard for fifteen years came into the meeting I was holding at Augusta, hopeless, despairing, and lost. One afternoon he rose for prayers, but when asked to come to the altar said, with a shudder, "Me go to the altar! I am not fit to sit here by the door." He drooped for two or three days, like a wounded brute, but one afternoon I gave a Bible reading on *Redemption*—what Jesus *is* as a *Redeemer*. I saw the struggle of hope in his face, so marred by years of sinning, and as I passed him I said, "O, brother, do you not see your help!" "Yes, I do," he said, "and I am going to him," and he did. I saw him not long since, strong, clean, saved.

A Roman Catholic, who was a drunkard for twenty years, but who now, with his whole family, are in Simpson Methodist Episcopal Church, Detroit, had *delirium tremens* when I began my work there last January. He raved about the streets in his delirium at night, then drank and slept in the day. He signed the pledge, and then, Catholic as he was, fled to our revival meeting. In a few nights he came to the inquiry room. It was a struggle—out of the mists of rum and Romanism together—but God came to him in a wonderful way. When he said his sins were forgiven and the chain of appetite broken I trembled; it seemed so much even for God to do; but he said to me, "You are surprised, but let me tell you what God did for me the night I took the pledge. I had not slept for nights, and again I felt the awful horror coming over me, and I got down on my knees and said, 'O, Lord, save me from this just to-night, till I get strength to try and be a man,' and the Lord heard me, and I slept almost all night; so when I asked him to save me I knew he would." He stands like a rock, and has been persecuted by some of the Reform Club for talking Jesus too strong.

I was holding a meeting at Mason, Michigan, when one night the sheriff's son, a young man twenty-eight years old, came to the altar. When I spoke to him as he came I saw he had drank recently, for his breath was strong with it still. He knelt in deep penitence, apparently, and went over the whole struggle of appetite and the future as only a strong soul can. After a time he lifted his head and said to me, "Jesus Christ must be absolute victory to me, or I cannot go any farther." I assured him that was what *Christ was* to any soul. He found the victory, and went down on the street corners among his old companions to tell it with wonderful effect.

There is a little English family now living in Ann Arbor, who at the beginning of the revival there three years ago were in squalid poverty. The wife and mother washed to support the family, and the father drank to terrible excess. He finally, after his wife's conversion, came among the crowds to the meeting, and was saved fully from his bondage. Their home is full of comfort now, and I am told the Lord has wonderfully prospered them.

One old man who was a Catholic, and was a sot with tobacco as well as rum, was converted in Detroit last winter, fully saved from his past, and made a happy, triumphant Christian.

My experience with tobacco has been quite singular—a great many have given it up, and God has saved them from it. I have had for

23

two years a special mission on this line, and God has blessed me. The greatest triumph I saw among the camp-meetings last summer was Colonels Hoy and Barry putting away that sin at Lake Side—I sent you an account—and they publicly and privately said I was the instrument which brought them to the decision. I do not like to write of myself, but I want these truths before the public—

> " 'Tis Jesus Christ the first and last,
>   He saves, and he alone."

I could write a book myself just of what I have seen Jesus do for this class. Tell the world he is mighty to save, and that you know one woman who would pledge her life that Jesus Christ will save any drunkard clear out to glorious liberty who will come to him for that kind of salvation.   MARY T. LATHROP.

JERRY M'AULEY AND HIS WATER-STREET MISSION.

Although this is not strictly a temperance reform movement, it has its place in this volume by virtue of the fact that its leaders, both Jerry and his wife, are reformed and converted drunkards, and that the mission under their direction deals almost entirely with men and women who are of the same class as their former selves. The writer of these pages has again and again listened to the testimonies of these simple-hearted, happy, triumphant sailors, stevedores, porters, truckmen, etc., some of them from the lowest parts of the city of New York, of various nationalities and saved from almost every depth of degradation ; and this is the almost universal note of praise, " Jesus saves me from drunkenness, and from the appetite for liquor;" while a good many add, "from smoking and chewing tobacco," "from thieving, from blaspheming," and from almost every other vice.

The following sketch, first prepared for the columns of the " Christian Advocate," is here republished, as giving a striking picture of this most interesting and successful mission :—

SOME MODERN MIRACLES.

Respectability is a vital thing in society, though, if we may believe Jerry M'Auley and the converts at his Water-street Mission, it counts very little in religion. Society grades and classifies sinners, making great differences between them; but it may be that to the Eye which looks through hats and skulls to see the thoughts of men, and through silks and satins, flesh and bones, to watch the feelings of women, there is less difference among impenitent sinners than good people are apt to imagine.

One thing is certain, both from facts and logic, namely, no appreciable amount of depravity makes any difference in the ease with which Almighty grace can save the soul who turns from sin to God; and it seems to make no difference in what part of the man the sin has settled, whether in body, mind, or soul, faith in Jesus Christ as the human condition, and the work of the Holy Spirit as the divine response thereto, takes the sin clean out of him, and makes the old man over into a new one.

"But that would be a straight miracle," says some weak brother, whose philosophy has got the better of his faith.

Yes, and why not?

"O, the age of miracles is past!"

But, brother, what do you mean by the "age of miracles?" They belong to all ages. The Old Testament is full of them; the New Testament is full of them; prophecy declares that the last days shall be full of them; and our Lord himself gave his followers permission to work them whenever they could make connection with the Infinite by means of faith and prayer. Besides, the facts are against you.

This new brick building, at No. 316 Water-street, close by the pier of the great bridge, jostled by dance-houses and brothels, and fumigated by beer-shops and gin-mills, is the Mission of the Helping Hand—perhaps I ought to say hands, for there are two pairs of very helpful hands here, that is, Jerry's and his wife's; besides which there is a Hand that is reached down from above, and many a poor lost one, by means of one of the former, has managed to get hold of the latter, and they are "all right," as they say.

This gentlemanly person, with sharp eyes, a long, sharp nose, and a grip like a vise, is Jerry—the "miah" was lost long ago—as wild an Irishman as ever fought in a street row or ground his teeth in rage behind penitentiary bars. He used to be a river-thief as a regular profession, varying his labors with gambling, prize-fighting, and stealing on shore. For years he was the terror of Water-street when he was drunk, its pet and pride when he was sober, carrying the warmest heart and the heaviest hand of any general "sport" in the profession.

This man was converted to God in Sing Sing prison. He has been guilty of every crime except murder; and, with that warm heart and heavy hand sanctified and consecrated, he is the watchful pastor of the strangest flock of lost-sheep-found that ever Chief Shepherd brought home from the mountains and the sea.

On the lamp over the door—which is always open from six in the morning till eleven at night—are the words, "JERRY M'AULEY'S PRAYER-MEETINGS," and in this neat little hall, opening directly from the street, the praying and helping goes on every night and every Sunday afternoon all the year round.

"We start the meetin' sharp at half-past seven," says Jerry; "the man who reads the Bible takes till a quarter to eight—if he is a long-winded feller he stretches it out till eight—then I take hold of it, shut the speeches down to one minute, and on we go for three quarters of an hour with testimonies."

Jerry is a pretty good Methodist, and knows what is the value of "experience" in a meeting. He knows the blessedness of brevity, too; therefore he is inexorable on the one-minute rule.

Who is that sweet-faced woman playing the little organ, and leading the preliminary singing? She looks as if she belongs to the Society of Friends, with her hair combed so smoothly over her broad, handsome forehead, her blue eyes full of love and happiness, and her whole face and form marked by a quiet repose. O, she can't be a Quaker, though, for there is a knot of bright blue ribbon in her bonnet!

That lady is Miracle Number Two, counting Jerry as one: Mrs. M'Auley, who used to be as much worse a drunkard and a "bummer" (vide Water-street vernacular) than Jerry, as a lost woman is worse than a lost man. You can't believe it. It is true, all the same. She was born in sin and raised in iniquity; she and Jerry were "mates" in the old days, though it was not till the days of grace that they were married. After she found the Lord, who gave her a clean heart for the foul one, a pleasant voice for the harsh one, a Madonna face for the bleared and bloated one, she was full of a desire to be helpful; so, besides keeping the mission house as neat as a pin, being the queen of housekeepers for Jerry in the snug tenement overhead, and doing the offices of a Christian sister and mother to an endless procession of ruined men, broken-hearted women, and neglected children, it occurred to her that she might help Jerry a good deal more if she could only play the organ at his prayer-meetings; therefore she laid the case before the Lord, who seems almost to have put the music into her fingers, in so short a time did she learn it; and now Jerry says, "She beats half of them professionals," and, so far as organ music for actual worship is concerned, he has the right of it.

It is half-past seven "sharp." "Twelve!" shouts Jerry, and without further ceremony the singing begins—a little faintly at first, for the room is not quite full yet. "Sixty-nine!" he calls out again, adding, "Don't be afraid of your voices, boys: sing!"

Glory! How they sing! And to think that every one of these voices now singing,

> "Jesus, lover of my soul,
> Let me to thy bosom fly,"

used to be cursing and brawling in the Water-street groggeries!

The next number is eleven:

> "Only a step to Jesus."

A pretty long step, you think, from the position of drunkards, thieves, vagabonds, and men with the stripes on, to that of saved believers, conscious of God's favor, and of their claim to eternal glory! Yes, but did you never see a tall man and a little boy running together, the boy held up and lifted along by the strong hand of his father? What long steps those short legs take! Well, this is the *rationale* of it.

Now a rough but clean-looking lad rises from his place, goes tremblingly to the platform, kneels a moment in silent prayer, and then opens the Bible, and begins to read the lesson:

"Therefore, being justified by faith, we have peace with God through our Lord Jesus Christ."

He has some difficulty with the long words, but he tugs away at them, and so pulls through without damaging any thing. Then he expounds the lesson thus:

"That ends the chapter, and I found it all true. For nine years I was a drinkin' and theivin'. In them nine years I was locked up eight times; but now my sins is all forgiven, and Jesus saves me to the uttermost; saves me, too, from thievin', from lyin', from cursin' and swearin', from drinkin' whisky, and chewin' and smokin' tobacker,

It was the 15th of Febuary last that I first got the invitation to Jerry's meetin', up in a den in the Bowery where I used to hang out. A young fellow up there says, 'Come down to Jerry M'Auley's meetin'; it is a good night's fun.' So I come. When I got here it was sort o' strange like ; but one after another they got up and said Jesus saved them from this, and saved them from that, and saved them from the other thing ; and I says to myself, 'Some of them fellows used to be just as bad as me, and if Jesus can save them, he can save me, too.' By and by Jerry inquired who wanted to be saved, and I said I did. So we went down on our knees, Jerry and I, and a lot of other poor fellers, and the Lord Jesus Christ gave me a new heart right there, took all the love of liquor, and tobacker, and the the-*a*-ters, and sparrin' matches, and all that, out of me, and now I am a-tryin' to do every thing to the glory of God."

Shall we mark this lad Miracle Number Three?

Sometimes a wicked fellow will come in to make sport, but Jerry is too smart for him.

Up rises a sailor, evidently half drunk, and stammers out :

" Jesus (hic) saves *me*, too ! "

" That aint so ! " cries Jerry ; " Jesus don't save any man that is full of gin ! "

" You've made a (hic) mistake, Brother M'Auley. It wasn't (hic) gin, but rum, I had."

Then Jerry, who is his own police to a large extent, takes the fellow by the collar and puts him out—an operation requiring quite a good deal of that bodily exercise which used to profit him so little, but which now stands him in good stead.

" I haven't never had to hit any one," he says to us, by way of explanation, "but I have had to squeeze some of 'em pretty tight." And one look at those bony fingers is enough to show what that means.

The next testimony is : "God has taken away my appetite for liquor and tobacco, and I haven't felt any thing of it for eight years."

Then a Dutchman : "I vas a poor lost sinners, und I didn't know ver to go, so I had to go to Yesus, and den I vas all right. Amen."

The next man has a sorrowful and disgraceful confession to make, but he does it thus : "Yesterday I told a lie. Pray for me ! I have an awful temper, and I need your prayers."

Poor fellow ! He has just been converted, after serving a fourteen years' sentence in State-prison, which great salvation from the ways of the world accounts for his unusual sensitiveness over any thing so common as lying.

And now Mrs. M'Auley rises in her gentle, pleasant way, to reach out a helping hand to this poor penitent thus :—

" I am glad that we who love God know when we offend him. Before I was converted I could tell lies by the yard, and my conscience would not trouble me a bit, but after I was saved I grieved over every sin. I know what it is to lead a miserable life ; I led it for years, but to-night I am saved."

Who is that poor girl on her knees, weeping as if her heart would break? That is one of the inmates of a dance-house just up the street, who used to come in and disturb the meeting, but she was not driven away. We will leave her for the present. She is reaching out after the heavenly Helping Hand.

After the meeting was over, at which there were a great many testimonies, any one of which would have been enough to kindle an ordinary respectable prayer-meeting into a perfect glow of delight, Jerry took me up to see his home over the chapel. It was a little paradise. Every thing was in the most perfect order ; and no one would have imagined, if he had suddenly woke up and found himself there, that he was in the midst of one of the lowest and vilest regions of New York.

" How is this for a poor miserable drunkard who, with his wretched ' woman,' used to live in a damp basement, with no furniture to speak of, except a sack full of dirty straw for a bed?" Thus spoke Jerry, as he saw the effect of his charming home upon the face of his delighted visitor. "O, but we have had hard times now and then," he continued, "when the devil gets to raging round here. You see, I was born a Roman Catholic, and all these people hate me for a turncoat. But it is no matter what they call me, for I get a chance to save some of 'em now and again."

" How about these converted men and women? do they stand pretty well?   .

"Of course they stand. For instance : A young sailor-boy found the Lord here one night ; he got soundly converted—got it clean through. Well, a few nights after he came back, looking rather down ; so I says, ' What's the matter, Bill?' And he told me that at his boarding-house, when he knelt down to pray, one of the roughs in the room lifted him up by his heels, and turned him completely over.'

" ' Did you hit him?' says I.

" ' No,' says the boy. ' I didn't, but I felt just a little mad ; ' and it was for feeling just that little 'mad' that he was so down in the mouth. You see what a fine thing it is to have a tender conscience.

"There was another one of the boys whose drunken old father was so furious at him for being converted at our mission that he seized a spider full of liver, that was frying on the stove, and threw it at his head; the boy ducked and saved his face, but the thing struck him on the shoulder and made a horrible mess, and—would you believe it?—that boy didn't behave in the least onhandsome! Stand? why they stand all sorts of abuse and persecution; but what they have to stand for the sake of religion is nothing to what they have had to stand in the ways of sin."

"Some of them backslide, of course?"

"Yes, a good many of 'em are sailors, and when they get away from us they sometimes go wrong; but when they get back to New York they come right here the first thing, and we treat 'em just as the Lord told us to. If one of 'em gets drunk a few times, we try and help him up again—seventy times seven is the rule. But pretty much all of 'em hang on before they come to that."

"Do they join the Church anywhere?"

"Yes, some of 'em join the Church their mother belonged to—a good many of the boys have had praying mothers. They join the Presbyterian Church that is over here convenient, and a good many go down to old John-street Methodist; but they mostly always comes back here again to meetin'—they say it is more like home."

"Sometimes we have uptown folks in silk and kid gloves seeking Christ right among these stevedores, sailors, river thieves, and what not; but it's my observation that the hardest cases often get saved the easiest."

"How do you account for that?"

"Well, you see, a thief, or a drunkard, or that sort of a chap, knows he hasn't any thing good about him, and he is ready to get salvation any way—no matter how, so as Jesus will take away his sins; but these goodish people can't get down; they are too proud, and too respectable, and all that. One day one of them Church people came in and took a front seat—we always give the high-toned people the front seats—and when sinners was asked to come to the altar for prayers, my wife went to this lady, and inquired if she was a Christian.

"'O, never mind me!' said the lady; 'you go and talk with my son. He is back there; may be you can get him to come.'

"'But how about yourself?' says my wife. 'Are you saved?

The woman confessed she wasn't saved.

"'I am a Church member,' she says, 'but haven't got any religion that amounts to any thing.'

"'You had better come forward for prayers yourself,' says my wife, 'and when your son sees his mother coming to Christ it will be the best sort of invitation for him.' So she came and knelt down, and began to seek the Lord in real earnest; and, sure enough, when the son saw her he came, too, and both of 'em was saved right there. But that don't happen every day.

"I tell you what," says Jerry, "some of these ministers make a big mistake. They preach all the time to the back of the meetin', when there are some of the worst sinners in the front pews."

On the subject of those modern temperance miracles, namely, the sudden loss of all appetite for liquor and tobacco, Jerry, who professes that experience himself, has this to say:—

"You see it is something like this: Blow out a candle and it is *out*, but the candle is there ready to be lighted again. Jest so it is with the drunkard's appetite who gets converted all over: the candle is out. The devil stands ready to light it again, but so long as the convert stands fast in the faith the old enemy can't do it; but just let him commit one sin, no matter what it is, and the devil will out with his brimstone and touch off that appetite.

"Mebbe I can put it in another way, so you will understand it better. You know about these men they call lion tamers? Well, now, would you rather go into a cage of lions along with the tamer, or would you rather go in alone? Jest so the old lion appetite is tamed by the grace of Jesus Christ, and as long as you stick to him you are all right; but the minute you try to go within reach of any sin *alone*, the old lion is on you, teeth, claws, and all."

"There's lots of religion in a good, hearty shake of the hand," said Jerry in his opening remarks to the boys one night. "Lots of sympathy in it; lots of love in it. And then, too, there's lots of religion in a beef-steak, if you give it to the right man at the right time. Last Thanksgiving day I got a sailor into the kingdom of God with a bowl of soup and a couple of bits of bread. It was a raw, chilly day, and this poor fellow came in ragged and cold. He had an eye like a black snake—a bad eye. I didn't like it. Found out afterward that he had just been in the Tombs for mutiny. However, I went up to him, and says to him:

"'Didn't you have a good mother?'

"One of the boys gave me the wink, so I went and brought him a bowl of Thanksgiving soup—we had made a big pot of it out of a

23*

great pile of chicken bones and turkey carcasses that had been sent in—and that reached him. He took the soup, and as he ate it the tears began to run, and right away we had that poor sailor, who used to be hating every body in the world, down on his knees praying to Jesus to save him. And he did save him.

"You see, boys, it was the soup that did it. Soup in his hungry, hungry stomach, then Christ in his lost soul."

Among other strange, sweet histories, Jerry related the following, first bringing out the photograph of a beautiful child by way of illustrating it:—

"Isn't that a nice little girl? And her little sister is prettier than she is. That's Molly, and her sister's name is Jenny.

"You see, these ignorant Catholics round here are no friends of mine, because I used to be a Catholic myself in the old days, and their children used to make all sorts of disturbance outside while our meeting was going on. But one night Molly came in, and stayed through the service, and the next night she brought Jenny with her.

"Before the meetin' was out a drunken Irish woman came to the door, furious with rage, and wanted to know if her children was in there, and, when they were sent out, as she ordered, she seized them by the hair, one in each hand, and began to shake them and curse them for going into that Protestant turncoat's place. The next night they came back again.

"'Are you not afraid your mother will beat you if you come in?' asked the usher.

"'To be sure she'll beat us, but we want to come in all the same.'

"Sometimes they came frowzy and dirty, and sometimes combed and clean, according as the mother was drunk or sober. The liquor always roused her anti-Protestant fury, and we could always tell the condition of the mother by the looks of the children.

"One night the father, who was a sailor, came home drunk, and turned wife and children all out of doors, and they had no place to sleep; but Molly said, 'Mother, I think Mrs. M'Auley would let us in.'

"'Do you think so, child? Well, go and thry.'

"We gave them shelter, and next morning gave them all their breakfast at our own table, and after that the little girls were beaten no more for coming to our meeting.

"But pretty soon the father went to sea again, and out of his advance wages the mother got so drunk that she was seized with the *delirium tremens*, and Molly came over for my wife, saying, 'Mother is going to die.'

"My wife went to see her at once, calmed down the poor wretch, fixed up her house, took care of her as if she had been her own sister, and it was not long before the wicked woman came to meeting herself, repented of her sins, and found peace in Jesus. O, how happy she was! how she loved my wife for saving her! and how her old Catholic friends tormented her!

"She is dead now; died at Dr. Cullis' consumption hospital in Boston; died happy, trusting in the merits of Christ. During her sickness some Catholic women found out that she was one of the children of Rome, and they tried to frighten her back into the old Church.

"'You'll go to hell sure,' said they, 'if you don't have a priest!' but she answered them calmly:

"'When I was a lost sinner no priest took any notice of me, but Jesus didn't forget me. He came down and saved me, and washed away all my sins. So I think I shall do very well now without the priest, since Jesus stays by me all the while.' And so she died in the faith, and Molly and Jenny are still living with Dr. Cullis."

Jerry M'Auley's prayer-meeting is known all round the world, very much as Father Taylor's Mariner's Chapel in Boston used to be. It is also coming to be quite a popular religious curiosity of late; so much so, that people with gold rings and fine raiment are in danger of crowding "the boys;" but they take it good-naturedly, knowing that it is quite according to the Bible that he who is forgiven much loveth much, and that he is naturally an object of interest to the man who only loves a little, because, according to his own reckoning, he was only forgiven a little.

CHAPTER XXII.

THE TEMPERANCE PULPIT.

IT would be false to history and unjust to the men who have not only done garrison duty, but also have stood in the front line of battle in this reform, to pass by the regular, steady, efficient, though often inconspicuous work which has been done for temperance in the pulpits of our country. The regular clergy have very naturally been occupied with other themes than total abstinence, it has been presumed that attendants at church are not, as a class, so likely to become drunkards as others, and only as a pastor has extended his labors beyond the limits of his regular congregation has he been liable to come in contact with the worst forms of this vice and the worst sorrows of its victims.

There are also to be found among some sects of the American clergy those who regard the ministry as an official and traditional profession, and who oppose the idea of total abstinence, avowedly on the ground that its doctrines tend to infidelity, but really because they forbid a habit of self-indulgence in which these gentlemen have been reared. But the great body of the Christian ministry in the United States, ever since the days of Dr. Lyman Beecher, have been teetotalers; they have preached hundreds of thousands of temperance sermons along the line of their accustomed work; they have been the men to invite, assist, support and defend those temperance

REV. THEO. L. CUYLER, D.D.

CHARLES H. FOWLER, D.D., LL.D

advocates of both sexes who have made a specialty of
this work, and there are men among them who are
towers of strength, not only in temperance literature,
but on the temperance platform. It is through the
evangelical ministry of America, after all, that the great
movements in the history of this reform have been possible ; and though it has been the habit of some reforming
laymen to criticise somewhat severely the slowness of
their clerical brethren, yet they have usually found in
them a solid line of reserve upon which to fall back in
time of emergency ; a line, too, that has been steadily
and irresistibly on the advance. The limits of this volume exclude a multitude of honored ministerial names
and faces, as well as multitudes of other local temperance workers. Perhaps no two better ministerial temperance advocates could be chosen as representatives
than the two whose portraits appear at the head of this
chapter.

Rev. Theodore L. Cuyler, D.D., for many years pastor
of the Lafayette Avenue Presbyterian Church, Brooklyn, N. Y., is a man without whom no great temperance
assembly east of the Alleghanies is complete ; a man
whose pen has furnished effective temperance campaign
documents, that have been widely circulated, both as
tracts and in the columns of the newspaper press, both
in America and Great Britain ; and whose own pulpit
has been a stronghold of teetotalism for many and many
a year. As specimens of the spirited and clear-cut
temperance articles which he has been constantly con-
tributing to this reform, two only can be given in the
pages which remain. The readers of this volume will

prefer to have them both, though in smaller type, rather than only one, in the standard letter of the book :—

A SHOT AT THE DECANTER.

BY REV. THEO. L. CUYLER, D.D.

There is a current story that a Quaker once discovered a thief in his house; and, taking down his grandfather's old fowling-piece, he quietly said, "Friend, thee had better get out of the way, for I intend to fire this gun *right where thee stands.*" With the same considerate spirit we warn certain good people that they had better take the decanter off their table, for we intend to aim a Bible-truth right where that decanter stands. It is in the wrong place. It has no more business to be there at all than the thief had to be in the honest Quaker's house. We are not surprised to find a decanter of alcoholic poison on the counter of a dram-shop whose keeper is "licensed" to sell death by measure. But we are surprised to find it on the table or the sideboard of one who professes to be guided by the spirit and the teachings of God's word. That bottle stands right in the range of the following inspired utterances of St. Paul: "It is good neither to eat flesh, *nor to drink wine, nor any thing whereby thy brother stumbleth.*" This text must either go out of the Christian's Bible, or the bottle go off the Christian's table. The text will not move, and the bottle must.

The passage itself is so clear that it can hardly admit of a cavil or a doubt. It teaches the lofty and benevolent principle—that abstinence from things that are necessarily hurtful to others is a Christian expediency that has the *grip* of a moral duty.

This sounds, at first, like a very radical doctrine; but so conservative an expounder as Professor Hodge, of Princeton, has defined the text as teaching that things which are not always wrong *per se* are to be given up for the sake of others. He says that the legal liberty of a good man is never to be exercised where a moral evil will inevitably flow from it. We are never to put stumbling-blocks in the way of others. Good men are bound to sacrifice any thing and every thing that is counter to the glory of God, and destructive of the best interests of humanity.

It would be easy to prove unanswerably that alcoholic beverages are injurious to those who use them. The famous athlete, *Tom Sayers*, was once asked by a gentleman, "Well, Thomas, I suppose that when you are training you use plenty of beefsteaks, and London porter, and pale ale?"

The boxer replied, "In my time I have drunk more than was good for me; but when I have *business* to do there's nothing *like water* and the dumb-bells." After retiring from "business," he took to drink, and died a sot. Cold water made him a Samson; alcohol laid him in his grave. As a matter of personal health and long life, "it is good not to drink wine;" as an example to others, *total abstinence is a Christian virtue.*

The inherent wrong of using intoxicating drinks is twofold. 1. It exposes to danger the man who tampers with it; for no man was ever positively *assured* by his Creator that he could play with the "adder" that lies coiled in a wine-cup without being stung by it. 2. It puts a stumbling-block in the way of him whom we are commanded to love as ourselves.

We lay down, then, the proposition that no man has a *moral* right to do any thing the influence of which is certainly and inevitably hurtful to his neighbor. I have a legal right to do many things which as a Christian I cannot do. I have a legal right to take arsenic or swallow strychnine; but I have no moral right to commit this self-destruction. I have a legal right to attend the theater. No policeman stands at the door to exclude me, or dares to eject me while my conduct is orderly and becoming. But I have no moral right to go there; not merely because I may see and hear much that may soil my memory for days and months, but because that whole garnished and glittering establishment, with its sensuous attractions, is to many a young person the yawning maelstrom of perdition. The dollar which I gave at the box-office is my contribution toward sustaining an establishment whose dark foundations rest on the murdered souls of thousands of my fellow-men. Their blood stains its walls, and from that "pit" they have gone down to another pit where no sounds of mirth ever come. Now I ask, What right have I to enter a place where the tragedies that are played off before me by painted women and dissolute men are as nothing to the tragedies of lost souls that are enacted in some parts of that house every night? What right have I to give my money and my presence to sustain that moral slaughter-house, and by walking into the theater myself to aid in decoying others to follow me?

Now, on the same principle, (not of self-preservation merely, but of avoiding what is dangerous to others,) what right have I to sustain those fountain-heads of death from which the drink-poison is sold? What right have I to advocate their license, to patronize the traffic or even in any way to abet the whole *system of drinking* alcoholic stimulants at home or abroad? If a glass of wine on my table will entrap some young man, or some one who is inclined to stimulants, into dissipation, then am I thoughtlessly setting a trap for his life. I am his tempter. I give the usage my sanction, and to him the direct inducement to partake of the bottled demon that sparkles so seductively before him. If the contents of that sparkling glass make my brother to stumble, he stumbles over me. If he go away from my table and commit some outrage under the effects of that stimulant, I am to a certain degree guilty of that outrage. I have a partnership in every blow he strikes, or in every oath he may utter, or in every bitter wound he may inflict on the hearts of those he loves while under the spell of my glass of "Cognac" or "Burgundy." I gave him the incentive to do what otherwise he might have left undone. The man who puts the bottle to his neighbor's lips is accountable for what comes from those lips under the influence of the dram, and is accountable, too, for every outrage that the maddened victim of the cup may perpetrate during his temporary insanity.

In view of this question, is it too much to ask of every professed Christian, and every lover of his kind, that they will wholly abstain from every thing that can intoxicate? For the sake of your children, do it. For the sake of a brother, a husband, a friend; for the sake of those who will plead your example; for the sake of frail, tempted ones who cannot say, *No!* for your fellow-traveler's sake to God's bar and to the eternal world, *touch not* the bottled devil, under whose shining scales damnation hides its adder-sting!

It is old-fashioned total abstinence that we are pleading for. We ask it, as Paul did, for the sake of those who "stumble." O those stumblers! those stumblers! We dare not speak of them. It would touch many of us too tenderly. It would reveal too many wrecks—wrecks that angels have wept over. It would open tombs whose charitable green turf hides out of sight what many a survivor would love to have forgotten. It would recall to me many a college friend who went down at midday into blackness of darkness.

And to-day I see this social curse coming back into our houses, into our streets, into our daily usages of life, with redoubled power. Would that every parent were a "prohibitory law" to his family! Would that every pulpit and every platform would thunder forth the old warning-cry, "Look not on the wine when it is red, when it giveth its color in the cup, for at the last it biteth like a serpent and stingeth like an adder." At the *last!* at the LAST! But, O! who can tell when that "last" shall ever end? When will the victim's last groan be heard? When will the last horror seize upon his wretched soul?

The second selection is "A New Year's Tract," prepared by request of temperance friends in Scotland, who had learned to admire and love this generous whole-souled American minister during his tour in that country.

Hundreds of thousands of these documents have been circulated on both sides of the ocean, and they still hold rank among the most serviceable temperance literature of our times.

A NEW-YEAR'S EPISTLE FROM AMERICA.

BY REV. THEO. L. CUYLER, D.D.

"Send us a New-year's Tract!" This is the message that reaches me from a group of warm-hearted friends in old Scotland. It would be ungrateful to refuse; for every day since I sailed out of the Clyde, last June, my thoughts have gone back to the happy hours passed among Scottish homes and hearts. Next to my native land, no spot on the globe is more dear to me than that pasture ground of poetry, history, and heroism that lies between the Tweed and the Pentland Firth.

I am surrounded with Scotland here. Many of my flock were born "or the heather." The majestic face of Thomas Chalmers looks down upon me from the walls of my American home; beside him are the gnarled and knotty features of the heroic stone-cutter of Cromarty, Hugh Miller. On my table lie the matchless songs that were first sung by a plowman on the banks of the bonnie Doon; they have been moistened with tears; for if Rabbie Burns had let the accursed drink alone, he might have climbed to that peak of renown where Milton and Shakspeare sit. And the same enemy that robbed poor Burns has robbed the land that was Burns' pride. If all the dram-shops in Scotland were massed together they would make a town as large as Edinburgh? If all the drunkards were gathered into one host they would outnumber the army which Bruce led at Bannockburn! If the death-roll from drink in 1872 could be printed on one huge sheet, it would be enough to set every church bell in

Scotland a-tolling! There is tenfold more money spent for ales and whisky in the land of John Knox than for all your Churches, and schools, and institutions of charity. The adoption this year of a "solemn league and covenant" against the drink-demon would make Scotland a "garden of the Lord."

While in Edinburgh I went down into the Cowgate to see the little chapel in which Knox once preached, and on whose table the bloody form of the brave Argyle was laid two hundred years ago. But every Saturday night human life is taken in the Cowgate! Fathers and mothers are murdered there by inches. Laboring men who have worked all the week for moderate wages spend the earnings that belong to their families in buying the poison that kills body and soul. And your authorities *license* the slaughter-pens in which death is dealt out by the dram. What is seen in the Cowgate may be seen in every one of your large towns. O, "brither Scots!" is it not a sorrow and a shame that, after three centuries of civil liberty and Gospel light, the New-year's sun of 1873 should rise upon such a sight?

1. Some apologists excuse this wide-spread intemperance on account of your race and your cold climate. They say that you belong to the "Anglo-Saxons, who are a race of drunkards," and that you live on certain parallels of latitude where men instinctively take to alcoholic stimulants. This is solemn nonsense. Our heavenly Father created Scotland and Scotchmen too; and I don't believe that he gave a climate to the one, or constitutions to the others, that *require* the use of alcoholic poisons. If your race and climate are fatal to sobriety, then every man ought to be a tippler. But the fact that so many among you are healthy abstainers proves that every one might be a teetotaler. No climate requires the habitual use of wines or whiskies. In frigid Siberia tea is the best warmer. In torrid India Havelock's men out-marched and out-fought their comrades on cold water. Our American soldiers (during the late war) found that good food, good sleep, and good coffee were better than all the "fire-water" of the rum-casks. A pilot on our wild Atlantic coast once told me that when he drank brandy he could not stand severe exposure as well as when he used only hot coffee. Suppose that every reader of this tract should begin the New-year by substituting tea or coffee for "brown-stout" and "mountain-dew." *Try it.*

2. Some people, both in your country and mine, charge all the drunkenness upon the dram-sellers. I offer no apology for the men who make their living at the mouth of hell. But if the dram-shops make drinkers, it is equally true that drinkers make the dram-shops.

If you buy a bottle of wine, you sustain the wine-merchant. Every one who buys a quart of intoxicating beverage becomes a partner in the liquor traffic. That destructive traffic can never be put down by law while a majority of the people have a partnership in it. You cannot outlaw what fashion makes respectable. We, in America, have never been able to close up a drinking-house by law except in those localities where a majority of the people were total abstainers. It is commonly slow work and hard work to bring a majority in any community over to the side of entire abstinence. But it is the only sure work. We have a town (in New Jersey) of over five thousand population that has never had an open dram-shop! The town was settled by teetotalers; it has always been the *fashion there not to drink*. The tiger has never been unchained in that peaceful, prosperous community. In Bessbrook (Ireland) teetotalism has starved out the publicans. What a happy New-year's day will dawn upon that town in Scotland which has barred up the last drinking-den!

Let me say a brotherly word to the working men of Scotland. Your brawny arms make "Glasgow flourish." Your sweat drives the looms of Paisley and Dundee. I see in yonder harbor of New York the splendid steamer you launched on the Clyde. Yet the great mass of you have a hard pull to live, and but very few ever grow rich. And the simple cause of most of this poverty is that the bottle burns a hole in your pockets. You cannot support your own families and a liquor-seller besides. Scotland is the birth-place of *savings'-banks*. How much did you deposit in them during the year just closed? Your cities and villages are full of *banks for losings*, in which every depositor *gains a loss*. Nothing is paid out but disease, and drunkenness, and disgrace, and death. Wont it be a "happy New-year" to every mechanic or laborer in the land o' cakes who resolves that, with God's help, he will not spend a farthing this year over the counter of a drunkard-factory? The best savings-bank for your money is a total abstinence pledge. The best savings-bank for your affections is a pure woman's heart. The best savings-bank for your soul is a trust in the Lord Jesus Christ. I wish that every young woman in Scotland would resolve never to offer a glass of strong drink to a friend, and never to marry any young man who is not a teetotaler.

3. But the drinking customs in your country or mine are not confined to the "working-classes" They reach from the rich man's mansion to the pauper's hut. Drinking is made *respectable* by the example of refined and Christian people. A majority of your Church members, and even a majority of your ministers of the Gospel, are not

avowed abstainers. The curse of dear old Scotland to-day is her drinking customs. They do more to hinder the elevation of the masses and the salvation of souls than all other evils combined. The dram-shop has been overmatched for the Kirk; and for the simple reason that the drink-usages find so many allies among the church-goers and so many supporters among the teachers of religious truth. If the Churches of Scotland were to make one year's thorough work for total abstinence; if every pulpit would open its batteries against dram-drinking; if every professed Christian would banish the ale-cup and the wine-bottle from his table; if every Sunday-school would adopt the motto of the "Bands of Hope," and every Church of Christ would hoist the temperance standard, Scotland would be revolutionized in a twelvemonth! Your "Leagues," and "Orders of Good Templars," and "Alliances" are doing a grand work; but no moral reform can ever win full success without the Church of the living God. There will be no diminution of crime, no decrease of pauperism, no general amelioration of the masses, while the demon of strong drink finds a sanctuary behind the altars of Jehovah. Will Scotland's Church draw sword upon Scotland's deadliest enemy?

I make no apology for the earnestness of my language. Your influence upon my own country is prodigious. A descendant of one of your Highland clans sits to-day in our presidential chair. With the importation of Scottish genius, industry, and piety, came also Scottish drinking customs and Scotch whisky. One of my cherished friends, but lately reformed from his evil habits, went down to visit friends in his native Forfarshire, and was tempted back to his cups!

In conclusion, I exhort every householder to banish the tempter from their boards during the holiday festivities. If your own children are not in danger, other people's children are so. A runaway horse was once seen dashing through the streets of a town, dragging a wagon containing a lad screaming with fright. As the wagon came crashing to the pavement, a crowd hurried to the spot. Among them came an old lady, with cap-strings flying, and the utmost distress depicted on her countenance. "Is he *your* son?" exclaimed a by-stander. "O, no!" replied the true-hearted woman, "but he is *somebody's son*." Kind friends, the social glass you offered at your holiday entertainment may send somebody's son to ruin! Start the New-year with the banishment of the fatal cup from your house, and you may hope for God's blessing to rest upon it. Hang your pledge of total abstinence upon your walls on the first day of January; and there shall be at least one lover of "auld Scotland" to wish you A HAPPY NEW-YEAR IN THE LORD!

Of the relation of the Church to the Temperance Reform, Dr. Cuyler says :—

The pastor's aid and sympathy are indispensable. A Church seldom gets beyond its own pulpit; and if the devil can smuggle a demijohn of choice wine into the pulpit, it is pretty certain to trickle out into all the pews in the sanctuary. Next to the pastor's co-operation, success will depend upon having the right sort of men and women to handle the ropes. Managers should be appointed who are zealous enough to arrange frequent public meetings, and discreet enough to select the right kind of speakers and singers, and wise enough to steer clear of reckless methods and of sensational buffooneries in the name of the Lord. No righteous cause has ever been so sadly damaged by fools and fanatics as the cause of temperance. The wisest heads and the most godly hearts in every Church can find no better field for their best efforts than in the difficult conflict with this hundred-headed hydra of strong drink.

*　　*　　*　　*　　*　　*　　*　　*　　*

The temperance reform is really as yet in its experimental stages. So far from being a veteran giant, it is as yet but a ruddy stripling, confronting a giant with but five smooth stones from the waterbrooks in its slender scrip. In its early, experimental stages our holy cause has suffered severely from some unwise methods, but is gaining wisdom from every reverse or blunder. Our severest sufferings have come from the indifference or unbelief or open opposition of many who "profess and call themselves Christians." In regard to the temperance enterprise the American Churches actually stand to-day where they stood in regard to foreign missions threescore years ago. Only a few individual Churches here and there have introduced our weapons into their armory, or organized their opposition to the most colossal curse on this continent. Only a few Churches have efficient total abstinence societies; only a few comparatively have introduced temperance literature into their Sabbath-schools.

What shall the Church do? She must do what she has never yet done, and has hardly yet begun to do to-day. To-day the brightest sign of the age is that the Church of God is beginning to awake to her duty. The very inebriates that are coming up will preach sermons that will rouse, I trust, even a dead Church. What must the Church do? Do what the Church of Scotland was told to do when they sent to our Yankee brother, and asked, "What is the best way to arrest intemperance in Scotland." He gave them a glance like a shot from his eye, and said,

"Let the ministers and Christian people put the bottle from off their own table."

That answer set Scotland to shaking. He never said a wiser or a truer thing than that. I would have the Church of God, from the pulpit clear down to the pews, clean from complicity with these drinking habits. To begin with, I will go right into the pulpit. ' You will never get a Church higher than the pulpit, and if the devil can smuggle a demijohn into the pulpit, it will be sure to leak out into the pews.

I have noticed another thing: that the minister taking wine on social or other occasions tempts more young people to ruin—I don't care what you say about light wines or inoffensive beer—than all the utterances of the pulpit can save. Another thing: when a man puts alcohol into his mouth, and endeavors to get temperance out of his mouth, there is a strange collision of trains here in the throat. Let every minister resolve, as a fundamental principle, that if wine comes where he is he will never touch it while the world stands. How dare a minister stand up and look in the face of Christ Jesus, who gave his life to save the world, and say, "Lord, I will give up every thing but my glass—not that, not that!"

There is not a well-organized Church in America that hasn't got a temperance wheel in it. A temperance wheel well constructed balances the rest of the machinery, and makes the Church more complete. Without it the Church isn't complete. Men must understand that it is part and parcel of the Christian Gospel. Men who don't merely burn pine shavings, but who feel in their hearts the deep red glow of the anthracite fire that comes of a thorough love of Jesus, have a hatred of sin and a love of souls. Those are the three essential requisites for a good Church organization: love of Jesus, hatred of sin, and a love of souls.

Rev. Charles H. Fowler, D.D., formerly the leading Methodist preacher and platform speaker in the Northwest, the ex-President of the North-western University, and now editor of the "Christian Advocate," at New York, is a Canadian by birth; a man in whom are concentrated the powers both of nerve and brain of a long line of brave and vigorous ancestors, trained under the best advantage which the schools of America could furnish.

A natural leader, he was not long in coming to the front in Chicago, not only as a minister of the Gospel, but as a patriot and a reformer. His eulogy on Abraham Lincoln, his defense of the Bible in the schools, his splendid leadership at the time when Chicago lay in ashes, his grand address on The Impeachment of King Alcohol, and his more recent arraignment of the theories of one of our antitcetotal temperance reformers, are all worthy of permanent record in the history of his country, his Church, and of the temperance reform.

The sermon here presented (in smaller type that it may be given entire) has a history of its own. It was printed and immense numbers of it circulated in Ohio just previous to the beginning of the Crusades in that State, and its author, then on a visit to Cincinnati, was privileged to be the volunteer chaplain to that brave company of Crusaders who were taken to jail in that city by order of its antitemperance mayor, for the offense (?) of the public worship of God in the neighborhood of certain haunts of the devil :—

THE IMPEACHMENT AND PUNISHMENT OF ALCOHOL.

" Look not thou upon the wine when it is read, when it giveth its color in the cup, when it moveth itself aright. At the last it biteth like a serpent, and stingeth like an adder. Prov. xxiii, 31, 32.

We are here to confront the great enemy of our time ; to handle the greatest living question. This monster has " the world " for a home, " the flesh " for a mother, and "the devil " for a father. He stands erect, a monster of fabulous proportions. He has no head, and cannot think. He has no heart, and cannot feel. He has no eyes, and cannot see. He has no ears, and cannot hear. He has only an instinct by which to plan, a passion by which to allure, a coil by which to bind, a fang with which to sting, and an infinite maw in which to consume his victims.

I impeach this monster, and arraign him before the bar of public judgment, and demand his condemnation in the name of industry robbed and beggared; of the public peace disturbed and broken; of private safety gagged and garroted; of common justice violated and trampled; of the popular conscience debauched and prostituted; of royal manhood wrecked and ruined; and of helpless innocence waylaid and assassinated.

In examining this case we shall appropriate whatever we can find of service in the labors of chemists, jurists, compilers, scholars, in every branch of the subject.

We now approach to-night the most difficult part of this subject— The Correction of the Evil. Even a child may accurately determine when it is sick, while the most skillful practitioner may utterly fail in his prescription. Your stable-boy may know that your horse has been stolen, though Pinkerton and all his band may not recover him. The public mind has only to glance at this criminal to be certain of his guilt. For he goes about armed with all malignity, concealed behind all craftiness, seeking with infinite cunning to entrap the unwary and destroy the feeble. Like a blood-hound, he scents his victims afar off, tracking them with patient and infallible instinct across fiery sand-fields and over the the barren rock-waste. Once on a young man's track, with one sniff of his heel, nothing but the running stream of living water can check his pursuit and give the fugitive rest. In dark rooms and dingy cellars, in secret conclave, he devises his plans and mixes his drugs. By night and by day he draws out the catalogues of crime. With hands polluted with blood, and locks that wriggle and crawl and hiss; with purpose fixed for slaughter, and with heart unpitying and unrelenting, he presses his infernal work. With the gold his crimes have brought him he seeks to secure friends in the halls of legislation; to put his judges upon the bench, his advocates at the bar, his witnesses on the stand, and, to make surety doubly sure, his views in the public mind. He would control, if he could, not only our almshouses and prisons, but also our legislative halls and our public presses. He would fill not only our cells and grave-yards, but also our judgment-seats and our police commissions. This is our foe—cunning as a fox, wise as a serpent, strong as an ox, bold as a lion, merciless as a tiger, remorseless as a hyena, fierce as the pestilence, deadly as the plague. To condemn and correct such a criminal is not the pastime of an hour, but *the manly, hero-born, martyr-bred work of a life-time.*

The Legislature of Illinois has given us a law with which we can handle this monster. I will read the distinguishing features:

SECTION 1. *Be it enacted by the people of the State of Illinois, represented in the General Assembly,* That it shall be unlawful for any person or persons, by agent or otherwise, without first having obtained a license to keep a grocery, to sell in any quantity, intoxicating liquors, to be drunk in, upon, or about the building or premises where sold, or to sell such intoxicating liquors to be drunk in any adjoining room, building, or premises, or other place of public resort connected with said building: *Provided,* That no person shall be granted a license to sell or give away intoxicating liquors, without first giving a bond to the municipality or authority authorized by law to grant licenses; which bond shall run in the name of "The People of the State of Illinois," and be in the penal sum of three thousand dollars, with at least two good and sufficient securities, who shall be freeholders, conditioned that they will pay all damages to any person or persons which may be inflicted upon them, either in person or property, or means of support, by reason of the person so obtaining a license selling or giving away intoxicating liquors; and such bond may be sued and recovered upon for the use of any person or persons, or their legal representatives, who may be injured by reason of the selling intoxicating liquors by the person or his agent so obtaining the license.

SEC. 5. Every husband, wife, child, parent, guardian, employer, or other person, who shall be injured in person or property, or means of support, by any intoxicated person, or in consequence of the intoxication, habitual or otherwise, of any person, shall have a right of action in his or her own name, severally or jointly, against any person or persons who shall, by selling or giving intoxicating liquors, have caused the intoxication, in whole or in part, of such person or persons.

SEC. 8. For the payment of all fines, costs, and damages, assessed against any person or persons, in consequence of the sale of intoxicating liquors, as provided in section five of this act, the real estate and personal property of such person or persons, of every kind, except such as may be exempt under the homestead laws of this State, or such as may be exempt from levy and sale upon judgment and execution, shall be liable, and such fines, costs, and damages shall be a lien upon such real estate until paid; and in case any person or persons shall rent or lease to another or others any buildings or premises to be used or occupied, in whole or in part, for the sale of intoxicating liquors, or shall permit the same to be so used or occupied, such building or premises so used or occupied shall be held liable for and may be sold to pay all fines, costs, and damages assessed against any person or persons occupying such building or premises.

SEC. 10. In all prosecutions under this act, by indictment or otherwise, it shall not be necessary to state the kind of liquor sold, or to describe the place where sold.

We urge the maintenance of this law *because it is the only available system that will reach the case.*

24

I can see but *five possible* courses of action, one of which must be followed. The first and the easiest in seeming, but not in fact, is *to sit still—the do-nothing policy*. I need not argue this case. It is not admissible. Indeed, it is not long possible. We cannot sit still if we would. We are on the crusted crater of *Vesuvius*. Its eruption is only a question of time. Soon it will belch, and we shall find such a grave that no future antiquarian will more than dream of our existence. The tiger is at our throat. Sit still, and we are dead. *We must act ; we must move*. All that sin ever wants is to be let alone. The thief has his hand in your pocket, and asks you to hold still. If you move, you may put him to more trouble, or disappoint him of his gains. The assassin is in your chamber, stealing, with clinched dagger, up to the crib where your child slumbers. All he wants is time. The work of reform is always aggressive, and wearisome, and dangerous. It must have its convictions from above, be in league with God, move by a command so supreme that no human veto is heard. It can have no fellowship with conservatism. Cautious it may be, but never cowardly. It takes bold and strong strokes to liberate an angel from a block of marble. Every advance is fatal to the old forms. Even the serpent's worn-out skin creaks and rustles when the inhabitant moves out. Like cinders, it is crisp and crotchety while it lasts. God sent his Son into the world not to bring peace, but a sword. It is an old war against an aggressor—sin. He must be *driven* out of the world, and this means conflict, and struggle, and woe. The sooner we settle down to the conviction that we are to endure hardness like good soldiers, the better it will be for us.

Another line of action that has been presented, tried, and exploded, is just now practically brought forward as an amendment to this law —to except wine and beer. It is the *substitution of wines, lighter drinks, in the place of alcohol or strong spirituous liquors*. To pave the way, it is stated by Ex-Governor Andrew, of Massachusetts, in his pamphlet for which he received $10,000 from the Liquor Ring, that all peoples that have arrived at any degree of civilization have been drinking peoples, have invented some kind of intoxicating drink. It is, therefore, most bravely concluded that strong drink is a civilizer. A grog-shop, then, is a center of civilizing power. Need one argue against such a statement? It reminds one of Lord Brougham's case concerning Tenterton Steeple and Donneby Sands. In former times, there was a harbor at Donneby; the sea filled the channel. Meantime, a church with a steeple was built at Tenterton. A meeting was called to consider what should be done about the channel, when one man said that he noticed that as soon as they built that steeple at Tenterton the channel filled up, and moved that they tear down the steeple. All peoples that have become civilized have drunk strong drink : therefore, strong drink is a civilizer. Mark another fact. All peoples that have become civilized have stolen, been licentious and adulterous, and have lied ; therefore, stealing, licentiousness, adultery, and lying are civilizers.

Now, let us look at the facts concerning domestic wines and their influence upon drunkenness in the countries where they are raised and made. This will be a fair putting of the case, to put it at its best. Paris, the city of *wine*, where the light wines abound, where more wine is consumed than in any other city in the world, in 1863 consumed seven gallons distilled spirits for each man, woman, and child. That surpasses us. She produces 1,089,000,000 gallons of wine in 1865, yet consumes more brandy and other distilled liquors per head than any other nation on earth. This indicates that wine does not wean men from strong drink. If it does, they had better not be weaned, judging by the poverty, wretchedness, and godlessness that characterize France, especially the wine-growing sections.

There is an impression that France is a temperance nation. Men ride through the country in the better class of cars and see little of it, because the matchless police remove the nuisance ; but let them live there, and live with the people, and they will change their minds. Listen to the witnesses :—

Our author, J. Fenimore Cooper, says : " I came to Europe under the impression that there was more drunkenness among us (Americans) than in any other country. *A residence of six months in Paris changed my views entirely.* I have taken unbelievers about Paris, and always convinced them in one walk. I have been more struck by drunkenness in the streets of Paris than in those of London."

Horace Greeley wrote from Paris : " That wine *will* intoxicate, *does* intoxicate—that there are confirmed drunkards in Paris and throughout France—is notorious and undeniable."

M. Le Clerc says : " Laborers leave their work, derange their means, drink irregularly, and transform into drunken debauch the time which should have been spent in profitable labor."

A French magazine says : " Drunkenness is the beginning and end of life in the great French industrial centers. At Lille, twenty-five per cent. of the men and twelve per cent. of the women are confirmed drunkards."

The Count de Montalembert, Member of the Academy of Natural Sciences, said in the National Assembly of France : " Where there is a wine-shop, there are the elements of disease, and the frightful source of all that is at enmity with the interests of the workman."

M. Jules Simon: "Women rival the men in drunkenness. At Lille, at Rouen, there are some so saturated with it that their infants refuse to take the breast of a sober woman."

Hon. James M. Usher, Chief Commissioner of Massachusetts to the World's Exposition in Paris, in 1867, says: "The drinking habit runs through every phase of society. I have seen more people drunk here than I ever saw in Boston for the same length of time. They are the same class of people, too."

Hon. Caleb Foote, of Salem, Mass., writing from Paris, after large investigations, "denies, in toto, the theory that the people of the wine-producing countries are sober."

Dr. E. N. Kirk, of Boston, says: "I never saw such systematic drunkenness as I saw in France during a residence of sixteen months. The French go about it as a business. I never saw so many women drunk."

Surely there is no lack of testimony. Look at other wine-growing countries:—

Rev. E. S. Lacy, of San Francisco, six months in Switzerland in a wine-growing section, says: "Here more intoxication was obvious than in any other place it was ever my lot to live in."

Before the Legislative License Committee of Massachusetts, Dr. Warren, of the Boston Biblical School, seven years a resident in Germany, says: "Drunkenness is very common; every evening drunken people stagger by my house."

Rev. J. G. Cochran, missionary to Persia, says of a wine-producing section: "The whole village of male adults will be habitually intoxicated for a month or six weeks."

Rev. Mr. Larabee, another missionary to Persia, confirms the statement. Even priests coolly excuse their own irregularities by the plea of drunkenness.

How is Italy? Cardinal Acton, Chief Judge of Rome, says: "Nearly all the crime in Rome originates in the use of wine."

Thirty-five or forty years ago England attempted to suppress drunkenness by licensing ale and beer. More distilled liquor per head now than then. The consumption of distilled liquors has increased in the last fifty years one hundred and seventy-five per cent.

Turn to America. How fares it in California? The experiment fails. A State convention of the friends of temperance, in October, 1866, resolved against wine-growing. Conventions of Congregational

ministers and lay delegates, same month, reached the same result.
They are fully convinced that the hope of temperance based on wine
is delusive. This case has been tried till the State exceeds, perhaps,
all others in corruption.

Com. Wells: "California, with her cheap wines for temperance, in
the year ending June 30, 1867, sold fourteen times, per head, as
much alcoholic stuff as Maine did, and more than any other State."

These are the facts concerning the wine-growing countries. The
idea of a substitute of wine for alcohol in the interest of temperance
is absurd. I have protracted this part of the argument because the
enemies of this law are seeking to have wine and beer excepted from
the law. But do it, and you kill the law; and this is what they seek.
Beware! If you make wine and beer abound, drunkenness will
much more abound.

Against this evil plan we can only thunder the facts that the countries that manufacture and drink most wine use most distilled liquors,
and have the largest per cent. of beastly, wife-beating, child-beating
drunkenness. Husbands may tell their ragged and pleading wives
that they can stop. They guess they know who drives. They can
stop if they will, but the fact remains. The 60,000 drunkards that
annually die were all moderate drinkers before they settled down into
old tubs. They all tippled a little before they guzzled. There is no
disguising the fact: once drinking, there is no way out but to face
about and let it alone, or go through into hell. When a pair of dice
are thrown, and 999 out of 1,000 turn double sixes, you are bound
to believe the dice loaded. This awful game of perdition turns up
death 60,000 times a year. Are you willing to believe that any dose
is safe? Will slow scuttling keep a ship afloat better than no scuttling? You who tipple are the ones that need to be alarmed. 'Tis
not the worthless sot that desolates the land; it is the respectable
drinker. This is where the evil is conceived and born. Beware of
the beginnings of evil. Wines can never advance the temperance
cause by being substituted for distilled liquors.

The third mode of treatment is that practiced in Illinois and many
other States. It is the LICENSE SYSTEM. This justly assumes that
the traffic is wrong, and must be controlled. I am bold to say that
this is the chiefest if not the only virtue in the entire system. I object
to the license system, that *it does not control the trade*. It does not
limit the sale of liquor. Do you ask for proof? You can have it on
this very block, within a stone's cast from this spot. There is not a
section of this city where there is any dearth of saloons. There are
in Chicago two thousand—one for each one hundred and fifty people.

There is not a man living in this city whom the law has restrained from drink. It does not restrain the business.

Again: *It helps to make this systematized murder respectable.* Good citizens do not engage in killing their fellows. Reputable men do not go into this work of making criminals and paupers. This awful work is disgraceful. License legalizes it, and cloaks it with public sanction. They become public servants, doing the public will.

Again: *It is an unjust monopoly.* If it is right for one man in one hundred and fifty to sell liquor, the other one hundred and forty-nine have the same right. If it is wrong for the one hundred and forty-nine, it cannot be right for the one. Legislatures have no power to make rights. Rights are as old as God. And no conclave, no Congress, no Parliament, no Sanhedrin, can give a man a right to murder his fellow for his money, even though he does drop a part of the price of his crime into the public coffers.

Again: *It involves the right to license gambling-houses and houses of ill-fame.*

Again: It becomes itself a school of vice. The law is a public educator. If it proscribes a crime, it puts the fatal seal upon that crime, and the children grow up with the conviction of the evil of that crime. Establish the prize-ring by law, and your sons will be more apt to be bruisers. This is fearfully true of the license law. Therefore, for these reasons, the license law fails, and must forever fail.

The fourth course *is by prohibition.* I will not discuss this, for it is not now within our reach. But allow me to say, I believe in prohibition. We have the right by the law of self-preservation. Again, the Supreme Courts of some of the States have decided in its favor. The safety of the State is the supreme law. *Moreover, it is not a failure.* It actually empties jails, almshouses, and poor-houses. It stops the sale of three fourths of the liquor, and stops nearly all the crime. Take the general statistics. Maine, Vermont, and Massachusetts, with 2,250,000 population in 1860, sold, under prohibitory law, $43,022,754 worth of liquor during the year 1867. New Jersey, Rhode Island, Maryland, and Wisconsin, with 2,225,000 population, sold the same year, under license law, $137,886,445 worth of liquor. Prohibition is not a failure.

We now approach the last experiment, as embodied in the new law. Three questions arise. First, Is it right? Second, Is it wise? Third, Is it possible? Let us answer in detail: It is right, because all that favors prohibition favors this, as the greater includes the less.

The first fact is this. Intemperance is *an evil*, therefore this restraint can do no harm. The experiment is safe. It is the case of a man on a burning vessel—it is entirely safe to take to the landing. Whatever comes, to stay is to die. The change here can do no harm; we take no risk. Again, we have the right. This inheres in us; we have the right to protection. A man tries to bring his cattle from Texas to our market; we stop him because they infect and damage our herds. A man tries to bring the quintessence of ruin into my home to infect my sons. I have a right to stop him; are not my sons as sacred as my oxen? An assassin crawls into my room and raises his dagger above my wife. He dies, if God gives me grace and strength to kill him. A wretch crawls up to my brother and undertakes to poison him. Have I not a right to stop him? A man comes to my hen-coop to steal my chickens. The law says *Joliet*.* He comes to my angel-coop to steal my angels. Have I not a right to protect them? Have I not as divine a right to defend my children as I have to defend my chickens? More than this, the Supreme Courts of many of the States declare this right. The people are *sovereign*. They have supreme right to stop crime. Prohibition is an old right: China forbade the use of wine eleven hundred years before Christ, and it is a stranger there yet as a beverage. Carthage banished it from the camp. Plato approved this law. Lycurgus made it shameful to use it; slaves were intoxicated and exhibited to the youth. Romulus sentenced women to death for intoxication as the beginning of adultery. Mohammed prohibited it twelve hundred and fifty years ago. Governments have always had the right to punish and prevent crime.

This is not all vague generalities. This law is based on the principles of common justice and common law. A leading jurist of this city, Hon. Judge Goodrich, has given me his opinion of this law since its enactment.

He says: " It is justified upon principles fundamental to all social and governmental organizations. In entering into society, every individual surrenders certain of his natural rights, such as the vindication of his wrongs, the protection of life and of property, in consideration that society will insure to him the peaceable enjoyment of his unsurrendered rights, and indemnity for all wrongs done to him.

" One right surrendered is the privilege of doing any thing, though personally beneficial, or pursuing any occupation, the natural or probable results of which are, or are likely to be, injurious to other

---

* State Prison.

members of society; and society in return is bound to prevent such acts, and provide for remuneration for all damages occasioned by such acts. This right and remedy should be extended to wives, mothers, minors, as well as to men and adults. Unless society afford this protection and these remedies, it cannot be maintained, for it fails to keep its terms of the compact.

" Hence, if a man erect on his premises a dangerous or unhealthful business, or nuisance, society can remove it, and the injured party can recover damages resulting directly from the same.

" So we say, If the natural result or probable result of the sale of intoxicating liquors to minors, or persons liable to intoxication, is to inflict any injury upon the person purchasing them, or upon other persons, society is bound to prevent it, or afford to the parties injured adequate compensation for the injury sustained.

" If it takes away the means of maintenance from those dependent upon the party to whom sold, or maddens his brain so that he inflicts injury upon others, society is bound to give them a remedy of compensation.

" This law is just to the vender, and is founded on well-established principles of the common law.

" The law holds a man responsible for the consequences of an act which he had reasonable ground to know would be the result of the act, and, doing the act with such knowledge, is held to have intended the consequences ; therefore, as a vender of intoxicating drinks knows its sale to a minor or habitually intoxicated person usually produces acts of violence, pauperism, etc., he should be regarded as having intended to produce such results, and liable for the injurious results."

This is definitively stated, vol. i., " Starkie on Evidence," p. 51 : " In case of crime, it is reasonable to infer that a man intended and contemplated that end and result which is the natural and immediate consequence of the means which he used." *Therefore, for the foregoing reasons we conclude that the law is right.*

Next, *Is it wise?* Is it a law that, enforced, will reach the object aimed at ? In my judgment, it is wise, because it *treats the business like any other crime.* It does not dignify it by the name of law, nor protect it by the arm of the Government. It does not turn the rumseller loose in society as a teacher, on the footing of public approval, to mold and educate our children. It brands him as an enemy. It does not let him lift a hand or a foot till it takes hostages from him for good behavior ; and thus it says, " This monster must be watched. He may slay or ruin somebody. Beware ! " It looks on him as a mad dog in the highway. It runs after him, crying, "Mad dog, mad dog!" This puts a sort of Cain-mark on him, to start with. Society says, "I am not able to slay him, but I will cry after him, wherever he goes, Murderer! murderer! so the youth in the land may not be deceived." It is like a certain old English livery-stable, in which a police-officer was stationed. Of some gentle horses he said to the owner, "Hire them, and make a living, and be blessed." Of one black, untamed beast he said, "If you hire him out, you shall pay damages." It discriminates against the black beast. A man can sell groceries, and the law says, "Amen, good citizen;" but if he sells alcohol, it says, "Dangerous! beware of the black beast."

It is wise, *because it strikes the rumseller where he lives—in the pocket.* It wastes no strength in sentimentalism. It moves to conquer. It means business. It comprehends the character of the enemy. Nothing but striking the profits can be understood, so it aims low; and, if I mistake not, it will slay these things, rumsellers, by the thousand. The law accepts the situation, admits that every sentiment of humanity is dead, that moral obligation has lost its power, that honor has long been forgotten, that common justice is only a myth of the past, that there is no footing in such a soul but in the low sense of loss of the bloodstained gains.

So the law is wise in striking the rumseller where he lives—in his pocket. Touch the profits, and he feels; make it unprofitable, and it will cease. It is not a missionary enterprise, it is all for gain.

It is wise, because it applies the recovered money to the injured. It does not put this money into the public pocket. I have little faith in the policy that will allow a man to destroy a whole neighborhood, send a hundred men to jail and a hundred families to the poor-house, and stop a score of factories, for the small income the murderer pays on his booty. Nor do I see how the State can innocently barter the blood and health and character of my brother or son for a few dollars for the treasury. I have more faith even in the poor wretch who, in the confessional, while confessing and paying a few pence for absolution, was stealing the priest's watch and purse. It is here a penny in, and a thousand dollars out.

But this law gives its recovered plunder not to the State, which has but doubtful right to it, but to those who suffer the wrong and need the help. It keeps that mother from pauperism. It feeds and schools those helpless, innocent, wronged, and robbed children. It applies the funds exactly where they are most needed, and, therefore, we conclude *that it is wise.*

24*

THE TEMPERANCE REFORM.

It is wise, because it cuts down through all subterfuges, and *makes good its securities.* Wherever it is possible to sell or give away this deadly drug, there it can seize the very soil for damages. It stops not at the cat's-paw, but it reaches all the parties. The landlord who divides the profits in rents must now divide the responsibility and damages, as he has always shared the guilt. Nothing can be clearer than that the man who furnishes the den is a *particeps criminis,* and should be so held. Some men rent their buildings for dead-falls, and fancy that they are free from guilt. But I can see no moral difference between your letting a saloon into your building and your tending the bar yourself. In both cases you pocket the profits, and your hiring some widow's son to dose out the poison for you does not lessen your guilt. The victims sinking into a drunkard's hell may fasten their frenzied hands upon you, and crying, "Thou art the man," drag you into the same condemnation. This law recognizes this great fact, and holds the property liable, and *so is wise.*

Again, it is wise in making no distinctions in liquor. Chemists are not needed to define the various kinds. It is one simple question : Did the man who drank your liquor do any damage? If beer and wine do no harm and don't intoxicate, then there will be no damages. If the man who drinks beer does not break down my fence, you will not have to put it up again. Why do these men resist ? It is because they know that wine and beer are dangerous and ruinous, and ought to be held responsible.

Again, it is wise in *touching off this shell with a six months' fuse.* It gives its friends a chance to rally against a foe already in the fort and always ready.

Is it possible? Can it be enforced? That is the leading question. I wish to answer that it *can and must be enforced,* because it receives the *support of all good men of all parties.* It was introduced into the House by one party, and into the Senate by the other. Sometimes party spirit carries men over into opposition to a good thing, because it is of the opposite faction. But in this case it breaks into all the old party lines and makes a party for itself, and comes to the people with a tremendous indorsement from the strength of the State.

The fact that it is a law of the State must be its surety. It is purely a *public sentiment.* If the people are convicted for the law, all the powers of lager and whisky and of darkness cannot resist it. Awaken the people, impress them with the majesty and authority of the law, set them for its defense, and its victory is inevitable. I think we need a revival on this question of law. The way to despotism is through anarchy. Law is our only safety. Let me sail on a sea of fire rather than on the sea of chance and chaos. We are drifting toward the breakers. In the *home* there is a letting down of authority. Children are certain they know more than their parents, and, by the pulseless hand with which the parents guide them, I think the children are right. God has put you in charge. They are not your guardians. They resent correction as an insult. All this must be cured. In the home must be laid the foundations of the law and authority. The best thing a people can have as insurance for the future is a solid conviction of *authority of law*. It is not a question whether my personal rights can be served, but what is the demand of the public good. My sidewalk may hold me, but it must hold also the public. My cellar-way may be sufficiently guarded for me, but it must also be safe for the stranger. The public good is the supreme law. And enacted law is the judgment of the majority as to what is the public good. So the individual can have no alternative but to obey the law while it is the law, or suffer the penalty. Let this be instilled into every mind, and there will be no difficulty in enforcing the law on temperance or on any other subject. It is purely a question of public opinion. This is always resistless. Government is always the creature of public will. The government of the Celestial Empire would last in America about one sixteenth of one second—just long enough to touch ground. It would hold this Yankee nation about as long as a sheet of tissue paper would keep down an eruption of Vesuvius. The public sentiment is absolute. No law can be valid without this support. Let the mayor issue a proclamation forbidding Christian people from assembling to worship next Sabbath morning because he was opposed to it. What would happen? I can tell you what would happen. Unless such action was demanded by the public good, on account of some plague or peril, and so had the approval of the people, next Sabbath would see us all in our places, and such a mayor in his place in Jacksonville or at Elgin. The public will is supreme. This is always the final arbiter. This makes the people invincible. " You may destroy the cities to the last hamlet, desolate the country to the last cabin, wipe out the press to the last page, and you have done nothing. There still remains the human mind, pure as the light and unapproachable as the sun." And in its supreme decisions are the decrees of destiny. Thus you may burn the buildings from Jefferson-street to the Lake, and from De Koven-street to Fullerton Avenue, and you have not burned Chicago. All that is not Chicago. Chicago is in the heroic bosoms of the heroic people, in the everlasting purpose, in the almighty energy that camped like savages on the prairie, without stool or tent—planned by the light of the burning fortunes new railroads, new depots, new elevators, new hotels, new churches, a new city, and a new civilization. Fix this sentiment for this law, and then the gates of hell shall not prevail against it. The whole question is one of public opinion. This, I think, is right, or can be righted by the first of July.

Suppose I indicate how I think it can be done. First, on the general questions of respect for the law for the long future. Teach your children to respect it, teach them to respect your authority, and teach them to respect the law while in school.

Again: Let *your influence be solid against excusing great criminals.* These local aldermen that have sold themselves and the public trust should have fair trial and fair chance like any other thieves, and, if convicted, suffer the extreme penalty of the law. They have nominally served the public for nothing; now make them do it actually. This is not so harsh. If it seems harsh, that seeming is proof of its necessity. This poor day-laborer is sick, and so without income, and his babes are hungry, and in desperation he snatches a man's money, and runs. He is dogged into the penitentiary. These scoundrels steal the city poor, and take away public confidence, and breed contempt for law. I say, in God's name, do not shield them, but send them to their reward. To secure this, let men in trying places know that they have your sympathy and support. Without regard to party, let honest men say to the faithful judges and officials, "God bless you," and "We will support you."

The press have a large share of responsibility in this matter of public opinion. There is great hope in the general tone of the press on this law. Some editorials have been clear and manly for the law. These forces mean victory in July. The Press is the Third House, but the people are the Fourth House.

Another fact: You come in contact with large numbers of laboring men. You meet them in their shops and at their work. A few words judiciously spoken will prepare them for right action when the time comes. If the law is to be resisted, men must be found to leave their work, and mass and combine against it. Now, you can prevent many from doing this. If the great working-class say that the law shall not be enforced, its execution will be difficult, if not impossible. But if they say, "It must be obeyed," or even keep out of the crowds and at their work, its enforcement will be as certain as destiny. Every man do his duty like a man, and this benign and equitable law will hedge this awful traffic with mortal and fatal disabilities.

Mobs may threaten, but they must finally obey. I would put deliberate emphasis upon this. If men cannot obey the law, the way is open. They can return to the old despotisms, and they can go without passports too; and they can take the fortunes they have made here. But if they stay, they must obey the law. I had rather be a thousand years longer in reclaiming the wilderness, than see it seized by brutality, and beastliness, and crime.

Possibly some of you are saying, "I approve the law, but my family is safe, and I will not take any risks of ill-will by taking sides. Let those who are exposed enforce the law." Brother, you are exposed. This traffic is an infernal machine stored under your bed. Your thoughtless boy may light the fuse when you least expect it. There is no safety with the thing about the premises. Is it just the fair play which we all approve and demand to ask our representatives to take the chances of defeat or censure in enacting a good law, which we approve and the public safety demands, and then we ourselves shirk the responsibility and leave the law unenforced? Is it manly for us to send them out on the forlorn hope, and then, when they have made the breach and hold it, we desert and refuse to march in with the main army? All honor to the men who have breasted the storm and secured such advantage to the cause! Blessings from many a humble widow whose son shall be saved to her, and from many a poor orphan thus furnished with protection and possible schooling, shall come upon their heads. In the humble homes of poverty, where piety and virtue struggle against want and degradation, where God's tall and tender-footed angels keep mightly watch, there their names shall be mentioned. And yonder, when the reckoning comes, think you this vote shall be forgotten? I tell you, Nay. The Judge himself shall say, "Inasmuch as you have done it unto the least of these my little ones, you have done it unto me." I had rather have my name on that affirmative vote than be the representative of a compromised and drunken constituency for a thousand years. All honor to the men who enacted the law, and let us show ourselves worthy of such representatives. To-night, brother, after this long survey of this momentous subject, I call upon you, in the presence of this great criminal—in full view of his malignant character; of the vileness that stamps the poison itself; of the frauds that are practiced in its manufacture; of the deadly counterfeits that deepen its malignity; of the insanity that makes its victims fairly fly to ruin; of the 1,000,000 wrecks that stagger, and ooze, and leer, and bloat, and fester, and fall downward; of the 60,000 poor creatures that yearly fill drunkards' graves on their way to the drunkard's doom; of 2,000,000 children that are left worse than orphans, cursed with an inheritance of rags and shame; of the 3,000,000 of women who have millstones tied about their necks and are thus cast into the social sea; of the 200,000 broken-hearted ones that yearly march to the poor-house; of the 200,000 convicts that are annually sent to jail; of the 200,000 orphans annually bequeathed to public charity; of the 450 suicides that are caused by this evil spirit; of the 700 murders that horrify the year; of the 1,350 rapes that are committed by this demon; of the 12,000 lunatics that are made in this fire; of the great company of idiots that are spawned by this monster; of the millions of homes ruined and all the homes threatened by this invader; of the public schools, robbed of 2,000,000 children; of seven-eighths of all the crimes of the land committed by this evil inspiration; and of the enormous sum of $2,607,491,866 annually taken from the public comfort and expended in wretchedness and crime—in the presence of all these fearful facts, I call upon you, in this day of probation, in this house of God, by the absolute need of prompt action, by the utter failure of indecision, by the worse than failure of many substitutes, and by the right of self-preservation; I call upon you, in the name of the countless victims who are bound in this wretched habit, in the name of the wearying, watching mothers whose sons are imperiled, in the name of some young men here to-night who may yet wreck all beauty for time and all hope for eternity, in the name of some fair and hopeful maidens here to-night who may yet mourn and pine in the squalor and misery of the drunkard's hovel, in the name of earth desolated and heaven forfeited by this crime, and in the name of Almighty God, whose eye is upon us, and at whose judgment-bar we must shortly stand—I call upon you to maintain and enforce this law at all costs! Out of these awful responsibilities we cry from our hearts forever and ever, "Everlasting war against rum, and eternal death to alcohol!"

E. C. DELAVAN.

CHARLES JEWETT, M.D.

SECTION IX.
TEMPERANCE LITERATURE.

CHAPTER XXIII.

MEDICAL AND CHEMICAL TEMPERANCE.

SO obvious and powerful an argument in favor of abstinence from intoxicating drinks as that furnished by their injury to the health was not likely to be long overlooked.

In olden times drunkenness was regarded either as the result of weakness of the head, that is, inability to "stand the liquor," or as the effect of deliberate indulgence therein; and the man who could carry the most alcohol without staggering or stammering was regarded as a person of great head power, and among his boon companions was treated with distinguished honor. As Robert Burns has it, in one of his drinking songs:—

> "Wha last beside his chair shall fa',
> He is the king among us a'."

To drink deep without drunkenness was an accomplishment most highly coveted by men in all grades of society. Old admirers of that distinguished Massachusetts statesman, Daniel Webster, will not fail to remember in this connection that, along with his peerless fame as "The Defender of the Constitution," there was often coupled this other distinguished honor, (?) namely, "Old Dan can carry more brandy than any other man in America."

In those days the ruinous effects of alcohol upon the

physical constitution were regarded as among the common ills of mankind, and the verdict of a coroner's jury in the case of a person who suddenly died in a drunken debauch would be, "Died of the visitation of God." Such a view of such a case implies not only the most absolute blindness to the crime of drunkenness, but a dense ignorance of the laws of health as affected by alcoholic drinks. The medical prescription of St. Paul to his young friend Timothy, "Drink no longer water, but use a little wine for thy stomach's sake and thine often infirmities," was held by simple people to contain the sum and substance of domestic medical practice, the kind and quantity of liquor to be varied to suit varying tastes and conditions. Liquor was necessary to keep out the cold, it was equally required to keep out the heat. If one were weak it would strengthen him, and if he were strong he could stand it without danger. For women it was needful to drink gin, especially at or near the time of child-birth, and to such an extent did this idea prevail among the common people of England, that it has been said, that most of the poor of that country fifty years ago were born with a liking for gin, the mother being usually half drunk on it when the baby came into the world.

No less useful was liquor thought to be for comfort and consolation in times of severe mental distress. "Is any merry?" says that same St. Paul, "let him sing psalms. Is any among you afflicted? let him pray:" but this also, if one might judge by the common practice, had been varied so as to read, Is any merry? let him drink punch and toddy; is any afflicted? let him drink brandy and hollands.

But at length some of the medical profession in America began to study the effects of alcohol upon the muscular and nervous systems, and to this temperance agitation do we owe a large and valuable class of medical discoveries.

In 1794 Dr. Rush, of Philadelphia, published a volume of medical inquiries into the effects of ardent spirits upon the body and mind, and even in that early day preached the doctrine of total abstinence as the only successful safeguard against intemperance.

As usual, the doctors were divided on so great a question, some declaring that alcohol was a healthy stimulant, aided digestion, and toned up the nerves, while others, abandoning all argument from the old medical authorities, commenced to observe for themselves. It was not long before it was discovered that alcohol taken into the system was neither digested itself, nor did it help in the digestion of any thing else, but that, after flying about along the nerves and often into the brain, it was expelled from the system again *as alcohol*. Thus it was demonstrated once for all that ALCOHOL IS NOT FOOD. On this ground the temperance men intrenched themselves, and prepared for a further advance.

In 1842, in the midst of the early success of the Washingtonian movement, Dr. Thomas Sewell, Professor of Pathology in the College of Columbia, D. C., published a series of colored diagrams taken from drawings made as the result of dissections of the stomachs of drunkards who had died in different degrees of alcoholic diseases. These plates were indorsed by Dr. Warren, of Boston ; Dr. Mott, of New York ; and Dr. Horner, of Philadelphia ;

and form the basis of a considerable lecture system on the hygienic questions connected with the temperance reform. They have done good service to the cause for over thirty-five years, and are still in active use.

Figure 1 represents the mucous coat of the stomach in a healthy state, which in color is slightly reddish, tinged with yellow.

Figure 2 represents a part of the internal portion of the stomach of a temperate drinker, a man who takes his grog daily, but moderately, the effect of which is to distend the blood vessels of the inner surface of the stomach, or, in other words, produce a degree of inflammation which makes the blood vessels visible.

Figure 3 represents the stomach of a habitual drunkard—a hard drinker. It was drawn from life, or, rather, from death, of one who had been such for many years, and the stomach resembled what are called *rum blossoms*, which are sometimes seen upon the face of the hard drinker.

In this state the inebriate is never entirely satisfied unless the stomach is excited by the presence of alcohol, or some other narcotic poison, and whenever these are withheld he is afflicted with the loss of appetite, nausea, gnawing pains, and a sinking sensation at the stomach, also lassitude and temporary disturbance of all the functions of the body.

It is under these circumstances, and in this condition of the body, that the drunkard finds it so difficult to resist the cravings of his appetite, and to reform his habits—difficult, but not impossible. Thousands of those far sunk to ruin have reformed, and thousands are now undergoing the experiment; but it is only by total abstinence that reform can be accomplished. No one may hope to reform by degrees, or to be cured by substituting one form of alcohol for another. So long as he indulges in the smallest degree, so long will his propensity to drink be perpetuated.

Figure 4 represents the inner coat of the stomach ulcerated, as the result of alcoholic inflammation.

Figure 5 is the drawing of the stomach of a drunkard who died immediately after a long debauch. It shows a high degree of inflammation, and the color is changed to a livid red.

The last of these plates represents the internal coat of the stomach of a drunkard who had died with the *delirium tremens*. The fearful effects of the alcoholic poison, as thus shown in color, are inde-

DIAGRAMS OF THE STOMACH IN VARIOUS CONDITIONS.

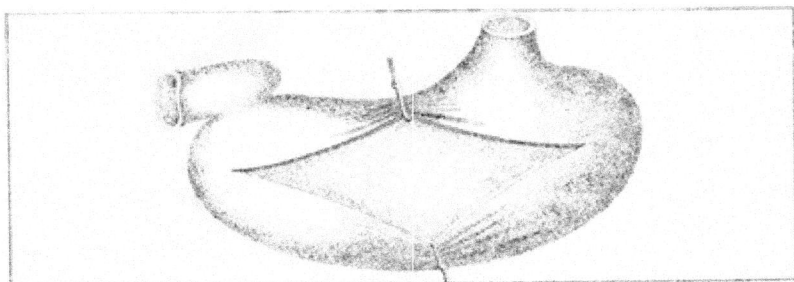

Healthful

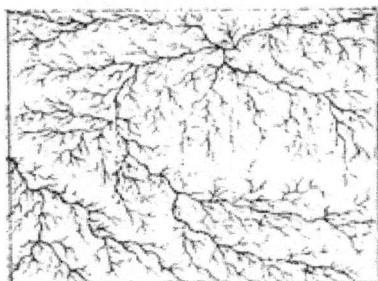

Moderate Drinking

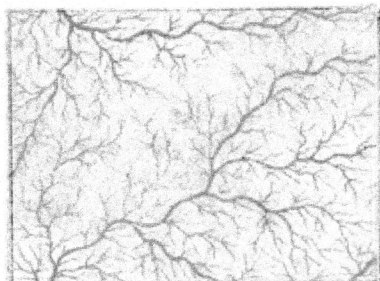

Drunkards

Ulcerous.

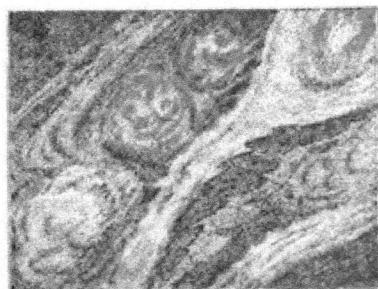

After a long Debauch.

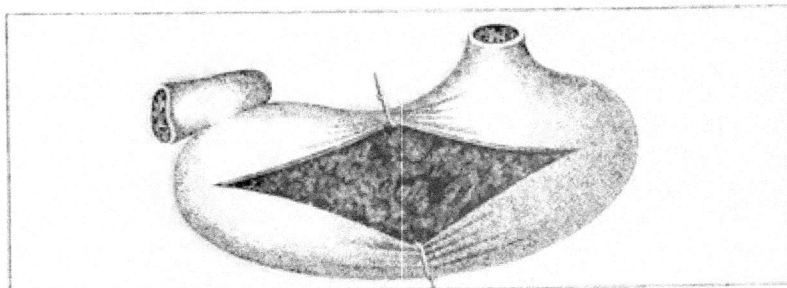

Death by Delirium Tremens

scribable in words. In some places the coats of the stomach seem even to be in an incipient state of mortification.

Question. What takes place in the stomach of the reformed drunkard who abandons the use of all intoxicating drinks?

Answer. The stomach, by that extraordinary power of self-restoration with which it is endowed, gradually resumes its natural appearance. Its gorged blood-vessels become reduced to their original size, and its natural color and health insensibly return. A few weeks or months, according to the observations I have made, will accomplish this renovation; after which the individual has no longer any suffering or desire for liquor.

It is true, however, and should ever be borne in mind, that such is the susceptibility of the stomach of the reformed drunkard, that a repetition of the use of liquor in the slightest degree, or in any form, revives the appetite; the blood-vessels again become dilated, and all the morbid sensibility of the organ is reproduced.

Abstinence, therefore, total abstinence, at once and forever, must be the pledge of him who means to stand.

The use of wine, beer, or any intoxicating liquor whatever, the doctor declares, will produce the alcoholic disease. After giving some cases that have come under his observation, the doctor continues:—

But time would fail me, were I to attempt the account of half the pathology of drunkenness. Dyspepsia, jaundice, emaciation, corpulence, rheumatism, gout, palpitation, epilepsy, lethargy, palsy, apoplexy, melancholy, madness, *delirium tremens*, premature old age, compose but a small part of the endless catalogue of diseases produced by alcohol drinking. Indeed, there is scarcely a morbid affection to which the human body is liable that has not in one form or another been produced by that; not a disease but has been aggravated by it; nor a predisposition to disease which it has not called into action.

These are the reasons why the drunkard dies so easily, and from such apparently slight causes.

As regards the operation of liquor in its effects on the human body, the experiments of Dr. Perry, of London, clearly prove that liquor is absorbed into the circulation, and carried to the brain and other organs, immediately upon its being received into the system, where it remains unchanged until the abused organs can throw it off.

The "British Medical Journal" says: "On the face of it, the teetotalers have, from a scientific point of view, the best of the argument. Our greatest and most esteemed authorities have come to the conclusion that alcohol is not food, and that it is simply eliminated *as* alcohol from the body."

Thus the early theory of *Liebig*, that alcohol, though not a flesh-former, was burned in the blood, and so became a heat-former, is finally and entirely exploded.

As a further proof that alcohol goes to the brain of the drinker in an unchanged form, take this recent statement of Mr. George M'Candlish, Secretary of the Jackson, Mich., Reform Club, to the editor of this volume:—

"In the fall of 1867, during my drinking days, I was going home one night badly set up, and when I came to the High Bridge, between Oil City and West Oil City, I looked down and saw a man lying at the bottom of the ravine apparently dead. I was a good deal frightened, and went and called the chief of police; and along with two policemen and Drs. Seys and Harding, we picked up the man, and found that he had fallen over, in a fit of intoxication, and broken his neck. I was summoned as a witness before the coroner's jury, and saw the *post mortem* examination performed by these two physicians. After removing the top of the skull, for the purpose of examining the condition of the brain, they tested it for alcohol, by holding a lighted match near it; and immediately the brain took fire, and burned with a blue flame, like an alcohol lamp."

The following is a list of the principal inebriate asylums in the United States, which have grown up out of the idea that drunkenness is a disease :—

Binghamton, N. Y.—Dr. Willard Parker, President; Albert Day, M.D., Superintendent.

Kings County Inebriate Asylum, located in Brooklyn.—Hon. J. S. T. Stranahan, President; Rev. John Willetts, Superintendent.

Ward's Island Asylum for Inebriates, New York city.—Under charge of the Commissioners of Charities and Corrections.—Dr. W. R. Fisher, Resident Physician.

Washingtonian Home, 1,009 Washington-street, Boston, Mass.—Otis Clapp, President; William C. Lawrence, Superintendent.

Washingtonian Home, 570 West Madison-street, Chicago, Ill.—Charles J. Hull, President; Dr. J. A. Ballard, Superintendent.

Inebriate Asylum, Media, Pa.—Dr. Joseph Parrish, M.D., Superintendent.

THE CHEMISTRY OF STRONG DRINK.

Among the curious things brought out by the investigations of the temperance men is the system of manufacturing beverages under fancy names out of cheap liquor and a mixture of drugs, some of which are poisonous—and others by the use of acids; the whole together producing a mixture scarcely better than the " witches' broth " of Shakspeare.

Dr. Charles Jewett, in his admirable chemical examination of the liquors of the tippling shops, has this biting sentence : " Rum is alcohol and water, brandy is alcohol and dirty water." The latter definition will apply to a very large proportion of the two hundred and twenty different drinks, recipes for which are given in the " Bon-Vivants' Companion."

Among the interesting names for the drinks in this volume are : " Stone Fences, Bottled Velvet, Pope, Cardinal, Archbishop, Bishop,

Locomotive, White Tiger's Milk, Pousse L'Amour, etc. One drink, called the Blue Blazer, is concocted as follows: "one wine glass of Scotch whisky, one wine glass boiling water. Put the whisky and the boiling water in one mug, ignite the liquid with fire, and while blazing mix both ingredients by pouring them four or five times from one mug to the other, as represented in the cut. If well done this will have the appearance of a continued stream of liquid fire.

A beholder, gazing for the first time upon an experienced artist

BLUE BLAZER.

compounding this beverage, would naturally come to the conclusion that it was a nectar for Pluto rather than Bacchus."

The use of logwood, sulphuric acid, and other pungent and powerful drugs and chemicals, is among the common practices of the compounders of liquors.

The author of the "Manual for the Manufacture of Cordials," etc., proposes in his card to furnish the concentrated extract of any of the recipes in his book at a low price for cash; and when it is borne in mind that all manner of abominations, among which may be mentioned bilge water pumped from the hold of ships, has been used in the manufacture of these liquors to give them body, it is a wonder that the appetite for strong drink in these doctored forms has not long since given place to universal disgust.

Mr. E. C. Delavan, whose name was a tower of strength in the temperance movement in the State of New York, once made an attack upon the liquor interest, showing how malt liquors were made in Albany. In an article published in the "American Temperance Intelligencer," he charged that water was used for making beer out of the pond into which the offal of the city was thrown.

This charge produced great excitement, and Mr. Delavan was sued for damages to the amount of three hundred thousand dollars, but the case, after five years' delay, resulted in favor of Mr. Delavan.

His caricature entitled "The Lament of the Albany Brewers," in which all the horrible and disgusting details were set forth, was so very forcible and suggestive that the beer drinkers must have been possessed of strong nerves or of weak imaginations if, after seeing the picture, they could possibly swallow the Albany beer.

Mr. Delavan, to the day of his death, devoted large sums out of his ample fortune to the circulation of temperance literature, and much of his time to the organization of temperance societies, and to personal advocacy of the cause of total abstinence.

Along this same line it has been understood that one of the peculiar merits of the London *brown stout* was the Thames water used in its manufacture, a stouter fluid and with more "body" to it than commonly falls to the lot of waters.

Among the most dangerous forms of alcoholic drinks are the "bitters," "tonics," and such like, sold by druggists every-where as "medicines," but whose market depends far less upon any of their health-giving properties than upon the alcohol they contain.

In Michigan, during the recent sweeping temperance revival, when efforts were made to enforce the prohibitory law, the reformers were coolly informed, "If you take away all the whisky we can have all the sprees we want on Hostetter's Bitters." And why not, when every twenty ounce bottle of the stuff contains the same amount of alcohol as a pint of pure whisky?

These bitters are advertised in religious newspapers thus :—

"Hostetter's bitters are a standard tonic remedy in many Christian and temperance homes, and are so regarded by many of our best physicians who are both temperance and Christian men."

"It is not probable that a single case of inebriation can be authenticated which originated where the appetite for strong drink was occasioned by the use of Hostetter's Bitters."

"They are generally, and I do not know but always, admitted

25

by all religious and temperance papers where they have been offered."

Per contra, see the following table, taken from the official report of the State Assayer of Rhode Island :—

Richardson's Bitters................50	per cent. of alcohol.	
Hostetter's Stomach Bitters.......43	"	"
Plantation Bitters................30	"	"
Puritan " 25	"	"
Quaker " 23	"	"
Temperance " 17	"	"
Vinegar " 7½	"	"
Pierce's " 6⅓	"	"

CHARLES JEWETT, M.D.

Among the distinguished advocates of the medical side of the temperance reform brought out by the old Washingtonian Movement was and is Dr. Charles Jewett, of Connecticut; a man gifted with shrewd common sense, something of a poet; a man who, as he says of himself, " did not come in at the back door of his profession," and whose medical opinions, therefore, on questions connected with the use of intoxicating liquors are entitled to respectful attention.

In a volume of his speeches, poems, and miscellaneous articles, the latter chiefly for the temperance journals, he says at the conclusion of his preface. " I will say to the public concerning this book, as I have often said of a dose of medicine to a sick friend, " If you can only manage to swallow it, I believe it will do you good." By the kind permission of this genial and hearty veteran in the temperance cause, the following selections are made :—

THE ALCOHOL APPETITE.

" The law of artificial appetites is the law of increase. Their demand is for more, more. It is this law which, when a man has heedlessly formed an appetite for intoxicating stimulants, drags him down through a course of indescribable sufferings, to a grave of infamy. There is no such tendency in natural appetites for food and drink, though indulged, in to perfect satiety, and through the period of a long life.

I see before me a number of very young persons. Now, suppose you take one of these children and give him a plate of strawberries and cream. The child will eat them with a keen relish. Give him an apple, and observe with what evident gusto he will dispose of it; now you may place at his elbow a basket of choice apples during every succeeding day of his life, but the appetite for apples will not increase; he will not eat one to-day, two to-morrow, three next day, and so on until he shall gorge himself with apples, and, oppressed with the load, lie down like a brute and wallow in the street. Such results do not follow the use of these fruits.

The same is true of every proper article of food and drink. Great as is the pleasure with which we receive, when athirst, the pure cold water, a desire for it is not increased by continued indulgence. We do not find men drinking a pint to-day, a quart to-morrow, and so on increasing, until, urged on by insatiable thirst, they suck on to the spout of the pump, and there remain until, like the gorged leech, they can swallow no more.

This is not the law of the appetite which craves water, but it is the law of the appetite which calls for gin.

All artificial appetites are governed by the same law. Those which crave rum, or tobacco, or any other narcotic substance show the controlling influence of this law of increase.

Again, another peculiarity of artificial appetites is that they seem to disqualify an individual subject to their influence for sound reasoning on this one subject. I doubt whether it would be in the power of the strongest intellect to reason as soundly in relation to an unnatural appetite to which the individual had become subject, as upon other matters; at any rate I have never met with such a one.

"What have you in that glass, young man?" A little wine, or, may be, some brandy and water, or whisky punch. "But, young man, do you know that the use of that article tends to the production of an unnatural appetite, so fierce and insatiable, that it has often overcome the will of the strongest men."

O, it is melancholy to hear him reply, "Pshaw! a man is a fool that cannot drink a glass of wine or brandy occasionally, and yet govern his appetites. Do not give yourself any uneasiness on my account. I know when I have taken enough ; I can drink, or, if I please, I can let it alone."

Now, I without further evidence believe one half of that assertion ; I believe he "*can drink ;*" and I may believe the other half, that he "*can let it alone,*" after he has tried the experiment. Until then I am skeptical on that point. If he could but understand to what a tremendous power he is subjecting himself he would pause before he took another step in that direction. "Wine is a mocker, strong drink is raging." Suppose Appetite and the controlling power, Will, to be represented on two opposite scales or thermometers. In health, we will suppose that appetite stands at fifty on its scale, while the will stands at seventy. The will now governs ; but in such a case as I have described, that of a man recovering from a fever and feeling almost unnatural hunger, the appetite runs up on the scale to seventy, eighty, or a hundred, while the will, enfeebled by the infirmity of the body, especially that of the stomach and nervous system, has fallen below zero.

The man must now be controlled by forces from without, or he will destroy himself. Supply him with a little food to-day, to-morrow his strength of body and will has crept up five or ten degrees on the scale, while appetite is less clamorous, having fallen five or ten degrees. Pursue the same course daily for a few days, and appetite will come down daily until it answers to fifty on the scale, while will, or the governing power, has gone up to seventy. You may now relax your care of the patient ; he can take care of himself.

Not so with the drunkard. He is the slave of his appetite. His will is enfeebled by diseases of the stomach and nervous system, and the terrific power of an unnatural and fiendish appetite rules him with a rod of iron. O, my hearers, have mercy on the drunkard ! His wretched condition demands your compassion. Encourage him by kind words, and support him in every feeble resolution. Stand around him like a wall of fire to protect him from the merciless wretches who would profit by his folly and weakness."

On the subject of regulating the rum traffic the doctor says : " Physicians often speak of regulating the action of the various organs of the body ; they regulate the liver ; they regulate the circulation ; they regulate the secretions, and so on ; but you never heard a doctor, unless he were a quack, talk about regulating cholera, or cancer ! These ailments are enemies, which must be fought tooth and nail, and be driven out of the system by all help. nursing and medicine. Just as stupid is it for men to talk about regulating the appetite for alcohol, or regulating the traffic in strong drink. These are cholera and cancer! Call them by whatever name you will, they are diseases of the individual, or of society; and the thing to be done is not to regulate them, but to drive them out of existence.

"Ah, but you say, you cannot drive men, though you can persuade them. I marvel greatly that men can allow themselves to employ language so thoughtlessly, when neither common sense nor common observation warrant it. 'Men cannot be driven!' Can't they? Did you ever see men run out of a burning house, or seek shelter from a driving storm by running to some cover? Man, like other animals, is subject to the influence of fear, and he will fly with all the speed he can command from threatening danger.

"Some of our rum-sellers have proved the truth of that statement within the past few months, for when the sheriff has been seen approaching their premises, they have been seized with a sudden panic, and given leg bail for security! 'Men cannot be driven,' indeed! Did you ever read of the flight of the French from Russia? I will not waste more words on such miserable nonsense as is contained in the language I have quoted.

"Only let the statute-book declare this traffic to be what it really is, a crime, and affix to it a penalty proportionate to its enormity, and the extent of its mischief, and let the sober, intelligent, moral portion of the community stand by the law with a determination to see it respected, and we shall find that these men can be 'driven' as they ought to be."

SOME TEMPERANCE STATISTICS.

Among the later and more valuable publications of the National Temperance Society is the work of Dr. Hargreaves, entitled "Our Wasted Resources," in which the statistics and the cost of alcoholic beverages are given, in connection with other sources of national wealth and poverty. The income of the country from all sources, including agriculture, manufactories, commerce, railways, mines, and fisheries, is set down in round numbers at seven hundred millions of dollars per annum. The amount of liquors, on the basis of the year 1871, sold in the United States is estimated at six hundred millions of dollars, an amount exceeding the value of all the food and food preparations, and nearly twice the amount spent for clothing.

The cost to the consumers of these alcoholic liquors in thirteen years—from 1860 to 1872—according to the official reports, is, in round numbers, six thousand seven hundred and eighty millions of dollars, or about three times the amount of the entire national debt. When it is taken into account that this consumption of liquors is a total loss, and that it leads to a train of other losses—as idleness, crime, and pauperism—it will readily be seen how it is possible for a nation with such fabulous resources steadily to decline in financial prosperity.

The liquor bill of the State of Pennsylvania in 1870 is set down at sixty-five million dollars. That of Illinois for the same year, forty-two million eight hundred and twenty-five thousand. Ohio, fifty-eight million eight hundred and forty-five thousand. Massachusetts, twenty-five million. While even in Maine under the prohibitory law the cost of liquors for drinking was four million two hundred and fifteen thousand dollars.

The losses to the nation by the drink traffic, as estimated in money alone, are something fearful; besides which it is estimated that there are six hundred thousand drunkards in the United States, which seems to be no exaggeration, for it would only give four drunkards apiece to the licensed liquor shops in the country, to say nothing of the unlicensed ones. The amount of grain used in the manufacture of liquors is forty million bushels—an amount sufficient to make bread for the whole country.

It is argued that every bushel of grain that is made into liquor enhances the price of what remains in the market, and dear bread always causes bad trade; for the more people have to pay for clothing and other comforts or luxuries, the less they can buy.

The results are the same whether forty millions of bushels perish in the field by mildew, or are subsequently destroyed in the breweries and distilleries. In both cases prices will be raised, and in the latter case there is not only the destruction of the grain, but the destruction of the thousands of people who use it in its distilled form. This enormous waste of food is of itself sufficient to keep multitudes of our people in poverty.

The number of paupers in the United States in the year 1870 is given in the census returns as 116,102, out of the population of 38,558,371.

From the able paper of Rev. John M. Walden, D.D., of Cincinnati, the following statistics of the beer traffic are reproduced:—

In order that the extent of the brewing, malting, and hop trades may be fully understood, we present the following figures, based upon the most reliable data:—

Capital invested in Breweries................$88,806,290
   "   "   Malt-houses............... 24,094,500
Value of land cultivated for Barley............ 63,225,040
   "   "   "   " Hops 2,360,520

Total capital....................... $178,486,350

Men employed in Breweries	11,000	Annual wages	$5,772,000
"	"	" Malt-houses	2,500	" "	1,086,500
"	"	" Barley culture	15,806	" "	4,742,000
"	"	" Hop culture	5,901	" "	1,770,300

Total laborers....35,207   Total wages....$13,370,800

The percentage of alcohol in lager beer, ale, and porter varies from four to seven per cent. Calculating from this statement how much absolute alcohol is in one year consumed in beer throughout the United States, we find that 9,000,000 barrels of beer, containing on the average 5.5 per cent. of alcohol, yield 495,000 barrels, or 23,850,000 gallons of alcohol.

Whisky contains from 40 to 50 per cent. of alcohol; therefore ten pints of lager beer or seven pints of ale contain the same quantity of alcohol as one pint of old Bourbon; and one pint, or two glasses, of lager beer as much alcohol as half a gill—a moderate drinker's "dram"—of whisky; hence not a few of those who drink beer or ale become intoxicated by it.

The effect of the temperance reform on the beer interest appears in the following:—

The United States Brewers' Association, a powerful body, which aspires to national greatness, held an annual meeting in Cincinnati in June, 1875. The official reports show that there had been a reduction in the number of breweries during the year of nearly thirty per cent.

Mr. Lewis Schade, editor of the "Washington Sentinel," and special agent of the brewers in Washington, in an address before the Convention said: "Very severe is the injury which the brewers have received in the so-called temperance States. The Local Option Law in Pennsylvania reduced the brewers from five hundred in 1873 to 346 in 1874. This destroyed 154 breweries in one year. In Michigan it is even worse, for of 202 in 1873 only 68 remain. In Ohio the Crusaders destroyed 68 out of 296. In Indiana the Baxter Law stopped many more. In Maryland the breweries were reduced from 74 to 15."

Rev. Newman Hall, of London, says : " Thirty thousand members of Churches in England are slaughtered yearly through liquor drinking." Rev. Dr. Guthrie, of Edinburgh, says: "I have seen no less than ten clergymen with whom I have sat down to the Lord's table deposed through strong drink."

It seems pitiful that the votaries of the Christian religion should, as a whole, show a poorer record in the matter of intemperance than the believers in Islam and Brahmanism. With all these water is the universal drink, and under these designations we may include nearly half the race of mankind. Archdeacon Jeffries, a missionary in the East Indies, has declared, " That for one real convert to Christianity as the fruit of missionary labor, the drinking practices of the English make one thousand drunkards." There is evidently a good deal of missionary work to be done along the Gospel temperance line even among people calling themselves Christians.

CHAPTER XXIV.

TESTIMONIES.

THE Boston "Globe" of March 10, 1877, has the following testimonies of reformed men, as given at the Moody temperance meetings :—-

Mr. M'Elvry said he came here last Monday, helped in by two men, a perfect wreck. He had been drinking since Thanksgiving Day, and for six years had been under the power of this appetite, which he thought he would have been able to conquer by his own strength. He probably had as much will as any man in front of him, and he did not want to acknowledge that he could not conquer his appetite by his own strength. But he had done all that a man could do. He had belonged to the Reform Club, the Sons of Temperance, and had been to the Washingtonian Home; had drank cold coffee and cold tea; had ate cayenne pepper by the spoonful, and still rum was his master.

"Last Monday," said the speaker, "I came here, assisted by two friends of mine, and asked the prayers of the people. I went to the retiring room, and knelt with five or six of my friends, and they prayed with me, and I prayed for myself. My appetite was cured right there. I can go out in the morning now and buy my provisions without drinking any thing. I could never do that before. What I want to instill into your minds is this: that if there is one man trying to conquer his appetite in his own strength, it cannot be done. I have been able to do so for a few months, and then I would slip up and go on another spree, and that is what I have been doing for the last six years. I had drank previous to that, and didn't try to leave off, but six years ago I thought I would leave off. I have just told you the result; it was a failure.

"I came here to be cured through Christ, and Jesus Christ saved me. Just as long as I live close to the cross I feel that I shall have no appetite for rum."

Mr. Moody then called on Mr. Ayer to give his testimony.

Mr. Ayer said : " My friends, I stand before you a new man. Four

25*

weeks ago I was a wreck. For a great number of years I have been addicted to strong drink. I have a strong will and strong purposes in every thing but that cursed thing. I have given it up, and my appetite has entirely left me. On New Year's eve—that was Sunday—I was lonesome; the last day of the year I had been drinking considerably. I had slept most of the day in a saloon, and in the evening after I went down Tremont-street to one of my favorite haunts, but it was shut up. I passed along by the Old Granary buryingground, and, coming to Park-street Church, I found it open. I went in, and the sexton politely gave me a seat in the middle aisle. Dr. Withrow was preaching. In the course of his remarks—that sermon ever memorable to me—he made use of the expression from the Bible that no drunkard shall inherit the kingdom of God. I had heard that thousands of times, having been raised by pious parents and in a Christian community, and attended Church for years. I thought I never had it strike me so forcibly as at that hour. I shook all over, and then he was telling when he was in Europe the only drunken man he ever met on the Continent was an American, and he was so ashamed of him.

I left that Church a wiser man. I began to feel and realize the position I was in. Previous to this I had noticed my personal friends looked at me with a suspicion because my face indicated that I was a hard drinker. I was ashamed of it. I actually used to go out on the Common in the morning to walk away bleared eyes and get up something of an appetite. Any man in this audience who has been a drinking man knows what a terrible curse we have when we rise at three or four o'clock in the morning, all burnt up with damnable pain, and sneak out to see which rum-hole is open to get drinks sufficient to get up a morbid appetite; and then, after eating, the distress our victuals give in our stomach, and then in two or three hours we have to drink again, and then we have to go to bed with so many drinks in order to sleep. Any drinking man knows that. You know I have been there by these remarks.

"The next Monday night, which was the Week of Prayer, I went to the first prayer-meeting, which was held in the small vestry room. Mr. Moody came, and I went to the first and second meeting in the Tabernacle. Then they had a men's prayer-meeting in the Berkeleystreet Church. I went over there, and I think I was the first man that stood up on the floor of that church anxious to inquire the way to Christ. From that time I began to grow stronger, my appetite lessening; and I recollect that the next morning I got up thirsty and wanted a drink, and I went to the eastern window, and saw a beautiful star in the east. I could not help feeling I was sent to look at it, like the wise men who saw the star in the East. It struck me very forcibly at that time; and I thank God that was the turning-point in my life, and my soul became pure, and I was filled with hope. My appetite was taken entirely away, and I have not been troubled since.

" I hope that all you young men who are here, that are just tippling, will not go on with it and acquire that thirst. It was years before I acquired it. I was in the army nine years, a commissioned officer, and in the midst of rioting and debauchery of all sorts, and I kept on, and by and by I was a confirmed drinker. Those things are now past and gone, and Christ has promised that those who call upon him he will cast all their sins away and they shall be forgotten. When I look back there is shame, and I suffer with remorse. O, God help me and help all you drinking men to come to him, and he will take your appetites away from you ! ' "

The following letter from a Boston lawyer was read by the Rev. L. B. Bates at one of the Gospel Temperance meetings, as reported in " The Boston Advertiser : "—

My Dear Sir : It is with a degree of pleasure unequaled by any heretofore experienced during my whole life that I address you this note. For the past five years I have been an habitual drinker of whisky, rum, gin, brandy, and all liquors of an intoxicating nature. I found my appetite increasing as each successive year carried me nearer to the grave. During the past two or three months it has been so strong that I could hardly drink rum enough to satisfy it. Since I began to drink I have always been cognizant, fully so, of the degradation and misery that the cursed stuff was likely to entail upon myself and my family, and many, many times have I made resolves to let it alone, to drink no more. Perhaps I would for a few days, but a week at the furthest would find me again at the bar of some favorite grogshop, swilling down those dregs of misery, that rob men of their senses, their families of their happiness and homes, and fill our Penitentiaries, State Prisons, and alms-houses with its victims. After hearing the testimony given at the Tabernacle last Sabbath under your leadership, and having found, by experience, that by no resolve made between myself and my conscience could I baffle my desire for strong drink, I went home concluding to adopt the course recommended by those whom I had heard speak. I did so ; I went home and prayed to God, penitent for my past sins, imploring him in his infinite mercy to rid me of the terrible curse that was fast carrying me on to destruction and a pauper's grave. I prayed twice before retiring to my bed. On Monday morning I awoke, feeling a marked change—which no words of mine can explain. I ate my breakfast and went out to my business, and, strange as it was, experienced no desire to go in and get a glass of rum, before arriving at my office, as was my usual custom. The day wore by, not, however, without my receiving very many solicitations to drink ; but I had no inclination whatever, and found myself in possession of strength and courage to say " No ;" and I am happy to say that I went home that night (Monday) the first time for months that my family could not smell the fumes of the liquor in my breath. I was filled with courage, and before retiring on Monday night I prayed again. On Tuesday morning I awoke, and after breakfasting went to my business, again passing the door it was my custom to enter for a morning drink. Before reaching my office I felt myself absolutely free from my previous desire to drink. I spent another day experiencing no appetite for it. This is the third day, and still no desire for "rum" manifests itself. I now feel that I am entirely free ; that the fetters which once bound me to the demon are forever broken, and that I have been saved from a drunkard's grave by the teachings of the men whom I heard speak at the Tabernacle last Sabbath, and by your teachings, "to make one's will the will of God." I feel and know that God has answered my prayer, that he has given me abundant strength, and that my future life, instead of being one of debauchery and sin, shall be one of peace and happiness, acceptable in the sight of him who gave it. To you, and to the men whom I heard speak upon the great evil of intemperance, thereby spurring me on to Christ and victory, I extend my heartfelt thanks. May God give you strength to continue your labors, and may his blessings in the future, as in the past, ever rest upon your good work, is my sincere prayer ! If this letter can be of any service to you in teaching others the way, you are at liberty to use it, withholding my name. Should any one doubt its authenticity you are at liberty to send them to my office, where I shall be only too happy to confer with them, and in my poor way tell them of what God has done for me. I should be most happy to see you and converse with you. Am generally at liberty from three until four o'clock P. M., and if convenient would be pleased to have you call. Asking your prayers for my future welfare and the salvation of my soul, I am, sir, yours with esteem,

To Dwight L. Moody. * * * *

At one of the meetings of the Berkeley-street Church, near the Boston Tabernacle, Miss Willard related the experience of a man in Newark, N. J., who was brought to Christ by the efforts of the Christian women :—

"This man," said the speaker, "was a very hard man before his conversion. He formerly resided in London, where he was in the habit of frequenting low haunts and going with dissolute companions; but finally this man was obliged to leave London. He drifted to San Francisco, and subsequently to New York city. When in the latter city he was arrested for some grave offense, and sent to Sing Sing prison. When he was finally released, he went to Newark, N. J., and soon drifted into his old ways and haunts. One day he was proceeding up one of the principal streets in Newark, in the crooked way peculiar to drunken men. At some distance before him he saw a lady, who was slowly coming toward him. When the lady got quite near the drunken man turned out to the best of his ability to allow her to pass by; but the lady, instead of passing him, put her hand on his shoulder and asked, in a calm voice, 'Where are you going, my man?' The man was thunderstruck, so to speak, for those were the very words which policemen were accustomed to use when arresting him. The man endeavored to reply, but couldn't utter a word. Finally, however, he managed to say, 'Dear lady, as near as I can reckon I'm going as fast as I can to his Satanic majesty.' 'And I,' replied the lady, producing a New Testament, and laying one of her hands on it, 'am going, as near as I can reckon, to the Lord Jesus Christ. Don't you want to go along with me, brother?' The man hesitated, but was finally induced to follow her. She led her companion to a temperance meeting. The man was conducted to a seat, and then was prayed for by some of the ladies present. The prayers which were so earnestly uttered that night by three women undoubtedly greatly impressed the man, for before he left the room that night he was completely sober; and in a few days after was converted to Christ. So we can also do a great deal for Christ if we only think so."

AN INTERESTING LETTER.

March 22, 1877.

MR. MOODY: DEAR SIR: Some twenty-five years ago there was a rum-seller in Boston who seemed to be remarkably successful in his business. I think he owned several places in the city, and a hotel at Chelsea Beach—a fine-looking young man, and the envy of a great many thoughtless young men, myself among the number. His acquaintance was sought by many; in fact, he seemed to "flourish like a green bay tree planted by the rivers of water," but he gradually went down. I knew him by sight, and could see him as the years went by, till he got to be what the rum-sellers call "a bar-room loafer." I think it is about two years ago I read in the daily papers of a poor, miserable creature being picked up in the street—I think he was ragged and covered with vermin—giving his name, which was the former rum-seller. Since I have not heard any thing from him. This past week at the Tabernacle prayer-meeting Mr. Sawyer called on this man to speak, and then I saw the same man, clothed and in his right mind. I didn't catch the words that he uttered, but his manner showed there had been a remarkable change. We hear people speak in a sneering way sometimes of your stories, but I never heard you tell any more wonderful story than the above.　　　　　　　　(Signed,)

"A BUSINESS MAN IN THE CITY."

"Now," said Mr. Moody, when he had finished reading this letter, "I want this man just to speak and tell what great things the Lord has done for him." Thereupon a middle-aged man advanced to the front, and said he was the representative of the letter Mr. Moody had just read. He had been just what the letter had described, but through the grace of God had been saved. He urged those before him to follow his example, and then they will be men.

THE CONVERSION OF AN OPIUM-EATER.

After Mr. Moody's discourse on 2 Sam. xv. 19, a man, whose face was deeply furrowed with the marks of dissipation, arose and said :—

"I have struggled for weeks against a terrible appetite, but the Lord has carried me through, and now there isn't a happier man in Boston.

Mr. Moody—"Tell them how you went to the office, and came back."

The Convert—"When I rose for prayers I could hear my heart thump against my ribs ; but instead of going into the inquiry meeting I went to my office, but I came back and went right straight into the inquiry room, although I did not know where it was, and hadn't been in that part of the building before."

Mr. Moody—"I think you had better tell them what bound you, because it may set some poor captive free."

The Convert—"It was opium. It is the hardest habit in the world for a man to break off. I had a loving wife, lovely children, a kind father and mother ; but no power on earth could save me—nothing but the power of the Lord Jesus Christ. If any one is bound by his appetite let him come to the Lord Jesus Christ, and he will cure him. The way is simple enough."

Mr. Moody—"They didn't all hear you. He said it was opium, and if there is any poor slave of opium here to-day, talk with him, and let him pray with you, and the Lord will deliver the captive. I was perfectly surprised the other day to learn that there were hundreds of thousands in this country fast bound with opium."

A gentleman on the platform said he had held a position for four-teen years in the Custom-house, but he had lost that by his own fault. He had lost every position he had held in his life by his own faul⸱ His friends had placed him in different asylums, but he trusted in his own strength. He had tried different temperance societies, but nothing had saved him from the curse of the appetite for strong drink but the power of the Lord Jesus Christ. He had lost friends, but now he felt that he had gained a friend that was going to carry him through. He had got strength now, he said—such strength as he never had before; and he would say that he had experienced the divinity of his Lord and Saviour.

Mr. Moody—"Didn't you use to believe in it?"

Answer—"No, sir, I didn't. What religious belief I had—I was brought up a Unitarian, and I didn't believe in the divinity of my Lord and Saviour Jesus Christ. I had no conception of it; but now it animates my whole soul."

Mr. Moody—"Is there any change in your life?"

Answer—"A perfect change. My children at home asked my wife, 'What is the matter with pa? He seems an entirely changed man. He seems so happy.' Now I have family prayers, read the Bible and study it, and there's where I learned the divinity of my Saviour."

Mr. Moody—"Were you happy before?"

Answer—"No, sir; I was morose, cross—a perfect, miserable mis-anthrope. It seems as though I was deserted by both God and man; but I have found out since that instead of God and man deserting me I deserted them. Now all my friends are coming back to me. One of the influences that brought me to Christ was those sweet hymns, 'What a Friend We have in Jesus,' and 'I Need Thee Every Hour.' Those two combined I could not get out of my mind. They haunted me constantly, and I asked myself, 'Why shouldn't I find this dear friend, Jesus?' And, thank God, I have found him, and got him to-day, and I am happy—O, so happy!"

Mr. Moody—"Yes, what a friend we have in Jesus! I think we will have to sing that." The audience then sung the hymn with great earnestness and feeling.

Another case of opium cure is thus reported in the "North-western Christian Advocate," of Chicago, by the pastor of the lady in question:—

"I was an invalid, and for three years had been under the con-tinued influence of opium. I became convinced that to persist in its use was both physical and spiritual ruin. Under the direction of my physician I undertook to discontinue its use by decreasing the dose gradually. I succeeded till the tenth day, when, my will refusing to yield, reason was dethroned, and it was again administered in increased doses. After recovering from this terrible strain on my system, I attempted several times to abandon its use, but without success . . . I felt that I could not be free in Christ, nor could I offer myself to him while I hugged this idol to my heart. I finally decided to exercise what faith I could, and ask for wisdom from on high. I acted on this decision, and the answer was, 'Come unto me, and I will give you rest.' Duty was plain, but days and weeks passed by, and yet my idolatry was perfect. I had often weighed mentally one grain of this poison against my hope of future and eternal peace! I confess with shame that it was more to me than the 'bread of life.' Its value was 'above rubies,' so necessary had it become to me through five years of constant use. One afternoon in September, 1870, I was alone at home. I took in my hand the bottle containing the opiate, preparatory to swallowing my drug. I recollect so vividly how everything appeared about the house, the arrangement of the furniture, and of standing there holding the bottle from me as I would had it been a venomous serpent to prevent it from stinging me to death; and yet I could not let it go, for it was my life. O, the horrors of that hour! I remember summoning all the will power of my being, and of finding myself kneeling beside my bed, the perspiration starting from every pore. I know not how long I prayed, but this I do know, that for one second of time, Jesus stood by me, and I marveled at the glory, for that one glimpse was enough to quell the cravings of an awful appetite and break in that instant the fetters that were woven so strongly about me! I arose, and my chains fell off. I was free.

"A year passed by, and brought again the same hazy atmosphere, the same languidness of the system. I had scarce a temptation, and not once yielded; but now the tempter came, under peculiar circumstances and with fearful power. I felt that to yield now was to lose all. . . . At last the morning broke. I will not attempt to tell the joy that ever since has been mine. I have complete victory over my enslaving appetite. I have taken the opiate at two different times during sickness, since; but it has lost its charm over me—is no more to me than any other drug.

"As I recall the scenes of those years of trial, I feel that, though my experience was purchased by suffering and sorrow—aye, by the very bitterness of despair—it was not all in vain, if any poor soul now fettered by appetite or passion may from my testimony take heart, trust wholly in Christ, and prove to the world that we may 'do all things through Christ which strengtheneth us.'"

Another witness testified : "I was a great drunkard, had been so for years, but I brought my sins to God, and he saved me from them all. Some of my young friends began to ridicule me, and to say, 'You belong to Moody, do you?' but my answer was, '*I belong to God.*' They said, 'Any one is an idiot or a lunatic who will get up and speak in the Tabernacle.' But I said, 'Is it madness to get freed from the power of liquor? Is it madness to go back to a happy home at night instead of staying in a bar-room until three o'clock in the morning, playing cards and drinking? Is it madness to go to a prayer-meeting and praise God, and then go home and kneel at the family altar? If that is insanity, I am insane.' But just ask my wife how she likes the change ; she is here and can tell you?"

Mr. Moody—"If he is insane he has a good Keeper, and a good asylum at the end of the journey."

Mr. Stanley, a young man who had been a drinking man for twelve years, and for three years a common drunkard, said that he had lost place after place, until no one would take him; he was so much under the influence of liquor as to be unfit for business. Six weeks ago he came to the Tabernacle, and talked with one who had been saved, and he showed him the way to be saved also. From that time he had no desire for liquor or for tobacco, and he felt confident that God would enable him to lead a sober, honest life.

Mr. B. P. Palmer, of the Boston "Herald," was then introduced by Mr. Moody. He said that he believed there was no other name but that of the Lord Jesus Christ whereby we may be saved. "I want to say one other thing," said he, "and only one thing, and that is the importance of personal effort among our acquaintances. There is no one here but who ought to feel the dreadful curse that rum is. Every one who drinks at all has some friend that he may do something for. I have found that already in this short experience of mine. I am but learning my alphabet in this matter ; but I know that those who strive in the name of Jesus Christ will gain a power which will set persons thinking, if nothing more."

Mr. Moody—"How about your appetite? does it trouble you?"

Mr. Palmer—"It does not trouble me at all. It is either entirely destroyed or is wholly under subjection."

The following, from a letter to the editor, written from Dwight, Ill., will be of interest:—

"The first week in December, 1876, Dwight, Ill., was visited by Mr. C. M. Morton, State Secretary of the Y. M. C. A. of Ill.; a series of union meetings were commenced, which continued for a space of twelve weeks, which resulted in a great work in the village, and extended for miles in every direction in the country. One marked feature of the meetings was the work among the drinking class of our population. Perhaps the most notable case was that of Col. J. B. C., of Lexington, Ky., who had formerly lived here, and was still the owner of a valuable farm a short distance in the country; he had been a hard drinker for years, and since the month of June, 1876, when he returned to Dwight, he had scarcely allowed a day to pass over his head without a spree. He had become so low that most of his old friends and acquaintances had forsaken him, and the lowest persons whom he could find in our saloons were his only companions. His family were in Kentucky, and he lived in debauchery. When our meetings began he was confined to his bed, often delirious, and many supposed he would not recover. Mr. Morton visited him; he seemed penitent, but said that there was no hope for him, he was a doomed man; and he then left him feeling, indeed, that his case was sad and almost hopeless. His case was made a special subject of prayer, a better home for him was furnished, his shattered constitution seemed to rally, he finally was enabled to get out to the meetings, and came out manfully, and said he desired to quit the accursed thing. He felt the only help for him was from above, and he desired to seek it. The result was that he came as a penitent; the Lord heard his prayer, and we all felt that he was accepted of Christ; old things had passed away, and he felt he was a new man in Christ Jesus. He spent some weeks with us in our meetings, and was of great service to the cause; his testimony was always clear and positive, and certain changes seemed to have taken place in the man. Before leaving here he united with one of the Churches, and on his return to Lexington, Ky., united with the Centenary Methodist Episcopal Church, and we are glad to add that a letter, under date of Oct. 6, 1877, reports our brother doing well, an honor to our cause, a redeemed, and we think, a sound man. A family whose hopes had been blighted are reunited and happy."

JOHN N. STEARNS

HON. WILLIAM E. DODGE.

TEMPERANCE LITERATURE.

Among the efficient means for carrying on the temperance reform is the ample temperance literature, which has been produced and circulated in the form of books for popular use and for Sunday-school libraries; local temperance newspapers—of which there are about a hundred published in America; temperance tracts in great variety; and temperance articles, by the first writers in the land, which are constantly appearing in the columns of the weekly religious press.

Foremost in the department of temperance literature stands THE NATIONAL TEMPERANCE AND PUBLICATION SOCIETY, at New York, of which Hon. Wm. E. Dodge is President, and J. N. Stearns, Esq., is Secretary and manager, to whose fraternal courtesy and valuable assistance the Editor of this volume is under lasting obligation. It publishes "The National Temperance Advocate," which may be regarded as the leading temperance organ of those having no specialty, but devoted to all the interests of the great reform. Its list of books has now reached the number of seventy, while its supply of tracts, illustrated handbills, cards, etc., is very full and attractive.

Next in power and efficiency may be mentioned the temperance department of THE AMERICAN TRACT SOCIETY, whose temperance books have already reached the aggregate of seven hundred and sixty thousand copies, while its temperance tracts have been circulated to the number of nearly nine millions of copies.

The "Union," published by the Woman's Christian Temperance Union, at Brooklyn, is already a recognized power in the temperance world. Its sketches of eminent Christian temperance women are a notable feature among its many excellences, and serve to indicate a fact at once remarkable and hopeful—that to the Christian women of América has been committed, by the manifest providence of God, a field of usefulness and a grasp of power quite in fulfillment of the prophecies concerning "the last times."

To the long and honorable list of temperance writings this volume is added, with the hope that it may be worthy of a place among them, and that it may be of some substantial service, not only as grouping together the more prominent facts and persons brought out by the temperance movement, but also as presenting additional evidence of the power and grace of our Lord and Saviour Jesus Christ to save unto the uttermost all who come unto God by him.

THE END.

www.ingramcontent.com/pod-product-compliance
Lightning Source LLC
Chambersburg PA
CBHW022124020426
42334CB00015B/746